Into the Tiger's Jaw

Brigadier General Frank E. Petersen, as assistant commander, 1st Marine Aircraft Wing, Okinawa, Japan, during a command briefing. (USMC photo)

Into the Tiger's Jaw

America's First Black Marine Aviator

The Autobiography of Lt. Gen. Frank E. Petersen

with J. Alfred Phelps

★

PRESIDIO

Published by Presidio Press
505 B San Marin Drive, Suite 300
Novato, CA 94945-1340

Library of Congress Cataloging-in-Publication Data

Petersen, Frank E.
    Into the Tiger's jaw : America's first Black marine aviator / the autobiography of Lt. Gen. Frank E. Petersen with J. Alfred Phelps.
        p.   cm.
    ISBN 0-89141-675-7
    1. Petersen, Frank E. 2. United States. Marine Corps—Aviation—Biography. 3. Afro-American air pilots—Biography. 4. Air pilots, Military—United States—Biography. 5. Afro-American generals—biography. 6. Generals—United States—Biography. I. Phelps, J. Alfred.
VE25.P48A3   1998
355'.0092—dc21
[B]   98-26406
                                   CIP

All photos are from the author's collection unless otherwise noted.

Printed in the United States of America

Contents

Preface

During World War II, blacks learned, again, that fighting for their country brought them no closer to full citizenship. Trying to enlist, they were often summarily rejected. The Army accepted them only in a quota system linked to the proportion of the black population of the country, and then only in segregated units whose roles were primarily noncombatant in nature, except for certain "special" Army Air Forces units like the Tuskegee Airmen, set up only in response to civil rights campaigns. These were regarded as an "experiment," and were not expected to last.

Contrary to expectations, these units distinguished themselves in combat. Many of the men involved died. Generally, however, historical patterns show that blacks were usually allowed to serve only in times of crisis, when manpower needs surmounted the restrictions of racism.

In 1948, President Harry Truman issued an edict to the armed forces, requiring its integration. Blacks would be given equal opportunity. They were to enjoy the same advantages and opportunities to perform as their white counterparts. Blacks then on active duty viewed the pronouncement with elated optimism, but others moaned in sardonic cynicism, recalling that actions, not words, were the measure of progress.

When President Truman issued his edict, the Marine Corps, of all the services, was in the least enviable position for compliance. Not until May 1942 had it finally succumbed to political and public pressure and officially accept blacks into its ranks for the first time in its 150-year history. It was the last of the services to do so.

The first black Marines underwent segregated training at the Montford Point Marine Base, part of the massive Camp Lejeune Training Base. Initially assigned for duty to a composite defense battalion (a small, self-sufficient army that employed a maximum number of special skills ranging from infantryman to radar technician), the first recruit, Pvt. Howard Perry of Charlotte, North Carolina, arrived for duty on 26 August 1942. By the middle of September, 125 new black recruits were undergoing training under the leadership of white enlisted and officer personnel. Commanding was Col. Samuel A. Woods, who later wrote to the director of Marine Corps recruiting:

> Thank you for getting us some excellent recruits. They are most enthusiastic and I am sure they are doing their level best to make good. We have to train the organization to operate, maintain, and repair the equipment that belongs to the Composite Battalion; therefore we have to run our own schools. The men recruited have in general shown splendid aptitude for the service; at present we have probable rejections, but so far none of these has been for inaptitude.

After the blacks passed their trial period, plans were immediately made to bring more blacks into the Corps and to form more black units. By 1949, blacks in the United States Marine Corps numbered 1,633 enlisted and no officers on deck. By 1951 there were three black officers in the Corps, and by the end of 1967 officers numbered 314 with 23,046 black enlisted. (It is noteworthy that the number of black officers grew extremely slowly. Fred Branch, the first black to become a commissioned officer in the Marine Corps, was summarily discharged into the reserves the same day he was commissioned in 1945. As will be seen, the scaling down of the Corps after World War II dictated that the 245 men in his officers' candidate class were simply not needed.)

However, during World War II, a total of 19,168 blacks served in the Marine Corps. Of this number, approximately 13,000 served in overseas combat commands. The 52d Defense Battalion was organized on 15 December 1943. It saw service on Roi and Namur Islands, Kwajalein, the Marshalls, and Guam before returning to the States in 1946. There were a total of twenty such defense battalions in the Corps. The two black battalions (the 51st and 52d) were the last formed.

As the United States began to achieve dominance in the Pacific, the Marine Corps' need for logistics personnel supplanted the need for combat troops. Blacks were trained in logistics handling skills and formed into twelve ammunition-handling companies as part of the beach parties used in amphibious landings. Beginning with the Marine landing on Saipan, these ammunition companies took part in every major landing thereafter. The first black Marine to die in combat was Pfc. LeRoy Seals of Brooklyn, New York. He received fatal wounds shortly after the Saipan landing on 16 June 1944.

A future Marine commandant, Gen. Lemuel C. Shepherd, then commanding the 41st Provisional Marine Brigade, took the opportunity to praise the 4th Ammunition Company:

> You are commended for the splendid and expeditious manner in which the supplies and equipment were unloaded from the LSTs' group. Working long hours frequently during nights and in at least two instances under enemy fire [you] so coordinated your unloading [that supplies kept] flowing to the beach. You have contributed in large measure to the successful and rapid movement of combat amphibious operation.

General Shepherd was not alone in praise of the black Marines. General A. A. Vandegrift, then commandant of the Marines, noted: "The Negro Marines are no longer on trial. They are Marines—period." Major General William Rupertus, then commanding the 1st Marine Division, commended the 7th Ammunition Company for its action on Peleliu:

> The performance of the officers and men of your command throughout the landing on Peleliu and the assault phase has been such as to warrant the highest praise. Unit commanders have repeatedly brought to my attention the wholehearted cooperation of each individual. The Negro race can well be proud of the work performed by the Seventh Ammunition Company as they appreciate the privilege of wearing a Marine uniform and serving with the Marines in combat. Please convey to your command these sentiments and inform them that in the eyes of the entire 1st Marine Division, they have earned a well done.

In spite of these commendations based upon their performance in combat environments, blacks were still not allowed to serve in infantry divisions or Marine air units. There were no black women Marines or officers. As World War II drew to a close, the Marine Corps redefined its manpower requirements and restricted the number of blacks to a total of 2,880, divided among garrisons, service support, antiaircraft, and the steward's branch. By the end of December 1946, this number had dropped to 2,238. In the spring of 1947, blacks were given a final choice: Either transfer to the steward's branch or be discharged from the Corps. Some selected the latter course of action, but by September 1948, only 1,532 blacks remained in the Corps.

President Truman's Executive Order 9981 of July 1948 did little to change this policy. As late as May 1949, Marine Corps policy held that no black first-term enlistments would be accepted unless optioned for steward's duty only. The Corps found it difficult to fill these special quotas. Marine Corps inducements were introduced to increase black participation which included rapid promotions, guaranteed schooling, the closing of Montford Point, and the decision that all recruits would be trained at Parris Island. (However, they would be trained in separate units with black drill instructors.) These proffered inducements made little impression on the psyche of the black community.

In mid-1950, the North Koreans attacked across the demilitarized zone (DMZ), and America was at war again. By 1951, the black Marine population increased some 400 percent, to a high of 8,001 enlisted men and three officers. Combat necessity caused integration to be carried out at such a rapid rate that by the summer of 1952, the Corps had disbanded the last of its black units. The Corps, the last service to integrate, became one of the first to eliminate overt segregation from its ranks.

This era is where my story begins. Overt segregation and racism were supposedly on the way out within the Marine Corps, but there were to be considerable bouts of pain and discomfiture in the coming years.

Though unaware of much that had gone before, I was aware of the 1948 Truman edict and assumed that the playing field was level. In late 1951, upon arriving in Pensacola, Florida, as a trusting eighteen year old eager to commence flight training, I discovered that such was not the case. Nor was I aware that I had taken the first steps along a twisted path that would lead to a three-star, thirty-eight-year career.

Acknowledgments

We wish to thank all of the following that in one way or another contributed so much to the realization of this project. Bernie Bruce, Ph.D.; Ernie Douglas; TSgt. Robert (Bob) Doktor; Michael McLeod; Paul Tyler; Cork Milner; Lt. Col. Hubert Mitchell, USMC (Ret); Thomas (Tom) Kelly; Arthur Edwards; Adm. Samuel L. Gravely, Jr., USN (Ret); Gale Harlan; Dr. Dale Tipton; Dr. Eric Best; Anne L. Nickerson, Ph.D., sister of General Petersen; Gayle, Dana, and Lindsey; Frank Petersen III and Monique Petersen, General Petersen's children; Ellie Anderson; Alicia Downes Petersen; William Poulis Petersen, the general's brother; Maj. Gen. J. Gary Cooper, USMCR (Ret) and ambassador to Jamaica; Maj. D. K. Carpenter; MSgt. J. D. Black; Curtis Smothers, attorney at law; Lt. Col. William F. Gilliland; Ann Hassinger, History, Reference, and Preservation, United States Naval Academy; Frederick C. Branch, the Marine Corps' first black officer; Frank C. Brown; Paul Tyler; Col. Manfred Reitsch (Ret.); Jack Alexander; Shirley Williams, archivist, National Archives and Record Administration; Jim Gotti and Bea Kaya, *Honolulu Advertiser;* Jesse Brown; Lt. Col. Hurdle Maxwell, USMC (Ret); Lt. Col. Edward House, USMC (Ret); Jack Alexander; Brig. Gen. Clifford L. Stanley, USMC; Capt. Mike Neuman, USMCR; Capt. John C. Milliman, USMC; Brooks Gray, Montford Point Marines; P. F. Earle, master gunnery sergeant, USMC; Percy L. Corke, Montford Point Marines; Melanie W. Slan, Marine Corps University Archives; Col. Clarence Davis, USMC (Ret); Brig. Gen. George Walls, USMC (Ret), vice chancellor, North Carolina State College; Melissa Mantel, assistant librarian, *Houston Chronicle;* Michael E. Bragg, Margaret Simmons, and Sally Faubian, librarians in the Marian O. Lawrence Library in Galt, California; Don Gass, librarian in the Sonoma County Cotati Library, California. There may be some we haven't been able to include because of space considerations. These people are also heartily thanked for their contributions.

Prologue

Once I found out what being a United States Marine was all about, jumping into the tiger's jaw was just something to do. We'd been trained for combat. That's our reason for being. When the time comes, hell, stick out your can. Let's go. Let's see what that old tiger's got. Let's jump right into his big, old jaw.

That's what I was doing that day in Vietnam when that old tiger caterwauled and bit me. I was flying high. A lieutenant colonel. Marine fighter squadron commander. Keeper of the keys, Marine Fighter Attack Squadron 314. And to make it sweeter, our call sign was Black Knights. Hypothetical swords at the ready, I pulled that hot pad duty just like I wanted my men to do it. Five- to twelve-hour stints, depending on the threat and the type of call for assistance.

Tiger growled. We listened. Marine troops pinned down, deep in the DMZ. Twenty miles north of the Rock Pile, near An Khe. Target, fifteen miles into North Vietnam. We fired up the Phantoms, those big, powerful, weirdly beautiful F-4s—and flew right into that old tiger's jaw.

We took some pretty heavy fire on our first pass on target. I rolled in on my second pass, singsonging MK-84 five-hundred-pound bombs on top of some people on the ground. Although unfortunate, they weren't passive. They nailed us with hot 37mm rapid fire as I pulled my nose up through the horizon. I felt the hit. The F-4 shuddered. . . .

_____ Part One
Beginnings

1: Genesis

My hometown is Topeka, Kansas, and it sits along the Kansas River in the fertile Kaw Valley. The city is the state capital, and it resides smack dab in the middle of Shawnee County. My only sister, Anne, was born in 1930, and I came along on 2 March 1932. We were the oldest of four children born to a couple of folks named Edythe and Frank Petersen, Sr. My father came from St. Croix in the U.S. Virgin Islands. I remember how delightfully his words undulated in that wonderful meter of the islanders. His lips pushed out that Creolese patois spoken throughout the islands.

I recall as a child hearing him tell how he happened to come to the United States. It was something he'd always thought about. Perhaps it might be possible to earn a better living in America. Born in 1905 to Augustus and Ann Petersen in the town of Frederiksted on the western edge of St. Croix, he'd always relished the idea of freedom. It didn't exist on the island, which he considered repressive enough to leave if he could. But there was never enough money to leave. So the periodic visions of America were to percolate. The dream sufficed until his sister, Victoria Alicia, grew up, went to the United States, and suffered the "great disillusionment."

But before that, the family enjoyed life as much as they could, living on St. Croix and working on the Two Friends Plantation, where they were born. They knew all about harvesting the sugarcane fields around the Great House with its old slave quarters. They worked other fields on the far side of the stone fences patterning the hillsides. They learned about Campeche and tamarind trees—how both were used for dyewood and the tamarind was sometimes used in beverages. When the time came, they were both baptized and confirmed in the Moravian Church. Sometimes, in a somber, reflective mood at the end of a hard day's work, they'd sit looking across the road at the cemetery and see the name PETERSEN chiseled on the headstones glinting in the failing light as the sun set hugely and boldly into the blue seas behind them. Perhaps they wondered about the black Petersens and the white Petersens who were all together now under the greensward and how they related one to the other in times past.

They knew that the black ones had some of the same skills as they. Cutting and moving the sugarcane. In the olden days, donkeys carried the stalks to the mill to be unloaded and fed into the iron rollers. Then came the juice—the "cane squeezins"—sluicing down a concrete trough into the hissing still with its curlicued coils while vapors wafted into the vapid air. Finally came that clear stream of warm, reeking rum, dropping down beautifully into waiting calabashes. I think they knew that at one time not very long ago, those dead old Petersens danced the way they themselves danced on those occasions when the grownups sometimes lost it and the fiery rum moved itself about in the cup.

During the week, the children would go to school, then work the fields. On Sundays, they'd go to church. The cycle was a roundabout. Help harvest the cane, then process it.

Our family history has it that about 1922 my father's sister, Aunt Victoria, migrated to the United States and settled in New York City. It was a grand adventure for her, and she eventually married and had a son. But she found the practice of segregation particularly galling. She wrote my father about it. Based on her assessment of life for blacks in America, my father thought less about coming here. The conditions left a bad taste in his mouth. That is, until one day at the age of sixteen he found himself driving a taxi to accommodate the tourist trade in addition to his usual job as a garage mechanic for five dollars a day. That day driving a taxi proved providential. His fare for a tour of the island in the Model T Ford was none other than Frank P. MacLennan, the owner of the *Topeka State Journal*.

On a tour sponsored by the U.S. Navy for newspaper publishers, MacLennan wanted to get to one of the highest points on St. Croix to survey the beauty of the island set against the Atlantic and the Caribbean stretching away into opposite infinities. It was, in fact, a lucky day for him, for he'd engaged as his driver a man known as a most resourceful and intelligent individual. The day, the story goes, was hot, the humidity high, and the elected hill most steep. The Model T Ford groaned wearily. It heaved, hemmed, hawed, and refused the climb. MacLennan's hopes seemed dashed. But as MacLennan himself was to later note, "The brilliance of their taxi driver, Frank E. Petersen, Sr.," came into play and saved the day. In those days, if it got hot, the gas in the old Fords would evaporate and the engine wouldn't run too well. But Dad conceived the idea of turning the car around and backing it up the hill, reasoning that gravity would cause the gas to flow into the carburetor. That impressed MacLennan. In fact, he was absolutely overwhelmed that my dad showed such skill and knowledge in dealing with mechanical problems. MacLennan suggested that my father go to the United States, where he'd make more money and "have chances to advance."

Although the opportunity sounded good, my dad wasn't immediately convinced. The stories from his sister in New York about segregation in the United States worried him. He simply didn't want to face it. But MacLennan was persistent, assuring him he'd have no problems if he went to Kansas. Two years passed. In 1924 MacLennan sent him a ticket and money for the trip to Topeka. Dad decided to risk it.

He was on his way—I've since found out—to an area of the United States that early on had not seemed to find consensus on the subjects of slavery and blacks. In 1856, sixty-eight years before my dad's planned trip to Kansas, pro-slavery men attacked the town of Lawrence (which favored a free state). It was a stone's throw from Topeka. The newspaper offices and other offices were burned. Several people were killed. Down on Pottawatomie Creek, abolitionist John Brown led a raid against the little settlement, and several pro-slavery men were killed. They fought for months, until federal troops came in to ease the tension.

Although slavery was outlawed in Kansas in 1859, sixty-five years before my dad arrived, pro-slavery people were still about. The air was not entirely free for black people.

Of course, my dad knew nothing about all that and probably couldn't have cared less. After arriving in Topeka at the age of nineteen, he got a job washing cars. He was high on his future, totally believing MacLennan's promise that he would surely advance. When a mechanic left the garage in which he worked, Dad walked right up and applied for the job. He was turned down.

After talking with other black car washers in Topeka, he found that he wouldn't make a lot of money washing cars.

So he went to see MacLennan.

"I've got problems, Mr. MacLennan."

"What's wrong, Petersen?"

"Things just aren't turning out as I expected. You work and you work and there's no advancement. Doin' the same job year after year for the same low pay."

MacLennan gave him a job at the newspaper as a porter. But my dad was no ordinary porter. The whirring, clicking typographic machines were music to his ears. He yearned to operate them, and he rushed to tell MacLennan.

"I know I could run one in just a little while," he began excitedly. MacLennan regarded him for a long moment. "I'm sorry, Frank," he hedged, "but that's something you just can't hope for around this town."

I used to watch my dad's face as he told that story for the umpteenth time. Dejection hid under his brown skin. His eyes flashed. Because there it was again, big as an old hound dog: the racism, the prejudice, the denial of a chance to advance because of his color.

He had already been jousting with others about his inability to enter certain places in town. Wherever he looked, there were separate waiting rooms and bathrooms and segregated lunch counters. Status quo in the South at the time.

Even the Catholic Church, the church of Dad's choice, required sitting in segregated pews. He protested to the church fathers, decrying the unfairness of it, to no avail. The rule held. Although in those days Topeka was not totally segregated, the movies, restaurants, and churches were divided along racial lines.

Even as a child, I could see that segregation was an assault on Dad's innate independence, his pride, his need to get ahead and be somebody. Although he didn't have a gilt-edged education, he was intelligent and resourceful. He spoke six languages (English, Danish, German, Spanish, French, and the island patois) without a day in a classroom, having acquired them simply by growing up on the island.

There were probably times in my father's life when he thought about giving up or quitting. He didn't. Instead, he rid himself of his resentment and decided to stay in the United States and do what was needed to survive. Thus began the search for a job with a better future. People began to compliment him on the personal confidence he always seemed to exude. He'd flash that famous Petersen smile and seemed to glow with the significance of his Fourth of July birthday. With his flowing West Indian accent, he'd say: "That's what your America requires. You have to prove yourself every day. It's like a challenge—and I like it."

Even though I was young at the time, I remember the attraction of the challenge: to recognize and accept it. It had to be fun. Dad lived it. He became something of a whirling dervish. There was a stint at the Atchison, Topeka & Santa Fe Railroad as an apprentice in their railway shops as he worked his way up to freight car man. Now he could stand tall.

He bought himself some duds and a beautiful two-toned Model T Ford. Got clean. Wore a derby hat and a stickpin in his tie. Sported a high-collared shirt and those straight trousers over high-button shoes with the shiny, knobby toes, the ones the well dressed used to wear in those days. "Sharp as a tack," as black folks used to say.

Still single, Dad heard about all the pretties down at the University of Kansas in Lawrence, where the white folks used to talk about whether or not there ought to be slavery in the state. Lawrence wasn't far. Only a mere twenty-eight miles or so.

I remember seeing a picture of him taken about that time. He was standing in front of his shiny, new Model T Ford with his nickname in metal letters emblazoned on the front of the silver radiator. "P-E-E-T," the saucy letters announced. He was beaming.

Little did he know that he was about to meet a young lady down in Lawrence at the University of Kansas who not only would change his life but would marry him, have his children, and raise hell with him for years about not spelling his nickname correctly on the front of the radiator of his lovely Model T Ford.

2: The Gathering

My mother, Edythe Southard, came from the small town of Syracuse in the southwest corner of Kansas. Admixtures of blood ran in her veins. She was black, Indian, and Irish and pale of countenance. Her hair was long, her face a cross between almost caucasian and decidedly Indian, while the black peeked around the corners of her eyes. She stood about five foot four and was slim built and energetic, mentally as well as physically. Black folks would have described her as "one of them high yallar gals." In her youth, she was as fine as wine and could cook like an angel. She learned about that along with her two sisters early in life. They were all farm girls, raised on the high plains of Kansas.

The choice of Syracuse as a place to settle was one of studied necessity on the part of her widowed mother, who decided what was best for her girls. The family lived originally in the larger city of Wichita, until the so-called authorities decided that the school system would be segregated. This meant, of course, that Edythe and her siblings would attend an all-black school, a long walk across a railroad track, even though an all-white school was closer.

"No way!" exclaimed Mrs. Southard, the first Negro graduate of Friends University in Wichita, as she moved her brood to Syracuse. The logic was cogent. A segregated school system might have made sense to some purists in Wichita because of the sheer numbers of blacks in the city. It did not make sense in Syracuse, where there were no blacks at all until the Southards appeared, and the only school was the one-room schoolhouse where everybody in town sent their children.

That is how my mother and her sisters received their elementary education and grew up on the Kansas plains. (A little brother died in infancy.) Later, Mother graduated from Syracuse High School. From what I can understand of the time, there were few black friends because few blacks ever came to live in Syracuse. Although once or twice a black family showed up, nobody ever knew what brought them there and what made them leave as quietly as they had come. It was a mystery, like the sudden coming of winter and the silent frenzy of spring tiptoeing in on the cadences of melting snow washing down gullies. It simply happened. Of the three sisters, Mother was the only one who got a higher education. She left Syracuse and went on to the University of Kansas. And she went in style, in a buggy with a driver and all the things that went with that sort of excess of the day. Music glorified my mother's soul. An accomplished pianist, she played well enough to give concerts. Her arrival at the University of Kansas did not go unheralded.

As Mother was about to finish her third year of college, Dad showed up on the university campus. He undoubtedly was driving his glorious Model T Ford. From pictures I've seen of him when he was dressed in his "Sunday-go-to-meetings," he had to have been dashing, dressed to the hilt in his wide-lapeled suit, high-collared shirt, stickpinned tie with the sassy knot, handkerchief in the breast pocket—just so. His mustache was shaved with the greatest economy, leaving two precise, small islands of hair on either side of the natural channel between the nose and the upper lip. He had to have been smiling the Petersen special smile that takes over the face. We all got that from him.

As for Mother, I suppose she figured that fate had just walked up and met her, for suddenly there was no time to finish a fourth year of college. There was instead the care and assuaging of my dad, Frank E. Petersen, Sr. Years later, we were to see that love had completely taken her over when, among some dusty, fading family records, we ran across her university registrar transcript for spring 1926. Her grades began unaccountably to fall: Harmony—F, Exercise—F, Instrumentation—D, an incomplete in Practice Teaching. Things improved just a little in the fall months: two Bs, one A, one D. She had totally withdrawn from Harmony. Spring 1927 showed new resolve and intent with a full load of fifteen units. However, the transcript was blank.

Scheduled to graduate in February 1929, she chose instead to marry her newfound love in December 1928, over the objections of her sisters and even the objections of her suitor. They all wanted her to graduate first. But it was a characteristic of the women in her family to make up their own mind—regardless. They were married on Christmas Eve in Kansas City, then made their home in Topeka in a little house at 1110 Clay Street.

My dad thought that advancement had surely come his way after working his way up to freight car man. It was not to be. The high jinks of the 1920s came to an abrupt end with the great stock market crash of 1929. Dad was laid off from his fancy freight car job. Mother was pregnant with her first child. Things were tight; it was back to washing cars. Anne was born on 29 October 1930.

Dad began to notice possibilities in the new invention called radio that was sweeping the country. From the first radio broadcasts in the United States in 1920 through the early 1930s, the medium produced important new stars and personalities: Amos 'n Andy, Bing Crosby, Kate Smith, Eddie Cantor, Burns and Allen. Dad noted that these new radios would malfunction and need repair. He sensed opportunity. It was constantly on his mind.

He decided to take a correspondence course in radio repair. It cost sixty-five dollars, cash up front, or one hundred dollars on time. He didn't have the money, but Elmer Gutting, the man he worked for, did. Gutting not only lent him the money but encouraged him and promised to help get his business under way.

In less than a year, Dad was making more money repairing radios than he was washing cars. I bounced into the world in March 1932. I'm told that acquaintances used to look at me and say: "My goodness, y'all. Would'ja look at this boy? Looks like old Frank E. just spit 'im out."

I admit to an uncanny resemblance to my father. I was named Frank E., too, but Dad liked to call me Buddy, and it stuck. I found out later that it was the song "My Buddy" that folks were going around singing all misty eyed that prompted the conferring of the name.

Another son, William Poulis Petersen, was born in 1934. A little guy, he was called Billy. Seemed to fit.

Dad continued washing cars until 1935. Although the radio repair business he operated out of our home was prospering, he found an extra job at a department store as a salesman and repairman. When he left his old job, Gutting regarded him so highly that he gave him a bonus of two weeks' wages and told him he could come back to work for him anytime.

The Petersen clan was growing fast. Number three son's name was Hans Rupert McKinley Petersen. Momma tacked all this on him the minute he showed up in 1936. He was going to be the last, and she was trying to use up all the family names.

In 1940, the family moved to a better home at 1726 Topeka, where Dad set up his radio repair shop and announced its existence with an appropriate sign out front. I'll never forget the sign, because it gave us a certain prestige in the community. Not many black men in the South had their own business in those days. The shop extended across the front of the house for its entire width and was one story high. The sign, emblazoned across the shop, read PETERSEN'S RADIO. (Later, with the advent of television, the word "TV" was added.) The shop had a framed metal and glass front entrance and signs about the nature of the business in the window. A huge tree sheltered the right side of the shop and the house. A white picket fence separated the house from the driveway, in which sat Dad's Model T Ford. Grass grew in the small front yard. By now, radio not only helped put food on the table, it brought the family closer. My father was an avid sports fan and loved boxing. Although I was still young, I can remember when Joe Louis knocked out James J. Braddock. Whenever there was a big fight, Dad used to make it a family event. He'd go to the store before the fight and bring home a whole gallon of ice cream. We'd all sit around the radio as if we were really at the fight sitting in hundred-dollar ringside seats, whooping and hollering, feinting punches, laughing and clapping, eating ice cream. We were not that different from most black families across America who were listening, because Joe Louis was a definite role model. Where else but in the ring could a black man kick a white man's ass with impunity and walk away smiling with a pocket full of money? Louis was kicking ass and taking names, I do remember. It was like getting into the ring yourself. Envisioning ourseves big time champs. Ass kickers supreme. Name takers extraordinare. Boom! Boom! Boom! Oh, yeah, Bubba!

That wasn't all radio brought to the family. We tracked all the other popular entertainment, too: the Orson Welles thing, the Green Hornet, the Shadow, the Jack Benny Show, the guy named Lamont Cranston. When it came to Amos 'n Andy, though, Mother the schoolteacher stepped in. She was big on diction and education. We had to listen to Amos 'n Andy because they were an example of how we were *not* to talk.

The coming of age of Dad's repair shop wasn't the only outstanding thing that happened that year. According to a *Topeka Daily Capitol* newspaper clipping from Sunday, 31 March 1940, kept by my mother about Dad's success, "Frank Petersen, salesman for the General Electric Department of Crosby Brothers store, on March 6 was admitted to membership in the Toppers Club of the appliance and merchandise departments of the General Electric Company, and handed a plaque and lapel pin as tokens. Membership in the club is the highest honor that General Electric confers upon its retail salesmen. Only ten of one hundred salesmen in the Kansas City area qualified for the recognition."

The year 1940 was also when the United States okayed the sale of surplus war material to Great Britain and transferred overage destroyers to them for use in their struggle with Germany. A little more than a year later, Japan attacked U.S. forces at Pearl Harbor, sinking nineteen ships and killing 2,300 men. War was declared in 1941; I was all of nine years old. I remember FDR's infamy speech on the radio. I don't recall if everyone in the family gathered around the radio the way we normally did when something important happened, but I remember the sonorous sound of the president's voice. The thought crossed my mind that there was going to be a war, but I didn't understand what that meant, except that the Japanese had done us wrong. I was scared but happy that it hadn't been black people who'd done it. I remember that suddenly "Japanese" was a nasty word. We used to call them "Japs" with great derision. We held our mouth just so and adapted the correct body language when we said it, as if we were looking down at a fat caterpillar suddenly fallen from a tree. When we said it, everybody around silently agreed. The consensus around the black community seemed to be, thank God, they've finally found somebody they consider worse than us to hate.

I'm not proud that we jumped on the bandwagon so quickly, however, because it wasn't very long before genuine fear grabbed us as Detroit, Michigan, erupted into wild race riots. I remember a "they're coming to get us" kind of fear. I remember a hunkering down feeling and high apprehension when I was not in my own neighborhood.

Life suddenly seemed to be complex, even for a small fry. There was a lot of military activity at nearby Topeka Army Air Field. I was fascinated by the B-17s, B-24s, and B-29 bombers flying in and out. I was fascinated by all kinds of aircraft, as a matter of fact. I wondered how they worked. I dreamed of going into outer space and grappled with the concept of infinity. I built model airplanes. I loved fighter planes most of all and powered them with rubber bands. Although most of the fighters I built were American, I also built Japanese planes. I even built a German Stuka dive-bomber.

Electronics also fascinated me, and my discovery of that discipline was right up my father's alley. He insisted that I try to understand its concepts and began teaching me, starting me with simple tasks and explaining the basics of electricity. He explained how a flashlight worked. We'd experiment together with things like the tried and true "cat's whiskers," in which we'd move a fine piece of wire across a rusty razor blade to pick up radio signals through an attached earphone.

As I grew older, Dad insisted that I think about the concept of earning a living. His point of view was shared by the father of my best friend, Paul Tyler. Paul and I discussed ways to make our own money. One day, it hit us. Paul's dad had a lawnmower. My dad had shears and a rake. We would start a grass cutting business. A small lawn would cost twentyfive cents, a medium lawn fifty cents, a monstrous lawn a whole dollar. Neither of us was thrilled about our extra job, but we pursued it, until the night we washed off the lawnmower in the park and it "accidentally" ended up in the lake. After a few such episodes, the lawn mowing enterprise seemed to melt into the woodwork.

Paul and I were full of other mischief, too. Because we had to be at church every Sunday, sometimes all day and maybe even at night, we began looking for diversions. I remember asking questions of a little old lady who taught our Sunday school class. We'd done our own comparative analysis of what the Bible said about the age of the Earth and what new science said about that. The figures didn't agree. The Sunday school teacher was annoyed. Her response was, "Children should be seen and not heard." She actually quit. Another Sunday school teacher labeled us "precocious little beasts." We should've been ashamed of ourselves, but we enjoyed it.

Every Sunday morning, Paul and I sang in the youth choir at the AME Baptist Church. After puberty came along, we spent a great deal of time admiring the female figure. At choir practice and every Sunday morning, our lecherous gazes fell on the beauteous Juliet Parks, our choir director. Paul used to remark about how pretty she was. We fell head over heels in love. In 1993, I heard somebody say they'd seen Miss Parks as she was returning from a Caribbean cruise. More than seventy years old, she was reportedly still a fox, and I can truly believe that.

As time passed, my father did things that made me admire him all the more. On a repair call to Topeka Army Air Field, he so impressed the Army brass with his electronics skill and knowledge that the federal government sent him to a civilian training school in Omaha and later to Philadelphia to teach radio in the Signal Corps. During the war, he served as an instructor. When the base was taken over by the Air Force, he became supervisor for the maintenance of Air Force electronics equipment. He came home agog, telling us about a new invention called television, a tube that causes pictures to be transmitted through the air. For a moment, I thought that my father had lost it. "What's he talking about?" I rasped within earshot. "What the hell is he talking about?"

Then he began to explain it in great detail. I sat back as the admiration for my father grew by leaps and bounds. The excitement was catching.

His can-do attitude wasn't lost on me. Later in life, I would remember him as a focused and aggressive man who took racial discrimination in stride and handled it by being independent and confident that he could somehow beat it. He was from the islands, and people from the islands are proud and tough about themselves and life.

"A different kind of nigger," I've heard some folks say. I think they're right. My sister, Anne, says about Dad:

> Daddy was the one who put bread on the table and made sure we were taken care of. I saw him as a man ahead of his time for a lot of things he did. Just the sense of how he got to the States in the first place, that he had his own radio and television business way back then. He didn't work for others. He liked being independent, his own boss.

Mother was as much of a positive influence as Dad but in a different way. Anne remembers her most for her contributions in child rearing, whereas Dad was the perfectionist and disciplinarian. When Dad's discipline got too harsh, we were glad that Mom was around because she would intervene to protect her flock. When we copped a plea to get what we considered justice from Dad, Mom became our court of appeal. We'd go to her first so she could moderate. Most of the time, Dad would cool down. Mom was a peacemaker, quiet in manner but strong and innovative.

Mom had taken home economics in college and was a good cook. Dad would be thrilled when she prepared his favorite—fried fish—which reminded him of the islands. We'd all smack our lips when she'd cook fried chicken and bake lemon meringue pie for dessert. Mom could do chicken so well that we could hurt our stomachs because we'd eat with such abandon.

When times were hard financially for the family, Mom prepared meals for sale. On Sunday, after we'd all come home hungry after a marathon church service, she'd make us wait while she prepared and served people who came to the house to eat the meals they'd purchased. We were upset because we had to wait until those people got through eating "our" food.

I remember when I was about ten years old or so, Mom had us deliver a meal to a lady across town. Fried chicken, it was. As we walked with the chicken dinner, the smell overwhelmed us. My brother Billy and I looked at each other as we walked. Pangs of hunger grabbed us. Not a word was spoken as our eyes met and the wordless decision was reached to do the dastardly deed of purloining a piece of chicken. God, it was so good. With a smile on our faces and probably a bit of fried chicken residue still on our lips, Billy and I delivered the dinner to the hapless lady. We hadn't fooled her one bit. Before we were halfway home, the woman was on the phone to Mom complaining that some chicken was missing from her dinner.

Well, Mom didn't say anything, but she immediately dispatched us with replacement chicken parts back to the outraged lady. I'm sure that Mom knew what we'd done. But that was Mom: quiet, strong, understanding.

By the time we were twelve or thirteen, finances got better and Mom no longer had to sell cooked meals. So on Sunday, our typical routine would be going to church, then to the segregated movie theater down on 4th Street, then back home for the big meal and getting ready for school the next day.

I saw an achiever in Momma. She was more than vocal about pursuing education and intellectual interests. She went back to the University of Kansas and graduated. It was an extraordinary achievement in the 1920s for a black woman in the Midwest to earn a college degree. She'd done it and testified to the efficacy of education as she taught in the public school system and counseled her children at home.

She was responsible for more than our formal education. She helped us learn what the world was all about. A quiet intellectual, she put things around the house that made us think, like the poem that begins, "If you can keep your head when all others about you are losing theirs," which I constantly read and reread. It moved me so much that I memorized the entire thing. She exposed us to music and played "our" piano, an instrument rarely found in a black household in the 1930s and 1940s.

Mom was the reason that I became fascinated with reading, because she encouraged us to know books. My sister, Anne, and I used to enter the reading contests at our local library, which was about four blocks from the house. We'd win the contests from time to time. We loved to go to the library because it was one place in Topeka that wasn't segregated. (The buses weren't either, but schools, restaurants, and movies were.) Aside from the wealth of knowledge that the library contained in books, it was a sanctuary from the incipient craziness that was Topeka if you were black.

Both our parents demonstrated the importance of being your own person and coming out on top. We could get there, they seemed to be saying, only by recognizing what the priorities were. As for school, the priority was coming home and getting our homework done and maintaining a respectful attitude toward our teachers. From all this, there developed among the Petersen clan a kind of family pride involving a sense of dress, etiquette, manners, and speech. A kind of personal worth that said, "You're as good as, if not better than . . ." These are the ethics we carried with us into preschool at Buchanan Elementary and, later, Monroe Elementary. The edict was to always do well, bask in the recognition of the achievement of good grades (a C wasn't good enough), and understand that the only thing worth working toward was excellence.

The teacher I remember most was Eva Montgomery: black, buxom, strong willed, stern but also fair (but who dealt punishment with a ruler), and who connected well with parents.

I found out about the latter the hard way. If we transgressed in school, our parents knew before we got home. It was therefore necessary that we come up with a good excuse before we walked in the door, because there was no escape.

I remember "transgressing" a Miss Catherine King, who was directly in charge of my grade school classroom. I can't remember what it was I'd done, but I do remember that Miss King was of the same mold (cold, stern) as Miss Montgomery. In fact, all the black teachers in the then all-black school system were of that mold. I was only six or seven when I transgressed Miss King. Even at that age, I was feisty. When she chastised me for whatever I'd done wrong, she grabbed me and her fingernails dug into my arm. I kept my fingernails in the same spot to make the indentations even deeper. When Momma mentioned my "transgression," I dramatically unveiled the preserved indentations.

"See?" I said with great bravado. "Look what she did to me."

Momma, a teacher herself, undoubtedly recognized the scam, but it softened her up. I knew I was going to get it, but I had to try to lighten the punishment.

I know that Momma loved me because she showed it when my buddy Paul Tyler and I got bigger and became involved in the all-black Boy Scout troop. On encampment by Lake Shawnee in southeast Topeka, we were shooting for our merit badges in hiking. It was supposed to be only a twelve-mile hike, but we decided to walk around the lake. Unfortunately for us, with all the coves and inlets, it was more like a twenty-five-mile hike. So we were late getting back. Both our mothers were out in the car looking for their lost sons. Guess that's love, too.

I remember the Normandy invasion in 1944. I felt greatly forlorn and vulnerable because Dad was away. Nights and weekends, I'd listen to the airplanes coming and going from Forbes Air Force Base. I'd gotten so I could identify them by the sound of their engines. Although I built models, I wished I could build something I could actually fly.

Before I knew it, the Great War began to show signs of winding down. Roosevelt, Stalin, and Churchill were at Yalta. The U.S. Marines were on Iwo Jima. Two months later, in Warm Springs, Georgia, President Roosevelt died, and we all gathered around the radio again. This time there was no hollering and clapping, no feinting. Instead, it was one single, long funeral that made a big impression on me as the newspeople told how the casket rode on the black steam train, glistening in the heavy light up from Warm Springs. I remember that my parents didn't smile much. They would miss the president's wife, Eleanor, because they thought, as did all of us, that she had a feeling for what we all thought black rights ought to be.

Then Hitler bit the dust. V-E Day. People didn't raise too much hell in Topeka because of that. I remember thinking that the war was about to be over and I was tired of the various restrictions. Yet I appreciated my new latitude; Dad was away and I had a special permit to drive the car, although I was only fourteen. I couldn't drive at night, but I could drive all I wanted during the day. I had a green gas rationing sticker, so we had enough gas. I got to take Mom shopping. She would go to about eighteen different stores with her coupons so she could get the best deal. I had to go with her and wait for her, which drove me crazy. To this day, going shopping with anyone drives me stark, raving crazy.

A few months later, when the United States dropped two atomic bombs on Japan, "Japanese" stopped being a nasty word, and using the slang "Jap" became a shameful thing. Eighty thousand people simply disappeared. The power of such a weapon was incomprehensible. On V-J Day, Topeka people weren't nonchalant. Our house sat right on the highway between the town and the air base, and we could hear the celebrations.

With the coming of junior high school, an almost complete disenchantment with the school system, and Topeka itself, seemed to take hold of me. Paul Tyler and I were singled out because of our high intelligence test results, and we were put in the category called "gifted children." We were immediately pulled from the city school to attend the special course for gifted children. That made me angry, because to get to the "gifted student school," I had to walk five miles across Topeka, whereas the school I ordinarily attended was right across the street. On top of that, it took us a long time to find out our IQ test scores (they were between 135 and 140).

The course of instruction at the new school was interracial. There were some students we liked and some we didn't like. Some we've maintained contact with over the years. After a couple of sessions in this "rarefied" atmosphere, Paul and I rebelled and went back to our old school.

My sojourn at Topeka High School completed my disenchantment with the city. I didn't care if I went to college or not. I simply wanted to leave Topeka. All I could see was unhappiness down the road. If the high school reflected the real lifestyle in Topeka, I wanted no part of it. I hated the quasi-integration, which highlighted, even celebrated, the segregated way of living. Although youngsters of all races sat together in the same classrooms, underneath the "integration," social exception ran deep. There were two school proms: one black, one white. There were separate homecoming kings and queens. There were two basketball teams: one black (the Ramblers), one white. Football was integrated, probably to gain the brawn and speed realized by letting everybody play. The beautiful indoor swimming pool was closed, to prevent the possibility of white and black students swimming together.

Yet things were going on in the world that flew in the face of all this separateness. In 1947, when I was fifteen, black men did things of note—like Jackie Robinson breaking the color barrier in baseball.

Joe Louis and Jackie Robinson were my role models, because I was focused on issues of race. I viewed their success as a sign that things were going to change, that discrimination would soon be illegal. I wasn't a baseball fan then nor am I today, but I always listened to those kinds of events on the radio because I deemed them important.

My brothers, Billy and Hans, and I had grown close over the years partly because we were close in age. Hans was the youngest (we nicknamed him Hansy), and Billy and I had to protect him because, if nothing else, he was Momma's favorite. But Hans and I gravitated toward each other. I was the oldest, he the youngest. But we all knew how to take care of one another. It was a family. If we got into trouble, we got into trouble together.

Some black students seemed to thrive on the separate racial agenda at school. My sister, Anne, thought it was a great experience. The Ramblers were the only black basketball team. In Topeka, blacks didn't play white teams, so the fun for her, at least as a young person, was the bus trips with the Ramblers to Lawrence and Emporia and seeing other black teams play.

That didn't move me much. I ran track instead. I was big in the 880. Dabbled in the 440 and the high jump. But the 880 was my best event. Ran it pretty close to the state record.

During this period, I managed to fall into what I thought was love with a sweet little girl who was so fine and who would surely be the one who'd be bringing me my slippers when I got to be an old guy. I really thought she'd wait until I got my life in order. She became a definite plus in my life. Judy was her name. Sweet Judy, my first love.

Beyond that, the family involvement in St. John's AME Church may have acted as a palliative from time to time. Church every Sunday. Sunday school first, and then the main service. Singing in the young folks' choir. Youth activities late afternoon and early evening and then we'd try to sneak away. Making friends. Seeing Judy around. Cementing relationships. For the black kids, the church was our main source of social activity. Young blacks would come from all over town. It was our real hangout.

Even so, my disenchantment with Topeka was complete. I wanted to escape. Spread my wings. Go beyond the confines of Topeka's narrow world and see the big world. There were two oceans I had never seen. I knew I couldn't see the world without joining the military. So, at seventeen, the U.S. Navy beckoned. Friends who had come home from the Navy told me some good stories about the service. I felt myself to be a kind of fish in water. I wanted to see the ocean. What better place to be than in the U.S. Navy in order to do that?

Just the idea of it brought me into direct confrontation with my parents. In those days, it took the signature of both parents to enlist in the military as a seventeen year old. Dad was willing to sign at first, but Mother adamantly refused.

"No, I'm not going to sign," she said. Now Dad agreed. I was furious. The ultimate word was that I was going to get a college education and not go running off to join the military.

It was a traumatic time in the Petersen household. My brothers and sister were awed by my recalcitrance.

"Gee, whiz," they marveled. "Here's the brightest kid of the whole bunch, and he doesn't want to go to college. Wow!"

I'd even tried to talk my buddy Paul Tyler into joining up with me.

"Are you crazy, man?" he asked.

My father and I not only looked alike, we possessed the same volatile temperament, which was in evidence when he decided to back up Momma on the issue of joining the military. I was looking for independence and wanted to branch out. From 1946 to 1948, for example, I'd dug ditches on a construction crew. I wanted to do what I wanted to do when I wanted to do it. But there was Dad, staring me down, grinding out the "old school" rhetoric: "In my house, you do what I say or you don't stay here."

So at seventeen, after my senior year in high school, I enrolled in nearby Washburn University. The atmosphere was better than in high school. The student body was totally mixed. So was football.

Art Fletcher, soon to be a pro ball player and eventually head of the Equal Opportunity Employment Commission (EEOC), was there. Sam Jackson, one day to be a high-powered Washington D.C., attorney, was there. A highly qualified group, as I recall.

Even so, after a year at Washburn, I still strained against the imaginary shackles binding me to home. One day, my father and I stood in the house, glowering at each other. I will never forget the scenario.

"I believe," he said with great levity, "this house is gettin' a little too small." Then he walked away.

I didn't get the message at first. Then, suddenly, came the light. He was telling me to get out and see what the world was all about. I was eighteen, and I didn't need anybody's signature to leave or to join the military.

I raced down to see the Navy recruiters.

In one corner of my mind, misgivings erupted for a moment. The news from the Far East left a bit to be desired. North Korea had invaded South Korea. President Truman had sent in ground troops and authorized air strikes against the North in an attempt to secure peace in South Korea. I couldn't help but wonder if I was doing the right thing. But I'd made up my mind.

Momma might smile when I get ready to go and wish me well, I thought, but I didn't think it was going to be the happiest day of her life. Dad and my siblings would survive it. As for Judy, the love of my life, I thought about it and concluded, well, it's love, isn't it? That's the greatest thing of all. At least that's what I'd learned in Sunday school. So I knew she'd be here when I got back.

3: A Great Steward

It felt as if the entire world was opening its arms to me as I rushed down to the Navy recruiting office to take its entrance examination. The granite face of the old post office building scowled with age as I passed the front entrance, then climbed the steps to the second floor. The two semesters at Washburn University were far behind me. That place simply wasn't where my mind was. My grades showed it. I was not so much a student as I was someone warming a seat.

An overweight petty officer third class greeted me as I entered the examination room. Brusque in demeanor, he steered all of us would-be recruits to our seats. As he barked the examination instructions, it was clear that he fancied himself supremely important. The applicable lingo for him, I was to later find, was "Old Salt." He gloried in his role as the consummate veteran, bent upon impressing neophyte landlubbers that he knew what the Navy was all about. As far as I was concerned, the test seemed relatively unremarkable. I zipped through it, turned in the completed answer sheets, and went home full of confidence. Not more than two days later, the Old Salt was on the telephone.

The voice half growled, half cajoled. "Frank Petersen?"

"Yep."

"Say, listen, I'd like to talk with you about your entrance examination. You don't mind coming back in?"

"Well," I started, "what's—"

"It isn't serious. Won't take long."

"All right," I agreed, as all kinds of fears beset me. Did I really blow the damned thing? Was this guy trying to pull a shrewdy? Hell, in my view, the test simply wasn't that hard. And beyond all that, the guy's voice didn't sound right to me. It wasn't that official, sounded indifferent. The Old Salt timbre was missing. My guard went up.

I sauntered into the old post office building and climbed the steps to the second floor as my brain worked feverishly to solve this puzzle. What in the world was bugging this guy? Once inside, I saw that there was nothing indifferent about the fat little petty officer. Suspicious attitude sat atop his persona like a huge fly. How did Frank Petersen feel about this section of the text as opposed to another part of the text? Did he find it too hard to do? Did he somehow have outside help that the officer didn't know about? My back began to rise a bit. Although he meant to hide his intent, his questions pointed to the fact that he thought I'd cheated on the examination.

He tried a smile.

"Would you mind," he grated, "retaking the examination? Just to make sure?" My eyes lasered. I was right. It was clear he'd thought I'd cheated. The inference was there, written big, like God writes stuff in the sky when He's upset. You know, "There's no way in hell or in this world that a black guy could possibly do this well on this examination. Just no way."

A strange resolve overcame me. I took the examination papers and sat down. The Old Salt sat down, too, this time in the room with me. No roving about. No cigarette breaks. He just sat there watching me, like a little black-footed ferret watching a prairie dog.

I zipped through the test again.

He took my test papers, slapped down the answer key, and graded the exam on the spot. I coughed away the silence. He grunted. The silence shook. His cheeks and ears flushed red as he finished the grading. A smile helter-skeltered his face. Why, I'd scored the highest score he'd ever recorded in that recruiting station. Did I realize that? I'd done that on the first try, and did even better on the second. The Old Salt was impressed.

He took me aside, and as we walked, his voice assumed a kind of sotto-voce quality.

"Wow!" he enthused. "Petersen, my boy, the Navy has opportunities for guys like you. I like what I've seen here. My God, man, what a great steward you'd make."

He could not have insulted me more had he slapped me. I recoiled. Rage crashed through my system like a flash flood in the Mojave.

"I'm not going into the Navy if that's what the new stipulation is," I spat, and I bolted from the room, down the stairs, into the concreted world of Topeka, which assumed the properties of a strange kind of prison from which it was important that I escape on the first thing smoking. The outrage grew inside me, and I could hear Old Salt's voice: "Well, you know, the Navy has—er—good career opportunities. How'd you like to become a steward?"

Arriving home, I burst into my father's work space. Startled, he put down the electronics on which he was working. "Hey," I cried, "this Navy thing ain't gonna work, Dad." All of it spilled out. Passing the first examination. The disbelief. Retaking the examination. The suspicion. The looks. The insulting invitation to become a "great steward" in the United States Navy.

My father was visibly upset. He didn't say much. But then, that was his style. He never said much, but I knew that whenever any of the children had a problem, he'd quietly go around to that location and "drop a dime on the people." (It was the black folks' way of saying that an injustice has been done and somebody will have to do something to fix it, even if it means dropping a dime in the pay phone to call Jesus Christ Himself.) I knew there would be no backing off on the part of my father when it came to our family.

Nobody knows for sure if Frank Sr. put a bee in the Old Salt's bonnet, but there was a second conversation between the Old Salt and me. Amenable. Good-natured. No apologies, but no animosity in his voice. There were, it seems, other opportunities in the Navy, to be sure. The highest-level electronics technician school at Treasure Island, California, for example. How'd you like to go there?

In some respects, my father's quiet intervention reminded me of a more raucous one captained by my sister, Anne. Older than I, she was also Daddy's pet. Smarter than I, she would also be a sort of surrogate mom, worrying about and looking after us. And that is how she happened upon a scourge of my youngest years, the school bully, who was yet again assaulting and picking on me as I tried to get home from grade school. Perhaps only seven or eight years of age, I hadn't yet learned to defend myself, and this guy obviously thought that picking on me was tastier than the biggest ice cream cone or the biggest doughnut or the hugest piece of apple pie a la mode he could ever come by. That's when Anne finally jumped him. Told him to knock it off as she probably threatened a right cross to the chops. So I was thankful for my big sis. But, by the same token, she was also the first to report to our parents any transgressions that my brothers and I were guilty of. She was a kind of two-edged sword, I guess. But we all knew how to take care of one another. It was family, and if we got into trouble, we got into trouble together.

And family had helped do it again. That's how, on 6 June 1950, I got to sign up in the Navy with a guarantee of going to the El Toro electronics technician school after completion of boot camp.

• • •

Dawn seemed to jump-start the morning sun earlier than usual the day I left to join the U.S. Navy. On the one hand, I was glad to go, because it was the ultimate fulfillment of a yearned-for dream. To get out there in the world and be part of it. To see it. To do something grand, maybe. And if that didn't work, well, then, I'd come back to Topeka and do electronics, just like my dad.

Breakfast conversation assumed a strange kind of tentativeness. Were my bags all packed? Did I have everything I needed?

Suddenly, it was time to walk out the door. The troop train would be leaving within the hour. Mother wouldn't be going to the train depot. She would say her good-byes in the quiet serenity of our home. I felt the slackening of the apron string that young men feel when the time comes to leave the nest. I turned to say good-bye, and she was in my arms. Her eyes sought mine and I could see the great tears form, then well and flow softly down her cheeks.

"Oh, Buddy," she managed, "I don't want you to go."

I smiled at the nickname. Buddy. That name conferred on me long ago by my father was used by everyone in the family and everybody who knew us in Topeka. It gave me a warm feeling. Like an inside joke, you had to know the origins of it to latch onto the emotions of it.

"I know, Momma. I know." And I was sorry that she cried. It made for a gloomy feeling inside because I didn't know what awaited me out in the big world. I knew it was going to be an adventure. That's what I was hoping for. But somehow, my mother's tears highlighted the uncertainty.

My father went with me to the train depot. There was a kind of magic in that, because all of a sudden there was no longer just a father-son thing going on. Now there were two grown men mouthing good-byes on the station concourse. A sort of quintessential emotional control rode over it. Frank Sr.—Daddy—seeing his spitting image—his Buddy—off to be part of the world. My father tried to hold back the tears, as fathers were expected to do in those days, but a bit more moisture than usual gathered in his eyes. As the new, suddenly grown "me" boarded the train, I looked back at my father just in time to see him slip the porter a twenty-dollar bill, to "keep an eye on my son all the way out to California." The gesture made me smile. The warmth of it, just knowing that my father loved me, turned that bill into twenty-four-carat gold.

The train eased out of the Topeka station and began its measured clatter west. As I sat next to a window, apprehension and excitement grew. I could feel the porter's eyes on me from time to time, but I didn't care.

Watching the scenery rush past the window was more exciting and important. I'd never been very far from home. At first, it was simply a kick to see the names of the towns in Kansas I'd only heard about flash past, then I'd look away. But then I found myself looking out the window again. The countryside mesmerized me as I stared at all those places I'd read about in books. Denver. The Rockies. Salt Lake City. At every stop, more and more young men on their way to boot camp came aboard. All of us were young and leery of the others. Attempts at conversation stumbled.

But I just thought, adios, Topeka. I sang it quietly to myself. Long gone, and ain't I lucky? Long gone from old Topeka. The new song became a kind of singsong in my head, the rhythm set by the motion of the train surging along the rails as we melded into the startling sunshine. Flowers along the right-of-way seemed brighter, more colorful than they had before. Sometimes I could see crows sailing with abandon on crooked wings. I was leaving a place that, through no fault of its own, seemed to limit any view of distant horizons. My time as a young boy seemed to melt away as my life disappeared into another time that I was all too glad to let go.

Suddenly, the train broke out on the California coast up around San Francisco. I'll never forget that morning. Waking up and looking out the window. Seeing the Pacific Ocean for the first time in my life.

I stayed at that window as the train roared down the coast toward San Diego and boot camp. Beyond that, I was dreaming of that electronics technician school at Treasure Island. The rhythm of the train's steel wheels caressing the segmented tracks lulled me. I thought about my father back home and his TV and radio business. About how he recognized that his son, ever curious about electricity, was interested in the craft. About how my dad taught me the basics by showing me, then letting me practice on my own. The flashlight battery and figuring how the current caused the bulb to light. In my mind I could see my little room at home rigged with all sorts of battery cells. I soldered a piece of wire on the bottom and the top of a battery, touched the wires together on the bulb, and watched the bulb light up. My father's explanations about the components of a radio and what they did. Cutting up capacitors and pulling them apart to see how they did what it was they did. Learning how to put a charge on a condenser for fun, then taking it outside to throw at my buddies just to watch the damned thing discharge and give them a slight jolt. Great fun. Smoking out the theories behind the old radio tubes, how they were constructed, what each of their ele-

ments did, and how the current flowed through. Learning to use the
tools of the trade: the oscilloscope, the voltmeter, the analyzers. Putting
something in one end of a radio circuit and seeing how it would be
changed as it moved through the circuit. Learning the names of the radio tubes. Power tube. Rectifier tube. On and on.

Los Angeles sprawled before us as the train criss-crossed junctions en
route to Union Station. We'd been gliding along the railroad tracks now
for one day, one night, and another day. I was still at the window, drinking in all the history and projecting myself, albeit timidly, beyond Navy
boot camp, now just hours away.

As the train serpentined the environs of San Diego, I thought about
my sweet babe Judy, my high school heartthrob. I was at this precise moment crazy about the young lady. I thought about how we'd been together the night before I left Topeka. Spending the evening together
around the corner at her house. Vowing love that lasted forever. Love
that's set in concrete, won't ever change, and all that kind of stuff. The
"you know I'm going to be here when you get back" thing. Kisses, hugs.
She didn't come to the station to see me off, and maybe that was good
in the long run. That evening alone at her house was decidedly better,
I guess, and my Dad wasn't around, either.

A person could be happy about being in San Diego. The sun, sand,
and beaches warmed the heart. Navy boot camp, although stringent, was
a bit saner than its Marine counterpart close by, where I heard how they
drove you into the base in the dark on back roads, confronted you with
bright lights and mean-as-hell drill instructors in Smokey the Bear hats
just cussing, yelling, and screaming about wiping whatever smile you
might have off your face.

In place of that, I had a "good shepherd" drill instructor named Bunz.
Chief Bunz. New regimens changed my life. Marching everywhere we
went to cadences called by my new omnipresent acquaintance, a Navy
chief named Bunz. He ensured our initial isolation, the issuance of shoes
much too big (there was a method to the madness, because he knew
that our feet were going to swell with all the marching coming up). Issuance of uniforms and seabags, linen and blankets. A date with the barber where all our hair was buzzed off without so much as even asking
our permission. Instructions on how to make a rack (bed) the Navy way.
How to shower. Everything was taken away except for a small bag called
a ditty bag. Slung around our necks, it contained everything of importance—toothbrush, toothpaste, comb, razor. There were field days,

when washing our clothes and cleaning our shoes were the big agenda items. Hovering over all were the classroom instructors, the rifle range, the exercises. More isolation. The maddening sameness of it all. Into bed by ten o'clock every night, until we were lucky enough to catch the night fire watch duty. Two-hour shifts. Walking around the barracks. Being certain that all cigarettes were extinguished, inside and outside the barracks.

After a month, the Navy bent a bit and allowed us entry into the Gedunk—a small heaven of candy, Cokes, and other sweets. Established rewards based on the status of individual accomplishment. The sunlight seemed to peek through, if only for a moment.

First liberty. A night on the town, a short foray into San Diego. A chance to fly where the real sailors flew. Tattoo parlors beckoned. Maybe when I could stay in town longer, I could get that tattoo I wanted. That'll show Judy how much I care. Burn that old girl's name right into the skin on my forearm. Forever mine. Yes, sir, Buddy. She's my baby.

And before I knew it, we were back. Bunz. Marching. 'Cruit. Exercise of military custom. Reduce everything and everyone to the least common denominator. Bring them all in. Break them all down. Destroy our basic personalities and psyches. Teach us to come together as a unit. Achieve sameness of identity. Scare the hell out of everybody. Move. Move. March. March. "Whaddya mean, weapons? Yew don't need no weapons. Y'gotta learn how to walk first."

And then, one day, a rifle in the hands. A big rifle in the hands. An M-1 with leaded barrel so it can't be fired. But we could drill with it. Hook it in a tripod when we didn't need it. Carry it when we marched. Exercise with it held high above our head. March. March. March.

Civilian clothing was out. In uniform always. We were all a bunch of kids, and just a little scared so that the fear itself heightened the initial isolation. The isolation telescoped into three months of training. We thought when that was over, it would be time for a little dancing music. A little leave. To saunter and pose around the girls (with appropriate mental apologies to Judy back in Topeka). A brand-new sailor on the job for his country. And just across the border, just a few klicks away, the Mexican town of Tijuana beckoned.

But all that was denied us. Deep into 1950, the Korean War was on in earnest. Nobody was allowed to go on leave from boot camp. As far as Tijuana was concerned, none of us would have gone if we'd gotten the chance. Tijuana was not the place for the young and uninitiated. We were scared, having heard all those stories about what could happen to us over there among the garish lights, the painted whores, and the marijuana smoke hanging in the air. And if something didn't happen to us while we were there, the possibility was high that something of our anatomy that was very dear might just fall off when we least expected it. So we were scared to death. And because we were in uniform, we would have been easily identified. We were a bunch of kids fresh off the farm and just a little too unsure about getting out there to see some of that stuff.

The plan was, I seem to remember, that everyone in my training group was to go directly from boot camp to their next duty assignments. Although I didn't know it, the fact that I'd applied for electronics school meant that my time in San Diego was swiftly coming to an end, and I would soon proudly be Apprentice Seaman Frank E. Petersen. Not exactly the fulfillment of a dream, but a start.

After I finished boot training, I was held at San Diego for about a month prior to electronics school at Treasure Island. My work was burial details. Coffins and greensward. Tears and taps in the eerie quiet of cemeteries. Sometimes I wondered if this would be my fate. Home from the war in a box. But it was something to do until the opening of my electronics class at Treasure Island.

There was no leave. Straight to Treasure Island. The Korean War continued to rage. Back home in Topeka, a guy named Richard was eyeballing my Judy baby.

MUTUAL VOICES
Ernie Douglas, Childhood Friend

Yeah, I remember Frank. He was a couple of grades ahead of me, but you know, in an all-black grade school that didn't really mean anything. So we lived in the same neighborhood. I knew his brothers, sister, his mother, and his father. I can say that his father was definitely diligent and, I guess you could say, a guy who was persevering. Because, you know, for a black man to try and do a business in Topeka, Kansas, back in the forties or fifties—well, you know, that was a miracle as far as I'm concerned.

I guess that's one reason Frank couldn't wait to get out of that town. I kind of feel that anybody who had any get-up-and-go about them couldn't wait to get out of that town. There was nothing happening there for young blacks or even an old black. I guess the older generation kinda felt like they were stuck there. The war years were an exodus from Topeka for most blacks who were older or senior to me. Lot of them moved west, heading for California. Now you take Frank, for example. His kind had that get-up-and-go, I'd say. If there was anything I could really put my finger on, he wasn't somebody who'd sit there and let the grass grow, you know. I guess you'd almost say he was a leader—somebody who'd just get out there and show you that if there was something you wanted to get after, it was out there to get after.

_____Part Two
Trial by Fire

4: The Gauntlet

The sights and sounds of San Francisco made my pulse beat faster. The bus to Treasure Island crossed the Oakland Bay Bridge, spilled into a short tunnel, followed a crooked road accessing Yerba Buena Island, then led down sharp curves and across the causeway leading to the base. Opposite the causeway, destroyers and destroyer escort ships were docked, getting ready to hook up with the aircraft carriers and other big ships coming out of Alameda. Treasure Island lay in front of me like a postage stamp. Exactly one square mile in area, the island was the site of the 1939–40 World's Fair. It has been under Navy control since 1941.

The bus slowed to a crawl as it negotiated the main gate and the red shore patrol station on the right. On a long, low wall bending around the corner of the first intersection upon entering the installation, large burnished letters announced the facility: U.S. NAVAL STATION. The words "Treasure Island" were centered below the grand pronouncement. I looked over my shoulder. The Oakland Bay Bridge, cantilevered over the water on steel stilts, led toward the Oakland Hills and Alameda in one direction and gestured grandly toward the concrete buildings and streets of San Francisco in the other.

In those days, barracks and many of the classrooms for the electronics school I was to attend sat directly ahead on the right side of the main road. Hastily built in the shape of an H, the beige buildings were to be my home for weeks as I learned the skills involved in becoming an electronics technician.

The courses were relatively easy for me because of all the instruction I'd gotten from my father back in Topeka, along with his reminders of electronics theory afforded while we swam in the rivers and shot squirrels with BB guns. Here, it was essentially diagnosing a problem, then swapping a malfunctioning electronics part for a new one.

• • •

The San Francisco Bay area was a hell of a place for liberty. My buddy Merrill Scott and I went in together and bought an old, ratty gray-green '37 Buick. We had no money for insurance, and couldn't take it on the base. We'd park it in strategic locations, then ride the bus to get to it, then go and do our thing. Coming back onto Treasure Island at three in the morning was another experience as the wind turned wicked and whipped across the landscape.

We were afraid of the San Francisco jazz club scene and stayed away from the Fillmore in San Francisco, for example, because it was unfamiliar territory for us. Those wild jazz clubs were far too big and boisterous. Just being there put a damper on us and made us feel as if something bad was going to happen. When we did go there, our demeanor was low key. Most of our time was spent in Oakland because my buddy had relatives there. Meeting the ladies thereabouts was thus simplified. We worked part-time on our weekends unloading ships. His relative was a stevedore and ran interference for us. We weren't busting union. Because we were military, they let us go in and work. We'd unload ships from six o'clock in the evening until six o'clock in the morning. For the times, the pay was scrumptious. Big-time money. Fifty bucks for a night's work.

Late on a December evening in 1950 on Treasure Island, I lay sacked out listening to music and the news on my portable radio, as was my usual habit. That's when I heard about Ens. Jesse L. Brown, the black Navy pilot shot down over Korea. The first black man to earn the Navy's "wings of gold," Jesse manned his F-4U Corsair on the carrier USS *Leyte*, flew off on a mission to help free a trapped Marine division, and was killed. A posthumous Distinguished Flying Cross was awarded. I sat straight up. Possibilities surged in my mind. My first awareness dawned that blacks could, in fact, be a part of the Naval Cadet Program. It was a dream I'd harbored. Jesse had done it, so now it didn't seem impossible. Perhaps it could be done again.

Caution flags went up in my brain, because in those days, if you were black, you just never knew. Segregation had supposedly ended in the military, but the Navy and the Marines were the last people to even entertain the idea of integrating their forces. Nobody was running around flying flags at half-mast for old Jesse. But there it was. Jesse Brown had been the first black pilot to fly in the U.S. Navy, and that was the reason for the wide publicity that his untimely death received. I was sad over his death, but at the same time I felt a kind of joy. I knew that I, too, could try to become a Navy pilot. Jesse had done it. Why not me? The next day, jack out the box, I applied for Naval Cadet training. Yes, sir. Apprentice Seaman Second Class Frank Emmanuel Petersen defined his own reality by making a move. Somehow, everything seemed theoretical to me unless I acted in the moment. I would never become a pilot of any kind if I didn't act. I expected the usual problems linked to race as I applied, but there didn't appear to be any. I thought my age would be a factor, because I was still relatively young. But it was my sense that the Navy was looking only for the young.

Retrospectively, I understand that war changes things; ironically, war can make some things a little bit easier. Korea and a war spawned a need for aviators. Whether I was black or blue didn't seem to be of any consequence to the people taking my application. They proved it, too, because later I found out, much to my amusement, that the person taking my application simply marked it "caucasian," so inured was he to the fact that it had to be someone representing that segment of the Navy applying for the Naval Aviation Cadet Program.

Arrival at Pensacola Naval Air Station's Basic Training Command for air cadets in Florida was traumatic. I knew I had a problem as soon as I assessed the racial climate. I had fled my hometown to escape racism, only to find myself caught in a deeper kind of prejudice than Topeka ever knew. Separate water fountains in the gym. Designated latrines. The back-of-the-bus routine. I didn't know it at the time, but only three blacks had completed the Naval Aviation Cadet Program before my arrival: Jesse, who wiped out in Korea; a guy named Floyd, who was killed in a crash in Atlantic City; and Earl Carter, who was to have a successful career, only to die long before his time of bone cancer. It was pretty lonely, being the only black in a cadet corps of maybe two to three thousand.

New arrivals were put into an incoming battalion called Battalion X, or Bat X. We got preliminary instructions on marching and military protocol—shadings of routines covered in boot camp. Out of the rack at 0600. Calisthenics until breakfast. The classroom day began. Lunch break. More exercise and calisthenics. Dinner about five o'clock or so. Study, study, study. They tucked us in at ten o'clock. Taps. Lights out. Eight hours of sleep, then bite the bulldog again like you'd never bitten him before. Watch your back. Ward off the demerit points for not doing something right. Shoes not shined, mister. Your bed ain't tight enough, my friend. Your cubicle leaves a bunch to be desired, kind sir. And what kind of grade do you call that? I see right now that probation's gonna be the name of your game. Liberty's denied. You got up late this morning. Liberty's denied. It was tough. Four months of classroom work before our first flight.

We were billeted in rooms to which four to six cadets were assigned. It soon became evident that if you were black, you were watched closely. We had to wear our uniforms at all times. In preflight, we were required to go to Sunday sevices. We'd march in as a unit. This was particularly trying for me, and it turned out to be almost an insult, because as I walked in I could almost feel the nudging, the turning, twisting, and craning of the necks of the people there. Turning and looking at this "new one." This "black one." My sensitivity to the stares ran deep. It made me anti–established religion. I absolutely hated walking in there, being the only black in the entire place and somehow being "the show." I hate the memory of it, even today.

For many weeks I never saw another black cadet, but there was one named Dave Campbell in the class a year ahead of mine. He was brilliant academically. He heard that "another black" had arrived on station, so he looked me up and took me under his wing, introduced me to people in the city, and grounded me in what to anticipate. We became close friends. It was Dave, in fact, who pointed out to me that never, in the history of the U.S. Marine Corps, had there ever been a black pilot, let alone a black fighter pilot. It was a goal he had in mind for himself, and he convinced me that I should also try to break the barrier. We swore, one to the other, that if one of us didn't make it through Naval Cadets, the other would give the Marines a try. If I didn't make it, I was to try to convince the next black coming through the program to try.

Weeks later, Dave left to go to Texas for advanced flight training. While he was there, he was busted out on his final attempt in carrier landing qualifications. I was alone again. The fact that Dave didn't make it scared the hell out of me. I figured they would get me, too.

Things got busy quickly, and suddenly there wasn't enough time to worry about the history of black cadets. Signs in the aircraft hangars and the ready rooms were enough to mess up your mind, especially if you planned to be the best pilot in the whole U.S. Marine Corps. One sign pumped you up. In big black letters, it read: "Can Do!" The other one could scare your socks off, depending on how you felt on any given day. It read: "What you don't know won't hurt you—it will KILL you." I never forgot either one of those damned signs.

Gray flight. We were in the airplane at long last, an SNJ two-seater trainer, comparable to the Air Force AT-6 trainer. It shook me up. Airsickness. Found out I had a problem with heights—acrophobia. Helluva thing if I was ever going to be a pilot. I wasn't about to let this thing get the better of me. So I figured I'd just mentally take the ground up there with me in the airplane. No matter how high or low or what the attitude, the ground was always going to be just below my feet. Acrobatics. Formation flying. Simulated carrier landing protocols coming up fast. Going in, I'd at least found another buddy in the person of Edgar A. House, from Memphis, Tennessee, another black naval cadet and a pretty sharp one at that. We ripped and ran together all around the black sections of Pensacola. The Sugar Bowl. Slim's. Meeting the schoolteachers, because we figured they knew everybody in town who was anybody. Evelyn DuBose, for example. She was a good friend, never anything more than that. We all went out, danced together, had fun together.

Although all the fun and games on liberty were heady, I was getting exceedingly worried about my ability to successfully finish the Naval Cadet Program. I had an instructor who dogged my heels unmercifully. A Marine captain. Big, husky, beefy, a loudmouth, J. A. Blair seemed to be just laying in the weeds for me, just waiting to do me in on my solo check ride, one of the most important times of an aviation cadet's training. If you blow that, your can's in the grass. The party's over.

On liberty the weekend before my scheduled solo check ride, after I had just completed a particularly rigorous part of my training, I wandered into the Sugar Bowl. Disconsolate, I just didn't know how I was going to survive those aviation instructors. I was certain that the harassment, at least J. A. Blair's, was based on race. All of a sudden I saw a tall black Army Air Corps captain across the room. I thought I was seeing things. After what I'd been going through, I was convinced that I was looking at an absolute miracle. More than the rank, my God, he was wearing tracks *and* wings.

He was Dan "Chappie" James, destined to be America's first black four-star general, holding forth at the Sugar Bowl bar on one of his trips home. I was feeling pretty down, and we talked for about two hours. I told him about the hard times, the racism, the possibility of never making it because of that. I laid it all out there, including the fact that the black guy just in front of me had been wiped out. I felt that "they" were simply waiting to wipe me out, too. There weren't any more blacks coming into the program. It was a lonely existence. Eight months, and where are the blacks?

Chappie stayed so long that he had to cancel his civilian flight home. He could've run. He didn't. He stayed there and listened.

He didn't say an awful lot at first, except that I could make it if I wanted it badly enough. Hang in there. I could do it. Just don't give up.

I looked at him and somehow felt new resolve. I mean, here was a living example that it could be done. I had a role model now. He patted me on the shoulder, then he said it again: "Just don't give up." That audience with Chappie helped get me through.

My solo check ride day seemed particularly bright. Old J. A. Blair seemed nastier and louder than usual. We took off and I did it. Blair was growling when we came back.

"Ya did evuhthing wrong," he exploded.

My heart sank. This guy was going to give me a "down," meaning that I hadn't qualified.

"Ya know whut?" he continued. "Yer totally, and ah mean totally, unqualified. Do ya want me to repeat that? Ah sed, totally unqualified. Do ya read me, cadet? Ah don't see no way in hell yer evuh gonna become a pilot, 'cause ya just cain't hack it, period."

I felt that the instructor was a little too quick to condemn.

The next day, without flying any further training flights, I was assigned a new instructor, who took me out, supposedly to restart that particular phase of training. Except he climbed out of the airplane and said, "Go fly it." I didn't know it at the time, but the instructors had taken a consensus among themselves and removed the instructor who had given me a "down." I never went back to J. A. Blair. My next solo check ride went off as smooth as silk. It was heartening, given the fact that in those days racial discrimination was evident almost everywhere.

MUTUAL VOICES
Evelyn DuBose, Pensacola Friend

He was like a part of our extended family. We had a big family and there were always lots of people. Our door was always open. I recall that my sis and niece went to [some affair] and I couldn't go because of the hay fever being so bad. They met him and maybe brought him by the house— I don't know—I just looked around and there he was. I think one of the reasons he came to our house so much was there was really no place else to go. There weren't any decent places open, except hanging on the blocks and that kind of thing. We could just look at him and know that it had been tough. I remember one day he came in and he looked kind of sad. We asked what the matter was. And he told us how, in the billets that day, he'd been combing his hair and some [white cadet] had made a disparaging [remark]. You know, like: "What's that you're combing?" And I could tell that emotionally, he'd been touched by that. When there was something that

*meant a lot to him, it was projected in his conversation. We would just
ride it with him and tell him he could do it and tell him we were there and
just know it's going to turn out all right. [We did] all the things you do
to support a person.*

No matter where I was, on the ground or in the air, that old racism
bug always seemed to jump up and bite me. Things weren't too bad at
the Aviation Cadet Recreational Club (ACRC) on the air station. Beers.
Ping-Pong. Pool. That kind of stuff. Everybody was in there, no matter
what the color of their skin, except for Sundays, of all days, which I found
particularly galling.

Liberty could be even worse. Southern hospitality abounded, but its
face was definitely either white or black, with damned few in-betweens
downtown in Pensacola, the only game in town when it came to taking
liberty. I guess it all started on base. For instance, we could ride the bus
on base, but once we reached the main gate, we were under local laws
as opposed to federal laws, and we had to get up and move to the back
of the bus. Conversely, coming back into the base at night, if we were
in the back of the bus, we could now move up to the front, which we
did religiously both ways. In interstate travel, we had to sit in the back
of the bus.

The movie theater in town was segregated. Blacks sat in the balcony
(called "peanut heaven" by the locals); the good seats elsewhere in the
theater were reserved for whites. It was insulting and embarrassing, especially walking up to the theater with a date and seeing my roommates
there in the same line with their dates.

"Hey, Frank," they'd yell when they saw us walk up, "are you going to
see the movie?"

"No, no," I'd lie, a half-smile straining my face, "just going for a walk."
I'd pretend I wasn't going to the movie because I knew that once we were
all inside, they would be seated on the first floor and my date and I would
be pointed to the balcony. That was really a low point. Lots of those white
guys didn't know the Southern laws. They just didn't know, and nobody
explained it to them.

And there was the San Carlos Hotel, "their" big hot spot. Their hangout. Big parties. Dances. Black cadets simply couldn't get into the place.
So I spent my off-duty time in the black portion of Pensacola and made
close friends with several of the people in the area.

Back on the base, my flight instructor was giving me fits. The infer-
ences were that I wouldn't make it through the course of flight in-

struction. "Downs" were frequent. Don't get me wrong. Naval Cadet training is meant to be tough. But the white cadets could lean on one another. Camaraderie was real and present for them. The issue of race and color were not real factors. Until I was near the last quarter of my training, I was the only black on site. I caught hell.

Then a black guy named A. L. Lamb came into the program. Unfortunately, Lamb didn't make it through. But while he was around, we became pretty good buddies and did lots of running around together on liberty. Things were beginning to look up, because President Truman ruled that interstate travel could not be segregated, and we were about to take off on a weekend to Mobile, Alabama, just across the state border aboard an interstate bus.

The Florida law, in spite of the presidential ruling, was still that blacks could sit in the "white section" of the bus when the "black section" was full and the white section was not, by moving forward row by row. There was a line, I think, or perhaps it had to do with the placement of the rear door, but everything to the right and front of that line was white.

When we got on, we sat in the white section because the black section was full. The white passengers protested to the bus driver, who promptly ordered us to go stand in the black section, even though there were no other whites up front. We knew that this was pure intimidation; this was an interstate bus and we knew what the law was.

"I'm not moving," I spat.

"Git on back theah," the bus driver rasped, adding fuel to the burgeoning fire, "or I ain't movin' this bus no further."

I heard shuffling and movement behind me. Looking back, I saw that the black people were moving their belongings so we could go back there and sit with them. I hated to see my people literally bowing and scraping to this bus driver, who obviously considered himself "the Almighty," hell bent for election to ignore the law regarding interstate travel.

Then we heard some absolutely beautiful words escape the bus driver's mouth. He said: "Git off the bus now, or ah'm gonna throw you off."

That sounded to us as if he wanted to kick our asses. Oh, what a joyful noise he made with that statement. Me and A. L. rose up like one man.

"Well, that's fair. Come on," I hollered.

"Yeah," A. L. enjoined. "Why don't you try that?"

We both assumed the position, glowering at this bus driver, who was about to be very, very unlucky. And that's when he opened the door, went inside the terminal, and called the cops. I looked toward the back of the bus again. My folks were doing what they'd been conditioned to do for decades: pushing and shoving one another, trying to make room for us, punching their little, greasy paper bags into smaller entities so as to eke out just a little more room. I felt sick in my stomach.

We got off the bus. Knowing that he'd have reinforcements due anytime now, the driver came back talking big, bad, and loud.

"Don't run, don't run," he yelled, trying to frighten us.

We stood our ground as we glared at this driver person.

"Nope," I growled, "we're still waiting for you." He stumbled back a step or two. A crowd began to gather, including quite a few blacks. In the middle of this gathering of humanity was one individual I will never forget: a black kid about ten years old, just a little guy, leaning on a baseball bat, a smile a mile wide gracing his face—just waiting for the fun to begin.

Fortunately for us, I suppose, the shore patrol arrived on the scene first. They put us into the back of their wagon and took us two or three blocks down the street. At first, we thought we'd had it, that they were going to take us back to the base. But presently, one of the shore patrol officers stopped the van, came around back, and opened the door. He was young and had a New York accent, and very calmly he began to talk some sense into me, because he knew that I had been ready to rumble.

"Frank," he said, and it shocked me that he knew my name, "I know you're about to graduate. I know it has been a long, hard struggle. It's been tough on you, and you have a helluva temper. But just keep your cool. Just listen to me—finish the program and get on. Now, where are you guys going?"

"Well, we were going to Mobile," A. L. replied, "but the party's over."

The shore patrol dropped us off in the black part of downtown Pensacola.

"Hey, enjoy yourselves, and keep your cool," the officer said as he clanged shut the rear door of the van. Before he turned to go, he looked at me and said again, "You get through this program."

There's no question that this was a stroke of luck. The police could have sirened up first, in which case there would have been a monstrous fight.

In retrospect, I have to admit that I was wound up pretty tight by then. Dave Campbell had been washed out, A. L.'s stuff was getting a little rancid, and I'd been through several of those tense, race-related experiences. Some I never forgot, like when my training flight section had flown an SNJ prop aircraft cross-country to one of those small, dirt fields in Alabama. The plan was to land, have lunch, and fly back to Pensacola, as the guys had done many times before. Order up lunch, climb back into their airplanes, and head off into the blue.

Well, as we entered the restaurant, a typical shack with a creaky screen door and lazy dogs lying around in the dirt, the faces of the guy and gal behind the counter suddenly scrunched up at the sight of me, the only black in the crowd.

"He cain't come in heah," they chorused, advising my flight leader (an officer) that I would have to eat on the porch, that I could not be served inside.

I quietly and angrily exited to the designated porch, where my flight mates joined me in mutual, angry hunger.

"I'm not going to eat this hamburger," I said, "because they might have spit in it."

That was an old trick in those dark days in the South. I sat there and got angrier and angrier. I'd had enough. So I asked the flight leader if I could be the last one to take off. He okayed the change. The dirt runway was fairly close to the restaurant. We taxied around. Off went the rest of the flight as I pulled my airplane right up in front of that old raggedy shack, aimed its tail at the screen door, and went to full power, blowing dust and tumbleweed. Looking into my rearview mirror, I could barely see through the dust storm as those old dogs ran amuck, the flimsy screen door flapped right off its hinges, and the restaurant owner cowered behind the counter, his apron blown over his head in the prop wash. As I let the brakes go and hauled ass, I hollered, "Engine, please don't fail me now."

It was about this time that I was hit with another downer that had nothing to do with Naval Cadet training. Or maybe in another way it did. I found out for sure that Judy, my first love, wouldn't be any of that to me anymore. My brother Hans called to tell me that she was going out with someone else. A guy named Richard stole my first love away. Maybe they deserved each other. Both were heartbreakers, because Judy stole Richard away from another young lady named Eleanor, with whom I'd grown up. Being a cadet was hard enough, but this news hurt even more.

We flew the SNJ for the remainder of basic flight. The routine was to culminate with six carrier landings, then graduate from basic and go on to advanced training. It was here that we built up to actual carrier landings by doing what is known as field carrier landing practice (FCLP), about a month's worth of practicing carrier landings on a simulated deck painted on the runway. What's drawn on the runway is an outline of the actual carrier deck. Our instructors then gave us a system of airspeed, altitude, and turning points, all in relation to the landing point on the deck. The name of the game was to fly the airplane about five knots above stall speed, controlling altitude by adding power or taking power off in minute amounts as we got in closer to the deck. It's a continuous turn from the 180-degree position, which is abeam the landing spot with a descending left-hand turn all the way down. On the ground, the landing signal officer (LSO) judges each approach and actually directs our movements in the cockpit. Our concentration quotient goes way up. Paddles in front of him in a V means we're too low. Above his head in a V means we're too high. What we want to see is him holding the paddles straight out from his shoulder, which means we're right on the glide path. But we still have to watch, because if we see the paddles in front of him but he brings them back in a rush, that means we're slow and have to add airspeed. We've arrived when we see him drop a paddle directly in front of him. That means cut power, we're in our landing position.

On 13 May 1952, I would actually land on an aircraft carrier for the first time. Fly that old SNJ right on down the chute onto the deck. All those landings in the FCLPs scurried around in my brain. All those instructions. The ruddy faces of my instructors, many of whom didn't really seem to believe that I could even fly an airplane, let alone land one aboard an aircraft carrier. I tried to shut out visions of those guys and substitute the protocols. Five knots above stall speed.

Don't sweat it, they say. After doing it four or five times, the rest is simply fun. Remember, while you're doing this, there's no room for a single thing other than what you're doing. Concentration, me bucko, concentration. And when that airplane finally stops, you're gonna say, Wow! I did it. And that's when it's gonna be fun.

Right. But I want to testify that when we were off Pensacola, Florida, and the USS *Cabot* was down there bobbing in the water with its wooden decks, it was a whole other scenario.

So they put us on the ship, and our training officers assigned us certain times to fly. It was time for "hot feet," meaning that as one cadet lands and exits the aircraft, the engine is left running, the throttle is back, chocks are put in front of the wheels, then another cadet gets in and becomes the new pilot. Six, seven, or maybe more airplanes are involved, and while they're hotfooting some cadets on the deck, others are orbiting, waiting to come in and continue the hot feet cycle until the entire class has completed qualifications.

Each individual needed six landings to qualify. If a cadet was not performing well, he would be sent ashore for more training, to return another day. This was my day. I was a "hot foot." I remember getting into the cockpit and strapping in. There was the signal to launch. My heart leapt; my throat constricted. Things are moving too fast, I thought. Suddenly, I was off the front end of the carrier, then turning downwind, setting up for the return approach and looking down at the carrier.

When I saw that tiny deck, my heart got stuck in my throat. A prayer escaped: "My God, I can't do that." I don't figure that God laughed or anything like that, but maybe He at least shrugged his shoulders and kind of smiled as my entreaties gained momentum. "Lord," I said, "it's just impossible. It is just impossible—they really don't mean for me to do this."

That postage-stamp-sized deck was still there. Bobbing in the water. Waiting for me. If I recall correctly, I was either number two or number three in the pattern.

Once I saw the guy in front of me make it, it all automatically began to fall in place, and I settled back into the routine in which I'd been instructed. I was a little shaky on my first pass. They waved me off and I came around again for the next pass. Suddenly, I became a kind of mechanical thing, a self-directed robot doing specific things by the numbers, things I'd been trained to do. I wasn't really thinking, just following the routines. After the fourth or fifth landing, going around for the sixth and final one, I was smiling to myself and heard myself exulting in macho abandon: "Hell, this is a piece of cake." I sat her down the sixth time, and I couldn't wait to do it again.

Back on shore, everyone had a beer to mark our success, our transition into the world of the advanced student. We changed our shoes from black to brown. Brown shoes, because now we were aviators, and only blue-water sailors wore those damned black shoes. I was proud to throw away those old black shoes. That night, my friend Ed House and I got together with a couple of old friends for drinks and conversation. I didn't tell them anything about my qualifying. But I had on my brown shoes. Nobody noticed. So I kept crossing and uncrossing my legs. Still nobody noticed. I kept crossing and uncrossing my legs until Evelyn

DuBose, my schoolteacher friend, after seriously considering whether I'd lost my mind, finally noticed my shoes.

"Oh, my God, look. Frank's got on brown shoes. Frank's got on brown shoes!"

"Damn, Frank. Congratulations, old buddy. You're now a real aviator, a flier," Ed enthused.

I was so damned proud. I'd done it. Now I had status among the cadet population because I'd qualified aboard the carrier. I thought about the shore patrol officer and his counsel to keep my cool. Advanced flight training lay ahead, and I would need all the "cool" I could muster. It was also time now to officially apply for designation as a Marine Corps aviator. So in January 1952, I made the necessary application.

5: Into the Fray

We were flying the F-8F Bearcat when I entered advanced flight training. It was really a sweet, powerful, wonderful airplane. If you wanted pure flash and dash, the F-8F Bearcat still held its own. It could sometimes be cantankerous because it was so fast. On takeoff, for example, when the big old prop started digging in with all that power, you had to open up the throttle and automatically straighten your right leg, to hold the torque generated by the powerful engine. If you didn't, it could pull the aircraft into a sharp turn right off the runway. So many cadets were killed flying them that the Navy decided to swap out the F-8F Bearcat for the tried and true F-6F Hellcat, a memorable World War II workhorse that practically dominated Pacific airspace as the war ground toward conclusion.

By now, I'd learned to handle my fear of flying. I'd been flying for almost a year and I was more than comfortable in the air and a lot more self-assured. Then, as now, I took that ground right up there in the clouds with me. Airsickness, on the other hand, was quite another thing, involving the melding of the body's reactions to the motions of the aircraft itself. It, too, often as not, becomes nonthreatening as one begins to fly and learns to anticipate the bodily changes, so it is pretty much a way of life.

The name of the game in advanced training was cumulative flying time. Cross-country. Getting really familiar with fighter aircraft and how to maneuver them.

We found ourselves on the ground in Dallas one October evening. Knowing that we'd remain overnight, we decided to have a beer or two under the lights in the city. Not one of us really thought anything "racial" about the decision. We were just a group of cadets out on the town with dry throats after a long cross-country flight. But the good citizens of Dallas (at least some of them) in those days took great exception at the temerity of a black man, naval air cadet or not, who had the gall to even think he'd have a beer in their hallowed recreational halls.

In downtown Dallas, my entire flight of eight guys walked into a night-club. I was the only black, and right away they said they couldn't serve me. So my guys bought the drinks and we all went out onto the sidewalk in front of the nightclub and proceeded to get schnockered while sitting on the curb. The cops came by and asked what was going on and we told them. Turned out they were ex-military themselves, so they parked nearby and stayed until we left, making sure nobody harassed us.

I suppose I should have begun to feel better about being the only black in the area. In the history of the Marines, in combat or postcombat, there essentially had been few black officers, if any. So some of the guys I teamed up with were just straight shooters, but there were also plenty of the "other" kind who would try to make my life miserable. It sometimes seemed that the white guys were choosing up sides as far as I was concerned. Some wanted to be sure that I was oppressed; others wanted to be my champion.

Back in Pensacola, it was now time for final carrier qualifications. Because we were flying the F-6F, I was stationed on board the carrier, the USS *Monterey*, as opposed to flying out to it. During World War II, ex-President Gerald Ford had served on the wooden-decked carrier, which now lay off the coast of Pensacola.

On 13 October 1952, after a catapult shot, I got one landing in, only to have the guy behind me have an accident. It was so bad that the deck was closed and we flew our planes ashore. Actually, I had gotten in front of a bunch of people by doing a little politicking. It wasn't the first time I'd done that kind of thing, but I found it beat the hell out of sitting around interminably waiting for something I desired to happen. I'd cor-raled the steward who served the captain of the carrier and engaged him in a private, "just-between-us-guys" conversation.

"Hey, old pardner," I postulated.

"Yeah? What can I do for you, man?"

"You can really help me out, if you will."

"What can I do for you?"

"I'd like you to talk to the captain for me."

"Say what? Talk to the who for you? Get on away from here."

"Hey, man, this is no joke. Really."

"Well, what is it?"

"Look, if I can qualify earlier, then I'll be promoted earlier. I'll get that second lieutenancy long before some of these other dudes. Can you help me? You see the captain every day. Why don't you put a bug in the dude's ear for me?"

He looked at me for a long time. For a moment, I thought all was lost. "Well," he drawled, "lemme see what I can do, okay?"

"Okay. Thanks, whether it works or not."

"You got it, cadet."

So he talked to the captain of the ship, and what do you know, I was moved forward to qualify. We flew out to the carrier on 14 October and, having already had one successful landing, I aced five more.

I was now qualified to become a second lieutenant in the U.S. Marine Corps. I had successfully completed Naval Cadet training, to include carrier landings in both primary and advanced flight training. I felt privileged. Less than half my cadet class graduated. It had been tough, what with segregation and prejudice winking around almost every corner. I was sure I'd done everything necessary to become a commissioned officer, at least as far as I knew.

Shortly before graduation, the Marine Corps suddenly seemed to have a problem with the color of my skin. Somebody had goofed and recorded my race code as white, but here I was, looking at them, waiting for my second lieutenant's bars, as black as I could be. Baffled flight school officials asked Headquarters, Marine Corps, if I could be commissioned if I was black.

The message to Marine Corps headquarters sizzled.

DE BESPC S4 1622Z FM CMABATRA TO COMDT USMC/ CODE DGK/ GRNC REQUEST AUTHORITY CORRECT ITEM 2 OF APPOINTMENT ACCEPTANCE AND RECORD NAVMC 763-PD CASE

FRANK EMMANUEL PETERSEN TO NEGRO VICE CAUCASIAN X PETERSEN WILL BE COMMISSIONED 22 OCT

CFN 2 763-PD 2216/2234Z OCT BESPC

A reply came back in typical, no-nonsense Marine language: "We've got to start sometime. Let's do it now."

The Marine Corps headquarters response by message was as terse.

URMSG 162232Z AUTHORITY GRANTED TO MAKE CORRECTION.

The commissioning ceremony was scheduled to take place on 22 October 1952 in the base theater on NAS Pensacola. It was a Wednesday morning. I'll never forget it. A rear admiral named J. P. Whitney, USN, chief of Naval Air Basic Training, presented me with my commission and designation as a Marine aviator. I remember thinking I'd joined an elite group of black military men. My role model, Ens. Jesse L. Brown, USN, had already been killed in Korea. The second black naval aviator, Lt. (jg) Earl L. Carter, flew his Panther jet off the carrier *Bon Homme Richard* on strikes against Pyongyang and hydroelectric plants in northeastern Korea. The third black naval flier, Ens. Albert Floyd, was assigned to the fleet all-weather training unit at NAS Key West. I'd fulfilled Campbell's dream and my dream—I was a black Marine aviator.

I had no sweetheart in the area, and no girlfriend either, to fulfill the tradition of having one or the other pin on my wings. So I called Evelyn DuBose, a lady I had become close friends with during my stay in Pensacola. My pal Ed House had introduced me to Evelyn some time before.

The ceremony was all very nice. The oath of office. The pinning by Evelyn. And now, who would take my first salute? The custom is that whoever gives a newly commissioned officer the first salute receives a dollar from the officer. After sending Evelyn home, I left the theater and ran into a battery of photographers who were taking pictures of all the new officers while jostling for position in order to get the dollar. I simply wouldn't give the dollar to these guys. I had other plans, and besides, I needed a new pack of cigarettes. That's why I walked across the base toward the base exchange. I waited until I ran into the first black sailor who saluted, and I gave him the dollar.

It was about then, I guess, that I was really hit by the significance of being the second black man to accept the commission of a second lieutenant and the first to be designated an aviator in the U.S. Marine Corps. I realized that what was coming could really be confusing if I allowed everything in my mind to be evaluated by and linked to social position and color. A tightrope walk of the first magnitude. A proud moment but fraught with myriad unseen obstacles.

MUTUAL VOICES
Evelyn DuBose, Pensacola Friend

When it was time for his wings to be pinned, [his friends] drew straws [to see which of us would do it]. I was chosen and when it was time to do it, I lied. I was supposed to be working and I told a white lie that I was sick. And I pinned his wings on. The publicity was all over the TV and radio. It was really embarrassing because I didn't realize he was the very first black Marine pilot, and that he was the first black Marine officer on [active duty]. As I said, there was lots of publicity related to that. But they turned it into a joke and it wasn't bad for me, except for the old tradition [which had it that a girlfriend or sweetheart should be the one to pin on the wings]. And there were lots of people who said, "Oh, my God. Are they really?" The local newspaper, the Pensacola News Journal, let the complete cat out of the bag. Under the headline "First Negro Cadet Gets Marine Corps Commission," it noted: "Present at the ceremonies was Miss Evelyn Du-Bose of 6ll West Jackson Street, Pensacola, who pinned the Navy wings on Lieutenant Petersen's uniform."

[No matter what the gossips said], he was a very dear friend. The really good thing about [our friendship] is that we didn't have very much, but we also had a lot, because it was a friendship that was honest, real, natural, and good. We did small things. Went to the beach, made campfires, sat around them and sang songs. [Other nights, we] watched the moon glisten on the water. Or [if it were daytime] watched the waves come in and just sat for hours, then walked down the beach. We had very little money to spend, [so] we'd go back home. But we had a good time. But, you know, we had each other, and that was about all we had. But we had a lot.

The significance of becoming the first black aviator in the Marine Corps was fully understood when I was designated a naval aviator and accepted the commission as a second lieutenant in the Marine Corps reserves. All this was prior to the civil rights movement, and we were still operating in a segregated environment. It made for a strange bit of mental confusion if I allowed myself to evaluate my new social position by the color of my skin.

Almost immediately, a problem erupted as far as my initial assignment was concerned. I received orders to Cherry Point Marine Corps Air Station (MCAS) in North Carolina. There was no way I wanted to go there. I wrote a letter asking not to be kept in the South. I'd had enough of it. I'd heard how things were for blacks in North Carolina in those days, on base or not. I copped a plea. I said, "Please, please, send me someplace other than the South." The Marine Corps was all too willing to comply with my wishes.

That's how I ended up with modified orders sending me posthaste to El Toro, California, where fighter pilots were being trained for combat replacements in Korea. The message was straight up:

DIRECT YOU REPORT AIRFMFPAC MCAS EL TORO/SANTA ANA/CALIF FOR DIFOT WITH TEN DAYS DEL. UPON COM-

PLETION. . . . ALL WEATHER FLIGHT NAS CORPC TEX X
PARA SEVEN MODIFIED ACCORDINGLY.

My pulse quickened as I realized I was on my way to Korea and combat at the ripe old age of twenty.

Ironically, it turned out that early exposure to combat would bene-
fit my career overall. I didn't know that then, so I confess to concern
over my future and whether or not I'd have one. Not to worry, though.
With one week's leave, I grabbed a flight home to spend some time with
my family and connect with the brand-new Chrysler my father had
arranged for me to buy. It was nice seeing the family. We hugged, talked,
and reminisced; there was a party or two. I saw Judy around, but of
course she'd already gotten hooked up with Richard. When my week's
leave was almost up, I said my good-byes to family and friends and
headed the Chrysler toward the West Coast.

In those days, it could still be chancy for a black man driving across
the United States. In the first place, the accommodations just weren't
there, except in the larger cities where on occasion some black person
had opened a motel or hotel, or you could stay with friends along the
way. It was best to play all your cards right driving across the country.
You either had your uniform on or you hung it in the window on the
driver's side so if a policeman stopped you, he'd see that right off. The
name of my game was to concentrate my driving. The nonstop express.
Topeka to El Toro in thirty hours.

When I arrived at El Toro, I was pretty tired and certainly not up for
any funny business from anybody about anything.

As I drove up to the main gate, "funny business" in the form of er-
satz racism was exactly what I got.

November winds were blowing. A slight shiver rode the air. In a way,
I suppose I could have tried to understand the gate sentry's point of view,
except I was definitely not in the mood to be that gracious because he
didn't seem to be inclined to render the necessary salute when a commissioned officer drove, walked, ran, or crawled up to his station. When
I drove up, the color of my skin seemed to mesmerize the sentry, who
just stood there, glaring. I was ready to return his hand salute, but he
rendered none at all. Now, I realize that I was probably the only black
officer that Marine had ever seen, and certainly the only one assigned
to his base. In point of fact, I think I was damned near the only black
officer in the entire Marine Corps at the time. So I bailed out of my car
and commenced to verbally confront the sentry about the protocols of

saluting a commissioned officer when one is encountered and certainly when one is passing through one's sentry post. "When," I wanted to know, "did the Marine Corps decide they were no longer going to salute officers?"

I'm sure my visage was horrible; I intended it to be. After a great deal of stammering and apology from the sentry—and a damned fine salute, I might add—the matter was settled. Wherever that gentleman went after that, I'd wager he saluted a commissioned officer, no matter what that officer looked like.

But the problems were just beginning. After checking into the base on this first night aboard, I thought I'd have a drink at the bar in the officers' club. As I stood at the bar after ordering, a guy walked up to me and began a rather weird conversation. From the tenor of it, I knew right away that what he was doing was checking to see if I was really an officer and an aviator. He was a captain, I believe.

"Harumph," he began. "Where did you get your wings?"

"Pensacola," I replied bemusedly.

He then presented me with a long list of places and establishments in and around Pensacola, all unfamiliar to me because they were places that white people primarily frequented. I thought I'd play the game, too.

"Hey, Captain, you ever been to the Sugar Bowl? Really great bunch of ladies around there."

Silence. A negative shake of the head.

"Oh, you've never been there? Well, then, how about Slim's? Really great place."

The captain continued his catechism, his voice growing louder and louder. "Okay, okay. Where did you go to school?" he fired. "Where did you go to flight school?"

"Pensacola," I repeated, but nothing seemed to assuage his verbal attack.

The upshot of all this questioning of my authenticity was that he decided I was impersonating an officer. He called in the duty officer. But he didn't appear to think this was going to be a good bust and hesitated for a moment. I'll never forget his reaction.

"I know there is one," stammered the duty officer, "because I saw one check onto the base this morning."

Before I could open my mouth, my accusers multiplied. Strangely, I was the one charged with causing the uproar in the club, just by coming into it. The duty officer promptly placed me under house arrest. All I had done was stop in for a drink, only to be put under arrest the first day on station.

The next morning, my commanding officer had me on the carpet bright and early.

"What's this ruckus I hear you caused at the O club last night?" he growled.

Well, when he got the full details, he got pissed. My skipper was understanding and knew what was going on. After an apology, that captain was sent overseas early.

Perhaps it was the public information people on El Toro who made a press release to the local *Santa Ana Register* announcing my existence—that there was now a black officer and aviator in the Corps and, more than that, he was right here on El Toro. In its 6 January 1953 issue, under a picture of me climbing into the cockpit of a Corsair fighter and a headline reading "Marine's Only Negro Pilot Now At El Toro," the article detailed my duties involving "final checkout" before Korean combat in F-4U and Skyraider aircraft. Most importantly, however, the article went to the crux of the racial problem in an effective manner.

Being the Marines' sole pilot of the Negro race has often resulted in minor complications—none too humorous. . . . He is frequently stopped by Marine military policemen at El Toro and in Santa Ana who "refuse to believe I'm actually a pilot. They always ask for my identification. Then they're more embarrassed than I am when they learn the truth. . . . I've solved that problem. . . . I wear civilian clothes in town."

My fellow pilot friends also gave statements of attestation to the fact that "enlisted men frequently refused to salute the Negro officer as required by military regulations." I didn't give the latter statement credence one way or the other, electing to leave the matter alone.

Even so, that was a low spot for me, especially after Pensacola and throughout the South, then to go to California for my first duty station and run right into full-blown prejudice. That tightened me up a little bit.

But there was no time to remain uptight about it. I had been assigned to VMAT-10 at El Toro, my first Marine Corps experience. Luckily, I began to run into white Marines who didn't play the "race card." They were just regular guys who accepted me as I was, a regular guy—like them.

One of these was a gentleman named Gale Harlan. We both headed for Korea, and because I'd logged more training time than he, I would probably ship out first. But the point was that we became good buddies.

We used to hang out in bars together. Gale was to become one of my best friends.

There was a lot to learn in a short time. Air cadre, because of the replacement requirements of the Korean War, didn't go to the Marine Basic School, as is the usual route for every Marine officer, and especially one coming from another service. The idea was to keep the fresh pilots coming to frontline bases. Today, all Marine fliers are required to take a platoon leaders' course or officers' candidate course, then Basic School at Quantico, Virginia. To learn about teamwork and sacrifice. Duty and honor. Being an officer and what that Marine attitude called *semper fi* (always faithful) is all about. Esprit. Some of my compatriots were selected to go back to Basic School for refresher courses or defense courses. I missed those as well. But, believe me, although lots of it was through osmosis, I learned in short order how and what it meant to be a Marine and was damned proud to be one.

January 1953. El Toro MCAS was about training for combat. Adrenaline pumped. Even though a bit edgy about the future, I was happy about one thing. I'd finally gotten my hands on that famous World War II fighter, an F-4U Corsair. Actually, we began training in the AD Skyraider, then shifted over to the Corsair, the baby we trained in. It was mass produced in World War II. Some of the models I was to fly had no floor in the cockpit. We'd unbuckle and stand in the bottom of the airplane. Our head would be just above the canopy rail, but we could still see out. It was a fast plane. There were models up to about two- or three-stage superchargers, which could get up around forty thousand feet.

Our nickname for the Corsair was the bent-winged, hose-nosed widowmaker. That was because of the excessive power it had, especially in the landing pattern. We had to be careful when making a landing. If we got into trouble and needed to power our way out, we had to add the throttle slowly, or we would encounter what we referred to as torque roll, when the big prop biting the airstream would tend to give a counter-roll to the airplane. So we learned to be extremely careful as we were doing our go-arounds.

That never happened to me, but I was really scared of that damned plane. I had one accident at El Centro, where we went for gunnery practice. After fighting the thermals and coming in too fast on the landing, I hit the brakes and the plane skidded right off the end of the runway. The main gear dug in and the aircraft flipped over and slid in the sand upside down. I dug myself out and took off like a scared cat. Didn't get hurt, but the airplane had to have some repair work done. We quickly learned to respect her on the takeoff roll as well. We never added full power on takeoff. We'd gradually add on the power; otherwise we'd have the torque effect and tend to cock the airplane off to one side of the runway. It was a sensitive little devil.

We flew out to the Mojave Desert to NAS El Centro for practice in live firing: strafing, bombing, zapping rockets through the ether. Combat training in the Corsairs. I loved flying the airplane. To quote "Pappy" Boyington, "She was a sweet-flying baby if ever I saw one." For us gladiators of the Korean War, her capabilities were upgraded—the ultimate air unit, with four 20mm cannons and up to four 1,000-pound bombs. Or six .50-caliber Browning MG 53-2 (M-2) machine guns plus eight 5-inch rockets. Enough to make any targeted guy on the ground wet his britches, no doubt about it.

My time to enter the Korean War approached faster than I thought it ought. I had just turned twenty on 2 March. The war in Korea seemed pretty much stalemated along the DMZ, but we were still going north to hit their supply routes. And, too, by the time my assignment to Korea was about to happen, the Marine Corps had gone through a huge adjustment period. It had expanded and, as pointed out by Allan R. Millett in *Semper Fidelis: The History of the United States Marine Corps* [p. 508–9], roles for both women and blacks in the Corps had changed significantly. Women Marines now numbered almost three thousand, with no change in duty focus. American forces were fighting in Korea in integrated units for the first time. Integration of blacks had increased by leaps and bounds unheard of in the annals of Marine Corps history, which resulted in a new look at them in terms of rank and abilities. "From a June 1950 strength of 1,502 [representing only 2 percent of the Corps]," Millett noted, "the number of black marines increased to 14,731 [or 6 percent] by 1953"—my witching hour. Blacks not only left the relatively constricted assignments of security detachments and other menial jobs but were assigned to "integrated units and for the first time commanded white troops."

This war I was about to enter, although reputed to be a "stalemate," did not, I later discovered, give the Chinese their proper due at the time, for history shows that 40 percent of Marine casualties of the entire Korean War happened between April 1952 and the end of the war [Millett, 108]. Of course, I had no way of knowing all of this in April 1953, when orders came to report to the commanding officer of VMFA-212. Job: squadron pilot. Arena: combat.

Just enough time existed for a quick trip home to visit family and friends and verify that the young lady I thought I was in love with had really chosen someone else. It was nice seeing everyone, then it was back to California and on to the adventure of combat.

April 1953. In a special news release to the *Call and Post,* El Toro public relations announced the departure of the "nation's first and only Negro Marine pilot . . . for Korea about the middle of April." It wasn't clear, the article went on, as to whether I would "fly across or go by boat." In point of fact, about twenty replacement pilots and I were sent to Korea aboard a four-engine C-54 transport aircraft. We island-hopped across the Pacific—Hawaii, Midway islands—two days' travel in those days by propeller-driven airplane. When I got off the plane on Johnston Island, about eight hundred miles southwest of Honolulu, we'd been in the air perhaps three days. I was scared to death they'd go off and leave me. Less than half a square mile, the place seemed small and isolated, even though it had been enlarged with coral dredged from the nearby lagoon so as to make an airfield. There was water, water everywhere. A seabird refuge since 1926, the island was home to gooney birds, the dumbest birds in the world. They'd have to run and flap their wings to get airborne. Then once they were aloft, they'd look down and see the heat reflecting off the pavement, which resembled water, and then they'd dive into it. That seemed to be the only entertainment on the island.

Our next stop was a place called Itami, on the Japanese island of Honshu. We were sorted out and assigned to a squadron. In early morning, we replacement pilots were flown out of Itami in a DC-4 (an old, twin-engine Douglas airplane) across the Korean Strait directly into Marine air base K-6 to join my squadron at Pyongtaek, Korea, about thirty miles south of Seoul. I imagined that my arrival there was going to cause quite a stir, because there'd never been a black U.S. Marine aviator. This was going to be interesting. The name of the game, I thought, was to keep cool even though I knew it would probably be tough. The focus for me was just to do my job and do it damned well.

Even so, I was apprehensive. I was the only "blood" aviator in the entire USMC, so I watched the so-called veterans, to make sure that I was going to be able to follow the "professionals." I had no idea just how the color of my skin would haunt the remainder of my career as a Marine officer. Korea would be only the beginning.

6: Fresh-Caught Fighter Pilot in Korea

VMFA Fighter Attack Squadron 212, The Devil Cats

I was more of an oddity as a second lieutenant than the lowest-ranking Marine when I landed at K-6, the Marine fighter base outside Pyongtaek, Korea. Second lieutenants were a rarity. So many units had been deactivated after World War II that President Truman had found it necessary to activate reserve units for the Korean War. That was enough for the "seasoned" troops to talk about, but when curiosity about my race and the color of my skin was added in, the fact that I was the Marine's first black pilot and fighter pilot seemed inconsequential.

As I stepped down from the transport airplane, wrestling my B-4 and seabag onto the metal airstrip, I looked about. The humidity was high; the air smelled fertilized. Groups of pilots ambled by in the distance, shuffling off toward what I imagined were ready rooms. Some of the pilots wore old leather flight suits and goggles, others wore scarves and cowboy boots. The base was what I envisioned a combat, frontline environment to be. Sparse. Tents. Quonset huts for living and working. An officers' club made of stone, prefab maintenance shacks, the runway of glistening Marsten steel matting. Lots of manual labor in evidence in terms of loading ordnance. A seemingly relaxed bunch involved in some really serious business.

We were met by squadron representatives who took us to our billeting areas and made sure we had all our combat gear and were bedded down in our assigned Quonset huts. So I was understandably apprehensive, not only about watching the "professionals" so I wouldn't make operational mistakes, but my radar was constantly on to bag the occasional racist electing to make a run at me. I did have some friends, however. Guys I'd known while attending Naval Cadets in Pensacola. Joseph Christian Anderson, Gersitz, Chuck Pavlich, and a couple of others.

Once billeted and settled with our rather meager gear—essentially just our military dungarees and flight gear—we met with the commanding officer. At first, it was a gentleman named Hanby, then (maybe it was because Hanby's time was up) it was Maj. E. C. Kicklighter from Pasco in southeastern Washington state. I guess you'd call it a kind of welcoming to the squadron, a wish for good luck and good hunting. I felt better after meeting the commanding officer, but then I saw a major sauntering by with a look in his eye I hadn't seen too much of since I'd left Topeka. That look said I really wasn't welcome in the vicinity, and if he had his way, I simply wouldn't be there. I was the only black in VFMA-212 and the only black aviator in the whole damned Corps. But his demeanor was just something to note for the moment and file away for future reference. He was somebody to watch. Given the tenor of the times, for me to do otherwise would have been foolhardy, I thought. The need was to take my cue from the place I was in. This was the "Land of the Morning Calm," as the Koreans liked to call their country, and this spoke volumes for me where racism was concerned.

Our squadron orientations consisted of briefings about targeting systems, which areas were safe, and what the battlefront consisted of on the DMZ, important because we were just to the south of it. Combat training flights began, which were stair steps into real combat. We were up around seven o'clock in the morning and performed ablutions in a washbasin. Showers came in the evening, because taking one in the morning was too awkward. There were makeshift showers and makeshift toilets, featuring the ever-popular "piss tubes" for quick relief.

Then we were down to the flight line to begin training for bomb delivery on the Suwon bombing range, located about fifteen miles west and near the ocean. After three or four days of practice bombing and strafing, we were placed on the flight schedule for actual air operations in a combat zone. It was laid on fast and tried to be all encompassing. Whatever, our lives were going to ride on that training. Combat indoctrination flight couldn't be far off.

My instant "bright spot" around the squadron area was the main dining hall—an officers' dining hall—for breakfast. Although spartan in equipment and decor, it was perhaps the greatest place on K-6 for me because most of the mess stewards were black. I was probably the first black Marine officer (and certainly Marine aviator) they'd ever seen, and each time I entered the dining hall, it was something special for them and me.

There was an instant, unspoken camaraderie between us that transcended rank. They expressed great friendliness toward me and I reciprocated. Funny, that wire between us was missed by many. If I needed extra chow, it was always available. It was a kind of silent celebration, a plus—for being black, an officer, and an aviator. There were also one or two other guys in the squadron I'd known in flight training. One was Edison W. Miller, who was to seem star-crossed somehow, because he would become one of the infamous seven accused of collaborating with the enemy at the Hanoi Hilton during the Vietnam War. Then there was a guy named Dick Gersitz. We'd been friends before, and quite close during training. Just knowing that these guys were there helped ease the strangeness of being around all those World War II pilots recalled from the reserves.

There were other interesting characters in the squadron, mostly (except for us fresh-caught fighter jocks) recalled World War II veterans. There was a lot of resentment on their part about being called back in, as opposed to using America's regular forces. But all the services had drawn down to the point where Truman found it necessary to activate the reserves. So these guys had been pulled from their various communities and their livelihoods and returned to uniform and put back into the cockpit. Many of them had a very "civilian" attitude about them. Their bottom line was that they just didn't want to be in that war. So they were cavalier about it, although they were getting the job done. They were humorous. In fact, they were some of the funniest guys I've ever run across.

One of the funniest was a guy nicknamed Thunderlips (his real name was Ed Schaeffer). He was about six foot three, weighed about 260 pounds, had reddish hair and a big laugh that came up out of a naturally huge, gravelly voice that sounded like a foghorn. I think he came from the Seattle area, where most of these reservists lived.

There was another guy (I can't recall his name) who was a real oddball. He'd been an embalmer in a mortuary and was an alcoholic. Drank more than a fifth of bourbon a day and he still flew—every day. The flight surgeon took him off flying status the day he fell asleep, again, where he sat. While I waited for my indoctrination combat flight to be set up, I watched the guys try to wake him up. He had drunk so much whiskey that we all thought he was dead. But the doc hit him with a needle full of something and he came back.

The World War II "retreads," as we younger pilots called some of the veterans, were a different breed of cat. Thunderlips showed up for

Christmas breakfast wearing long johns, a derby hat, a red scarf, and galoshes. Although challenged by the squadron commander, he matter-of-factly replied: "Sir, this is the way I always dress for Christmas. Why should I change?"

I'd just turned twenty-one when the day finally arrived for my combat indoctrination mission. A real, live mission, where it was entirely possible that people would be shooting at me. Could kill me, maybe.

As I rolled in, the excitement of that coursed through my body. Actually, it wasn't supposed to be a big deal. We weren't expecting lots of gunfire or opposition because we were going into a "soft" area. The name of the game was to get us new guys broken in. Blow up a bunch of buildings and come home.

As we taxied out, I couldn't help thinking about the history of VMFA-212 that I'd dredged up. Where the squadron had been and what it had done. From activation in Hawaii to patrol in the South Pacific. Sixty-four and a half enemy planes destroyed. Vella Lavella, flying strikes in support of ground forces on Bougainville. The Devil Cats. Helping MacArthur recapture the Philippines. Convoying missions to Mindoro and over the Sulu Sea. Strafing targets of opportunity on Luzon and patrolling Leyte Gulf. Flying close air support during the invasion of Okinawa. One of the first land-based Marine squadrons to conduct operations from Kimpo airfield near Seoul.

Now I was a Devil Cat. A fresh-caught Devil Cat who didn't feel particularly devilish at the moment. The name of the malady was fear, embedded in the uncertainty of being in a combat zone and not knowing what to expect. My first time in war was a bit traumatic. We locked down, spooled up, leapt into the sky, and droned north until we found ourselves near the Yalu River, bombing what targets we could find. Basic stuff, then back to base again for assignment to really serious combat strikes.

The first few flights were eerie because the gun emplacements on the enemy's side had been sighted in easily and weren't moved around very well. One guy became rather notorious with us. We called him One Shot Charlie. He was firing a 90mm, and although all he would do was fire one shot, it would come awfully close as we droned by. We'd be flying along and everything would be smooth, then suddenly a big black-red cloud would erupt close by. We'd frantically begin evasive maneuvers in order to avoid shrapnel. Our ground attacks would primarily be gun emplacements—troops that were dug in and supply movements we could spot. After twenty to thirty combat flights, it became routine to fly out to attack the fortified areas around the large North Korean cities and hit hydroelectric plants and industrial complexes along the Yalu River.

MUTUAL VOICES
TSgt. Robert (Bob) Doktor

> *I was there when he joined our outfit as a young lieutenant in Korea. He was a guy everybody loved. We had a couple of rednecks out there, of course, who didn't. They [spouted] the typical thing. "Nigger in here," and that kind of thing. They pissed me off. But anyway, he was one fine gentleman. We used to walk across the street to get in front of him and salute, because he was a good man and he was a Marine. He didn't have too much flying time then because we had a real rednecked major, the executive officer, with whom I unfortunately served at Memphis.*

Our mission was the conducting of tactical air operations as requested by higher command. Interdiction, close air support, rescue combat air patrol. We were getting pretty good at it, too. Then the Communist forces challenged the hell out of us as they slammed against the 1st Marine Division's right sector then in the area of the 5th Marines. They raked their outposts Reno, Vegas, and Carson with withering artillery fire, and at night they continued to fight; they slashed at the Marines with infantry assault. The battle raged: attack, defense, counterattack. A plethora of artillery duels, shells from both sides snuffing out the lives of American and Chinese soldiers alike. The nights grew garish in the glow of flares while star shells stammered across and stung the denuded hills. Men lay dead in bunkers that seemed so safe just hours before [Millett, p. 516].

We Devil Cats flew 482 combat sorties that month. Everybody sent fighter strikes against the enemy. Navy, Air Force, and Marine fighters, stacked eight deep, waited to descend, like growling, moaning dragons of destruction spitting death. More than 820 combat hours in the air. We flew close air support missions 181 times, 248 interdiction missions, and more than 60 hours of rescue cap flights. Probably a good portion of our flying time was spent in close air support for the 5th Marines. The battle lasted for five days, and when it was over, outpost Reno was gone. Vegas and Carson held. Fifteen hundred Marines were counted dead or missing. The Chinese losses were twice that.

One of the scariest missions for me was one into North Korea. We could see our target ahead and were gearing up to attack when we were jumped by a Communist MiG. The sucker hit one of our aircraft with cannon fire as he dove through our flight and imploded the canopy of the airplane he hit. The pilot panicked, came on the air, and began screaming for help. The canopy glass had shattered and cut him all over his face. He was bleeding. There was nothing we could do.

My initial reaction was to immediately make a hard turn and see if I couldn't get a shot at the Commie pilot. But when I heard this kid start screaming, I lost all courage right away. Our only defense in those days was to form what is called a Lufberry Circle, an old German maneuver from World War I. Normally, with twenty-four planes in our squadron, when we encountered a MiG we'd form a circle with the idea that if the attacking jet went after the guy in front of you, you had a shot at the MiG—a commitment that took considerable nerve. To do that, however, we had to regroup.

I was cut off and separated from the rest of the flight, so I immediately rolled over, dropped my bombs, got right down on the deck—and I mean down, like ten feet off the ground, with full power—and drove out to the west coast of Korea, over water. Found out where I was, then went south, back to my base, alone.

The MiG, I understand, made two or three passes through the gallery and then bugged out across the Yalu, China, and safety. We couldn't follow. That was sanctuary. Not that we could've caught him, because he was flying a jet and we were in conventional propeller-driven airplanes. Frankly, we were glad to see the son of a bitch go. A MiG encounter was fairly serious business. We could outturn but couldn't outrun one. Getting clear was simply the better part of valor.

In the officers' club back at the base, I discovered I had a real enemy in the person of the pilot whose airplane got hit that day. A first lieutenant, this guy always tried to give me his particular brand of hell. No matter what happened, if there was something wrong he'd always try to wriggle that sucker off on me. After he was jumped by the MiG, I was stupidly rehashing the event that night in our hut. I said, "Well, who screamed? Some guy came on the radio and screamed just like a woman in labor pains."

"That was you, goddamnit," came the angry retort from the stricken lieutenant. "We all know who it was."

Uh-oh, I thought. Another burr in my saddle.

That was just the beginning. It seemed that one of the older pilots—one of the disgruntled reservists—took the opportunity to play his racist card as well. When I wondered aloud about the kid screaming when he got hit, the older pilot sounded off, too.

"Hey, what did you do? Huh? You ain't nothing but a coward, that's what. There was gonna be a fight, and you ran away, that's what. You bugged out of that fight, that's what you did."

Well, the fact of the matter was that we all bugged out when we found ourselves attacked by the MiG and heard that guy's blood-curdling scream. The appearance of the MiG threw everyone into turmoil, and that's when everything went to hell. We were all scared to death. I was ready to take up the cudgel in my own defense, but some of the guys who always took my side cautioned me to let it go. I salved my wounds and went back to my hut. I don't know what happened after I left, and I never tried to find out.

Some nights at the officers' club could be mellow and relaxing. Sometimes, we'd toss down a few and shake the flimsy bar as we sang fighter pilots' songs, some honoring the esteemed University of Pusan—"Old Pusan U"—or one of my favorites (for those of us who had been lucky enough for some rest and recreation in Japan), that old classic "When the Ice Is on the Rice in Southern Honshu." Been years since I've hummed it. Something like, "When the ice is on the rice in southern Honshu / And the Saki in the cellar starts to freeze / And she looks at you and whispers 'How I "ruv" you' / Then you know you're just a skoshi Nipponese." Ah, yes, magnificent. Brings back the memories.

Those interludes helped, but as time passed there were lots of "little" things going on. Initially, for example, the question of who was going to sleep in my tent kept surfacing. Even socializing with me was cause for small discussions, although these guys were few and far between. And every time the issue of race came up, one of the others would intercede and threaten to knock some guy on his ass if he didn't come off it. The most memorable example of this happened while on rest and relaxation in Itami, Japan, at a geisha house that had belonged to a very nice Japanese officer.

We'd all flown a lot of missions by now. Chuck Pavlich, his buddy John Harelicek, and a couple of other Devil Cats fighter pilots agreed that it was time to have a little fun. It was also agreed that part of the fun ought to include ladies, no matter how fleeting the connection.

So we all got the permission, spruced ourselves up, and jumped on board the sturdy C-54 for a quick flight over to the Marines' playground around Itami. It was lighthearted, as though we were on our way to a high school football game. I forget which of us started the singing, but before we knew it, everybody was singing along: "Ishi Bashi 258, yeah, yeah, yeah. Ishi Bashi 258. Ah-h-h-h-h so." If you were in the know, you recognized the telephone number of the local Japanese geisha house, where all sorts of gorgeous, shapely, soft, and good-smelling creatures hung out.

Once on the ground, we didn't waste much time getting on target. In uniform, we headed straight to Ishi Bashi 258, situated in one of the better Japanese homes in the residential area of Itami. It had been converted into an officers' club and had been Americanized. A bar had been put in, and American-type food was to be had. On top of that, Mama-San brought in a whole bunch of honeys to act as "hostesses." So it was the place to be.

We were greeted with the usual Japanese courtesy and considerations. We four Marine officers had, in fact, just ordered our first drinks and were clustered at the far end of the bar, talking. I figured I was a kind of main attraction around there, because none of Mama-San's "chillun" had ever seen a black man before. Besides, I could boogie (as the saying was in those days). Yep, I could get on down. So the honeys were smiling in anticipation and I was grinning and talking back, thinking what a blast this was going to be.

We'd only just begun to relax when in walked six Navy officers. There were only four of us Marines (unusual, because the geisha house was near a Marine base). The Navy officers didn't waste much time injecting some good old down-home rhetoric into the setting.

"What's he doing in heah?" twanged one of the Navy gentlemen. "We don't drink with his kind."

My Marine buddies and I looked at one another as the Navy pilot's words struck home. It was the old innuendo game again. Noises that suggested I shouldn't be in the place.

"What's he doing here?" growled one of the Navy pilots again.

"Why doesn't he understand that this is our place?" another said, his visage growing darker by the minute.

"We think the SOB should leave," came the ultimate suggestion from the Navy folks. Temperatures began to rise as the Marines considered the Navy's suggestions.

"They should shut the hell up," said one of my pilot buddies, perhaps Chuck Pavlich.

"Hell, they should be the ones to leave if they feel that way," shot another one of the Devil Cats.

Well, the Navy pilots obviously did feel that way, because their reaction to our side of this sotto-voce conversation lit the fuse.

"Nobody's gonna make us leave," the Navy pilots fired. "Like to see you jarheads give that a shot. Ho-ho-ho."

That challenge was a serious mistake. The Navy pilots postured as if to think about a fight or to savor a fight or to have a fight or whatever it was they thought they were going to do.

It was about this time that "my guys" grabbed them by their collars and their coats, picked them up, and literally threw them over the stone wall behind the bar. The Navy pilots thrashed about in the air for quite a while as they fell, because it was an eight-foot drop to the ground. We braced ourselves. Perhaps the Navy would return. No such luck. It was kind of stupid on their part, because Itami was a Marine stronghold and they were actually the interlopers.

That's why being the only black in a unit like the Devil Cats was always an enigma. You just never knew. Sometimes people fought your personal wars for you. I sat there absolutely amazed, my mouth open. I found myself in these sorts of situations on more than one occasion, even in flight school, when we'd flown to Texas on cross-country.

The morning after the first night I stayed in Japan, I awoke to find this little honey rubbing my face, and rubbing my face again, then looking at her hand, her face a great puzzlement. At first I thought the child had lost it, but then I began to get the drift when I heard: "It's real. It's really real," then giggles. She'd never seen a black man before. We had a long talk about the different colors of people on the planet. She'd come into town from the country to find work. There were few black Marine officers at that time, and seeing me was a real first for her. I still chuckle about it.

There's not much more to say about our time at Ishi Bashi 258, except that we all needed petting from time to time. To be spoiled. A little gentility. A little touch, a little loving. You could get some of that at Ishi Bashi 258. We had a grand time, and left singing that old song again in praises of the ladies there: "Ishi Bashi 258, yeah, yeah, yeah. Ishi Bashi 258. Ah-h-h-h-h so."

7: In Search of Shining Armor

Before we knew it, we were back at K-6 Marine Air Base outside Pyong-taek, looking at the low-hanging clouds and blue hills framing the far horizon. The gull-winged F-4Us awaited, lined up along the edges of the metallic airstrip, their four-bladed props still and silent. The foray into Japan to party with the pretties had to suffice for a while.

We were still going up north to hit the North Korean supply routes. But the enemy had learned of it and found a partial solution fairly quickly. Their heavy traffic was suddenly not on the roads anymore. We ranged far and wide behind the enemy's lines, taking out trucks, trains, and other targets of opportunity. We'd take out anything moving, including oxen. Recognizing the animal as a form of transportation for them, we'd get down low and kill them on the road. But being in a vehicle was even deadlier for the North Koreans, and they knew it.

Of course, there were days when it didn't pay to get out of the sack—dreary, inclement days combining fog, rain, and low ceilings. Our navigational systems weren't state of the art. If weather closed in, it kept us on the ground. If we were airborne when it hit, we couldn't be effective because, with the F-4U, our targeting was primarily visual. If we couldn't see the target, there was no point in even launching.

But then the sky would clear and we'd head out to taunt the MiGs up along the Yalu. Initially, we didn't think much about the risk factor. The MiGs ventured out only for targets of opportunity. More times than I care to remember, we seemed to be that target. Sometimes, they'd come storming out of the sun and make a savage pass at us. In May, we lost Capt. A. J. Verrant and 1st Lt. R. G. Hipple on a combat mission. We didn't know whether they survived; they were listed as missing in action (MIA). My personal opinion is that we Marines were used as bait by the Fifth Air Force on more than one occasion. The MiGs would jump out, seeing the propeller-driven F-4Us. We'd be up there doing yeoman's duty as directed, hitting those urban rice paddy dams. Then here would come the MiGs. I can recall that on some of our missions, we could see a Corsair in a long, steep dive trying to escape a pursuing MiG, and an American F-86 would be coming in behind the MiG. When we got those missions, everybody would say, "Oh-h-h-h, shit, we know what this deal is gonna be." Maybe that old saying about everything being fair in love and war applied in these situations.

When I first checked into Korea, it was not at all clear in my mind that my performance as observed by my superior officers was A-1. For example, the commander at NAS Corpus Christi didn't say a lot, but how could he? The period of observation was short. So I took the evaluation of my regular duties as "average" with something of a grain of salt. The guy even tagged my "attention to duty" rating as average. The overall name of his game with me seemed to be average initiative and judgment. He evaluated my presence of mind as "not observed," as were my ability to think and effectively act under stress, my forcefulness, leadership loyalty, personal relations, and economy of management. Oh, he thought I cooperated very well, and that he rated as excellent, as was my conduct. But the one I was really after changing was his answer to this rating question: "Would you want this officer under your command in wartime?" His answer: "Not observed." Ouch. "His general value to the service?" "Not observed."

Things hadn't gotten much better at El Toro, except that I began to pick up some notations of "excellent" in the areas of regular duty performance, endurance (above average), cooperation, initiative, judgment, and ability to think under stress. Maybe it would all have been better had I not had my little aircraft accident. Frank Bowker was the rater, and although his word picture was good, he nailed me. "A fine officer," he wrote. "Except for one accident in an FG-10 aircraft which was by poor technique on his part, his attributes as a pilot are far above average 2d Lieutenant."

In Korea I went after those "average" and "not observed" ratings. After I flew thirty-one combat missions, the commander, L. R. Siminick, recommended me for promotion, and the new commander, E. C. Kicklighter, concurred, recommending me for the Gold Star in lieu of the fourth Air Medal and for jet training upon my return to El Toro after my tour. Most ratings were tagged as excellent. Military bearing and loyalty, "outstanding." The only "not observed" was "economy of management," and in combat, I wondered a bit about that.

For all the combat flying and fighting I'd been doing, I figured it was about time to apply to the Corps for transfer of my commissioned rank from that of reservist to the regular Marine Corps. "Integration," they called it. It was, after all, the career path I'd chosen. So on 29 May 1953, I applied for that, with a Certificate of Educational Equivalency Test Results (I hadn't completed my college work but had enough smarts to pass the course requirements of a two-year college) and the rousing endorsement from my commanding officer, E. C. Kicklighter, who did a special fitness report.

On 18 June 1953, I'd completed fifty combat missions. By mid-August 1953, my first turn-down for admittance into the regular Marine Corps came back. General Lemuel C. Shepherd, Jr., then Marine Corps commandant, wrote:

> Your application . . . has been given careful consideration by the Selection Board. . . . It is with sincere regret that I must report you were not among those officers recommended for integration. May I assure you that the Board gave full consideration to the qualifications and potentialities of each applicant. . . . A large number of individuals with somewhat similar qualifications applied, which necessitated highly competitive selection. I regret . . . the authorized strength of the regular Marine Corps does not permit the selection of all applicants who have served their country so well in both peace and war.

I felt somewhat rejected and dejected, immediately thinking that perhaps the color of my skin was the real issue. But, actually, the majority of the officers in my category were also turned down the first time they applied. It did make a modicum of sense. The Korean War was about over, and the Marine Corps was scaling down and returning the active-duty guys and reservists back to civilian life. Everyone was downsizing, and the Marine Corps was no exception.

Perhaps the mission that really helped define my entire career as a Marine officer happened while I was assigned to the Devil Cats. I'll never forget 15 June 1953. I had maybe a little more than forty combat missions under my belt. We were on a mission into North Korea. It was a four-plane division, and I had the second section. My division leader lost his radio. As a section leader, I automatically took the lead. Checking in with the forward air controller, I received necessary attack information, then led the attack, pummeling the enemy positions with bombs and a 20mm strafing pass.

On pulling up, I took ground fire, delivered the stuff on target, kept the guys together, and returned safely. A couple took a few hits, as I recall. My commanding officer thought that was quite a feat for a brand, spanking new second lieutenant to have led a division on target and brought it back. He wrote me up for the Distinguished Flying Cross (DFC).

I don't know if initially there had been a reluctance to award me the DFC because of who I was. I do know that once the word got out, the 1st Marine Aircraft Wing (1st MAW) commander, Maj. Gen. Vernon E. Megee, personally flew down to Pyongtaek from his headquarters to make the presentation of the Distinguished Flying Cross to me on 20 September 1953. Maybe the general had a kind of "prevision." It was probably one of the most memorable days of my life.

I'd already received three Air Medals (one per ten combat flights flown) and had been recommended for the Gold Star in lieu of a fourth Air Medal. These were nice to have, but to have the Distinguished Flying Cross after just turning twenty-one years of age was almost scary. My breath caught in my throat a little as tall, thin Major Kicklighter walked with me to the flight line. The starched folds of my utilities argued with one another as I walked.

The whole of VMFA-212 stood tall along the flight line as Major General Megee's transport arrived. He was on the ground now. The band played; commands were shouted. My breathing went shallow and the sweat rolled down my neck while I stood at attention. The citation was read over loudspeakers. The president of the United States, the voice said, took pleasure in giving me the Distinguished Flying Cross. Then the citation—crisp and loud—so everybody could hear:

> For heriosm and extraordinary achievement in aerial flight as Pilot of a Plane in Marine Attack Squadron TWO HUNDRED TWELVE during operations against enemy aggressor forces in Korea on 15 June 1953. Leading a division of attack aircraft on a close air support mission against heavily defended and well-entrenched enemy positions situated in proximity to friendly front line units, Second Lieutenant Petersen promptly located the camouflaged objective in mountainous terrain and initiated a bombing and strafing assault in the face of intense hostile antiaircraft fire. Despite severe damage to his plane from the increasingly accurate

enemy fire, he resolutely pressed his attack to low altitude, and, after scoring direct bomb hits that clearly marked the hostile mortars and automatic weapons positions, skillfully maneuvered his battle-damaged aircraft to direct the flight in a successful bombing assault that inflicted heavy casualties on the enemy and destroyed a major hostile strongpoint. . . .

The rest of it seemed far away, like a dream sequence in a big-screen motion picture. I heard the words but didn't really hear them, I was so full emotionally. "Exceptional accuracy and exemplary leadership," and "courage, superb airmanship . . . devotion to duty . . . great credit . . . in keeping with . . . Second Lieutenant Petersen."

Before I knew it, I was drafted to become a forward air controller (FAC) up near the front with the ground troops. As swiftly, I found myself up at P'ohang, air wing headquarters (K-3), attending Forward Air Controller School. At least there was one bright spot. Upon arriving there, who should I run into but my old buddy from El Toro, Gale Harlan, also drafted for FAC duty.

There wasn't much time for fun and games, though. This was serious business. Forward air controller familiarization training. A week of total concentration. Coordination. Who talked to whom. How to deliver verbal instructions to a pilot as you're observing his drops. Determining the direction of the aerial attack while considering vectors for safe breakaway, ideally over friendly lines. Communications and how they worked; being able to describe a target area to the pilot so he can identify it from the air. Getting smoke on the target where possible to facilitate that. Team composition; equipment needed. Then it was back to K-6; pack up and head for the front. The 5th Marines were across the Imjin River; the 1st and the 7th were behind.

The Korean winter was frigid up around the thirty-eighth parallel, just below the DMZ, right above the Imjin River near Liberty Bridge. I've never been so cold in my life. I'd been assigned up there with the infantry as a forward air controller with the 2d Battalion, 1st Marine Division. We slept in tents. We couldn't make a fire to keep warm. That would be a gift to the North Korean (NK) artillery. We'd be wearing our halo and wings before we knew it. So I slept in my clothes, hand warmers on inside the sleeping bag. Cold was walking and the duty absolutely miserable as my four-man crew, including one radioman, tried to be comfortable out there in the boonies with our gear, jeep, and backpacks.

Because the war had wound down, what we were doing was primarily a training session. Call out targets correctly. Report the kinds of fire our guys were taking. Conjure up heat on the enemies. Rook them around with artillery support. Decimate them with our fighter sweeps. Pop smoke telling our guys where the enemy was. Grid coordinates. Marker rounds. Call down the high explosive (HE). Scream safe vectors for our own incoming.

Sometimes I wondered how I'd feel calling in a nape (napalm) strike on human beings. I'd dropped it myself, and often wondered how anyone could survive the fury. It burned hot, sucked the air out of the area, and was the end of the road for any person caught in the middle of the firestorm. I just wondered how I'd feel doing that to another human being whom I probably could've seen from a distance before I called for his execution, even though it was a battlefield.

To maintain my flying status, I came back to K-6 from time to time to fly a mission or two. It was nice seeing some of the old guys who were there when I first arrived a few months before. But I also met some interesting individuals up on the front lines.

The same thing applied up there as it did in other places when it came to race. Some guys would be in my corner. Others wouldn't. The guys who would were the straight shooters, like the guy I met from Louisiana, a Cajun named Weege Lenoir. Weege was a bad boy. An infantry combat leader. He was the type of guy who'd pull his .45 on you and threaten to shoot you if you screwed around too much. And he was on my side, of all things. Imagine. A Cajun and a brother back in 1953. A helluva combination.

Every now and then, I'd get a chance to talk to Harlan over the radio. It was nice to hear a familiar voice every so often. There was also another guy in the same battalion who became a good friend: Big Ernie Cheatham. Ernie and I were lieutenants and were both to retire as flag officers at the end of our careers. Ernie was sort of a pro kind of football player. We were to become close over the years. When we met, Ernie was a second lieutenant, a platoon commander, and we were living (when we weren't riding one of those cold hills) in what we called hootches. Just wood frame tents with double liners—an inner liner because it was so viciously cold.

I not only had trouble with the cold that far up front during this period, but some Korean customs and traditions continued to get to me. My duties sometimes took my team into nearby Korean villages, where the dress, the cold, the theft (disadvantaged by the war, many Koreans would steal whatever they could get their hands on), and the food sometimes seemed more than I wanted or could stand. Perhaps that's understandable when you consider that it was the first time I'd been overseas in my life, so when the people began to show me what Korean life was all about, I eagerly wanted to participate. They loved me, it seemed, and invited me to dinner one evening in their village. All went swimmingly, until it was obvious that the main entree was a dog they'd put in a gunnysack and beaten to death with clubs right in front of me.

Then they cooked that sucker, and I was given first choice of the pot. Everything inside me seemed to go into utter rejection. A good retch didn't seem awfully far away. They watched me with great interest, smiles all around. I tried smiling back, although I'm sure it was at best a sick smile. My driver was with me and watched the scenario wide eyed, hardly breathing. There was a brief commotion behind me.

"I'll wait for you outside in the jeep," my driver said as he hastily exited, "—sir."

Well, I had to sit there and eat a little bit of that dog and a whole bunch more kimchi, a cabbage dish. I don't know how to describe the taste of dog. I do remember thinking about Mama-San, my own pet dog I had over there. About how she faithfully followed me back and forth from the campsite area down to the water hole where we had the battalion laundry. Mama-San would growl at any Korean who got close to her, and I now understood the reason. I could see them eyeing her as they walked by, and she would just freak out. I often think of that little, fat tyke and wonder how long she lasted after I came back to the United States. She probably never lived to see a ripe old age. And I think she knew that I was her temporary salvation in a land where she was a main course at dinnertime.

The fighting was slowing down perceptibly. Our FAC routines continued to be primarily practice. We weren't far from the bridge where the first prisoner exchanges took place as a result of the negotiations at Panmunjom. Big Switch and Little Switch. We took a jeep over to observe the exchange from a distance. A big six-by truck brought the guys to be exchanged down. We saw their bad guys go across and our good guys come across, with the United Nations troops sort of forming an honor guard for them.

One day, I got in touch with what real soldiering looked like from another perspective. A contingent of Gurkhas was brought down for prisoner exchange as we watched from our vantage point on a hill some distance away. We could see the pride, the soldiering, the esprit de corps of those guys all the way from our hill. It stirred the soul and made us proud to be on their side.

On 27 July 1953, Thunderlips and I drew a mission. He was flying lead, and we were taxiing out just as the announcement of the cease-fire came over our headphones. Thunderlips was turning out onto the runway. I was following. He simply stopped his airplane right in the middle of the runway, cut the engine, slid back the canopy as the propellers slowed, then got out of the ship, a huge smile on his face. I couldn't believe my eyes.

The infernal war that Thunderlips didn't want to be involved with in the first place was over. He was through with it. As he walked away from the airplane, he began throwing off pieces of his equipment. His helmet, his goggles, his piece. You could follow his trail right off the runway. As far as Thunderlips was concerned, when it's over—well, hell—it's over. That's all there was to that.

I taxied my ship back on the line and parked it. I was glad it was over, too. I'd survived the thing. Gotten a promotion, the Distinguished Flying Cross, six Air Medals, and, in the short time I'd been in country (eighty days), had flown some sixty-four combat missions.

I was reassigned to the 1st Marine Aircraft Wing for about a month before rotating back to the States. I was something of a "catch" in that I got all sorts of dirty work—"lieutenant" kinds of things. Laundry officer. Shower control officer. Then there was a stint in an embarkation school, which at that time was nothing more than cutting out paper dolls and making sure they fit into the hold of a ship. There was one bright spot, and that was that my friend Gale Harlan was also there, partaking of these menial duties for a spell. We were there because we still had time left on our tours. I had about two months before returning to the United States and Gale had three or four months left. As Gale has since said, "They gave us a bunch of shit jobs." No matter, I guess they were imbuing us with character. Didn't feel that good at the time, though. Still, as Carlisle Cornelius noted in the *Washington Post* of 28 February 1989 [B-8], "Korea was a good war. You knew who you were fighting." I absolutely agreed with his next statement: "I learned a lot as a young guy about life and what life was all about."

Ain't no doubt about it. I had begun my military sojourn in a magic year—1950. A time when American forces were fighting in Korea for the first time in integrated units. And there had been no black Marine pilots. I'd wanted to take a shot at it, and I'd done it. It didn't get much better than that. I felt a bit like Prince Valiant—a kind of knight in shining armor. I'd gone to Korea to fly a fighter plane in combat. I'd done that, and flew sixty-four missions before the truce was signed. It was a brief taste of combat, but it was more than enough.

Home was to be El Toro Marine Corps Air Station in Santa Ana, California. Just lucky, I guess. It could have been Cherry Point, North Carolina. Even though it was California, I was to find out exactly what it meant to be a black officer, the only black aviator, in the United States Marine Corps during the 1950s. And it wasn't to be all fun and games.

In fact, my first assignment was to a jet squadron that was flying the F-3D aircraft, manned by a crew of two. Second crew members were enlisted men called radar operators. When I hove into view, these fellows decided, amongst themselves in a closed meeting, that none of them would fly with me. Except for one guy named Joe Lollar, who gave them a piece of his mind.

"You're all full of shit," Lollar growled. "I'm flying with him, and no one's gonna tell me differently—I'm a Marine."

Well, Joe and I became the closest of friends. We were to fly together for more than three years. Our families were also to become friends. I took him to my home in Topeka to meet my family as we flew cross-country flights.

Part Three
Entering the Real World

8: Cauldron

*If white people do less for us than we think they should, there are really only
two solutions: we can complain . . . or we can help ourselves. And we already
know from the Proverbs which path the Lord favors.*
—Stephen L. Carter, *Reflections of an Affirmative Action Baby* [235]

Marine Corps Air Station, El Toro, California, 1954–60

As the only black aviator on station at El Toro from 1954 to 1960 (and
I felt, sometimes, the only black officer in the entire Marine Corps), I
often addressed the need to get a handle on what higher-ranking white
officers were thinking about my future and performance. For the most
part, it was illogical to believe, I thought, that I would ever get a straightforward fix on this face to face. For this kind of intelligence information, I relied heavily in the early years of my assignment on the black
enlisted men, who were often privy to conversations of white officers
while at lunch, dinner, work, and other affairs on base. These were the
Montford Point guys, some of whom had been in the Marines since
World War II, when the Corps was more than segregated, and had not
only survived but achieved a fairly high enlisted rank. I leaned forward
and formed the kind of relationships we probably wouldn't have enjoyed
had they seen other black officers around. As an aviator, I can only say
that knowing these men was invaluable and helped me, a fighter pilot
with a need to survive in the air by always knowing what's coming up
behind my airplane, to keep my six o'clock clean.

A reservist (before integrating into the regular Corps), I never felt
quite right going into the officers' club. As insurance, I was always with
a bunch of my squadron buddies. Guys I flew with, so I knew there
wouldn't be any crap. Laguna Beach, for example, was a neat place, but
problems could erupt there like a sudden windstorm if I wasn't careful.

I had several friends who were white. One was a gentleman named
Jerry Sproul. Well, he and I walked into a restaurant in Laguna Beach
called The White House run by another buddy of mine. I'll never forget a tall kid sitting in there. Turned out he was from someplace down
around San Diego. Jerry and I were sitting at the bar drinking. Picture

it. I'm the only black face in there and this tall kid is sitting about two stools down from me, checking out the situation.

"I didn't think we were letting them drink with us," came the guy's slurry voice. He mouthed off a couple more times. I turned, facing him, half off my stool, ready to fight my own battle, when Jerry stepped in front of him.

"Friend," Jerry growled, "finish your drink and get the fuck outta here."

"Who're you?" the tall guy wanted to know.

"I'm a friend of his," Jerry shot back.

"I don't hafta take that shit from you," said the tall guy, who looked as though he'd like to square off. But before any of that could begin, the bartender, who was also the owner of the place, was heard from in no uncertain terms.

"Oh, yes you do," the owner roared, "'cause he's also a friend of mine."

Before the tall guy knew what hit him, he found himself surrounded by about six guys, stalwart Marines all.

As the weeks and months passed, a few black Marine officers appeared. A gentleman who was to become one of my good friends, a young lieutenant named Dale Tipton, who I tried mightily to talk into going to flight school. That wasn't to be, because he had his eye fixed on medical school and a career as a doctor. My old civilian friend Frank C. Brown was also still around. It was pretty obvious that we weren't particularly welcomed at the "official" officers' parties, dinners, and teas. So to save ourselves the embarrassment and troubles, we spent time at Frank's parents' home, barbecuing in the backyard or just hanging out. It was a home away from home. When we were feeling really macho and adventuresome, we'd head out to the fabulous old Watkins Hotel for black folks down on Western and Adams. Hanging out in its Rubiyat Room, checking out all the pretties, watching and listening to all the headliner entertainers who'd be there. And if you were clean, smelled good, and looked as good as you could, it was almost a lead pipe cinch you'd be picked up by some gorgeous lady.

You could also meet legends there.

It was at this very bar, before I went to Korea, that I met and became close friends with John "Mr. Death" Whitehead, one of the famous and esteemed original Tuskegee Airmen—that group of intrepid fliers who'd become America's first black fighter pilots during World War II.

The first time John and I met, we were both in uniform, he in Air Force garb. His major's leaves gleamed dully in the subdued multicolored lighting; my second lieutenant's bar made a kind of pipsqueak exclamation mark. John never let me forget the differences in our rank on the night of our first encounter. In short, he was an Air Force major; I was a second lieutenant and a Marine, to boot, so he took great pleasure in a little unofficial hazing. He was a test pilot at the time, testing the new F-89 fighter. He'd come into town on weekends and, because his sister lived in an apartment right across the street from the Watkins Hotel, he'd come to the Rubiyat Room, tie one on, then go across the street and get some sleep. This was the man who taught me how to drink scotch. I never will forget that. I wasn't into scotch in those days. Once we became friends, I used to marvel at how much John relished the stuff.

"Well," I'd say, "why do you drink that stuff, John?"

He'd just look at me for a long minute. Once he said, "Hey, if you're gonna be a gawd-danged fighter pilot, let me show you how to drink some whiskey. Go on," he commanded, "take a sip or two."

I sipped. It tasted awful, I thought.

"John," I said, almost gagging, "this is some of the nastiest stuff I've ever tasted in my life."

"Keep at it," John asserted. "You'll get it. You'll get it."

John's gone now. But he was a legend in his own time, not only because of the scotch he could drink (he could put away a bottle of the stuff at a sitting) but because he was one helluva fighter pilot and gentleman. I loved the guy, and it was a pleasure being invited into a small window of his life.

Some weekends we'd pile into a car and head for San Francisco and the corner of Turk and Hyde, to hold forth in the Blackhawk Club. We'd hear Errol Garner. The "Take Five" guy, Dave Brubeck. And, from time to time, the Modern Jazz Quartet, known simply as "the MJQ." A couple of times it was a foray south of the border into Mexico. Ensenada. Fishing. Horseback riding.

All these good times were had against a backdrop of "other things" on El Toro. I remember it as vicious infighting, done to keep your head above water if you were black. Just to be able to survive. Later on, we were to see the strange plight of a black doctor who needed to examine a patient who happened to be white and female. There would be a hellacious uproar if that patient was asked to disrobe for "that black doctor."

Such were the points of view in the early 1950s. But I couldn't let downers like that get in my way. There was work to be done and other things to do with my life and career.

I yearned to go home to Topeka on leave. To see my parents and friends. Go to a party or two. In December 1953, my friend Frank Brown and I drove the Chrysler back to Topeka. By now, of course, my first love was comfortably dedicated to a new guy. It was nice seeing everyone, and then we headed back to California.

However, Frank Brown and I didn't know how close to stateside combat we were going to come just trying to get back to California as we cruised down toward Oklahoma City, intending to hook up with Route 66. We elected to bypass Oklahoma City and instead swing over by Vance Air Force Base and on down the line, hanging a right at Kingfisher, moving smartly along in those wide-open Oklahoma spaces. I think we even hummed a bar or two of that famous Nat King Cole hit about "O-O-k-la-homa Ci-i-ty looked mi-i-i-ghty pre-teee."

The highway beckoned, and I heard it as I took the Chrysler through its paces. The speedometer teased eighty, then ninety plus miles per hour. We had to keep moving, because in those days there were no black-run motels or hotels in which we could stay except in the larger cities. White-run motels wouldn't accept us as patrons. We drove the way the name of the game dictated. Do what you have to so you can get where you're going. It was grueling. Hours on end behind the wheel. Sometimes twenty hours or more at a crack.

Brown luxuriated on the backseat, catching a wink or two of sleep, his .45 automatic riding close at hand because we were two black men riding high through the South in a relatively new Chrysler early in the 1950s. We'd just zoomed through Watonga, a little town of about three thousand souls, when it happened.

The big red light flashed and the raucous police siren caterwauled as a highway patrol car materialized behind us as if it'd come from outer space. I pulled over and stopped, my Marine Corps uniform still crisp and clean, the knees a bit baggy from sitting. I got out of the car as the two patrolmen approached, one up front, the other hanging back a bit. From the corner of my eye, I saw a suddenly animated Frank shoving the gun down into the seam of the backseat.

One of the patrolmen glared as he looked me up and down. It was cause for suspicion, this thing about telling him that I was a Marine Corps officer. "Never saw a black one of those. So yer supposed to be a Marine pilot? Get outta heah. Yer not really a pilot in the Marine Corps.

Where ya stationed, anyhow? Don't know if ah quite believe yer story. Show me yer ID. Well, sir, there it is, sure as shootin'. Just one thing more—just what kinda airplanes you fly? Well, there's allus somethin' new under the ding-busted sun. Tell ya what, though. Gonna let ya go— this time. Don't let us catch ya speedin' like that long as yer in Oklahoma—yew unnerstan?"

And so, that, too, passed. Frank Brown wiped his brow and counted his blessings there in the backseat. I wore a slight smile on my face at the sight of the retreating highway patrolmen, still shaking their heads at the very idea of a black aviator in America's military—and in the United States Marine Corps, to boot. What was the country coming to? We pulled off. I could see the highway patrol car do a neat U-turn and go back to its hideout, waiting for the next unwary driver.

As we headed down toward Amarillo, Texas, and the foot of the Rockies at Albuquerque, I thought of the year of training at El Toro, and particularly the extracurricular stuff. The room I'd rented from a local black couple. Visiting with Brown's parents. Sojourning in the City of Angels. The beautiful ladies we'd met in the Rubiyat Room of the Watkins Hotel. Party time. Just walk in there in uniform and stand by. No questions asked. Beaches and dancing. Lovely loves. Hanging out in all-white Laguna Beach with my old partner Gale Harlan and other Marines. Quaffing at the Sandpiper. Nibbling hors d'oeuvres at "Normal" Norman Peterson's White House. The parties. Weekends in San Francisco at the Blackhawk Club. The steadfastness of the gate sentries when it came to failing to salute a black officer. The questioning of our right to sit in the officers' section in the base theater. Nobody wanted to believe our right to exist as Marine officers unless it was verified.

Even so, we were damned glad to get back to California and MCAS El Toro. Racism was there, all right, but more muted than in the rest of America at the time. It was also time to fix that infernal tattoo on my forearm celebrating the two-faced lady back home I used to think so grand. I went back to that tattoo artist one day and had him change the name to Buddy, my own nickname. So it was catch as catch can when it came to the ladies for a long while. There was no doubt that I belonged to the United States Marine Corps, lock, stock, and barrel, but there was no lady who could make that claim. It was, to put it mildly, a great deal of fun.

Not a lot happened regarding a woman in my life until December 1954, when I stopped over on leave in Denver, Colorado, to visit my sister, Anne, and her family for Christmas. While there, I patronized the local soda fountain in a nearby drugstore, and there she was. The electricity sizzled. I'd grown up with her—Eleanor Burton. We'd gone through school together. She had been enrolled in the University of Kansas when I went off to the service. And now here she was in Denver, visiting relatives. Ellie the pretty, hard at work at her first job ever behind the counter. Looking good. Young and vivacious. Looking ready. She invited me over to her house. The courting started and got really heavy. It seemed the most natural thing to do. She was almost like family, because our families knew each other. Her older sister and my mom had been in college together. We'd all lived nearby back in Topeka. I was still a bit blue about being jilted by the girl I considered my first love, and it seemed coincidental that Ellie—that's what everybody called her—had also been jilted by her longtime boyfriend. In even more of a crazy coincidence, her old boyfriend had fallen head over heels for my first love. When those facts hit us, it seemed like poetic justice. Maybe the two of them deserved each other. They'd hooked up, so why shouldn't we? We did. It was good. Maybe we deserved each other, too.

At El Toro, the Marine Corps didn't fool around about getting all of its prop pilots who could qualify transitioned into jet aircraft. That was fine by me. We were flying the F-9F, and once we finished the transition, I went right next door to the instrument training squadron, where we were flying the T-33. The things I found remarkable between flying a propeller-driven airplane and a jet were the ease of handling the jet aircraft (with tricycle landing gear for one), plus the difference in operating characteristics in terms of accelerating for takeoff. And, too, the jet engines seemed a lot quieter than the prop-driven airplanes because we were sealed in an air-conditioned environment inside the jet. Jet performance capabilities were about twice that of propeller-driven aircraft. Jets even smelled different, because a different kind of fuel is used. The joke went that we jet pilots took a small vial of jet fuel with us when we were assigned to a desk job, and took a sniff every now and then, just so we wouldn't forget it.

As the jet transition training progressed, it became obvious to me that the coming aerial wars would be light years away from what I'd been through in Korea. There, you had to see who you were fighting. You were literally face to face. Now, since the advent of jet fighter aircraft and improved weapons technologies, you could achieve a kill miles away.

It got so that my cross-countrys would always end up at the Navy installation at Olathe, Kansas, just down the road from Topeka and closer still to the University of Kansas, where Ellie held forth. I put my foot right in it. I asked the child to marry me, but not until I at least had been successful in being transferred from the Marine reserves to be "integrated" into the regular Marine Corps. I'd tried once and been unsuccessful, and on the eighteenth of the previous May I'd again applied for integration into the regular Corps. Nothing happened that time, either, but the answer from Marine headquarters was indeed encouraging. It advised that "former aviation cadets appointed to commissioned rank during calendar year 1952 would be invited to apply."

Boy, I could've jumped for joy. It was my time. The air base commander at El Toro gave me a hearty endorsement. He wrote: "Officers and enlisted men with whom he comes in contact accord him the greatest respect and admiration and constantly strive to emulate the qualities that make Lt. Petersen a distinguished Marine." Positive endorsements were added as the application went up the line to Marine headquarters.

Finally, on 21 December 1954, the answer came back. "The Secretary of the Navy," it read, "advises that the President of the United States, by and with the agreement of the Senate, appoints you to the grade of lst Lieutenant (temporary) in the United States Marine Corps with date of rank of 12 August 1954." A letter from the Marine Corps commandant contained instructions as to how to make it so. No doubt about it—I was now a regular Marine Corps officer and a first lieutenant. I could feel the juices flow.

There was even more cause to celebrate: the decision by the Supreme Court on 17 May 1954 outlawing racial segregation in public schools as a violation of the Fourteenth Amendment to the Constitution. It resulted from the Brown v. Board of Education decision based on a case emanating from my hometown of Topeka, Kansas. Perhaps now the city would not need two basketball teams, one white, one black. Maybe now it would not need two homecoming queens or two junior-senior proms. Maybe now the school officials would open and activate that beautiful swimming pool at the high school and make it possible for all the students to swim—together.

The Supreme Court decision appeared to be the most significant governmental act since the Emancipation Proclamation for black people in America. I was impressed and hopeful, even though from time to time

I had to produce my ID card at the base theater in order to remain in the officers' seating section because not many people wanted to believe that I was indeed a Marine officer. Sometimes I'd demand that they check the ID of everyone sitting in the officers' section. It gave me a bit of satisfaction, if I must say so myself.

Underneath the hopeful impressions, I was also somewhat dismayed. I remembered in great detail what the school I had attended in Topeka was like. I knew what the teachers and students were like. I also knew that if it was to be integrated, it would lose some of that community flavor. (Indeed we might lose the school itself—and, in point of fact, we did.) It was a two-edged sword, this togetherness and abandonment of separateness. The ending of separateness is ultimately necessary for a strong America, but I feared for the loss of that sense of togetherness the blacks had, even in the face of the most awful racism. A truly great country cannot have separatism in the long run, but I am sure that black people somehow must revive those things that are peculiar to an African American community. We sawed them off. We're in a multifaceted melting pot, but somebody forgot to light the fire; somebody forgot to stir the stew. These thoughts haunted me as life continued to beckon and beg to be lived.

It was lonely out there in the big world. Fighting the dragons. Deflecting the racial slurs. Running. Seeking. Wishing. Maybe what I needed was a wife. Family. Children.

9: Sharing the Pain

I didn't know it, but my attention to Eleanor had been thoroughly discussed within her family. Her sister had married an Army fellow and she knew about the service life. Based on that experience, the family thought our marriage would be a good match. Not only that, her family thought the guy she had been seeing (whoever that was) was for the birds. So it seemed that I was in the catbird's seat.

After that Christmas leave, we wrote each other constantly. I remember how my first California earthquake influenced the correspondence. In my next letter to Eleanor, I told her how it wasn't Mother Nature shaking that ground, it was my great love for her. Yessir. Every chance I had to do a cross-country, I'd drop in at Olathe, Kansas, to steal a look at ground-controlled approach (GCA) operations and the lady who'd soon be my wife.

MUTUAL VOICES
Ernie Douglas, Childhood Friend

One of the things I remember is when he was doing his cross-country flight, he had to fly into Olathe, Kansas. When he left, we were all over at his house. Of course, his folks took him down to get his plane to get ready to leave and he came back and circled the house. Yeah. And then he put that afterburner on. And he shook the whole damned neighborhood. He lit it UP, you know? He was gone. In a second. He was gone. And that was the talk of the town for most all the fellas, you know, that hung out in South Topeka. Man, we talked about that for days. He hit that afterburner and that thing said: "Pumpf"—and he was gone.

Although the usual juices that drive young people to the marriage altar were flowing normally with Eleanor and me, we may have been more relaxed about taking our wedding vows had it not been for two sets of circumstances that served to drive us into getting the marriage done as soon as possible. One was my work as a Marine and the commitments linked to that. The United States, the world's leading atomic power, continued its testing of atomic bombs apace. Testing had become critical, because Russia now possessed the bomb and had begun testing its first megaton-class hydrogen bomb as late as 1953. In response, America detonated six nuclear weapons in the Pacific. The British were itching to join this august group.

Intrinsic to all of this was the very real question of how would men, weaponry, and matériel survive these awesome weapons in a battlefield environment? We were tasked to fly our F-3D fighters in orbit twenty miles out and around the next scheduled detonation at Yucca Flats, Nevada, to observe the blast from a distance. The problem was that the test kept being scrubbed. We'd fly out, and be recalled. This seemed to go on interminably. So being on station for these scheduled flights was necessary and part of my duty. Second, Eleanor was Catholic, and Lent, the religious season observed by the church, was fast approaching. It began on Ash Wednesday, forty days before Easter (excluding Sundays), and ended on Easter Sunday. We were already deep into January 1955, and if we were to be married with any alacrity, we'd better get something together quickly that might fit between these two pressing requirements. Nobody knew when the orbit mission to Yucca Flats would be on. Lent stalked the church and us. Lent would mean fasting. Penance. The giving of alms. Abstinence from amusements and definitely no solemnizing of marriages.

So we figured we'd just do it. I double-checked to be sure that Eleanor had really said yes, then began to set up for our marriage in California to be performed at the base chapel on El Toro Marine Corps Air Station. A squadron mate, Capt. John Walsh was to be my best man. The eighteenth day of February 1955 was to be the big day. Eleanor had her ticket to fly out to California.

I began to sweat a little, as I usually do when things get a bit tight. Truth was, we were just going to barely slide by that Lent thing. Lent, in 1955, would begin on 3 March and end on 18 April. We were going to beat the prohibition for solemnizing marriages by a scant fourteen days (twelve days, if you don't count the Sundays). So you can see why the sweat.

An old friend and I went up to Los Angeles International Airport to meet my gorgeous bride. I don't remember what the weather was like that day. I didn't care at that point in my life. I was on the verge of one of my greatest experiences. Strange how life tends to repeat itself. My father pulled my mom out of college before she could graduate. I was doing the same thing to Ellie. But all that tended to get lost in the magic of the moment.

MUTUAL VOICES
Ellie, First Wife

When the airplane landed, I can remember that I was just excited. Just excited about being there. Excited about being in California. He met me at the airport with one of his friends who was a helicopter pilot. [If I had any concerns] they probably went to the [fact that] the Marine Corps and my background were different. I had gone to Catholic School, which was integrated. I hoped that the differences wouldn't be overwhelming.

Folks in attendance were some of the guys and gals from my squadron. The parents of my good buddy the helicopter pilot lived in Los Angeles on Westside Drive and were kind enough to give us a wedding reception in their home. It was a good day. Late in the day, we finally got away from the people and all the well-wishers. Time for a little love stuff.

Later, we moved into our quarters, which sat in that little oasis on the far corner of El Toro Marine Corps Air Station. Our married life began at 13541 Wake Avenue, Santa Ana, up the little hill on the other side of the runways.

Startled, we looked at each other as the telephone rang so hard it threatened to jump off the nightstand. Who could be calling at this hour, and on our wedding night? It took a lot of nerve, if you asked me. A little annoyed, I picked up the receiver. The squadron. The atomic test was on again. After hanging up the telephone, I rolled over in the bed.

"Gotta go," I announced.

Eleanor simply stared. "What?"

"Gotta go. The bomb's gonna go."

"What bomb's gonna go? Are you kidding me? On our wedding night? You mean, you're just going to walk out of here on our wedding night because of some bomb test?"

"Yep."

I began sliding into my socks and shoes and uniform. Actually, I was damned glad that the previous missions had been scrubbed. I didn't particularly want to see the bomb go off anyway because I personally felt that those folks down on the ground didn't really know what they were playing with. And I thought that the short distance we were orbiting from the bomb was a little too close to ground zero.

Ellie's voice pierced my consciousness.

"Well, Frank, I never. You're really going to leave me here—alone—on our wedding night?"

"Don't get so upset, Ellie. You knew who you were marrying when you married me."

That remark seemed to really make her mad. At any rate, I had to go. Duty called. Period.

We flew out again. They scrubbed the test again.

I guess the decision was that the bomb test had been cancelled so many times before and our flights scrubbed that the Marines decided to simply put some men out in the desert on the ground. So almost a month after I got married, they bussed us out to Yucca Flats. Several busloads of my outfit were directed to predetermined positions. Infantry was positioned in trenches much closer in to the site. We turned our backs toward the expected blast. The countdown marched ahead. Then the thing went off.

That bluish white flash. The hellish heat. Even at our distance, it felt as if someone had struck a match across the back of my neck. Then the wind shifted, blowing fallout in the wrong direction, putting us all in jeopardy. I can remember what was said by one of the enlisted guys in a group of fleeing men.

"Oh, man," he cried, his voice at full tremor. "Let's get the fuck outta here. I'm getting away from this muddahfuckah."

There was just about pure, bald-headed terror among the people. It was such an awesome sight. We couldn't look at it. We'd turned our backs when they'd set the sucker off, then we were told to turn around just as the fireball formed and was starting to rise.

That was the last time for me out at Yucca Flats. I suppose the training was successful—letting the troops know how these things looked. I'm here to tell you, I'll never forget it.

If you pick up a good encyclopedia, you can read about those American atomic bomb tests. In the middle of the Cold War with Russia, the Soviets exploded their first thermonuclear device during Korea and followed that with its first hydrogen bomb detonation in 1953. Perhaps the bomb test I witnessed was one of several prompted by that display. At any rate, I understand now why I felt searing heat on the back of my neck. By the time the heat from the fireball reaches maximum diameter, every section of its surface is radiating three times as much heat and light as a comparable area of the sun. No wonder that trooper wanted to get away from it. Hell, it was a scary thing.

I always wanted to accept any challenge thrown at me, take any kind of opportunity I thought would be on the success path. Even with my flying, I would spend at least half of the weekends in a given month out in an airplane doing cross-country flights to maintain my proficiency. Because I worked in several areas of base operations in addition to my other duties, I thought it might not be a bad idea to find out about the nuts and bolts of the operational aspects of the ground-controlled approach (GCA) system.

The system fascinated me. It was a "talk-down" landing approach system developed during World War II that used ground-calibrated radar. The ground operator follows the path of the aircraft and, by voice radio, gives the pilot his heading, distance to go, and descent instructions. On final landing approach, the operator indicates the final glide path for descent and landings.

I wanted to be an expert in that area, so I requested attendance at the GCA school at Olathe. It was to last eight weeks, and Ellie and I bundled up our belongings (as Ellie used to say, "Everything we owned at that time we could get in a car") and took off to Kansas a little after mid-March 1955. We lived with my parents in Topeka while I pursued this course of instruction.

While we were there, I was to find out about a joyous secret Ellie had been keeping from me. One evening we were sitting with my folks at the dinner table. Dad made a couple of explicit remarks and gestures that could mean only one thing. Ellie was pregnant with our first child. I went into complete shock, because it was only shortly after we'd married. Words failed me, but I remember how the thought flashed through my mind—Well, I'll be darned.

Ellie was a bit put out, because she'd wanted to tell me personally. Dad just sneaked it in before she could open her mouth. Mom didn't say much about the matter. She always seemed to take second fiddle to Dad.

For the moment, things couldn't have been better between my new wife and me. Warm. Fuzzy. Excited at the promise of the imminent arrival of our firstborn, representing our melding.

It was good to get back to Kansas for both of us and regroup, so to speak. We got along fairly well living in my parents' home, although I think I detected potential mother-in-law troubles just beneath the surface.

• • •

I was busy on several fronts. Ellie bustled in anticipation of the coming blessed event. After transition into F-9Fs, I went over to VFM(AW)-542 and was a squadron pilot again, doing what I loved the most—flying the F-3D. I taught tactics for a spell. After instrument training in the T-33 and night fighter school, I was to spend a little more than a year as an instrument instructor in VMAT-10 (fighter attack squadron). Once in a while, I'd take a buddy along with me on a cross-country flight. Not only was it fun, it was part of getting the job done and honing my skills as well. Some of these experiences I'll never forget, like the time when my old buddy Gale Harlan went with me back to Forbes Air Force Base outside of Topeka.

MUTUAL VOICES
Gale Harlan, ex-Marine Fighter Pilot and Friend

His brothers, Billy and Hans, picked us up [at the airfield]. I'd never been to Topeka, so I stayed at his family home there. I met his parents. They treated me as if I was one of the brood. It was a Friday evening when we arrived. We went out for a spell but were in early. Next night was Saturday and that was a different story. We went bar-hopping. I was hanging with old Frank, and that night I never saw another white face. I was it. I was in the black end of town. [I'll never forget] walking into this one bar—Frank was ahead of me—and I was talking to somebody behind, or maybe he was talking to somebody and I went on into the nightclub. Anyway, I'm about ten or twelve feet into [the place] and—Jesus—all of a sudden I'm lifted up into the air. These two bodyguards—these bouncers—had me under the arms. [They were] BIG guys—I'm pretty good size myself—and I'm up in the air and they turned me around and we're headed out and we ran into [Petersen] on the way in. Pete saved the day. "Oh," he said, his arms outstretched in a restraining fashion, "wait a minute. He's with me." These guys hesitated for what seemed a lifetime, then they set me down like I was a precious vase or something. I'm thankful to this day that Pete was there, because my ass was headed out.

Next morning, we were so hungover—you know—one of those mornings when you wake up and you're not sure whether you're gonna puke or not. We walked out into [the kitchen] and his mom had laid out this table. God. There was everything. A complete breakfast—and then there was fried chicken and ham and mashed potatoes and gravy. It was like a huge brunch. Really, though, all I wanted was a cup of hot coffee and a ciga-

rette. Frank, too, because he was about to turn green. We kept telling his mom, "No, we're gonna fly back to El Toro this morning." But his mom, and she was a big lady, insisted that we sit down and have a full meal. And we did, while Frank's brothers, Billy and Hans, laughed their asses off because they knew how bad we felt. Hans knew. He'd gone with us. Billy had begged off. He was a fireman and had to go to work.

Gale Harlan and I were always going off on cross-countries. Once, we dropped into Pensacola Naval Air Station to see his brother, who was attending flight school. We popped the F-3D in there and parked it. Went into downtown Pensacola and hoisted more than a few. Saw his brother. Next morning, we were back in the F-3D, flying back to El Toro, when not too far from Pensacola, around Shreveport, Louisiana—Barksdale Air Force Base, I believe—Tuna (that was his call sign) got sick. For the uninitiated, that Air Force base belonged to Strategic Air Command (SAC) during the time when old iron pants, Gen. Curtis LeMay, was its commander. He ruled it with an iron fist. No shenanigans, period. So, here we were, two Marine officers coming in for an unannounced landing. In true Strategic Air Command style, they were coming out to meet us, armored car and all. We sat the bird down and were taxiing in when Tuna threw up in a barf bag, flipped back the top canopy of the F-3D, and threw the damned bag out the top onto the runway. I thought, this guy just threw a barf bag full of barf stuff out onto one of Gen. Curtis LeMay's runways. Legend said that LeMay was the only living person who would dare walk out on the flight line next to the bombers parked there with a lit cigar in his mouth, and the damned thing wouldn't dare blow up. Hell, I just knew that the both of us were going to jail in one hot, little minute. Lucky for us, General LeMay was someplace else that day. But if he had been around, we would have gone straight to the hoosegow—ain't no question.

But even that was lightweight compared to the day I dropped in on Little Rock Air Force Base in Arkansas in an F-3D fighter along with a neighbor of mine. I'd gone back east to return to El Toro. We landed at the base right at the time they were having the riots over integrating the schools. We got out of the plane and I walked into operations, where the Air Force people looked at me as if they couldn't believe I was the pilot. Their expressions conveyed volumes, as in, Look, now they've even got their own Air Force. They even followed me into the room where I filed my flight plan to see if I knew what I was doing.

The gentleman who was flying with me was a white guy. The fact that we were one black and one white Marine officer together somehow seemed to temper things. But I look back at the history of those times and I think, Jesus, it's amazing that we've come as far as we have. Therein, I suppose, lay the hope of the whole damned thing.

It was while I was a member of VMAT-10 that I began to sense the slight beginnings of change in the Marine Corps as far as the consideration of racial mores was concerned. Put another way, it was a shift in attitude regarding integration and the people most affected by it. The commander, Lt. Col. H. D. Raymond, got my attention because he took my side of an issue when he very well might not have. It was his call.

I'd had an incident where we were bringing a T-33 back on an emergency. Its cockpit indicators showed a fire somewhere in the bird. I tried opening the aircraft canopy on touchdown, except that the canopy came halfway open and stopped. I could get out, but the guy in the rear seat couldn't. That's when I blew the canopy. Later, there was considerable controversy among certain of the pilots as to whether I had done the right thing, because subsequent investigation disclosed that there had been no fire. What I had done, they said, was unprofessional and, more than that, I had panicked—pure and simple.

The commander simply stopped all the rhetoric cold with the pronouncement, "If Petersen made a decision to blow the canopy, he was right." That kind of backup from my commander indicated faith in my judgment as an officer and meant worlds to me. I was even more determined to go as far as I dared in the Marine Corps.

I couldn't learn enough about what I'd chosen to do as a military career, so I also flew the T-28 and worked at the base operations shop as a GCA controller and airfield duty officer. Even so, military instruction and classes weren't enough, I figured. I had to complete my education on other fronts as well.

I began going to school at night because it was evident to me that the one year of college I came into the Marine Corps with wasn't enough to ensure the climb up the career ladder I wanted. Once I was pretty much in place dutywise after I returned to El Toro, I volunteered for the night watches and swapped my schedule around so I could participate as a full-time day student. By flying at night, I could go to school during the day. My day started at two o'clock in the afternoon and ran until about ten o'clock at night. I carried something like twelve units at Santa Ana Junior College. My duty day was still eight hours. From the F-3D squadron, I went to stand watch as a control tower officer, and that's where I did most of my watch swapping. It worked out pretty well.

It was while I did my stints in the base operations control tower that I began to hear rumblings of discontent from black enlisted men on station. I was approached by several black enlisted people who wanted me to petition their causes in the operation of the enlisted club. They were having typical problems whereby things weren't geared to the minority trooper in those days. Not their kind of music, for example, on the jukeboxes. Country western music carried the day. On top of this, they felt themselves harassed to a certain degree by some of the white patrons.

So when I was working in the base operations control tower, I occasionally got the staff duty officer (SDO) assignment. As such, I'd check the base, would be on call, and would make it a point to tour the enlisted club in uniform. It was during these tours of duty that the problems often lay exposed right in front of me. It was obvious that it wasn't just the country music and incidental racial harassment, but harassment that was more pointed, because it was becoming more and more common for the black troopers to approach white females who happened to be visiting. I found myself breaking up several fights relating to this issue. No matter, the duty did create a presence that the brothers could see, as well as the others.

When I was on duty as SDO, I had the full power of the commanding officer. This was when they'd come to me and bitch about being harassed and the ways they were being treated by some of the white guys. So I went to the group commander and told him what was taking place. Malaised treatment. Fighting. He invited me to make the presentation to a group of his squadron commanders—majors, lieutenant colonels—about the problems on the base. Apparent racial friction. Touchy fallout from the fact that the blacks were beginning to band together in order to solve the problems their way. Failure of club management to recognize their needs. Obviously, something needed to be done to avoid larger problems.

It could have been intimidating. A junior officer briefing a roomful of senior Marine officers about a touchy subject like racism. I figured that as long as the group commander was present, I'd lay it on that roomful of majors and lieutenant colonels. And I did. From that point on, these officers were much more aware of some of the problems that their young troops were facing. A kind of new awareness seemed to surface for a moment. Things calmed down at the club for a short period, although once the advisory had been made and it was felt that the problem had been "handled," things slowly returned to the way they were before. I also found that some of the black troops who had asked for assistance were now afraid to come forward to give testimony to commanding officers. The name-calling resurfaced; fistfights erupted as a result. Some black troops who were pretty good with their dukes went in from time to time, and if something happened, they would slug it out right there.

As SDO one evening, I found myself in the middle of such a melee and thought that I was actually taking my own life in my hands as I waded in to break up the confrontation. The situation never reached an official investigatory stage. Fear of retaliation ruled the day for the youngsters.

Disrespect for black officers also continued at the main gate, because some sentries simply refused to salute. I would just sigh hugely, get out of my car, and read each and every one the riot act: "Since when did you stop saluting officers? Is that a new Marine regulation or what?" I'd jack them up every time.

As the mid-1950s rolled around, other black officers were beginning to show up. Navy doctors. Marine pilots. It was the beginning of a new era, a new togetherness, because it was more than obvious that, even though on board, we simply wouldn't be considered part of the mainstream of Marine social life at El Toro Marine Corps Air Station.

10: Menagerie

During the mid-1950s, it was refreshing to see so many black officers appearing on El Toro. At least four or five within a few short months. Eric Best, who these days lives in Albuquerque. Dr. Dale Tipton, now in San Francisco, who showed up as a young second lieutenant, went to Korea in 1954, got out, and completed medical school. A guy named Don Moore, who died before his time. Don and I were very close in North Carolina many years ago. All of them had families; all had children. A guy named Art Edwards, a pilot out of Philadelphia. He and his family lived next door.

As black officers, we weren't usually included in many of the social events taking place at the officers' club, so we banded together, socialized together. We had to, because we weren't being invited out. We had no place to go. We weren't part of the mainstream. And, frankly, many of us didn't feel comfortable on that level with "them."

Nevertheless, in addition to the newly arrived black officers, we did have a group of close white officer friends who were our neighbors. True, we all did lots of "hanging out" at the bars in Laguna and Los Angeles, but once we were married some things began to change. It was more family-oriented stuff. Dinners and Sunday brunches. We were all so close that this kind of thing was almost spontaneous. We'd see one another in front of our houses or meandering in our backyards and the dialogue would begin.

"Hey, what're you guys eating tonight?"

"Jeez, I dunno—we'll think of something."

We'd all throw something into the mutual pot. After all, we were living dang near next door to one another. A kind of testament to how it can be in this world, I guess.

Even though some of us were able to put the "race problem" on the back burner, because we were neighbors in the military housing area, that didn't mean that we black officers and our wives were automatically included in social events that took place on the base. When we were, it was rather like walking on eggs, because in one way or another, the racial aspect of things would crop up.

For example, I invited my civilian friend Frank Brown to a party in which I was involved at the officers' club. He was dating a black lady who was very fair skinned. The white officers, not used to being around black folks in the first place, became emotionally exercised at what seemed to be a white woman with a black man within their social cocoon. To add insult to injury, one of the white ladies got a snoot full of the firewater and rather insisted that Mr. Brown dance with her. He did. She completely lost her cool, all propped up against Mr. Brown and obviously getting drunker by the minute. And, horrors of horrors, I almost panicked when I realized that the lady in question was none other than the commanding officer's wife. The CO's eyes were fast becoming narrow slits, and I could hardly wait for the music to stop. When it did, I spirited Mr. Brown over to a corner of the room.

"Man, do you know whose wife that is?" I said quietly.

"Naw. Who was the chick, man?"

"That's the CO's wife. You trying to get me strung out to dry?"

"Oops. Guess I'd better watch it."

"Yeah. You'd better."

We turned to see the commanding officer none too gently steering his inebriated wife out the front door of the officers' club. We could see him avidly counseling her through the big picture windows. Obviously telling her whatever it was that white men told their wives in those days about dancing with a black guy, I suppose. As Marine officers, though, we knew that the major issue wasn't just dancing with my friend. She'd gotten drunk in a public place, and parties within the environs of the officers' club were generally conservative to begin with. Within that, there was a certain protocol that had to be observed. Retrospectively, I think that the lady in question had a drinking problem, and if that probability hadn't existed, the faux pas might not have happened in the first place.

Relative skin color wasn't a problem just at the officers' club. It was an issue that existed within my own house. Most people would not have pegged my wife as a black woman. We had grown up together, so initially the light complexion she was born with wasn't regarded as a problem, because in Topeka, there was the lightest and the darkest sides of the black folks' rainbow. But I was conscious of Ellie's light skin, and how others reacted to her. Sometimes, it could be funny. At other times, it could pose serious problems. I was sensitive about it and alert to all the nuances involved. I felt I had to be, as most black men have to be. It's part of our basic survival techniques.

Some of my white officer friends like Gale Harlan, Tom Kelly, and Jerry Sproul used to join me in our own little game meant to bamboozle the racists down in the all-white town of nearby Laguna. It was an interesting place to go, especially in winter, because patronage would be down and owners of the restaurants and bars devised clever ways to pack the house. In The White House, for example, owner "Normal" Norm Peterson decreed Monday evening as amateur chef night. On Wednesday nights over at the Sandpiper, the house special was abalone, and as the frolicking reached a fever pitch, the owner would make movies of what was going on. Thursday nights, the speciality was prime rib, with a similar scenario.

Because we knew that the racists and bigots were around (and we knew how the local populace felt about mixed couples in those days), we'd go to Laguna Beach, drive up to the Sandpiper or The White House, and intentionally mix wives before we entered. I would walk in with Gale's wife on my arm, Gale would walk in with Ellie on his arm, and Tom would have somebody else's wife on his arm. We'd crack up watching the people flip out. We did it just to make a point. And it did. We'd chow down and have a few drinks, sometimes more than we should have. Sometimes the tips we left while under the influence were quite large. I fondly remember how my wife took exception to that practice one evening. We were all flying high, tipping the waitress (a friend of Harlan's) quite extravagantly, when Ellie decided enough was enough and began picking up the tips we'd left and returning them to the tippers because she thought it was far too much to give that girl.

MUTUAL VOICES
Gale Harlan, Friend and Ex-Marine Officer

He never spoke to me about it. Sometimes though, I could tell. Yeah. Sometimes he'd make remarks and—well—the guys that we hung around with would just say, "Ah, forget those guys. They're assholes." And, you know, it wasn't a big deal, because there are assholes everyplace. They're in the Marine Corps, too. So we'd just ignore the bastards. They weren't going to hang around with us anyway. The guys Frank and I hung around

were guys [who didn't care about] color. It didn't matter. If you were a good
guy and just one of the guys, you just fit in.

Sometimes the hazing because of the color of my skin would get my
goat. No doubt about it. It was difficult to contain practically and emotionally. I think that my wife probably perceived all of that differently,
from what I remember. But she was my bulwark and talking tree. Where
else could I go when the going got tough? I was very sensitive about the
racial slights, but Ellie probably didn't feel the lance as much because
of her light skin. I think she was always amazed at the stuff I'd pick up
on my mental radar that never bothered her. Retrospectively, she might
be prone to overdramatize my feelings of those days. They were real,
nevertheless. Harassment on and off the job. Slurs. Slights.

MUTUAL VOICES
Ellie, First Wife

He had all kinds of stories [that meant] he'd been harassed on the job.
He'd come home and what he'd been through would be so painful. He'd
tell me some of them and some he couldn't even tell me. Sometimes, he'd
come home pretty much in tears. And I always wanted to say: "How can
you take it? Let's stop this." But he wasn't about to. These days I'm still
often mistaken for Italian or Spanish. But in California, it didn't seem to
matter at first. [But when we went out] to social events, there were times
he made us the target. Yeah. Naturally, we're going to look different. He
was much more sensitive about slights and comments.

Of course, in those days all conversation, no matter how it started,
would revert to race. We found ourselves explaining the racial question nine
chances out of ten when we did go out. He'd go to the door and it'd be an
insurance salesman [who'd] say, "Well, Sergeant" or [look] shocked to see
him. He'd be stopped for impersonating an officer, or he'd always have to
show his ID card. It wasn't great in those days to be harassed like that.

December 1955 crept toward us through the Southern California fog.
Before we knew it, it was time for the delivery of our first child. The excitement of the coming birth made our pulse beat faster—our firstborn
was on the way into the world. Even though pregnancy was grossly uncomfortable, perhaps a modicum of relief was in sight and appreciated.
That pressure in the body. The balancing act. The trouble sitting, getting up, and moving about. Then the coming of the ancillary pains sig-

naling the beginning of labor. In the back, in the front. The pains swash-buckled, almost doubled her over as the downward pressure began to build, until they began to crank in every fifteen minutes or so and it was time. Time to grab her things and help her to the car, time to outfox (if we could) the breaking of the water and drive like a demon to the Navy contract civilian hospital down the road.

The baby leapt into the world on the eighteenth, and we called her Gayle Marie Petersen, after my good buddy Gale Harlan. We liked Gale and his wife, Paula. We were all very close. So we just made a female version of his name. He seemed pleased with the idea. He and his wife just had their first kid.

Gayle was light skinned, like her mother. The hair was blond, the skin exceedingly pale. When we brought our new citizen home, our neighbors and friends didn't fail to notice that fact. It was quite the interesting phenomenon. Didn't matter. She was my firstborn and I loved her in spite of what people said.

MUTUAL VOICES
Ellie, First Wife

> *It seemed that now the racism aspects of the place [El Toro] really began to show themselves as the children began to come. My first child, my daughter, was born here. [Frank] would ask the people, "How do you like the baby?" They'd say, "Well. That's the cutest, pinkest little baby." Then they'd say, "Man, you can't have no pink baby." Then they'd all come filing into the house to see this little pink baby.*

I don't remember things quite the way Ellie remembers them. For example, I never heard anything like that about how outsiders regarded Gayle. It's possible, I suppose, that I may have forgotten those things. I was color conscious, that's for sure, but Ellie seemed to outclass me in that area from time to time—even about her own light skin color. In fact, I used to tease her about it. There used to be a soft drink jingle called "Mellow Yellow." I used to sing that little "Mellow Yellow" jingle to her, and she'd go off.

At any rate, regardless of what my daughter's skin color was, she was my daughter; I loved her and was glad to have her aboard. Period. She was a source of great joy and wonderment as 1956 settled in.

In December 1956, it was our pleasure to have my younger brother,

Hans ("Hansy"), out to visit. It was great to see him again, and to celebrate his presence as well as the coming of Christmas. We threw a big party at our house. Hans was his usual affable self. I had hoped that the vaunted and new reputation of the military as far as the relative absence of racism was concerned would be borne out, at least in front of my brother, but I was to be disappointed.

White officers came by. Hans was there with the rest of us. The officers' women gave the impression they weren't used to being around blacks (and they probably weren't). But after a few drinks they seemed to want to hug and kiss everybody in sight—and they weren't selective. You could see the novelty thing happening in their visages. It was a different thing for them, being around blacks, and they were sort of bold with their flirtations. Hans came in for his share of attention. What made matters worse was the fact that, although some of these women were married, some of their husbands were away from El Toro on tours of duty elsewhere in the world.

In January 1957, the word aboard the Petersen ship was that Ellie was pregnant again. I hoped that things in America would be lots better for my children now bouncing into the world. There were signs. In April, Congress approved the first civil rights bill for blacks since Reconstruction, ensuring them the right to vote. It was a very emotional time, just to contemplate having the opportunity to finally vote, a thing denied me in many places in America. Not that I allowed myself to be caught up in politics, per se, but I viewed events like this as steps in the right direction, not only for my wife and me, but for my children as well. Even so, I wondered where it was all going to end.

This was especially true for me as National Guardsmen were called out by Governor Faubus of Arkansas, hell-bent to bar nine black students from entering previously all-white Central High School in Little Rock. On 21 September 1957, a federal court removed the National Guardsmen. The children entered the school on the twenty-third, only to be withdrawn as threats of violence seemed to escalate. President Eisenhower sent in federal troops to enforce the court's order on the twenty-fourth.

Dana Charlette Petersen, my second lovely daughter, was born on 30 September 1957. She came in like Gayle Marie did. White skin and blond hair. Folks were always wondering. Our close friends would come in and we'd all sit around and discuss it, almost as if the happenstance of the birth of my children was a kind of social science experiment in living color. I don't know exactly how my dear wife regarded all of this at the time, because I don't think Ellie realized how people tended to relate differently to her because of her skin color versus their reactions when we were together. The same attitudes and reactions were happening with our children's debut into the world. If anything, I grew even more protective of them.

My captaincy had been conferred by now (1 June 1956), which made me the senior black officer on El Toro Marine Corps Air Station. As other black officers were assigned, Ellie did a wonderful job helping to see that they were welcomed on station and into our community. I can remember guys like Bernie Bruce (now a professor at Brown University) running into Edgar House and me lazing over in Laguna at the Sandpiper one weekend afternoon. Bruce remembers that he was surprised to see us—black officers sitting there in uniform—and was amazed that he had run into number one and two black Marine pilots in one place. We black officers all hung out together. Partied together. Hooked up with Los Angeles area connections when required.

Ellie was magnificent during this period of our life. "Something of a magician," Bernie has called her, "just making things happen with all the kids and everything. Quite a lady." And she was. Ellie made sure that every new black officer reporting to El Toro met everybody. She'd either call them or their wives. She would arrange a picnic or a backyard barbecue and all of us would get together, get to know one another. It was an invaluable opportunity for us black officers. It gave us a chance, during our discourse, to check one another's six o'clock.

In spite of the trials and tribulations linked to racism, the major work of being a Marine and doing what the Marine Corps required of us went on apace. In line with my need to try to expand my area of expertise, I applied for attendance at the Navy test pilot school at Patuxent, Maryland. Unfortunately, I wasn't selected. Regardless, I always felt the need to improve myself and my chances for ultimate success. I began picking up more college credits, building on what I'd done back in Kansas. It was Santa Ana College and English 1B (composition and literature), Speech 1A (elements of speech), and a course at Chapman College in elementary Spanish (Spanish I).

Life zipped along. Duty. School. Boss handball player for physical conditioning. In fact, I was to go to the Marine Handball Championships for about three or four years in a row. Became fourth or fifth in the entire Marine Corps. Cross-country flights for proficiency, popping into that open area set aside by the FAA as a military flight area. Just wandered in to see if there was anybody around who wanted to boogie. It was illegal, but we Marines did it all the time. Just jump 'em—see if they can catch you or you can catch them—and then the fight would be on.

Impromptu things like that were frowned upon because we were supposed to brief these flights before they started. But if we wandered across someone, we'd always give him a run. A little old lieutenant named Art Edwards who lived next door to me likes to fat-mouth about the time he popped up and jumped me in a dogfight. Unfortunately, I don't remember that encounter. I do remember, though, that he was the dude who always wanted to use my motor scooter to zip around El Toro. Can't imagine a motor scooter driver giving me a whipping in the air, though. It would be a wonder.

An opportunity to live life on the edge while showing that we humans can help one another regardless of the color of our skin stared me in the face on the evening of 11 October 1958 while I was on duty with the GCA unit. The weather that Saturday afternoon had been foul. Warm, moisture-laden air had blown fitfully over the colder surface of the nearby Pacific, forming thick, advection fog common along the California coast at that time of year. The entire area was socked in as the fog crept across the sinews of the land, muffling sound, cutting down visibility, inundating the air with water vapor. Airports reported zero visibility. Some closed to all air traffic as the fog spiraled and swirled high into the atmosphere. Caught in the frightening, swirling fog at about twelve thousand feet were twenty-eight-year-old Robert Throop and his family, returning from an aerial vacation in Spokane, Washington, in their light plane. Robert's wife, Gloria, clutched their two sons, Greg, three, and Bobby, five, in her arms as she tried to comfort them. Fullerton airport, their destination, was completely socked in.

Throop stayed at twelve thousand feet as a safety precaution, trying to find a hole in the fog bank to complete this second leg of their journey from Reno. He could find no opening. Enough fuel was left for perhaps one-half hour of flying time. He continued to search for a place to break out of the fog, to no avail. The fuel levels were now critical. Nothing remained to do but put out a Mayday distress call. The signal was picked up in the El Toro operations tower, but Throop couldn't be contacted because of radio difficulties.

I was on duty in El Toro GCA. We saw Throop on our scope. Luckily, I was able to raise him on our radio, and although he'd never made a ground-controlled landing before, I could keep him calm enough to stay on that glide slope. I kept talking, watching that scope. Throop kept making the course corrections. I kept watching that blip and its position in relation to the runway—until finally he was almost over it. Flaps down, now. An interminable wait, and then that welcome sound of wheels to runway. They were down and safe. His fuel tanks were almost empty. It was about five o'clock in the evening. The drama had been in progress for about one harrowing hour. Throop beamed when he completed his blind landing and swung down from his airplane.

"Radar," he sighed. "It's the greatest."

The next day, I handed Throop's oldest son up to him as he and his family prepared to depart the base. "It was," as the local newspaper, *The Register,* reported, "a happy ending to what might otherwise have been an aerial tragedy." The newspaper credited El Toro Air Base for "saving four lives," its 12 October headline reading: "Family Praises Base for Plane Guidance." And that was all right by me. They printed my picture with the family, their airplane in the background. That's what being a Marine is all about. Doing your duty as you ought. Kudos, if they come, are icing on the cake. The episode gave me tremendous satisfaction for having done my job well.

In July 1959, we all smiled to know that finally the Marine Corps assigned two black doctors to El Toro. A definite first. Ellie immediately invited Dr. Eric Best and Dr. Don Moore and their wives over for the usual "on-board" backyard barbecue and get-together Even with professional people like Eric and Don, it was sad to see what they initially had to go through. In addition to the unwritten maxim that black doctors would not be allowed to examine white women, it seemed difficult for the authority figures on the base to decide how they would utilize the services of these two doctors.

MUTUAL VOICES
Dr. Eric Best, M.D., Ex-Navy Officer, Phoenix, Arizona

Before Don Moore and I got on base, there were no black physicians. And for two weeks, they didn't know what to do with us. So they decided that the best place for Don and me was in enlisted men's sick bay. So in that way, one, we wouldn't have to contaminate the officers and, two, we wouldn't have to contaminate any of the dependents. [However] the problem they decided they couldn't deal with was that we had to take night calls at times. When you were on night calls, you were on sick call, too. You had to stay on base, and you had to take all comers. So they just didn't deal with it. As far as I was concerned, and Don, too—if you didn't want to see me, that was a plus in my cap—because I didn't have to work as hard. So they would just walk out when I was there. They didn't care who handled the enlisted men.

I liked to take as many ground officers up for a flight as I could, for familiarization purposes, you understand. And it was especially appropriate for Eric Best, because he was a naval officer in the medical division and undoubtedly needed to expand his horizons. So after the required briefings, I took Eric up in a Marine T-33 jet. It was instructive (and fun).

MUTUAL VOICES
Dr. Eric Best, M.D., ex-Navy Officer

I guess one of things [Marine pilots] like to do to people like me is to take 'em up there—and get 'em sick. Since the Marines are carrier trained, unlike the Air Force, they like to take you up to about twenty-five or thirty thousand feet, dive down, touch the ground, then pull back up with heavy g forces. [They like to watch you] and, since you're in the backseat, they keep asking you how you are. And you keep saying you're doing fine (although you really aren't). But when I got out of the plane, I didn't vomit because, you know, if you vomit, you have to vomit in your oxygen mask. So I just made it home—and when I got home, I just let 'er go. I was as sick as a dog. My wife thought it was great fun.

It was a bright spot, especially when the word spread. Eric's wife, Hannah, dropped a dime on him. Told everybody within earshot about how her hubby man threw up over everything and everybody after his first ride in a fighter jet.

But then, like life, a bright spot can suddenly turn cloudy. And it did, around Labor Day. We lost a guy who'd been participating in a flyover over Los Angeles in an A-4 around Labor Day. I was working operations. The crash site was off base. There was no need for a casket. The pilot was vaporized. Tragedy. Odd—nobody could remember the kid's name. We remember that he was black. One of us. We know, because he met us all, albeit cursorily, at parties, or a dance, or was it a barbecue?

But bright spots are for catching when they come calling, like a yellow sunrise edging mountaintops or majestically sinking into blue seas—mental snapshots, never to be forgotten. On 28 October 1959, there came one of these bright spots for Ellie and me—the birth of our only son, Frank Emmanuel Petersen III.

Art Edwards, that erstwhile lieutenant who always had his arse propped astride my motor scooter, thought it was a hoot to see my infant son nibbling on my nose as I held him in my arms. Hey, nothing wrong with that at all. Just teasing the new guy.

Made him think it was a nipple.

11: Hawaii

Marine Corps Air Station, Kaneohe, Oahu, Hawaii, 1960–63

During 1958–59, what would normally be a plum assignment for any good American military type just fell into my lap. My new base, Kaneohe Bay Marine Corps Air Station, was situated on the island of Oahu, Hawaii, a locale known far and wide as "The Gathering Place," touted as representative of the center of Hawaiian life. Two verdant mountain ranges rode the face of the island like monstrous spines, creating a wide valley between them. The Koolau Range ran the length of the northeastern side of the island; the Wainae Range paralleled the southwestern coast. Pineapple and sugarcane plantations lay in the fertile, rolling plains between. The scenery seemed unsurpassed, the climate mild. Waikiki Beach was considered by many to be the playground of the world, where the water temperature flirted with a daily average air temperature of 75 to 77 degrees.

While still at El Toro, during my early reconnoitering to determine what Kaneohe Bay Air Station was all about and what it had to offer, I discovered that there was an F-8U-1 Crusader squadron on station. That was right up my alley—to be flying fighter jets again. Problem was that I wasn't F-8 qualified, so I decided to check myself out on the airplane before I left El Toro. It turned out that this wasn't too difficult to do, because I had a few friends on station. I simply walked into the F-8U-1 Crusader ground familiarization training school and checked in with the instructor.

"Do you mind my sitting in on the course?" I asked.

"No, Captain, no objection at all. Have a seat."

So I sat in and completed phase I familiarization training, so that when I checked into Kaneohe, I'd have a pretty good stumping point to fly the airplane. I really wanted to be in their fighter squadron and would end up being assigned to VMF-232, the proud Red Devils, who had just won the top fighter award for that particular year.

It was deep January 1960 by the time we were packed and our entire family was on its way to Hawaii, having embarked in San Francisco aboard the luxury Matson cruise ship the *Lurline*. A five-day trip, it quickly turned into a series of personal minidisasters. Rough seas. One seasick wife. One not-so-seasick dad. Three children who didn't seem to be upset at all by the exceedingly rough seas and who cheerfully announced one morning that it was time for breakfast. Ellie was too sick to make the trip to the wardroom, so, holding my breath, I took them down. But before I could enter the place, I felt my stomach go queasy, execute a flip-flop, then do the dipsy-doodle. It was back to our cabin in a rush, three irate youngsters in tow. They immediately and loudly complained to their mother, once we arrived in the cabin, that I had every intention of starving them to death.

"Mommy, mommy," they cried, tears streaming, "we want to go to breakfast and Daddy won't let us."

The issue was resolved later in the morning as I regained my sea legs, as shaky as they were.

On the morning of the fifth day, we disembarked in Honolulu harbor and were greeted in the traditional manner of newcomers to Hawaii, each of us properly caressed by leis, then were met by Marine Corps staff from Kaneohe Bay Air Station.

We lived in temporary housing on station for more than a month while I tried to locate appropriate housing. On-base housing existed, but the wait for occupancy was excessively long. The fact that we were in Hawaii, and considering the makeup of that population, I didn't anticipate a problem finding a place for my family and me to live. Hawaii, after all, was generally regarded as one of the melting pots of the world. It was a community of people from many different backgrounds with admixtures of several nationalities and ethnic groups. The "real" Hawaiians were descendents of the Polynesians who first settled there, bronze skinned, possessed of large, dark eyes and flowing black hair. Thirty-five percent of the remaining population was of European ancestry, twenty-five percent of Japanese ancestry. Other groups were sandwiched into the mix—Chinese, Filipino, Korean, Samoan, Southeast Asian. Additionally, there were the whites and blacks from the mainland United States. A problem finding housing? You've got to be kidding, I told myself. We might be some of those folks they called a *malihini* (newcomer), but finding a house over here is going to be easy as pie.

I was as wrong as the proverbial two left shoes.

While I acclimated to my unit and squadron life, Ellie took the lead in poring through the newspaper real estate ads for an available rental. I was assigned to the fighter squadron (VMF-232) and, after necessary orientations, began my familiarization flights in the F-8U-1E Crusader. It was the only Navy/Marine fighter with variable-incident wings, hinged to the fuselage so that the leading edge could be raised for takeoffs and landings for greater lift. For high-speed flight, the wings were dropped back to their normal position. Mach 1 flight was no problem. After about five flights, I was certified.

The squadron was commanded by Lt. Col. Lou Steaman, who was a good airplane driver himself. Standing about five foot six, with the bushiest eyebrows I've ever seen, Lou was a good commander who understood people and was just a prince of a man. He could also be stern if the situation demanded that stance, but he could offset that with a propensity for a damned good party. He did the unit proud, leading it to capture the all-Marine air-to-air shooting competition for that year. Old World War II heads who'd manned VMF-232 would have been proud. Shades of prior glory. Midway and Espiritu. Guadalcanal and Munda. The first fighter sweep over Rabaul in 1943. Samar, and the liberation of the Philippines. It looked as if I'd really made a good choice coming down in F-8U Crusader country in Hawaii.

We'd answered myriad ads for a house to rent. The going was rough, with one turndown after the other. Reasons for the turndowns included the ages of our small children, but we knew that the primary reason was the color of our skin.

On 5 May 1960, Ellie answered an ad for an available house rental by telephone. The owner was more than responsive, even volunteering to place the utilities in our names. Ellie was ebullient when I arrived home from work. On 7 May I drove out to the owner's house, introduced myself, and attempted to close the rental deal. After she looked me up and down, the air seemed strangely charged with an extended, embarrassing silence. I heard a whiny female voice coming, it seemed, from some faraway place.

"I'm sorry," the now-faceless woman said, "but the house has already been rented. Thanks for coming by."

"Thank you very much," I said, almost choking with anger. I spun on my heels, turned away, and left. To do otherwise would have caused an unnecessary conflagration, because, please understand, I was absolutely livid.

For the next several days the experience tumbled end over end in my mind like windblown trash on a ghetto street. Anger assailed and caterwauled as I assessed the happenstance. I'd dedicated my life to my country because I loved her, and now this new anger jerked me around, made me rue the day I'd come into America's military, if this was the way I was to be treated by other Americans. And I was angrier because this had happened to me in Hawaii, where World War II essentially began for my country, certainly a war in which many black Americans had died. Here, in Hawaii, a state populated primarily by brown people.

I saw, I thought, the existence of racism within racism. The native Hawaiians, who didn't seem to get along with the Japanese, who didn't seem to get along with a bunch of other people. And they called this place the melting pot of the United States. Well, for my money, it simply wasn't happening.

After checking around in the squadron, I found out that guys in the squadron who were white were being beaten up big-time some nights in downtown Waikiki by native Hawaiians. I didn't know what these guys were doing, but I was shook.

"Holy shit," I remember saying aloud to myself. "This place is really screwed up."

What to do? I was a Marine Corps officer. Going downtown and knocking some heads together was completely out of the question. I wanted to go as far as I could possibly go in the Marine Corps, so that wouldn't fly.

Once, I thought about the National Association for the Advancement of Colored People (NAACP), wondering whether there was a local branch in Hawaii. It turned out that there was one, just activated. Its newly elected president was a guy named Willie Moore. We caucused, and it was apparent that he was looking for issues that would consolidate blacks on the island. My incident with the housing issue led him to suggest that perhaps one of the first positive things to do was to direct a letter to the editor of one of the Honolulu newspapers. It was the catalyst I needed.

So I sat down and wrote a letter. Actually, I did it just to get the anger off my chest. I mailed it—tongue in cheek, actually—because I had no high hopes that the newspaper would ever print it.

Boy, was I wrong.

In the 20 May 1960 issue of the *Honolulu Advertiser,* there it was, under the headline "Letters From Readers," asking in boldface type the question: "Jim Crow In Kailua?" It told the whole story, exactly the way I wrote it.

As a recent arrival in Hawaii, I have encountered some interesting situations that have caused me to wonder about the expression, "Hawaii, the Melting Pot of the World." The following is one such situation. On the 5th of May, my wife answered an ad in a local newspaper for a two-bedroom house available in the town of Kailua. The owner was very responsive and all arrangements were made by telephone, even to the point of having utilities placed in our name. Inspection of the house and signing of the lease were to be made on the 7th of May. I arrived at the house and introduced myself to the owner. . . . The owner, after a hushed pause, informed me that the house had just been rented. I thanked the owner and left. I am a Negro. . . . Later that same day, I had a friend place a call to the owner in an attempt to rent [the same] house. My friend was not only successful in renting the house, but verbally obtained a two-year lease of same. In the course of the conversation [with my friend] it was stated by the owner that she did not wish to rent to Negroes and that, in fact, a Negro had dared attempt to rent her house that same day. . . . Intolerance in the mind of an individual is very difficult to cope with and is, in fact, that individual's constitutional right. . . . However, when that individual practices intolerance in attempting to deal with the public in the role of landlord or hotel owner, I find that intolerance nauseous. . . . On questioning several friends, I find this situation is not restricted to the Negro alone. . . . Hawaii, the melting pot of the world? Who stirs the pot and when? I think the stew needs mixing.
Frank E. Petersen
Captain, USMC

Much to my continuing surprise, publication of the letter caused a stir on the base. Lou Steaman, my commanding officer, called me into his office.

"Frank," Lou wanted to know, "is there anything I can do to help?"

"I don't know, Colonel. That's the way things are around this part of the world, I guess."

"Well, Frank, why didn't you come to me in the first place?"

"Just used to standing on my own two feet, sir. Just something I usually am able to handle on my own—or should be able to do on my own."

"Well, Frank, if there's anything I can do to help, just let me know. If we can help you find a place, we'll do it."

I believe that Lou was as good as his word. A white officer went with me on my house-hunting missions. The experience rekindled my faith in my fellow Marines. I found that I had lots of good, close friends among the company-grade officers—the pilots.

We all knew what the routine was "out in the world," so to speak. It was at least interesting, if not disgusting—but it was the way things were. If a white went to rent, there'd be one story; if a black went to rent, there'd be another story. Hawaii in the 1960s was quietly discriminatory. And the hell of it was that it wasn't just the whites who were doing the discriminating. Hawaiians didn't really mingle with anyone else. The Japanese had their own community. It all was a definite eye-opener. The web of discrimination may have existed quietly, but it became a cacophony when someone tried to pierce it.

I will always believe that Lou Steaman probably had something to do with my getting base housing shortly after the letter episode. I think that through his influence, we might have been moved up on the base housing list. The fact that there's a housing "list" that one "moves up" on, based upon rank, service, et cetera, on military installations is something that a lot of folks don't realize. The basic reason for the list is to ensure fairness, where possible (although circumstances might alter cases), so housing isn't automatically available when someone arrives at a new station. We were glad to get the military housing, and we stayed in it for an extended period.

During the summer of 1960, I returned to my urge to ultimately complete my college education and enrolled in the University of Hawaii, slugging it out with differential calculus, with my eye on a bout with modern algebra come fall.

I didn't know it at the time, but I was about to meet someone who would become a lifelong friend, and he wasn't a Marine aviator. I didn't realize that we were both meant for brighter, bigger things. This guy had always wanted to be a Marine. He'd seen John Wayne doing his thing in the movie *The Sands of Iwo Jima,* and that had done it. He said he "wanted to wear that big blue uniform with the Marine emblem on it." So he joined up on 4 June 1958. Went up to Quantico, did Basic School and the rest of it, and was commissioned an infantry officer. This guy would also end up a reserve Marine lieutenant general and, ultimately, ambassador to Jamaica in President Clinton's administration. But that's getting ahead of the story.

MUTUAL VOICES
Maj. Gen. Gary L. Cooper, USMC (Retired), Ambassador to Jamaica, Circa 1996

One of the biggest thrills of my life was to become a United States Marine infantry officer. I mean, there were so few black officers who were able to get to be an infantry officer. Usually, guys would end up being assigned as supply officers or motor pool officers and such. And for a while, I was the only black infantry officer in the whole Marine Corps. There weren't ten black ground officers in the whole Corps. So you can understand how absolutely happy I was, after being posted to Hawaii, to find out about Frank Petersen—until my arrival the only black Marine officer on the whole island. And to find out that he was the first black fighter pilot the Marine Corps had ever had was another thrill.

I'd never known a pilot before and here was Frank. We'd go to the officers' club together, and we'd both be asked for our identification cards. And when we'd go to the post exchange, whether we were together or not, we always had the feeling that we were being followed. And we were—but we didn't mind. You see, we'd turn around suddenly when we got that feeling and we'd catch some rather embarrassed black enlisted Marines following us around—amazed at what they were seeing—real, live black Marine officers on deck. They couldn't believe it. They simply couldn't believe it. They had to get close, to see whether or not we were real.

I'd been aboard at Kaneohe Bay Air Station (AS) about six months when Gary Cooper hove into view. We became fast friends. We lived nearby in the base housing area, and our families also became close acquaintances. It was unusual for an aviator to be that close to a ground officer. Kaneohe Bay AS presented an unusual setting however, because, as Gary used to point out, "It was the only place in the Marine Corps where both infantry and air units were routinely stationed in the same areas."

Gary and I did a modicum of sight-seeing together in the local clubs and bars around the island. It was a lot of fun, although I would think our wives took a dim view of our collective "adventures," which the two of us termed totally innocent in nature. Gary had a conscience of sorts, though, which was evident in the slick way he dropped me off at my residence early one morning. "I remember," he chortles today about the incident, "coming home at three in the morning, and not stopping at his house, telling him to jump outta the car 'cause I didn't want his wife to see me." Big joke today. Not so funny back in those days.

But the few black officers who were assigned to Kaneohe found it necessary to stay close and socialize together. It was almost a carbon copy of what had happened at El Toro. It was almost as if we were invisible after duty hours. So we compensated by hosting social functions at our home and the homes of other black officers. The younger pilots, too—we were all in the same boat. I can't say it was all strictly by virtue of race, but I felt excluded. For example, it was protocol that the group commander meet an officer and his lady after their arrival at an installation. I was the only black aviator at Kaneohe and it never happened. I won't call it racism, but let's just say that Ellie and I were never invited to the commanding officer's home for that time-honored practice.

Just when I thought that things might be running along all right, somebody else would go ape with the racism bit, like the squadron leader (a major) who refused to believe I'd done as well as I had during gunnery practice. They brought the banners back in, which showed that I'd gotten some pretty good hits. In fact, the high for the whole squadron. From the squadron leader's point of view, my scores simply had to be a mistake, so he made a complete ass of himself, going down to the armorer's shop, demanding that they pull the records of my guns in order to show what color bullets I was shooting, then double-checking to make sure that the records hadn't been "misplaced." Of course, the scoring was accurate. He made such an ass of himself that even the enlisted armament people were upset. The interesting thing was that the flight crew guys were all white, and they were pissed off at him, too. You can bet your bottom dollar that the commanding officer knew all about his outburst, but nothing happened to this guy about his attitude. The entire issue was treated as "being a little off base," so to speak—and that, too, was interesting to me, to say the least. No matter, I'd torn up that target sleeve. And I was damned proud of my scores.

Retrospectively, I think a lot of these problems had to do with the location of the squadron and the composition of its officer complement. This squadron was isolated by virtue of being in Kaneohe. A lot of the old-timers resented me because, for one, I'd already been through a war. I'd flown combat in Korea. Then there was my performance on the gunnery range. I was never more embarrassed at the untoward reaction. All squadrons are close, and cliques among the old-timers were everywhere in the squadron and they didn't include me.

As disgusting as these kinds of things were, life in the Marine Corps is like life anyplace else. Something bigger than all of the petty stuff comes up and the little things suddenly don't matter as much. At times like these, you find out who your real friends are.

• • •

It was one of those rare Hawaiian days. Smooth air. Gorgeous temperatures. Mild winds aloft. I happened to be flying that day, and little did I know that a midair collision would mar the ambience of the Marine community at Kaneohe Bay. The surprising thing was that every one of my friends thought I'd been involved. My friend Gary Cooper remembered the scenario.

Frank had been up flying the day there'd been a midair collision. Three planes smashed into one another. None of the pilots made it out alive. We just knew Frank was one of them. I was at home when I heard about it. I'd been out in the field, all muddy and dirty. Full of that drinking likker. My wife called and told me about the collision. All the pilots were missing, she said. I called Ellie, and Ellie didn't know what was happening. We went over to Frank's house, where all the wives were. It was a somber time, but in my mind, there was no doubt that this sumbitch would be coming home—and he was the one who made it. I was right. He made it, I'm happy to say.

Helluva way to have your friendships validated. I was flying that day, but I was up with another squadron. However, I was glad to know that people cared and, more than that, had I been one of the unfortunate ones that day, it would've mattered.

I managed to spend about a year and a half in VMF-232, still cracking the books at the University of Hawaii. I took applied calculus in spring 1961, theory of equations in fall. About that time, Col. George Dooley came up to take command of the Marine air group. Dooley got our attention. His badly scarred face—the result of a nearly fatal searing in an aircraft accident—made its own statement of service and dedication to America.

I was transferred from the squadron to the headquarters of the air group to be the group adjutant. This was a weird thing, as far as I could see, because that job was normally assigned to a man who had done some work in the administrative field. At that time in my career, I'd had no administrative background. I protested against going into that job, preferring anything else, actually. For the period of time I was there, I definitely considered it a low point in my career.

Added to the embarrassment of not knowing a goddamned thing

about being an administrator, there was the uncomfortable situation of being caught in an obvious cross fire between the executive officer (who was really trying to make full colonel) and Colonel Dooley, who was a strong commanding officer. It was a bad situation to be in. After an appropriate amount of cajoling and tight-lipped politicking, I finally managed to get transferred to Marine Air Control Squadron 2, a radar control unit at Kaneohe. At least this was an area I knew something about.

There, I ran into another sensitive situation. In fact, this was one of the few times that I openly stated that prejudice was a factor in my commanding officer's assessment of my work as a Marine. After spending about six months with the unit, I received the lowest fitness report I have ever picked up as an officer. My commanding officer had himself a field day at my expense. This time, I was determined to fight back, and I sat down to write a long rebuttal to the report, only to be talked out of submitting it along with my fitness report by the executive officer, a Marine major, who seemed determined in his mission.

"Frank," he said, "this isn't really the way things should be done."

"Yes, I know, but I just can't let this thing go unchallenged."

"Look, Frank—for the good of your future career, it would be better if you didn't make this statement."

For a long moment, I just looked at the major and saw either a real or feigned earnestness in his face. It was obvious that he was in something of a bind. His approach was more of an attempt at negotiation rather than an order. If I had been a betting man, I would've bet a million dollars that the commanding officer involved had put him up to talking me out of submitting my rebuttal detailing the underhanded way in which he was trying to deal with me. It was a blatant attempt to avoid the pressures that were sure to come on him had my counteraccusations about him gone forward to the bird colonel (full colonel) group commander. In the final analysis, I acquiesced and didn't submit the rebuttal, which was filled with rhetoric that wouldn't have done the CO's career (and probably mine, either) any good at all. (Later in my career, when I was in a position to do so, I looked up the records of another black officer assigned to the unit at the same time I was. His name was Clarence Davis, and I found that, upon his departure from the unit, this commanding officer had also given him a similar fitness report.) I am certain that my rebuttal was an accurate assessment of the commanding officer's attitudes and mores concerning blacks at that time.

Although these experiences were downers, there were good things going on that operated to bring a little sunshine into my life. Shortly after we arrived in Hawaii, Ellie discovered that she was pregnant with what would be our last child. On 27 November 1961, as close to Thanksgiving Day as she could muster, another daughter, Lindsey Cecil Petersen, came into the world, letting considerable joy and light into our lives. Our infantry officer friend Gary Cooper joyously accepted the role of being her godfather. He was a great choice.

Beyond that, it seemed that the universal powers of cause and effect reached out for the commanding officer who'd been giving me the business. Shortly after the effectiveness report outrage, some Hawaiian kids broke into his off-base house, rifled it, and stole a government weapon, a .38 revolver. The civilian authorities also became involved, and he was experiencing deep troubles, not the least of which was having to explain why a government weapon was residing in his home and not on base where it belonged. Considering all that this gentleman had put me through, I must say that news was satisfactory, and I was pleased to hear about his travails, and may God forgive my almost untrammeled euphoria.

After about a year and a half of on-base living, we decided it was time to find a house of our own. It would not only give us the space we needed for a growing family but a degree of privacy we could not have while living in government quarters on station. I knew that we had to have our antennae up while we conducted our property search, because, as we already knew, Hawaii could be a weird place. We had to be careful, especially on Oahu, because there were all those little turf and ethnic differences. We had to be extremely astute.

Even so, it was not as if we were able to simply go out and rent ourselves a house. This time we didn't fiddle around alone; we arranged to have some of our white Marine friends go out and find a suitable rental for us. In fact, some of our Marine friends did find us a house and see that we were accepted. Actually, we wanted it for only a short period, because we'd also discovered a new housing development going in. We qualified for a new home and lived in our rental until the building of the new house was completed. Before we left Hawaii, we were to own two houses on that multiracial island in the sun.

I kept myself busy upgrading my education because I was convinced that it was the way to ultimate success in the Corps. In the summer and fall of 1962, I took physics with laboratory at the University of Hawaii.

While all this transpired, my children were growing like blazes. My son, Frank III, was a little over two years old and a source of constant amazement.

MUTUAL VOICES
Frank Emmanuel Petersen III, Son

Hawaii was just like a paradise. I mostly remember having to ramble through what seemed like woods to me, just like a forest. Going to the library, getting books and first learning how to read, things like that. Hanging out with my sisters a lot. Seeing the Old Man and some of the weather. Raining on one side of the house, and sunny on the other. And the Old Man put in a patio. I remember when I went in there and started swimming in the concrete he'd just laid on his new patio. He just loves to tell that story. Well, he had to start over and do it again, I guess. He seems to think that the kids who get into the most trouble are his kinds of kid. Kids who don't do anything, he thinks something's wrong with them.

I did laugh like hell when I saw him in that concrete. I wanted to go right in there and pick him out of it, but I knew it wouldn't start to burn him right away, so I just put the hose on him and laughed about it. His mother had a fit. But he was a boy, and I figured that boys simply will be boys. He's right. He was my kind of kid. I liked an aggressive display, a kid who didn't sit in a corner and suck his thumb. I liked youngsters who asked you questions, inquired, touched, felt, explored, and discovered. You know, kids who exhibit an almost wanton curiosity. Yes. I liked that in a kid. He now knew that wet concrete wasn't a medium in which to swim. He was very active and curious, as were all of the children. All tested as gifted. Sometimes, however, I'd make the girls mad, I guess, because when I was around, I always took him along whenever I went somewhere. I always put him in the car with me, to get that male influence—that male bonding thing going.

And, of course, there was the irrepressible daughter Dana Charlette, who, around age five, decided to parachute (like her dad) off the top of a picnic table. She received a slight concussion for her trouble.

Early in 1963, I knew that my time for another overseas tour was getting close. My mentor at Marine Corps headquarters verified that an assignment such as that was due, based on my overall officer development profile. I would definitely be going overseas from Kaneohe. I wanted to line up with a job that I thought would be pretty challenging and exciting, so I volunteered to go to the safety officers' school at the University of Southern California in Los Angeles. Unfortunately, it meant leaving the family alone in Hawaii for a short period, but it turned out to be one of the most enjoyable three months or so that I spent in the

Corps. It was an aviation military academic environment, with top-notch instructors who were some of the best men in the field. Of course, the campus itself was pretty sparkly, and it was just one hell of a good technical and professional school. Some of my fellow students, like Alan Bean, soon to be an astronaut and walk on the moon, helped add more dimension to the overall experience.

After graduation from the course in May 1963, orders came down for a short overseas tour in Japan. My posting was to Fleet Marine Force Pacific, Western Pacific, 1st Marine Aircraft Wing, MCAS Iwakuni, about thirty miles south of Hiroshima on the island of Honshu, the main island of Japan. Because the tour was to be only a year, Ellie and I discussed the wisdom of the family remaining in Hawaii while I did the unaccompanied tour in Japan. After looking at the issue from all sides, we decided it would be better for them to return to the United States. So with a thirty-day leave in my pocket, we departed Hawaii and moved the family home to Topeka, where they settled in with relatives.

Come June, I transitioned to Iwakuni and reported about the time the black civil rights leader Medgar Evers was shot in the back by a sniper's bullet as he left his automobile to enter his home. Blacks were marching in Jackson, Mississippi, and other cities in the United States. There was cause to wonder about the future of things in my country. But I was a Marine and duty called.

The duty was a total staff assignment. A brand-new major (as of 1 August 1963), I longed for the pulsating glory of being a member of a real, live fighter squadron. I was tagged to learn other things. Assistant airfield operations officer. Ground-controlled approach operations. Helping run the airfield. I did get to fly, however, to maintain my flight proficiency. I traveled around Japan when I had the time.

From time to time, I mulled over the brilliant "I Have A Dream" speech by Martin Luther King, Jr., delivered at the Washington, D.C., demonstration attended by more than 200,000 people. That speech pulsated around the world. Unfortunately, I couldn't see it on television or hear it on radio where I was, but I was privileged to read about it in *Stars and Stripes*. I was impressed and thought I could see an eventual solving of the racial problems in my country.

However, the civil rights revolution was heating up back home, and the shock waves were being felt all over the military as well. Senior officers were being called in by their commanders throughout the Marine Corps and asked to mediate, to be part of community programs where communications between the races seemed to be breaking down. The need was to try to calm down communities and the military community at the same time. Marine Air Station Iwakuni was no exception. Racial problems were beginning to bubble over. My station commander called me in.

"Frank, I need your advice. What can we do to settle some of these racial problems that are cropping up around here, f'God's sake?"

And then President John F. Kennedy was shot on 22 November. Very, very tragic. I felt a sense of doom when he was killed. I was very down. Here was a guy I thought was really the one who was going to get this crap squared away. And he was killed .

"So now, Major Petersen, what do we do about these racial problems?"

12: Race Doctor

I began to look around at what was going on racially at Marine Corps Air Station Iwakuni. I talked to many people, both officer and enlisted. I looked in on things around the station and off base, downtown where Marines hung out—black Marines in particular. Some of the problems centered around what was going on in downtown Iwakuni—basic, all-too-familiar stuff.

In downtown Iwakuni, blacks were confined to about two bars whereas the white troops enjoyed all the rest. This restriction was not due to Japanese national laws. The bar owners simply catered to white trooper clientele by ensuring that their racial preferences were observed.

I made it a point to take various white officers downtown and show them the miserable bars the blacks were going to on liberty and explained why they were going there. I will never forget a conversation with one station commander.

"Frank," he said, "what can I do to solve the problem?"

"Quite simply," I replied, looking him straight in the eye, "get the Japanese whores to sleep with the blacks."

"Well," he huffed, "I can't do that."

"Well then, you can't solve the problem," I grated.

Strangely, though, although it took several years after the above conversation, my recommendation is exactly where that part of the problem found its solution and is being done until this very day without any authoritarian "nudging." People are just doing what comes naturally between human beings.

The other part of the problem resided on the base, where almost daily fistfights erupted. I eventually labeled the causes of these altercations the "big threes"—promotions, job assignments, and the severity of punishments levied by commanding officers. These were the areas where racism was most likely to rear its ugly head for blacks then and, to some extent, still does today.

The problem with my role as "race counselor" was, of course, that I wasn't called in on a weekly or daily basis—only when the cauldron seemed about to boil over. But there was little I could do at that point, if for no other reason than the fact that I was a "fresh-caught major" whose voice didn't carry much weight.

The other side of the picture involved the blacks themselves, who would come to me for advice and counsel on what to do and how to maneuver. Time and again, I would talk with the young black troopers out on liberty. I'd stop by the "black bars" and would always be engaged in conversation, or I'd even be stopped on the base. I tried to make sure they understood that I couldn't fix things for them, but if they were to initiate complaints on their own, then as a group they could bring the complaints to the attention of the commanding officer. This, in my view, was how to deal. Work with the system and do something on your own other than simply bitch.

I could see and feel a rise in racial confrontation coming. This was when the Vietnam War was beginning to open up and race relations had gone through a traumatic change. Whereas in the early 1950s there might have been one or two blacks with a one-on-one type of problem, now blacks in general were voicing the same complaints about their commanding officers and what they felt was needed to solve the problems. They were becoming astute in terms of analyzing the problems they faced and were recognizing that the patterns of the problems were such that all of them were involved.

Within that, there was a great split between the black staff noncommissioned officer and the black junior troopers. Most people did not think about it in this light, but the black junior trooper and the black staff noncommissioned officers were having the same problems, except that the latter were fighting the battle their way. "Their way" too often meant disassociating themselves from the young black enlisted trooper. The older staff NCOs felt they had paid their dues. They'd been there from the beginning of the Marine Corps assimilation of blacks within its ranks. They'd survived, had accomplished something, and opened the doors. In their view, "the kids" didn't want the same things. It was done already. The kids were whistling Dixie.

For example, the late Sergeant Majors Huff and Johnson, in their final oral histories, indicated their belief that by this time in Marine history (fifteen years after Truman outlawed segregation in the military), anybody could do anything in the Marine Corps. More than that, all they needed was the opportunity, and now the opportunity was there. It simply came down to who had the leadership ability and drive. What's more, guys like Huff and Johnson had proven it, they thought. They'd gone through the fire and the brimstone, that place in Marine Corps history where racial prejudice was really vile, and they had whipped it by maintaining a stiff upper lip.

The late Sergeant Major Huff, remembering "those days," told how he got through them: "I bit my tongue so often it hurt me to the bottom of my stomach." Huff, Johnson, and other black senior staff noncommissioned officers simply didn't think that what the new junior black Marines were facing was "really prejudice," at least not representative of what they'd endured.

But the young black trooper still suffered from the old-line attitudes of established white authoritarian Southern officers and noncommissioned officers. Many Marine commanding officers of this era were veterans of some twenty-five to thirty years of service and had come from strictly segregated environments. Many of them had to learn a lot in two or three years about what race relations were really all about.

Unfortunately, many hadn't learned (or refused to accept the new racial amenities). Because of the new emphasis on equality in the ranks, many confirmed bigots were forced underground to operate in a more clever fashion.

Feeling the effects of prejudice was a lot like being blindsided. Often, it was difficult to tell just where the racism was coming from. The need was for eternal vigilance, a quality the young black Marines didn't seem to have in great supply because they didn't think it was needed in this "new" society. Those from the northern or western United States especially had grown up after the time to which their senior majority commanders and senior noncommissioned officers now stubbornly clung.

What the young black troopers, these "kids," wanted, in addition to being Marines, was an opportunity to be themselves and not be penalized because their white counterparts either didn't or couldn't try to accept the ways in which they were different culturally. There were those who either didn't give them credit where credit was due or, when they had transgressed, didn't afford them the same levels of punishment as their white counterparts. They came down on them excessively hard solely because their skin was black. To adequately address these issues would have taken a special kind of social engineering that was not immediately available at the time within the Marine Corps.

I was convinced that addressing these issues would have involved looking at the makeup of the young black troopers in two areas that significantly impacted their military actions, both preservice and initial service. Upon entering military service, the majority of black recruits lived in the urban ghetto. To be urban, black, and successful in transition to adulthood in an environment scarred by economic and social hardship required early and continued avoidance of confrontation with the police and a demonstrated ability to integrate into society.

That said, even the youth who "escaped" and entered the military from the ghetto were generally possessed of apprehension and mistrust of whites and an education that was probably below the national norm in quality. In addition, these youth were willing to use violence as a solution to real or imagined personal grievances.

Prevailing postures in the Marine Corps and other military services did not cause these attitudes to disappear. The young black troopers were somehow perceived to be different from their white counterparts. They were perceived to be militant, but that militance was not geared initially toward acts of violence for the sake of violence. Rather it was their way of demonstrating a desire to take positive, productive steps toward self-improvement. In short, this was a new kind of black Marine, a volunteer, who would not put up with what older blacks had gone though. All of that was couched in the burgeoning civil rights revolution and its new mantras. Martin Luther King, Jr., and his "I Have A Dream" theme. Black pride. Black awareness. The "I am somebody" chant invading the consciousness of young blacks all over America.

The posture of the blacks of yesteryear's Marine Corps, relying on the theories of the old school—kick ass, take names, hard work, perseverence, and the ability to take the "low" road to solve problems of discrimination—simply did not work for these young troopers. The black Marines of this era would, in fact, quickly resort to violence as an expression of their total rejection of any and all facets of discrimination. Hence the perceived increase in racial problems all around the Marine Corps and in all the other services.

Fueling these black troopers' attitudes were factors they faced almost immediately upon entry into the service. This was the beginning of the Afro hairstyle among blacks all over the United States. New black Marines immediately found themselves embroiled in an area where the Marine establishment saw them as miscreants flaunting its regulations, mandating that hair should be three inches long, neatly trimmed. To give a black Marine nurturing his new "Fro" three inches of hair growing room was to give him all kinds of space for "Afro" growth. A simple fact never dawned on them. When Anglo straight hair was three inches long, it lay down flat athwart the scalp. Unless a black Marine's hair is either naturally straight or has been chemically processed, if it's three inches long it's going to stand straight up—exactly what the new "Afro" hairstyle required.

Trouble for the black troopers had only just begun. Usually they'd be serving under a white commanding officer and had little or no contact with black officers. If they committed an act that made them subject to the Uniform Code of Military Justice, their legal advice would be provided by whites, because few black lawyers served in the Corps in that time. This lack of black leadership and guidance led to a sense of detachment and isolation from the mainstream Marine Corps.

Consequently, at the slightest provocation, questions were raised by the young blacks to ensure, as they put it, that "a game is not being run on the brothers." They needed the reinforcement of associating with their own in order to restore self-confidence and a feeling of security. Brotherhood unofficially replaced esprit de corps. The issue was confused by competing philosophies: aggressive black militancy points of view thrust against those of subtle and not so subtle white racism. The new black Marine would remain a black Marine. He rarely ascribed to the view that "all Marines are green." There were, in his view, white Marines and black Marines and yellow Marines and brown Marines and tan Marines—and each had his own identity, lifestyle, and mores that none had the desire to lose.

There was, for example, an American Indian officer named Chief Flynn, who'd been a combat pilot during World War II. Chief Flynn was known in Marine circles for his extraordinary stamina and strength. He went into downtown Iwakuni one evening to a popular bar frequented by officers. T. Harry's was run by a Japanese national. Chief Flynn sat down and ordered a drink. Around Marines, Flynn was an okay guy, well known and famous.

Presently, a group of Navy pilots came into T. Harry's and brought their own brand of racial prejudice with them. One of them decided that Chief Flynn should not be allowed in the bar.

"Hey, you."

"Who, me?"

"Yeah, you."

"What's the problem, sailor?"

"You gotta go."

"What?"

"I said, you gotta go. Now."

"Are you crazy, man? I've got a drink here."

"Don't matter. You gotta go. Now."

"Yeah? Who's gonna throw me out? You?"

"Yeah, if I hafta. This here's a white only bar. People like you don't belong in this here bar. Y'unnerstand? Leave, or I'm kicking yo' butt."

The Navy guy was known for his brawling and being a troublemaker.

"You gon' kick my butt?" Chief Flynn inquired.

"Yeah. Let's go, citizen."

Well, they say that Chief Flynn got up and the two of them moseyed out to the front of T. Harry's. There was a bunch of scritching, scratching, stuff falling over, and heavy blows landing. The fight lasted for thirty minutes, and when it was over, both of Chief Flynn's arms were broken. The medics came, got the Navy guy, threw him into the meat wagon, and took him to the hospital, where he stayed for a good long time. The doctor who saw him on board the base wanted to press charges against the chief.

"My God," the doctor is reputed to have said about the Navy guy. "I've never seen a man so brutally beaten in my life."

I saw Chief Flynn about a day or so later in the officers' dining room. He had both arms bandaged and in splints, and he was holding them gingerly across his chest.

"Chief," I exclaimed, "what in the hell happened?"

"Just an awareness test," Chief replied, "just an awareness test."

Nothing ever happened to the chief for his thorough thrashing of the naval officer. I guess his commanding officer thought that justice had been appropriately meted out on both sides.

On the one hand, there are young black troopers imbued with varying degrees of racial hatred and paranoia who have elected the Marine Corps as a way of life. There are young white troopers with similar characteristics also drawn to the Corps. Once inside the Corps, both groups seek guidance from ethnic leaders selected from their respective groups. If these selected leaders are black bigots or white bigots who are serving in positions of military authority, reinforcement is provided for the continuance of racial animosity.

Solutions to military racial problems have ranged from the far left to the far right: to return to a totally segregated force or to compose a force divided along racial lines, separate but equal. Historically, it has been shown that such extremes are not applicable to any military force required to perform effectively and optimally as a unit The clouds of war then building over the Vietnam issue would prove that thesis without a doubt, even though racial animosities reached new heights during that conflict.

I tried in many instances to explain to both officers and troopers alike that the problem of solving racism within the Corps was not just a black problem but a problem in which all races are involved. It is, in fact, a sociological, circular phenomenon. To "study" blacks in an attempt to isolate those factors supposedly peculiar to the black psyche, thus explaining what is largely defined as irrational behavior on the part of blacks, only comes back to ground zero. Theorist Dr. Price Cobb, writing on the matter in *Black Rage,* suggests that the very behavior seen as irrational in blacks was developed in the white world and is therefore not so much irrational as it is a defense mechanism adopted by blacks for the purposes of sheer survival when set upon because of it.

Young white Marines were often quick to complain that black Marines received more favorable treatment and caused incidents by banding together and practicing racial hatred toward whites. The problem, of course, was that the black troopers' newly found racial pride was interpreted by their white counterparts as black racism. Conversely, however, future studies would show that one of the prime and fundamental causes of racism in the military was white racism. In short, one kind of racism begot its counterpart. The universal law of cause and effect stalked the land big-time, or, put another way, what came around went around. Sometimes, a white military type in a position of authority could, by a wanton act of racism, almost write his own ticket into the afterlife but for the grace of God. (It could work the other way around, too.) I am reminded of such an account in a book by a couple of black Army GIs entitled *Brothers: Black Soldiers in the Nam* [Presidio Press, 1982, p. 6]; it is a prime example of a life being saved by an act of God.

Drill Sergeant Meckler came along and kicked me hard right in the side. He was a racist bastard and I really felt like shooting him down. All I had to do was just turn right around. That was what my mind started telling me. And then I started realizing that I wasn't playing anymore. This was a serious thing . . . I was into. This was reality. A man comes up who had the authority to just kick me in the God damn ribs because he was who he was. All I had to do was just roll over, and pull that trigger, and just blow that motherfucker apart. I never felt that way toward anybody before. . . . But I just pretended like he was out there at that target, and I blew him away that way, because I knew if I didn't do it that way, all was lost with my life.

An act of God, activating common sense. Fallout from a senseless, racist act that could've had disastrous results because nobody was minding the store. Perhaps the most pernicious type of racism is the kind of racism practiced by a person from one group, itself regarded a minority, against a person of another. At T. Harry's in Iwakuni, the Japanese bar owner himself, having assimilated the racist baggage of his American racist friends, served a young black Marine officer a glass of black shoe polish as the drink he "thought" he ordered. Whereupon the young Marine officer, to his credit, immediately stood up and broke T. Harry's jaw. The young officer's commanding officer must have thought it was a job well done. Nothing in the way of discipline was ever done in retaliation or punishment.

Near the end of my Iwakuni tour, I had an opportunity to observe one of the worst kinds of white racism in operation. This time, the racism was directed toward the Japanese people.

On liberty one weekend in Hiroshima, about thirty miles north of Iwakuni, I visited the now-famous shrine the Japanese built and dedicated to the dead lost on 6 August 1945, when the United States dropped a single atomic bomb over the center of the city. More than 4.7 square miles of the city was destroyed. An estimated 70,000 persons were either killed or were missing. Another 70,000 were injured by the blast, and an undetermined number later died of the effects of the explosion. The memorial shrine and the Atomic Age Museum and Exposition Center (with a destroyed building preserved as a reminder of the horror of atomic warfare) are visited by thousands each year. It was a Peace Park, and one cannot help but be moved emotionally.

In civilian attire, I visited the Atomic Dome, originally the Industrial Exhibition Hall, designed to display prefectural wares. I stood in Peace Park in front of this place, in deep introspection, thinking of man's inhumanity to man, the awesome damage, the tremendous force of today's weaponry, when my senses recorded a thing that brought revulsion from deep inside. Here came several of my fellow American servicemen, none of whom I knew, all white, drunk, putting on a display of arrogance and power. They paraded and strutted like peacocks around that sacred place. Like apes, they beat their chests and swayed there in an alcoholic stupor before the mourning Japanese people.

"Lookit us," they slurred. "We're the conquerooo."

"Just lookit what we done," another said, gesturing widely.

"Yeah, just lookit what we can do. Don't mess with us."

Uproarious laughter. American military on liberty in the Peace Park. Loud. Profane. Quite out of context with the Japanese customs of gentility and politeness. Not one shred of humility on the part of these American servicemen, or even a modicum of awareness of what it was they were seeing or what it represented. All they saw was conquest. All they knew was that they were white and American. "Look what we did to you—you yellow bastards." These Americans had done nothing. Their forefathers had done it, and not without many subsequent visitations to the sackcloth and ashes to ask God's forgiveness. For even though what they did saved millions of American lives, the act itself was a horrendous thing.

I remember thinking that, as a Marine officer of relatively high rank, I should've intervened. Stopped this sideshow. Counseled and lectured these people. Perhaps later in my career I might have. But then I thought the better of it. First, I was alone. Second, I was African American, which in those days would have made for instant conflagration. By the time I'd gotten through with them or they had gotten through with me, it would have escalated the situation much more than warranted.

I never forgot the actual atomic explosion, however. It is locked inside my brain. You can never know the horror of an atom bomb exploding until you actually see one going off. From time to time I still see in my mind that famous picture of Hiroshima in *Life* magazine showing the bridge across the Ota River. Etched in its surviving stone was the shadow of a man who had been walking there the morning of the blinding flash, the searing heat, and the swirling, poisonous mushroom cloud rising, lashing out at the city, a man-made tornado. The equivalent of thirteen thousand tons of TNT was *pikadon*, the flash-boom, as the Japanese called it [Lifton, p. 24]. I remember the country western song that Americans sang about Hiroshima and Nagasaki. To be at the hypocenter of the explosion in Hiroshima must have been a visitation in hell itself.

Racism. In its rawest, nastiest form, the descriptive terminology would apply regardless of the race of the perpetrators. These, of course, happened to be white Americans. That's the saddest thing. And those Navy enlisted men were not alone in their arrogance. Wilfred Burchett, in his *Shadows of Hiroshima* [p. 107–8], remembers how the same attitudes pervaded certain of the power players in the American military. "The power of the bomb," he wrote, "gave birth to an unprecedented arrogance among both the military and the civilian policy-makers. The American military plane on which I flew to England after the war . . . [produced the views that were] . . . replicas of Truman's. 'It's the American century!' they bragged, 'we've got the power and we'll goddamn well use it!'" If American officers felt that way, then of course the enlisted men couldn't possibly be that far behind. For shame.

Orders came down in May 1964 transferring me to the Marine base at Quantico in Virginia with thirty days' intervening leave. As I came home and readied the family for a move to my new station, the air in America seemed charged. The civil rights revolution pot boiled. The government reacted by passing an omnibus civil rights bill on 29 June banning discrimination in voting, jobs, public accommodations, and other areas. Although noteworthy and long overdue, it seemed pale somehow when held up to the grisly discoveries on 4 August of the bodies of three civil rights workers buried in a Mississippi dam. I felt a certain foreboding about race relations, as all African Americans probably did then. But I had my military career to think about, and my entire concentration went into how to make that a success and go as far as I dared.

After leave time in Topeka, the family packed and bundled our belongings for the trip to Quantico and the nearby Marine training installation. Marine Corps Combat Development Command lay thirty-five to forty miles south of Washington, D.C., on more than 56,000 acres of land. The base itself borders the small town of Quantico on three sides; the Potomac River forms its remaining border. Dominating the base is the Amphibious Warfare School, which was the immediate focus of my new assignment. Quarters were immediately available when we arrived on station. My family and I moved right in, and Ellie went about doing her usual yeoman's work of reestablishing a comfortable base and home for our family.

13: Quantico I: Prepping for Command

I can remember Quantico. It was the last place [in the Marine Corps] that wanted to give up segregation. I had a hard time in school. I remember teachers not calling on me. They'd ask a question and nobody'd know the answer. I'd put up my hand, but they'd look right through me and never call on me. I didn't understand. I wasn't allowed to play with any of the other kids. Everything was subliminal. I tried to figure it out. What's wrong with me? I was about eight or nine years old. I didn't tell my dad. I didn't talk about that stuff until I was in my thirties.
—Gayle Marie Petersen, 14 July 1993

They called it the "Junior School," and on 24 August 1964, I was up to my neck in it. Every company-grade Marine officer worth his salt had to become steeped in the philosophies of the Marine Corps Amphibious Warfare School. A time for in-depth study of the complexities of operating and directing amphibious landings, beginning with techniques to form an amphibious group and how to place the units aboard ship so they can land in the correct sequences. Ground troops, support arms, logistics streams. Projecting all that power ashore and, once ashore, learning how to plan and establish ground maneuver requirements and operations.

As an aviator, I was a smidgin put out that more emphasis wasn't placed on aviation. There was some data about it, but an operation like an amphibious landing was a ground Marine officer's playpen. At first, I thought the instructional approach a bit unfair, but my fears were unfounded. The course was divided, with ground officers getting more about aviation support and we aviators getting more about ground operations. The object, of course, was to be certain that all students, regardless of their orientation, received well-rounded instruction about amphibious landings. The school was also geared to take the junior-level officers and give them upgrades on strategy, tactics, and Marine Corps politics, thus preparing them for field-grade rank.

It was time, I thought, to make my final drive toward complete educational requirements, which ought to enable me, all things being equal, to go as far up the Marine hierarchical ladder as I possibly could. Accordingly, in December 1964, I requested assignment to the Marine Corps College Degree Program, as prescribed by regulation. After determining the number of college semester hours I'd already completed, then projecting the number of units I needed to qualify for my baccalaureate degree, I submitted my request for attendance at nearby George Washington University in Washington, D.C. Forty-four semester hours of undergraduate work remained, with a major in social services from the College of General Studies. (I had considered a degree in mathematics, but after I experienced the complexities of the upper levels of the discipline, I sought easier turf.) The university verified my credits and projected program with studies to begin in spring 1965. On 29 April 1965, approval was granted by the commandant of the Marine Corps with a period of attendance designated as 20 July 1966 through 20 January 1967. (The general military identifier for this type of program for service members to complete their education was called Operation Bootstrap.)

Amphibious Warfare School (AWS) exuded a strong academic environment. It was a challenge but at the same time a kind of vacation, too, because I didn't find the course content that difficult. I used most of my spare evenings pumping myself up for Operation Bootstrap. Before AWS began, I looked around for other challenges and discovered that a course in nuclear, biological, and chemical weapons employment was being offered starting 7 June 1964. I jumped aboard. Actually, I was just marking time until I would start amphibious warfare training and, ultimately, Operation Bootstrap.

In those days, I don't know if I could call Quantico "Marine Corps." It was more a kind of educational campus—just books, books, books, and more books. Because officers were coming there from all over the Corps, most were away from the close affiliations at their home stations. The mix of missions also served to highlight an estrangement among students. I did make some good friends with the ground officers while I was there, but usually my friendships with the ground side of the Corps were based more on curiosity at my being an aviator than anything else.

Even though I was only marking time at Quantico, the place was not without the usual challenges based upon the color of the skin of my family and myself. Retrospectively, Quantico, perhaps because of its geographical location, always had the same amount of racial tension (albeit suppressed) found at Lejeune, a Marine Corps base on the East Coast, or Pendleton, on the West Coast. Shootouts had recently occurred at one of those bases wherein a policeman had been killed. So we had to mind what we said and did, for the need was to be constantly on the lookout.

The town of Quantico, for example, was bad news for blacks. I met prejudice in bars, restaurants, and places of business in the downtown. It seemed to be a kind of prejudice based upon rank. If I went downtown in uniform, and it was evident that I was a major, there would be little or no prejudicial attitude. But if I went downtown in civilian clothes, I would be treated as I imagine a Joe Blow private first class whose skin was black would be treated, and I would run head-on into the racism, in the cleaning establishments, restaurants, bars—the whole bit. My family began to run into problems as well—Ellie at the hairdresser, for example, and my children in their school activities.

MUTUAL VOICES
Frank Emmanuel Petersen III, Son

Quantico was nice. I remember wanting to go to school real bad, but I wasn't quite old enough to attend regular school. The other kids used to get on the bus every day and I had to stay home. I was very upset, because at the end of the summer, the other kids would be going to school and I wasn't able to. Preschool would've been fine, except that, according to my mother, none of the schools wanted to have me. When one of the schools finally let me in, the other parents took their kids out. Yeah. Now, I think this was a racially oriented thing. Of course, then I didn't realize that. The lady who let me in that school is still down there in Quantico [in 1993]. I meant to go down there and thank her. I never did, though. She's still there, running her little old school. She's been there for years. She was white, and she taught us French and it was fun. She taught us how to tie our shoes. Yeah, it was interesting.

Racial problems aside, however, there was one good aspect linked to being at Quantico. It was the first time I'd had a chance to be stationed with a number of other black officers. There were about six of us there at the time. There was Hurdle Maxwell, who now lives in San Diego. There was a Capt. "Chappie" Hill, who continued to be stationed at Quantico for a time, and two or three lieutenants who were going through the Basic School. So we had a chance to commiserate, to compare notes and see who was doing what to whom. We found that the young lieutenants who were coming in were having a pretty bad bunch of hassles out at the Basic School (basic ground officers' training for in-fantry fighting at the platoon level). The fact that the rest of us had been in the Corps for a goodly number of years didn't exempt us from racism's barbs. I think Hurdle Maxwell had to punch out a couple of guys at the officers' club on two or three occasions.

Halfway through the Amphibious Warfare School, I received word through the Red Cross that my father was hospitalized and his condi-tion was critical. He was stricken with leukemia in his fifty-fifth year. The adrenaline surged inside me, because he and I were extremely close. I called my mom and she verified that he was indeed in the hospital. My brother Billy also called. The Corps granted me an emergency leave. I wanted to go home immediately, but I decided to take enough time to get clean uniforms and be sure the family was squared away. Conse-quently, I didn't get a flight out of Washington until the following day.

As I sat in the Dulles airport waiting for the announcement of my flight to Topeka, United Airlines paged me. I felt my heart sink as they ushered me into a private room and laid the news on me. Another mes-sage from the Red Cross. Dad was dead. It was so swift, happening less than forty-eight hours from the first notification.

Brother Billy picked me up at the airport. We looked at each other for long moments after we met.

"Dad's gone, isn't he?" I managed.

"Yeah, Buddy, he's gone."

"What the hell happened?"

Billy related how he'd taken Dad for his usual physical checkup to the family doctor's office and how the doctor had come out to him and said pointedly: "Take your dad to the hospital." He told me about the diagnosis. Leukemia. Acute. Incurable. The trouble down deep in the bone marrow where blood cells are produced. Excessive immature white blood cells, crowded out by cancerous, leukemic cells, made it impos-sible for the white cells to fight infection [Chasnoff, Ellis, and Fainman, M.D., *New Illustrated Family Medical & Health Guide,* 1991, p. 363]. Billy wondered whether the doctors had done enough or knew enough to help our dad. It had been a shock. He'd brought him to the hospital and they'd walked inside together. He'd been there when they checked him in and stayed in his room with him for as long as he could. Later, he'd been out in the hallway when he saw a doctor go into Dad's room, then come out, and later go in and out again. The last time, he walked over to him with that look on his face.

"Your dad is gone," the doctor said.

And that had been that.

I was depressed. The days seemed to drag by as we completed arrangements for the memorial service and the cremation of our father's body. Mom and sister Anne came in from Denver. We consoled one another. Our sorrow brought us closer.

I felt cheated, somehow. I hadn't been there to see him off. After all, he'd been there to see me off the day I bolted and joined the Navy. He even gave that conductor twenty bucks to look after me. I hadn't been home in more than a year. The depression stuck with me for a long time. After about two weeks with the family, I went back to Quantico. An important segment of my life had just wafted away.

Perhaps the issue that disturbed me the most in the mid-1960s was the Marine Corps' race relations problem. In 1964, the problem had reached such proportions that it was practically open warfare at many of the bases. It was obvious to me that we were headed for some traumatic experiences. I wanted to study the problem and make some observations about it. Looking about, I thought I'd found a method for doing just that.

One of the requirements for completing the AWS course of instruction was to write a staff study. I could think of no more contemporary and meaningful issue than the rising racial problem within the Corps.

Unfortunately, Col. W. F. Cornell, the director of the Amphibious Warfare School, didn't agree. He resisted the idea of my subject matter. He said: "I don't think this would be a meaningful study." But I persisted and wrote it anyway, and to my everlasting surprise, it was one of the staff studies sent to the AWS library for retention. I was proud of that. Later in my career when I came down to Quantico for other reasons, I looked in at the library to see how many times the staff study had been checked out. Christ, they'd worn out several control sheets tracking it. (In 1996, however, the Quantico library claimed that for some reason, the "report just seemed to have disappeared," although they still showed it as a holding.)

In that staff study, I'd concluded the obvious, that in the mid-1960s there was indeed a paucity of black Marine officers. Prevailing attitudes (learned mores regarding prejudice and racism) within the Marine Corps were such that blacks were not being accepted for the most part. That was the basic reason why many of them departed the service after putting in their minimum period of time. Because they were not being accepted, it was necessary for them to move into other arenas where at least a small measure of acceptance and human worth could be realized.

Discussion of this issue was, in a way, ironic, because the Corps itself probably would have not accepted the idea that racism was a problem, or certainly not a problem that it could not control. It would, however, get a wakeup call soon, because this was just before the racial furor erupted in Vietnam among combat units on the ground.

So I was really gratified that the study turned out as well as it did. But my insistence in the writing of it stuck in my AWS commander's craw. Colonel Cornell launched his barb in the only way he could. Superior officers have a way of doing that to anyone who goes against their advice. Just a little kick in the britches as you glide by. In his first endorsement to my request for assignment to the College Degree Program, he'd recommended favorable consideration, that I was capable and conscientious and had adapted well to the Amphibious Warfare School regimen. Then came the swift kick when he wrote:

> Although his initial academic efforts were below the class average, he has shown steady improvement and there is every indication that this improvement will continue. Because of the . . . heavy workload associated with the Amphibious Warfare Course, off-duty civilian schooling for our students is not encouraged.
>
> Major PETERSEN's determination to carry the extra load is clearly an indication of his motivation to complete his education. . . .

Well, somebody forgot to light his fire. Somebody forgot to stir his stew. The workload of the AWS or any other Corps duty wasn't the name of the game. The Corps granted approved applicants one year to complete the requirements for a college degree. Not to worry; I understood the colonel's need for the swift kick. I'd gone against his advice and against his grain. There wasn't a hell of a lot he could've done to keep me from writing that staff study. He knew it. Maybe the swift kick made him feel better. Anyhow, life went on, as I (like many other professional Marine officers) drove evenings, after Amphibious Warfare School was finished for the day, up to George Washington University in Washington, D.C., to take night classes.

These classes were more than interesting because participation in them brought me face to face with the students who were strong in their anti-Vietnam and antimilitary themes. I managed to meet quite a few of them, found myself in long conversations, and listened with interest to some of their ideas. A few of them went to cocktail parties to which they'd been invited by other Marine officers attending the university.

Their attacks on the military were never ending and could unsettle the unsuspecting. I can remember one cocktail party where a fairly senior Marine officer from Quantico was astounded by the antimilitary rhetoric. The civil cocktail conversation all of a sudden went blam! and there stood some very articulate kids giving him holy hell. It was done in a studious, reasoned fashion on the part of the students, but the stings wounded.

"You guys, as a group, are nothing but murderers," they caterwauled.

"America has no business being in Vietnam—period. This is a war that should not be fought," they postulated.

"You people are committing war crimes—all of you. Why can't you see that? Why don't you admit it?"

Well, some of my fellow Marine officers who had to listen to this had been in the Corps for a long time and were quite militant in their responses. It was a confusing thing for all of us. We were caught by what we felt were our duties, our orders—only to be told that we were committing war crimes. So it was all pretty weird.

I finally developed my own counterargument that seemed to serve me well. After listening to the students address me with their venom, I looked them straight in the eye for a moment, then asked, "Well, who did you vote for in the last election?"

Actually, it was kind of a trick question, because I really didn't care whether he or she had voted the Democratic or Republican ticket. I had my answer, and now I could pull my own rapier.

"Well, " I swashbuckled, "you're as guilty as I am—except that I have to suffer from the errors that America makes."

Didn't solve a whole lot, but it made me feel pretty damned good.

On 4 March 1966, I received notice from George Washington University that a reevaluation of my credits showed that I was one semester hour short for graduation in the month of June. An accommodation was obtained in which the university allowed me to reduce my final semester's unit load by three, then waiving the short semester hours provided I completed them at my next duty station (or the Armed Forces Institute). George Washington University would then allow them to transfer back, so I could receive my baccalaureate degree.

It was actually providential, because orders came down from the Marine Corps on 2 May 1966 to report to Willow Grove Naval Air Station in Pennsylvania. I was allowed to complete my study program at George Washington before departing.

Once at Willow Grove, we quickly found a house to rent in Warminster, Pennsylvania, while I began to settle into my new duties. Because of those duties, I was not able to get involved with off-duty educational courses immediately, which resulted in a small snit from Marine Corps headquarters reminding me of my failure to "enroll in off-duty courses or provide a record of grade(s) received from a local institution of higher learning."

Quickly snaring courses at Temple University in anthropology and history (with some financial assistance from the Corps), I ultimately qualified for graduation from George Washington University in the 21 February 1967 convocation. It hadn't been an easy road, but it was one I considered a necessity in order to continue to climb the promotional ladder within the Marine Corps.

With my bachelor's degree in my pocket, I saw no reason to slow the educational process down at all. It was full steam ahead, as far as I was concerned. The job I was assigned at Willow Grove Naval Air Station wasn't the most exciting group of protocols around—operations officer for a Marine reserve training squadron. Coordinating the scheduling of the assigned aircraft with the pilots. Planning for maneuvers. Being sure that the aircraft were up to snuff and operational. So in early May, I thought I'd strike out in a new direction, applying for more special education within the Corps—defense systems analysis, or management and industrial engineering, or financial management, or even that course called Technology of Management, No. 55. Anything that would give me the feeling that I was moving along. Well, that fizzled on me. As the Marine Corps put it, I was "considered, but not selected."

But not to worry, the Good Lord was smiling broadly. In October 1967, I received temporary promotion to the grade of lieutenant colonel with the date of rank as of the first of that month. I remember smiling a lot in those days. With the coming of those silver oak leaves, I knew it wouldn't be long before we'd be moving on from Willow Grove.

I began thinking about my next career move. Vietnam was where the action was—and the opportunities. The thing to do was to volunteer for combat duty. That didn't go over well with my wife. She was right in a way. I was never around the family very much. I also thought that my wife was wasting her time by not improving herself—by not going back to school to finish her education.

It was instant domestic war, I guess, with my proposing another voluntary tour for combat and the resulting cross accusations. I guess I simply opted out for a while and moved into the bachelor officers' quarters on the base to get away from the confusion. I was out of the house for almost a year. My marriage was tentative, a close, though sometimes verbally combative, thing.

Getting a squadron to command seemed more than just a dream if I could stay on the right career track. I'd heard rumors from headquarters that there was a need for a black lieutenant colonel to come and start the Negro officers' experiment job. I knew that there were no lieutenant colonels available. There was only a major, and that gentleman was overseas at the time. Not wanting to be bogged down, I petitioned to go overseas and into combat. It would be, I thought, one of the few shots I would have to get a squadron as a lieutenant colonel. If I were to go any further, I should have a commander's assignment behind me.

MUTUAL VOICES
Gayle Marie Petersen, Daughter, 14 July 1993

He's a nice guy, real sensitive. I remember seeing him cry. I saw him cry one time when my cat died. They didn't know what to do with me, and they sent me to him—and he cried. And I thought, Well, I guess it's okay for me to cry because he was a colonel, a light colonel. I guess it was from the hopelessness, the powerlessness you feel when your kid is hurting and there's nothing you can do about it 'cause you know you can't bring that cat back. He was never around, but when he was—he was a kinda funny family type of guy. Quiet. Real quiet—not talking very much. But when he did feel like saying something, he had a very good sense of humor, could make you laugh—and have you heard such a laugh.

But he's all about the noggin, so my mother said, "They used to kick your father's ass every day." She said they used to call him nigger, and he'd come home upset. Poor Dad. But maybe for some reason it was just God's will to go through all that. I've never seen anybody else like him. I've never seen another man who acts like him. Oh, when he was young, he was so handsome. He was funny and nice and tall and skinny—real built chest. And he used to walk around with his shirt off, just his jeans and flip-flops on and work on his car—that Austin-Healy, that white Austin-Healy. That was his favorite thing—tinkering on that car. That was the thing he loved doing. And while he was doing that, he loved to drink lemonade and orange juice all mixed together. I love my dad.

I finished at Willow Grove and was sent to Marine Corps Air Station, Cherry Point, down in North Carolina, to go through training. But once on the ground, I found out that what they had in mind for me was C-130 training. The big push was on to get transport pilots for cargo ships. Big, lumbering cargo ships. But I knew if I went into C-130s, I'd never get a squadron. A fresh-caught lieutenant colonel would have absolutely no chance of command.

Oh, I knew what the people making assignments were doing. They were just trying to fill some of those seats and they weren't looking at the big picture in terms of Marine Corps racial progress. So I protested to my immediate commanding officer, to no avail. Then I petitioned the commanding general through a commander's mast (the procedure through which an officer or other lower ranks can register complaints with the man in charge of things) with the air wing commander, who happened to be a two-star general. I went in to see him. I explained that it was my preference to go over to Vietnam in fighters, that I would have a better chance of becoming a squadron commander because, all things being equal, I was at the right place on my career track and by now should have been coming up for a possible assignment as a squadron commander. I didn't say it, although I wanted to, that hey, you know, giving a black a squadron—that would really be a leg up for the Marine Corps.

"Colonel," began the air wing commander, clearing his throat, "I'm sorry, but my hands are tied. I have to fulfill my quotas as they come from Marine Corps headquarters."

"But—" I began as if to protest further.

"So I really can't take any action on your request," he said. "You're going into transports." He had turned me down cold.

"Fine, sir," I acquiesced.

That was the end of that for the moment.

Well, there's no point in arguing with a two-star general. If you don't outrank him, you're going to lose. So I jumped into my car, drove up to Washington, D.C., to Marine Corps headquarters. There, I walked purposefully into the Aviation Department where some old friends from that other combat in Korea were now full colonels and running things.

"Well, Frank, what can we do for you today?" one of them asked.

That invitation was all I needed. I was just very straight up. I reiterated my belief that I would never have a chance to command a squadron if I went into the C-130s. I also knew that the Marine Corps was trying to fill some of those seats and they simply weren't looking at the big picture. Second, I noted that it was a wonderful opportunity for the Marine Corps to show that it practiced equal opportunity by placing a black as a squadron commander. That put the old bug in their ear. Then I nailed it.

"In addition to all that," I said, "I'm qualified. And I just don't want to get shoveled down that C-130 path." I knew that if I didn't make that stand then, I'd probably be flying C-130 airplanes until the day of my retirement. I'd seen others get caught in that. I also knew that it would lead to an inability to compete if I continued to seek higher ranks.

"So, hey," I went charging on to the end of my plea, "I want to go into the tiger's jaw."

I thought that would probably seal the thing, because the Marine Corps, in particular, is geared to combat. You train to go into combat, and when it's time to go into it, you'd like to go in the way you were trained. For me to go to Vietnam and fly C-130s (which I'd never flown before and which would be completely foreign to my nature, my makeup, and everything else) would have been a personal travesty. If you're a Marine, you've got to go where the war is, and for me, that was in fighters. That's what I meant when I looked at my friend and told him I wanted to walk into the tiger's jaw. That tiger's out there. Let's go see how big and bad he is.

"Well, Frank," my friend finally replied, patting me on the shoulder, "we'll take a look and see what we can do."

I went back to Cherry Point and finished the ground school syllabus taught by the VMGR-252 squadron. Not too long afterward, I got a call from Marine headquarters that gladdened my heart.

"Would you like to go into fighters?" the voice began.

"Very definitely," I cried, my heart leaping.

The next thing I knew, orders were cut from Headquarters, Marine Corps, transferring me from C-130 training to F-4B Phantom fighter training with Marine Air Group 32. That also meant that I was volunteering for a combat tour in Vietnam.

That was really great. My sense was that the idea of having a black fighter squadron commander had become popular enough so that everything was now in order to ensure that I would get a squadron.

Exactly what I wanted, except that now I had one really pissed Marine Corps major general over at the air wing just aching to verbally dismantle one little old black lieutenant colonel and throw his bones to the wolves. He summoned me into his office and put me into a brace (ordered me to stand in an extreme position of attention, unmoving, until he gave me permission to move).

"What do you mean," he growled, "going behind my back to Headquarters, Marine Corps?"

My eyes found and concentrated on a point somewhere in the corner of the room, far over his head. My knees locked, and I could feel the sweat run down around my ears.

"Sir," I said, "I don't know what you're talking about."

"Are you standing there telling me you didn't go to Marine Corps headquarters with your own little dog and pony show, just trying to evade my orders?"

"Sir, I really don't know what in the hell is going on," I insisted.

"Like hell you don't know, Colonel."

"Sir?"

"Dismissed."

"Yes, sir."

I took to my next assignment with gusto, although my relationship with my wife seemed to be slowly sliding farther downhill because of it. I'd moved the family to Washington, D.C., while I pursued the F-4 tactical conventional weapons delivery course at MCAS Cherry Point and then went for more hands-on stuff out west at the Marine Corps air station in Yuma, Arizona, over wide desert airspace.

The family radio and television business run by my father Frank Sr.

The Delta Sigma Theta sorority that my mother Edythe belonged to in 1935. She is third from left in the second row.

Family and friends in Topeka. Back row, L-R, Billy, Paul Tyler, and myself. Front row, Paul's sister Nancy, sister Anne and my little brother Hans.

Middle school football player. My friend Paul Tyler is in the center, second row. I am second from the left in top row. (courtesy Paul Tyler)

My father hard at work in his radio and television repair shop.

Part of the 1949 graduating class of Topeka High School. I am third from the left in the third row. (courtesy Paul Tyler)

Seaman recruit Frank Petersen in boot camp, San Diego, during my second month of training in July 1950.

Naval cadet Frank Petersen visiting home on leave with brother Hans and my father Frank.

Graduating from naval flight training, receiving commission in the Marine Corps Reserves from Admiral Whitney, as friend Evelyn DuBose looks on.

Helping with orphans during the Korean War.

Hosting orphans' visit to my squadron VMFA-212, Korea 1953.

Relaxing with new Petersen citizens, daughters Dana and Gayle Marie, in front of family quarters, Marine Air Station, El Toro.

Enjoying the day with my family. Next to me is my daughter Gayle, on her left is my daughter Dana who's standing next to my wife Eleanor. In front are my daughter Lindsey and son Frank.

Accepting regular commission as Marine Corps officer. Congratulations being received from Lt. Col. William Gentry Johnson, Commander, VMFN-542.

Accepting congratulations from Senator Barry Goldwater, Bob Hope, and the mayor of Houston Louie Welch after receiving the Robert M. Hanson award for the Most Outstanding Fighter Squadron of 1968 while assigned in Vietnam. On my left is Lt. Col. Lundine, former commander of VMFA 314. On my right is Lt. Gen. Frank Tharin. (courtesy USMC)

Jocularity on Mother's 70th birthday. My brother Hans is in center.

Showing off Marine T-33 jet aircraft to children during stopover while performing cross country. My nephew, Robbie, left, my niece, Laurie, and an unidentified relative or acquaintance.

Savoring the promotion to brigadier general with family. From left, son Frank III, daughter Monique, daughter Lindsay, myself, and my wife Alicia.

Posing with close friend California doctor Dale Tipton, M.D., after my promotion to brigadier general. (courtesy Dale Tipton)

Celebrating promotion to brigadier general with members of the famous Montford Point Marines.

Friends celebrate promotion to brigadier general. I'm standing next to my best friend, mentor, and boating buddy Jim Smith. Next to him is Wally Terry, author of *Bloods*, and Col. Fred Cherry, U.S.A.F. fighter pilot, who was shot down in Vietnam and held as a POW in the Hanoi Hilton for seven years.

In Iwakuni, Japan, I was then commanding general of the 1st Marine Aircraft Wing. I'm talking with Lt. Gen. Charles G. Cooper, Commanding General, Fleet Marine Corps, Pacific (center) and Col. D. J. McCarthy, commanding officer, MCAS Iwakuni. (courtesy USMC)

Preparing to receive an honorary doctorate degree after making commencement address at Virginia Union University in Richmond in May 1987. Accompanying me is my wife Alicia on my right and other well-wishers.

I accept the flag and command of the Marine Corps Development and Education Command from retiring commanding general, Lt. Gen. David B. Tohmey. (courtesy USMC)

My wife Alicia and I descend stairs into the ballroom of the Sheraton in Washington, D.C., at the Officers' Marine Corps birthday ball, 15 November 1986. (courtesy USMC)

Greeting Secretary of the Navy James W. Webb Jr. upon his arrival at Quantico Marine Base. (courtesy USMC)

Proud father spends quality time with son Frank E. Petersen III.

In the cockpit of F8U Crusader at Naval Air Station Willow Grove, Pennsylvania, where I served as operation officer. (courtesy *Marines Magazine*)

During a change of command ceremony, Sgt. Maj. Sterlewski hands the command colors to me so that I can pass them along to my successor, Lt. Gen. William R. Etnyre, new commander of Quantico, as I retire. (courtesy USMC)

My retirement ceremony, Quantico 1988. The commandant just advised me of the amount of my retirement check.

The final salute as I retire from the Marine Corps in July 1988. (courtesy USMC)

Attending graduation of our daughter Monique from Hampton University, in Hampton, Virginia.

I am reflecting on the honorable discharge of my great-grandfather, Archie McKinney, who served during the Civil War with the 55th Regiment of the Massachussetts Infantry.

Part Four
Tiger Country

14: Looking for the Tiger

On 17 March 1968, I started my love affair with the big, ugly monster the Marines called the F-4B Phantom jet. A powerful airplane, it was the best fighter in the Marine Corps and Air Force arsenal at the time. I liked the large cockpit. I was six foot one, and the fit was comfortable. I could maneuver my body, twist my head around, and take a look. Just a comfortable plane. But what was really significant for me was the awesome knowlege that I was sitting in a monster that could exceed mach 2 in the fighter version with the racks and rails off. I was in one of the best machines in the world. It not only had power but maneuverability as well. In fact, I used to play with it, see how high and fast I could make it go during the air-ground workups—just like a hot rock fighter pilot ought to do.

There were times I'd just stand back and look at her. She wasn't pretty. At best, she just looked quaint. A strange but sharp-looking airplane that appeared evil. But it'd take you where you wanted to go. It was the tactical airplane of the Vietnam War. The Marines used it primarily in the air-ground mode, working in support of its ground units.

We had to learn how to do a walk-around inspection before we could ever think about flying that bird. Lots of stuff to check. Gauges to know about in the wheel wells. Rails, pylons, racks, and tanks under its belly to nomenclature. Ordnance types, fuel. Speed brakes, auxiliary air doors, trailing edge flaps. In short, there were about a hundred things to look at before we could ever get into the cockpit.

Once in the cockpit and strapped in, there were the oxygen, anti-g-suit lines, and communications checks. Knowing the strap-in routines and the positions of almost a hundred switches. The radar intercept officer (RIO) learned to check his list. No time for shortcuts, because when the power goosed that baby there was no forgiveness if things hadn't been done right. She skedaddled down the runway, a kind of metallic monster in heat, the awesome acceleration inviting our feet to lift, threatening to desert the rudder pedals. I felt that, at any moment, she was about to fly off without us, except for the reality check engendered by the vibrations of the striations and bumps in the runway as the stiff struts ran them over. The stabilator grabbed air; the nose got lighter. The RIO called the airspeed as the nose gear deserted the ground. Gingerly, we learned to ease the stick forward, keeping that prescribed nose-high attitude. One hundred forty knots and—blam!—rack that gear handle into the "up" stop. Initial climb. Cruise. It was a beautiful ship to fly.

The familiarization training was superintensive. In some cases we'd fly three training hops a day. Air-ground work was hit hard because, in support of Marine operations, that kind of activity was our bread and butter stuff. We'd take off with a load of live ordnance, then fly out to a ground target and practice various kinds of dive-bombing. Low angle, high angle, napalm delivery. The day probably wouldn't have been complete unless we fired up a bit of air-to-air-intercept, squaring off one against the other—taking off into a real dogfight at the end of all that.

Out over the California desert, the weather was hot. As a consequence, such intensive training and flying would just wring us out. After landing, we'd climb out of our planes dripping with perspiration. The typical day would end around five or six o'clock in the evening. Time for a little chow, a little drink, then right into the sack. Dang near sunrise the next morning, we'd be up and into those cockpits. Very intense. A kind of *Top Gun* thing in miniature. I think it lasted for about a month and a half. Once in a blue moon, a bright spot would occur—a kind of worm hole, reminding me of that other dimension we'd left before coming to this place.

I'll never forget one training mission during which my wingman had a generator come loose. We didn't know what the problem was at the time. The closest airfield to emergency him down was the civilian airport at Palm Springs. I got on the horn.

"Palm Springs tower, I have a Mayday. Mayday. Mayday. Mayday. Request emergency landing instructions. Arrival time approximately fourteen minutes."

Palm Springs tower immediately responded with landing instructions. We circled for approach. All other air traffic was cleared from the landing pattern. We were given priority for landing. From the air we could see the emergency crash vehicles begin doing wheelies.

After my wingman landed, I dropped in behind him, taxied in, trailing my drag chute. We took a look at the problem and made arrangements for repairs in Palm Springs.

Past the emergency now, we spent an enjoyable few hours. The civilians were cooperative, and a lot of people wanted to come out and look at the airplanes. I hate to admit it now, but there I was, just swaggering around, proud to be one of the pilots. Well, it was one of America's premier fighter airplanes. It was a successful design. The Navy, Air Force, and Marines were all using it. I was pleased to be there to show it off.

"Frank, why in hell did you go in there with him?" one of my training buddies asked when I returned to Cherry Point.

"Do you think I'd pass up the opportunity to land at Palm Springs airport in a Phantom?" I replied, a huge smile on my face.

I graduated from the F-4 training course on 21 March 1968, exactly fourteen days before Martin Luther King, Jr., was assassinated in Memphis. On the day of his assassination, 4 April, I was visiting in New York with an acquaintance who was white. Suddenly, it didn't seem safe on the streets in the Bronx, so we holed up for a couple of days at my friend's place. Incipient rioting was a distinct possibility. It was a tragic thing. The day seemed somehow surreal. With the civil rights revolution in high gear, the war in Southeast Asia had become more complex for almost every American. In 1965, Martin Luther King had publicly denounced that war, and I'd found myself all at sea about that. I had wanted King to be above criticism, and now I had begun to wonder if he was betraying us.

Perhaps King's most potent commentary about the war in Vietnam had come one year before his assassination in front of a meeting of the clergy and laity at Riverside Church in New York City.

> We are taking the black young men . . . crippled by our society
> . . . sending them 8,000 miles away to guarantee liberties in Southeast Asia . . . they had not found in southwest Georgia and East Harlem. We have been watching Negro and white boys on TV . . .
> as they kill and die together for a nation that has been unable to seat them together in the same classrooms.

A year before, on 15 April 1967, King had asserted that President Johnson's goals had been "shot down on the battlefields of Vietnam."

I was sorely confused, but then I considered what I was about as a member of the United States Marine Corps. Confusion fled when considering our only alternative. We didn't ask to fight; we had to fight. It was odd, but it seemed that more and more blacks were joining the military, even as King spoke and the antiwar debate widened. Deeply moved, I watched the panoply of King's funeral flash across America's television screens along with everyone else as the country seemed to approach a flash point not seen in decades. I continued to wonder why King had taken the position he did, just at that time.

In essence, we sometimes took these political posturings without realizing that we were saluting a certain portion of the population, the Afro-American population, that had already done its thing—kicking down barriers, opening doors, and participating—whether it was the military, the National Guard, or whatever. It sometimes angered and surprised me when civil rights leaders didn't realize that many of their inflammatory speeches—about what blacks should and shouldn't do in terms of police departments, the National Guard, the U.S. military—were excluding those segments of their society that we really should be a part of so that we could exert influence and control. I mean, we've used the National Guard to quell civil rights groups; we've used them to patrol the streets in the riots; we've used them to help integrate the school systems—yet some of these guys are saying that blacks should not serve in the military; blacks should not do this or that. It's like trying to close the barn door after the creature has busted out.

My life rumbled into high gear. I was due in Vietnam in May 1968. Ellie's brother-in-law and sister gave me a clue as to where I could find housing for my family in Northern California while I did my Vietnam tour. After several flights to California and a bit of luck, I found a house in a new housing development in the Hilltop area of Richmond. It looked like a wonderful setting and was close to a huge shopping center.

My wife and I had tried to mend the rift between us. This tour could do nothing but enhance my military career. This volunteer assignment to combat was a case in point regarding my marital problems, which seemed to center on military life versus family life and how the military part of my life impacted my family. The big question seemed to be whether I could turn off the military part of my life when I did come home.

Well, not that I couldn't turn it off, but I always wanted to accept any challenge thrown at me, take any opportunity that I thought would be on the success path. Even in flying, in a given month—half of those weekends—I'd be out in an airplane doing cross-country. Of course, the family response was to wonder why I was never at home, especially when they thought they needed me. I tried to be home sometimes, but I probably fell short of the mark from time to time.

But we were going to try to see this thing through together in spite of our differences. So we packed the children and our necessary belongings in the family car and struck out for California. While the final negotiations regarding the new house were in process, the family stayed with old friends, Dr. Dale Tipton and his wife, Frederica. We had grown up together in Topeka. Dale was from Parsons, a town not far from Topeka. Then escrow finally closed on our new house, and our family moved to 3088 Belfast in Richmond.

It was a nice little house, actually. The living room, to the front, had a wide picture window. Immediately behind that was the kitchen. To the left was a passageway back to three bedrooms and two baths, all on a single level. As I recall, there was an L-shaped courtyard and a concrete patio.

I was able to spend only a few days in the house with the family. Then it was time to take my flight out to Vietnam. Ellie had the whole ball of wax and the chore of raising our youngsters until I could get back from the war.

MUTUAL VOICES
Ellie, First Wife

There I was, this woman with these little black kids, this woman who had no visible means of support. It evidently blew a lot of people's minds. The neighbors started yelling across the back fence: "We're gonna get rid of you niggers one way or the other." It was a new housing development and there were some black people there, but my kids were very inquisitive. They did what they always did. They banded together and went exploring. They had bicycles and they were all over the place.

Huey Newton, the Black Panther, was in jail then. I didn't know who he was, but the kids did. Through my brother-in-law, who was the Alameda County clerk, they all went to meet him, and before I knew it, they all had these "naturals"—the Afro—and they were black and beautiful. Then they started being chased home, getting into fights at school while the yelling across the back fence gained velocity: "We're gonna get rid of you."

Fortunately, the people at their school were helpful. They sent the police community people around. That helped for a while. But then, my son,

Frank, was elected president of his second grade class. The teacher refused to let him serve as president. Being cut from his father's cloth, he said, "Hey, this ain't gonna work. I've been elected and I'm gonna do it." Oh, he raised a fuss. They expelled him from the school.

A friend we knew from Topeka went down to the school and totally raised hell. They then assigned us to a school psychologist, whose assessment was that I was a permissive mother that had these four children who were these beautiful black stallions running all over the place, and that I was not strong enough to control the reins. His recommendation was that the school write the military and inform the children's father that he needed to come home. Well, I knew that was the last thing I needed. That would be the final nail in my coffin, if that man of mine had to come home and control those kids.

So, we got it together. As mad as I was at the school, it probably was the best thing that could have ever happened, because I began to use that famous Marine Corps language that Frank had used on me often enough. I even turned it on the police. "Pigs" was the nomenclature in those days. They'd come up and bang on our door. It was a common occurrence.

The higher Frank got in rank, the worse it all seemed to get. I remember my oldest daughter, Gayle, coming home from school one day very distraught.

"Mom," she said, "they always say I'm black." After she said that, she went and got a box of crayons.

"Well, what did you tell them?" I asked.

"I told them I'm not black, I'm flesh colored."

"Well, Gayle, where did you get the expression 'flesh colored'?"

She held up her box of crayons, and there was a crayon that was cream colored, called "flesh." It was the first time I had seen such a thing. And that was the way they had to learn to deal with these things on their own.

Maybe one of the worst days was the day they came home, their eyes wide.

"Momma, they keep calling us nigger."

"Well," one of my daughters said, "why don't you just tell 'em you're an Indian?"

And my youngest daughter said: "You can't tell 'em you're an Indian. You ain't got no hatchet."

Although I thought that my idea of the Marine Corps eventually having its first black fighter squadron commander might be popular enough to ensure that I would, in fact, be given a squadron once I arrived in Vietnam, I was mentally prepared for that not to happen. I thought I would simply go to Vieitnam and spend six months or so in a staff job and then go into a squadron.

That's about where I was mentally when Vietnam hove into view and I deplaned at Da Nang Air Base. I recoiled at the heavy, moisture-laden air, seemingly full of water vapor and a strange kind of dust mixed with jet aircraft fumes. A war was in progress. Not on that particular spot, but from time to time would come the thudding, rolling thunder of how-itzer batteries dueling to the east. There was something different about reporting to Vietnam now compared to Korea. In Korea, I was still a youngster, still a bit wet behind the ears, off to see the world and bask in adventure. Out to make a mark if I could. But since then I'd worked hard, improved myself, and now embarked on what I hoped would be a star track—maybe taking me to the top of my game—unless I slipped along the way.

MUTUAL VOICES
Lt. Col. Gale Harlan, USMC (Retired), Longtime Friend

I was assistant air officer up at Dong Hoi in the DMZ. I was in Viet-nam in January during the Khe San seige, and then somebody called me and told me that Frank was coming in. I got a hop down to Da Nang to meet him and ran into a little guy named [Lt. Col.] Jim Penny. Penny commanded an A-6 squadron at Da Nang. Together, we met Pete when he came in. Penny picked him up and I met him over at Marine Air Group 11 about noon, then took him over to the Air Group Officers' Club at Da Nang. We just sat around telling sea stories—just shooting the shit and drinking beer.

"Man," I said after about four beers, "to hell with the beers. I'm gonna have a scotch, because I've gotta go back tonight and there's no scotch in the DMZ."

"Boy, that sounds good to me," Pete said with a laugh.

"Nope," Penny says, "I'm gonna have another beer. I've gotta go up to Hanoi tonight, and I never like to drink the hard stuff when I've gotta go that far north."

Pete and I laughed our asses off. It sounded funny for some reason com-ing from a guy like Penny. We used to call him "The Midget Marine." Just a bare-minimum kind of guy. Maybe five feet. He was probably a hard-ass if you didn't know him, but when you got to know him, you just laughed your ass off—just blew him off. But it was nice to know that an old buddy like Pete was in the Nam.

Well, I got my assignment to a squadron, all right, but I didn't really know in what capacity until I was called in by Col. Hal Berge, the air group commander. It was an interesting conversation.

"Frank," he said, "I'm going to give you a squadron."

The words electrified. I have to admit now to a kind of ethereal, floating sensation, as if somehow I'd been lifted off the ground about ten feet. It was what I'd been shooting for, hoping for. I knew then that my trip to Washington had borne fruit. The word had been passed.

Underneath the elation, though, another feeling lurked that wasn't particularly great. It was a weird situation I was in, to be elated at the achievement of a cherished goal on the one hand, and on the other to know I was being assigned to that place by color rather than by qualification. I could only hope that my qualifications met what I envisioned as my personal goals—regardless of the color of my skin. The timbre of the colonel's voice brought me back to the present.

"Now, Frank—just one thing."

"What's that, sir?"

"Would you have any hesitation on taking over VMFA-314, the Black Knight squadron?"

"No, absolutely not. Absolutely not," I replied, feeling my body shift a bit.

I'd heard about the Black Knights. The squadron was named for its squadron emblem, the painting of the torso of a real knight in full regalia and mail—all in black. The emblem rode the fuselages of all its aircraft. The men in the squadron also had a little helmet they wore for various functions; it was a black knight's helmet, painted black.

Actually, I said, I would prefer VFMA-115, which didn't have as good a track record. I wanted something that would give me a goal to shoot for, whereas VMFA-314 was riding pretty high under its present commander. Colonel Berge thought about that for a moment.

"No, Frank, I think not. You take over VMFA-314 and relieve Herb Lundine."

That settled the issue. I was shortly to become the first black fighter squadron commander in the history of the United States Marine Corps. Not only that, it would be one of the hottest Marine fighter squadrons in the Corps. A squadron with a distinguished World War II record in the Pacific. Ewa. Midway. Ie Shima. Okinawa. Re-formed in 1964 after a Far East tour, it had been the first Marine squadron to receive and fly the Phantom II. An old, proud squadron. An outfit that seemed to thrive when there was a shooting war. Its members told themselves, and believed, that they were the Marine Corps' premier Phantom squadron. And I was about to be its next commander—the challenge I was always looking for and talking about. This had to be my fiery furnace. I pumped myself, starched up the backbone.

The time had come to fly down south to VMFA-314's base at Chu Lai in the southernmost sector of the Quang Tin Province. My new command was situated about eighty miles south of Da Nang, right on the coast. A medium-sized base, it was the home of the famous Americal Division, plus two Marine Corps air groups. Marine Air Group 12 flew attack aircraft. Marine Air Group 13, my group, flew F-4 Phantoms. There was also an Army helicopter squadron assigned.

As we circled for landing, I was struck by the magnificent beauty of Chu Lai, situated on a four-mile strip of land set against the South China Sea. A crescent-shaped bay defined its northern boundaries. Nature seemed to have fashioned it in lovely counterpoint. White sand beaches to the east. Old marshes and sand dunes struck dumb with man-made striations called runways. Red clays and green hills in the west as the sea painted ever-changing watercolors of sun-swept blues and blazing turquoises against foreboding, dark, angrier blues riding the air. To the west, the grandeur of the Annam Mountains thrust up from the coastal plains to become their own natural canvas transforming clear daylight to mist-driven, agitated thunderheads, growling down the sun.

I was to find out later that, on the ground, my tall, tough, bespectacled sergeant major had called together his staff noncommissioned officers and advised them that I was coming in as the new commanding officer. There were, to my recollection, no black staff NCOs. At any rate, the sergeant major had thought to deliver a kind of morale booster lecture in view of this rather major change—a black commander coming in. "We're going to have a good squadron in spite of certain prevailing attitudes. And now is the time to step forward to say your piece, if indeed one has anything to say about the matter, so we can get on with this business of fighting the war."

Well, the story goes, a couple of the noncoms stepped forward and spoke their pieces in rather uncomplimentary verbiage, challenging the ultimate wisdom of the assignment of a black squadron commander—stuff about the "black" and the black knight and other things related to the racial aspect of things.

So the sergeant major knocked them on their respective asses.

The adrenaline flow increased as the realization hit me that within a few hours, I would become the leader of a stellar group of Marine Corps fighter pilots. A special breed of cat. I knew about that. I was one. Guys who looked at life a bit differently. We didn't have a guarantee about anything, because we lived right on the edge. Most were type A personalities, and we lived in a world of aggression. We did that freely, because we chose it ourselves. We were pushers, always seeking challenges, competition. And running through all if it was something we usually didn't even talk about because it just was, that's all—that wild kind of spirit that goes with our particular kind of living.

Blue smoke surged as the transport's wheels hit the deck, then it wafted away as we blew by. I smiled to myself. Hell, this was going to be a blast.

15: Into the Tiger's Jaw

In battle, particularly during an initial strike at a defended target, you have to be prepared to take losses. If you want to avoid them altogether, you stay home; otherwise you go smoking in there loaded for bear and obliterate the enemy's capabilities the first time around, so that when you come back, he's got nothing left to hit you with. Go get 'em tiger! See you at the debrief!
—John Trotti, ex-Marine fighter pilot, in
Marine Air: First to Fight, 1985, p. 38

The change of command ceremony was quite a gathering. Short. Sweet. Get the formalities over quickly. This was a combat zone. Spend about five minutes saying Hi! then get back to work.

Actually, though, it was more involved than that. Although the change of command ceremony might seem perfunctory to the uninitiated, it is a Marine custom steeped in history. In front of the entire squadron, the squadron colors are passed from the old commander to the new. Herb Lundine, the outgoing commander, passed the banner to me. I grasped it. Herb dropped his hands. It was my squadron. We saluted, changed sides. He was relieved. I was in charge.

As the departing commander, Herb addressed the squadron, thanked them, wished them godspeed and continued success. I congratulated Herb and the squadron on the job they'd done. I looked forward now to accepting the challenge.

With Squadron 314 colors flying high, the troops passed in review as the lst Marine Aircraft Wing band set the cadence. I looked down the line through that hot, humid air that you could not only feel but smell, and I saw the F-4 Phantoms in their revetments, the Black Knight emblem riding their fuselages, and I was proud to be the new skipper. Group commander Hal Berge, Herb Lundine, and I met with and greeted the officers and my senior noncoms. I'd have reason to remember and work with that tall guy with the glasses—my sergeant major—the enlisted right arm.

As part of my initiation as new commander, the staff noncommissioned officers had me to a dining-in for dinner and drinks. An established ritual was involved, and at some point in the ceremony it was necessary to put on the Black Knight helmet and pose for the noncoms. A few valiant and kind words were spoken, then the helmet was removed and placed in the center of the main table. My eyes swiveled round inside that helmet like crazy trying to see if there were any jokers who thought my placing it on my head amusing. I'm proud to say I didn't see or hear a single guffaw or snicker.

I was not unaware of my new role as the commander of a Marine fighter squadron. Of first import, of course, was the squadron itself. It was a live entity, overpoweringly energized. It was equipment, skills, goals, assignments, personalities—all to be melded into a writhing, searing thing with a constant edge that could slash and cut as the ultimate arm that accomplished an assigned mission, whatever the call. It was noise, confusion, smoke, sorted into the attainment of air superiority and support of troops in desperate firefights down there on the ground or the accomplishment of any other kind of missions that Marine aviators may be asked to perform. And all of it was ultimately my call. As commander, I set the tone. How I acted and the rules I decreed helped define how all of it would jell so that we'd be a living, effective part of the air group. A kind of pinnacle had been reached, one I considered a definite correct step in an overall career as a Marine Corps officer and aviator.

I knew that I would be running a tight ship. One reason was obvious. The first black commander of a Marine fighter squadron had better run a tight ship. I shouldn't have had to think this way, but I did. I felt that I always had to look over my shoulder, to be certain that something or someone wasn't creeping up to snatch what I'd attained. In the final analysis, though, the color of my skin and my concern about what was about to happen "over my shoulder" had to be shelved. I was the commander of a Marine fighter squadron flying twenty fighter airplanes that were technologically light years away from those in which I first began flying. I was the kind of skipper who would never ask a subordinate to do something I wouldn't, so early on I resolved to set the example by flying missions, leading my men into combat, on regular strikes and pulling my time on hot pad duty as well.

"Bloods" was my call sign. I settled on that because of all the rhetoric in the wind about race and racism inherent in the ongoing civil rights revolution. In those days, American black men almost universally referred to themselves as Bloods. It was a symbol. A connection of unspoken togetherness among us. Solidarity. We greeted one another that way in the most casual of settings.

"Wha's happenin', Blood?" was the tie. A special singularity that replaced all of the rhetoric and made the eyes flash with recognition. It applied regardless of our individual stations in life.

Bloods. It worked for me.

My first Vietnam mission was flown on 5 July 1968 in South Vietnam. It was a fighter strike against dug-in enemy troops giving Marines a hard time. It was a routine mission for me, a kind of upgraded thing I'd already done scores of times when I'd flown combat missions in Korea. The difference was that I was now flying a state-of-the-art fighter jet instead of a propeller-driven aircraft.

So I didn't suffer from the first-time apprehensions that a brand-new fighter pilot would've suffered. After the usual briefings by the operations and intelligence officers, my RIO—I can't remember his name—and I simply went out, made a group of North Vietnamese soldiers very unhappy, and came home.

I had fallen in love with the F-4 Phantom during familiarization training at MCAS Beaufort and Yuma. Now I found myself responsible for an entire squadron of them, with the men, machines, and armaments to utilize them exactly for the purpose for which they'd been designed and built—to prosecute a war. It was awesome to contemplate.

They looked mean and nasty sitting there in the chocks. In the air, they came through as ugly and menacing but still as things of absolute beauty that made adrenaline pump and the skin go prickly when they fired by. When they were loaded down with weapons of war—bombs and missiles, racks and rails—they became even more awesome to behold. We were thankful they were our airplanes, for their appearance thunderstruck an enemy.

To watch the planes coming home to roost after a strike was yet another experience. Looking like eagles back from the hunt, the Phantoms howled like banshees, their maniacal screams from the boundary layer controls piercing the air, their wings akimbo, landing gears searching for the deck. Then came the final howl as they sat down, trailing burning rubber, blue-white smoke curlicuing the air as drogue chutes rippled the airstream in turn behind them, snatching the captive air with a monumental pop. Deceleration. Their noses bowed down. Silence, except for the minor whine of the engines completing the run home.

Part of my job was to lead the way and establish adequate methodologies for the use of these magnificent weapons. Not only did I intend to set the example and the pace, I found that I was concerned as commander about the welfare of the younger pilots. I wanted to be sure that they had the knowledge and skill to be able to come home alive. That's number one. Being a hero is fine, but their primary job, in my view, was not to kill themselves but to kill the enemy. In short, my new job involved all of the above while setting standards for squadron operations, providing leadership through planning, continuous training—all aiming toward what I perceived as top efficiency, utilizing the skills of the officers and men assigned to the squadron for maximum effect.

For example, we discovered that we had several shortfalls in our equipment. One resided in our primary air-to-ground work—close air support. For example, McDonnell-Douglas had put out a 20mm gun pod that we could carry down the centerline rack. The problem was that the damned thing had the unnerving habit of jamming after we'd fired about five rounds. And when we were down on the ground, getting close to target, we needed something forward firing, especially if we were dropping napalm. Almost before we released it, we had to really get in there on top of the target. So I instructed my ordnance officer to remove all gun pods from the aircraft, and we installed forward-firing high-velocity aerial rockets (HVAR) instead. Those rockets had about the impact of a 30mm shell going off. We could aim them and point them, almost like pointing a finger, and they would fly fairly straight.

I guess the most memorable occasion in which we used that tactic was one evening on the east coast of Vietnam. We were up north, just above the DMZ, going after some bad guys dug into a mangrove swamp right on the edge of the water. The sun was just beginning to set as we rolled in. I could see the winking and blinking of their guns firing at our flight. I popped the nose up, kicked off an HVAR, and brought the nose back down. By the time the HVAR arrived and exploded, I was right behind with the napalm. All of the winking and blinking stopped.

It was weird. I could generate all sorts of philosophies of pilot survival. But I used to tell the guys, "If you can see the flashes, think to yourselves that means you're looking directly at the muzzles of their guns, which means that the trajectory of the shell is either going to go beneath you or go above you because he doesn't have the right deflection. He's not leading you enough or he's not high enough to hit you."

So I came by all these little cocoons of logic. Sometimes they could make a man feel better about rolling in there on the enemy. They could impact on ultimate morale, often in the same category as my insistence that everyone carry his load. There were always some guys who'd like to fly as many missions as they could. Others liked to fly as few as they could. So I always made sure that the operations officer had mission assignments spread out so that everyone got their fair share.

Beyond that, I always wanted to be certain that the troops got the straight scoop about what was going on as opposed to reading about things in *Stars and Stripes*. In biweekly troop briefings, we'd get documents from wing headquarters that gave the outline of what had been accomplished the day before. There would be information on troop buildup, of course, but also information about what was happening back home. It was a way of letting the troops know exactly where they fit into the bigger picture.

It all went toward ensuring that the squadron did things together, operated as a combat family, so to speak. Cookouts for the troops. Making sure that the officers knew what their men were doing, not just during duty hours but off duty as well. Even though we were technically on duty around the clock, the need was to ensure that when the men were off duty, they had everything they needed. Bedding. Adequate food. The whole nine yards. This kind of monitoring by my officers could well avoid disciplinary problems in the long run, could avoid things like the misstep a young corporal took on one occasion when the sergeant major caught him selling marijuana in the squadron—a prevalent thing in Vietnam in those days.

"Okay, Skipper," the sergeant major gritted between clenched teeth as he braced the corporal in front of me, "we're going to run this one up the yardarm."

The corporal seemed to tremble slightly. He was basically a good kid, but an object lesson was definitely needed. I looked steadily at him.

"No, Sergeant Major," I said, "what we're going to do is this. We need a personnel protection shelter right outside my headquarters. Do you know what I'm saying, Sergeant Major?"

"Yes, sir. Got it. Let's go, trooper. You've got a little project to do."

So we had the corporal dig about a five- by five-foot pit right where all the troops could see him at high noon in the hot sun and cruel humidity. When he finished, we had him fill it in, then dig it out again. Afterward, the sergeant major brought him back into my office and put him in a brace. The sweat rolled down his face onto a rumpled fatigue uniform that stuck to his body like glue. Concern streaked his countenance.

"Trooper," I began, "I hope you've learned your lesson."

"Yes, sir."

"If you ever sell pot again in my squadron, I will have you court-martialed. Do you read me?"

"Yes, sir."

"And then it's right on down to LBJ—that big old Long Binh jail. Is that it?"

"N-no, sir."

"Dismissed."

Actually, although what he'd done was purely a misguided act, the fruit of his labors in digging that shelter was a major contribution to safety, not only for myself but for any other member of my staff who happened to be in the area during the daily rocket attacks from the North Vietnamese, who considered it almost ritual that our day end with a bang.

Our days began around five in the morning. It was breakfast and then down to the flight line. For me, it was a visit with the ordnance crews, the maintenance crews, and the pilots as they were strapping in. Making sure that everything was going all right. Handling administrative matters. Then it would be my time in the cockpit: at least one mission, and sometimes as many as three missions a day. When all of that was finished, it would be into the afternoon.

We ate our dinner early, then hunkered down for the night, because we knew that a rocket attack would normally come in sometime around sundown and at five o'clock the next morning. The rocket attacks were particularly unnerving because the rockets essentially had no aiming device. They were just a kind of scatter shot—into the field—and we never knew where they were going to hit. We couldn't say, for example, that they were going for the airplanes, and then prudently hide from them, because their targets were completely random.

Even though we had foxholes and reinforced bunkers, we took casualties. Just before I arrived at Chu Lai, one of these rockets hit the top of one of the reinforced bunkers, cracked through a four-by-four support, dropped the bunker's heavy timbers down on the occupants, and killed one of the doctors who happened to seek shelter inside.

It could really get gory. Just before sunup one morning as I was making my rounds, the rockets came firing in and struck the enlisted mess hall. Some men scrambled into one of the foxholes. One of them stood up to look at the damage just as another rocket exploded. It blinded him, wrecked one of his arms, and severely mutilated other parts of his body.

So although digging the hole caused the young marijuana entre-preneur some major discomfiture, he did us the ultimate favor by pro-viding one more shelter when the crazy, deadly rockets came zooming.

In April, probably as part of the tailings of the large North Viet-namese Tet Offensive (kicking off 29–31 January 1968), some 80,000 North Vietcong (NV) and Vietcong (VC) regulars were thrown against the garrisons of some 105 South Vietnamese cities and towns, includ-ing Da Nang, accompanied by rocket attacks [Allen R. Millett, *Semper Fidelis: The History of the United States Marine Corps,* p. 152]. It was sheer luck that, during this, a large contingent of NV regulars was dis-covered approaching just west of Da Nang. Bad guys, out in the open, coming down close to the Ho Chi Minh Trail. The country was hilly and rocky. They hid in caves. The forward air controllers called in air support from all over. On one occasion, we found ourselves stacked eight deep in the air, rolling in to pound those suckers for twelve straight hours.

For three days, we flew concentrated strikes against them, as well as against targets near the DMZ and in the Ashau Valley. Our attacks were vicious and attenuated. They had to be, because, as someone has said, "When you're fighting the North Vietnamese regulars, you don't want to go in there with a switch." Those fellows were known to kick some butt if we weren't at the top of the defensive game. They were worthy opponents. The grunts had a way of putting it: You call the VC "Char-lie Cong"; you call the NV regulars "Mister Charlie." We put a serious "hurt" on those gentlemen in those three days, I'm sure.

Whatever elation had surfaced in my psyche because of success in the air was somehow muted come the sad day of 5 June 1968, when Robert F. Kennedy was assassinated in Los Angeles. It was a depressing thing. It just seemed to be a sequence of events that was never ending. I mean, those three almost in a row—John Kennedy, Martin Luther King, and now Robert Kennedy. It was mind-boggling. It seemed to me that the country was on the verge of insurrection. It was hard for me to com-prehend. I could never figure out who "they" were—the people re-sponsible for all this mayhem.

In August, flying got crazy when the monsoon season began. Contin-uous rain—from several days in a row to as long as two weeks. With the field at Chu Lai at minimums, the weather could be a bigger danger than a potential enemy, with hundred-foot ceilings and half-mile visibility or less. It rained all the time. The runway had a high crown, so the planes had to line up pretty well on landing and use short field arrestments when it was that wet [Drendel, *USMC Phantoms in Combat,* p. 11].

We couldn't do close air support unless we could see the target. But monsoon didn't mean that it was raining everywhere, so often we'd get airborne under radar control, then vector out over the ocean and come back in under the cloud layers and use low-angle kind of stuff, like napalm and fin-retarded bombs that allowed us to drive in closer, then go back over the water, get a radar vector, climb up, go back down to Chu Lai, and come home. Sometimes, we had to do some weird stuff, including adhering to the rules of the game: If we were flying north, we flew at even-altitude numbers; if we were flying south, we flew at odds. It wasn't the normal way of doing business, not by a long shot.

Of course, the farther north we flew, the more rugged the terrain. There were rather significant rock outcroppings up near the DMZ. There was one just outside Da Nang called Monkey Mountain. Whenever we flew over it, it really zonked our morale, because we'd always see wreckage of aircraft that had flown into that sucker.

10 September 1968. The day I flew up into the tiger's jaw big-time. Setting the example, pulling hot pad duty just like I wanted my men to do it. Each squadron rotated the duty, keeping two aircraft armed, fueled, wired up, and ready to go with crews within minutes of the claxon. On station at five in the morning in all our flight gear. Start the aircraft, shut it down, get it set up for fast start. Five- to twelve-hour stints, depending on the threat. Waiting for a call from anyone who might be in trouble. Hot pad. Immediate reaction to vicious firefights on the ground in the field. Whenever the tiger growled, we listened. The claxon kept on screaming as we grabbed our stuff and sprinted like crazy out to our waiting Phantoms. By the time we were strapped in, we had both engines running. It was a practiced routine. Preset switches. The RIO handled radio information as to what the target and situation were. And if it was a really hot mission, our backup crew played twin hot pad crew—and maybe even other aircraft—all of us turning and burning. Our goal was to be airborne within four minutes from the time the claxon blared.

This was a hot one. Marine recon troops were pinned down deep in the DMZ, twenty miles north of the Rock Pile, near An Khe. Target: fifteen miles into North Vietnam. The plane captain was waiting. Up the footholds into the cockpit. External power, and the cockpit was reborn. Gyros went frenetic; dials danced, while the telelight panel told the conditions and positions of the aircraft's systems. She's hot, ready to go.

Throttles out of the cut-off position. The RIO and I became an instant team, cross-checking systems as we began to roll. Half-flaps for takeoff. Boundary layer valves open. Engine air ducts to the leading edge of the wings added energy to the upper wing surface air. We checked our wingman's aircraft. He checked ours. We were both in apple pie shape. I bobbed my head, released the brakes, and nudged the throttles up to military. Another nod of the head. Afterburner.

The Phantom roared. Initial climb, cruise. Combat formation. Target acquisition. Forward air controller flying around down below us doing his thing, down among the enemy as he pinpointed our targets with white smoke rockets. Dangerous stuff, but glad he was there.

The tiger's jaw opened wide.

We took some pretty heavy fire on our first pass on target. It looked like an instant black cloud with lightning for a center. I rolled in on my second pass, singsonging MK-84 five-hundred-pound bombs on top of some people on the ground. Although unfortunate, they weren't passive. They nailed us with hot 37mm rapid fire as I pulled my nose up through the horizon. I felt the hit. The F-4 shuddered, mortally wounded.

"Oh, shit," I growled.

"What's wrong?" Ed Edelen, my backseater, replied.

"I think we took a hit."

I was glad it hadn't been 90mm fire. It would've torn the airplane apart and us with it. We were in deep kimchi.

I felt comfortable with Ed, my radar intercept officer, in the backseat. We were a team and had flown together in the early 1950s. I broke for the water, as we'd been trained to do, because it's by far the safest area when you're over North Vietnam. Just as we made our break, our left engine caught fire. The empaneled fire light winked on.

"Boss?" Ed's voice was a bit strained.

"Yeah?"

"Let's make a run for the DMZ. It's about three miles closer."

Enough said. I cranked the Phantom over and headed for the DMZ. It looked as if we'd be home free, but halfway there, the right engine caught fire. I figured, what the hell, the left engine's been burning longer than the right one, so I shut off its fuel.

As the right engine burned, I began to lose some of my hydraulic system. It was hard to fight the panic, the feeling that said punch the hell outta this airplane 'cause you gotta know that here's two guys sitting in a goddamned airplane that's on fire and the only alternative is to punch out. But the alternative seemed more grim at the moment. It meant punching out over North Vietnam. Everybody knew what that meant—an unwanted check-in at the Hanoi Hilton for the rest of the war. So we elected to stay with the airplane.

I climbed to about eighteen thousand feet. Figuring to go for broke, I relit the number-one engine. I figured, if it's gonna burn, let her burn, or let 'em blow. I wanted speed in order to get us back into South Vietnam.

My last hydraulic system went haywire just as we crossed into South Vietnam. I dropped my emergency ram air turbine (RAT), and that gave me just a zip's worth of hydraulic fluid—enough for a modicum of control. It was about that time that I knew the control stick had frozen. I had absolutely no control over the airplane. I could hear her breaking apart as the turbine blades in the engines ground into their own special oblivion.

"Ed," I yelled over the intercom, "we're out of Schlitz here. Let's go."

"Gee, I really hate to do this, Skipper," Ed moaned.

"Ed, in about ten seconds, you're gonna be talking to yourself, because I'm getting outta this motherfucker."

We were zinging down through channels of air until we had eaten up 10,000 feet at better than 450 miles per hour. I was looking back at Ed to make sure his seat worked.

Ed didn't hesitate. "Here we go," he yelled as he pulled the ejection seat handle. His canopy separated, the seat fired, and he punched out. I looked over my shoulder and saw that he'd cleared the aircraft, then I punched out. But I was in an awkward position. I didn't feel it then, but I'd sustained some real hurt. I guess I was hypnotized by the automatic sequence involved in punching out of a stricken airplane. I grabbed the ejection seat curtain. Pulled. Legs harnessed. Shoulder harness locked in. Canopy blew; seat fired up the ejection rail. Drogue chute stablilized the seat. Main chute popped. Oxygen working.

I mentally froze, waiting for the parachute to open. When it did, I had some relief, but it's a terrifying experience to be hanging there in space on a piece of silk.

Some things began to function. I pulled out my emergency radio, set it on emergency beeper, hung it on one wrist, then wrestled out my .38 and wrapped the thong around my other wrist. I tried transmitting on the radio but could hear nothing, so I just left it on emergency signal.

Then I looked down and saw that I was headed for a rice paddy. Not far away, I saw a Vietnamese guy running as hard as he could toward my landing place. There were other people working in the fields, all looking up at me. Some began running, too. Panic welled. For a few moments, I thought they were taking potshots at me. I looked back at the first man still running like crazy toward my landing place. My brain wanted to define him. Label him friend or condemn him as enemy. So I tried to maneuver my chute away from that place, away from the rice paddy and the running man. But as I maneuvered the chute, it went into partial collapse. Everything inside me froze again. Somewhere in my head, I heard the words come loud, clear, and with absolute conviction. "Fuck it," they said. "I ain't gonna touch that anymore."

I landed in the midst of the rice paddy, up to my waist in the mud and guck. My revolver dropped into the guck, its thong still wrapped around my wrist. Not without a little anger, I pulled it out. I saw that I couldn't shoot it because the barrel was jammed with the muck. And I could see that Vietnamese man still running hard toward me. Running as if his life depended upon getting to where I was. I slushed and splashed toward the dikes that surrounded the rice paddy. About two feet high and four to six feet wide. I got down behind them, trying desperately to hide while I tracked that running man.

I heard it first, then saw it rising over the horizon and the verdant tree line. A Marine CH-46 helicopter glinted in the vapid air, pulsating, looking for all the world like a bulbous, three-legged frog. There was something wonderful and at the same time horrific about it—huge rotor blades whomping the acrid currents of air, sounding as if they were singing the Marine hymn in a kind of "do-wop" fashion. I was ready to do a little sing-along of my own in one hot, little minute.

The helicopter set down about a hundred yards away from my position. I maneuvered my body, trying to put those rice paddy dikes between myself and that guy I'd seen running toward me. A peek over the dirt parapet confirmed it. He was still coming, getting closer and closer now, running as if his very heart would burst. So I hunkered down. My brain switched into a kind of overdrive. I figured that if that running person was really a bad guy, the .50-caliber machine gun positioned on station in the side of the CH-46 would take him out.

Then I noticed that the guys in the helicopter were starting to run toward me—the crew chief, yet. So I figured that there was no immediate danger. Sluicing, splashing, slipping in the guck, I was finally up and running. It turned out that this man I thought was such a threat was only after the silk in my abandoned parachute. Silk pants for a year.

I ran toward the helicopter at full tilt, running in a kind of semicircular route to be able to dash into its rear ramp. In I went at full speed—stumbling, falling, sliding into the thing—until I was right up to the front end, where I looked into the smiling faces of a white pilot and a black copilot.

I guess I was somewhat infamous in-country—the only black lieutenant colonel commander of a Marine fighter squadron—with a reputation for running a tight ship. So they knew who I was. My squadron emblem, they knew, was Black Knight, my call sign, Bloods. Maybe because of those connections, and especially the Bloods civil rights inference, the black copilot turned to me.

"Right on," he enthused, smiling broadly. "Right on, Black Knight." He gave me the old black power salute. The inappropriateness of the gesture in the moment set me off.

"Captain," I scowled, "will you get this fucking thing off the ground? Later for all that black power shit."

Truth be told, we were extremely lucky that day. Another helicopter picked up Ed Edelen. Both choppers had been doing medical evacuations and had just dropped off some troops when they spotted us still hanging in our parachutes. They set us down at the nearest aid station, where a doctor assessed that nothing was broken.

Worrying about ourselves wasn't exactly what was on our minds in that setting. We'd be sore for a few days from the firing of the ejection seat and the fury of the chute in the driving air when we bailed out. We were lucky to be alive. What really held our attention was what was going on in that medical triage unit. Wounded troops everywhere. On stretchers. Arms and legs gone. Dead, dying troops. Guys crying. Guys screaming, extremities swathed in bandages.

We were alive and damned glad to be walking around. It was time to get back to the war. I didn't know it then, but my imagined demise was big news on the radio nets around the Nam.

"Did ya hear?"

"What?"

"They got the Black Knight, man."

"Yeah?"

"Yep. Shot the sumbitch right on down. Whoa. Ain't that a bitch, now."

16: More Tiger

"Hey, Doc," I said with a laugh. "Tell you what. You just get me a jeep. I don't need to be examined any further. I'm fine. My backseater's fine. Just take us to the nearest helicopter strip, and we'll work it out from there."

In actuality, I wasn't as fine as I thought. Things would manifest themselves later, but for the moment, all I thought I had was a sore nose, the ridge of which had been sliced by the visor as I exited the aircraft. Nothing more. Certainly nothing of consequence, I thought.

I guess in deference to my rank, we were given a jeep. When we arrived at the helicopter strip, the 1st Marine Aircraft Wing band was putting on a show for the guys at Dang Ho.

"Goddamn, they sent the band out to congratulate you," my exalted ego said.

It wasn't so. Not by a long shot. The commander feted us with a beer, called up a flight for us, and sent us back to Da Nang Air Base. A military transport ship flew us to Chu Lai.

Our group commander, Col. Norm Courley, met and congratulated us on our safe return and took us back to our quarters in his jeep. Several members of the squadron were also there to greet us. In the squadron area all of our flight gear was restored. My pistol, for example, which I'd dropped into the mud in the rice paddy, was taken immediately by the armorer to be cleaned to make sure it didn't get corrosion pits. All of our flight gear had to be repacked.

We finally had a chance to get cleaned up a bit after the ordeal. We heard that there was a USO show coming through the base that night, so we went to the officers' club to see it. The master of ceremonies immediately gave Ed and me a welcome back. Everybody in the club stood up and roared. The sound was so lusty, it seemed to rattle the thatched roof of the open-air building, held up by four wall supports around the exterior. We proceeded to get shit-assed drunk. A grand time was had by all.

The club was big enough to accommodate most of the crews from the three squadrons. It served hot dogs and hamburgers, steaks every now and then, and, of course, booze. It was a place to cool off, once you came in from a mission—like tonight. As often as not, there would be a floor show. They were all kind of crappy. But we were desperate. If they'd put a snake up on the stage and it moved to the music, it would've gotten a standing ovation. Sometimes we'd get an Australian show. We'd get one of those "big shows" about every six weeks. War does have its brighter moments.

Ed and I thought that we'd survived the bailout all right, but we had to be examined by our physician at Chu Lai. His examination showed that we were both beaten up a lot more than either of us thought. We'd been simply running on adrenaline, not really feeling all the cuts and bruises. After that examination, we were awarded Purple Heart medals, for wounds received in a combat action. I had to step in quickly, though, to prevent messages of our mishap to be transmitted to my next of kin, especially my mother, which would've unduly worried her. I was just in the nick of time, as casualty reporting was moving right along.

CASUALTY MESSAGE 18SEP68. SEVEN HOSTILE CASUAL-TIES. LCOP G. A. BINFORD (HMM-362, MAG-16.) 1MAW 8 MILES SOUTH OF DANANG AB, QUANG NAM PROV - CREW CHIEF OF CH-46 ON MEDEVAC MSN WHICH RECEIVED HOS-TILE SA FIRE ENTERING LZ - PFC T. L. GRIFFIN, GUNNER OF CH-46 BACK STATION; PETERSEN, F. E. LTCOL 058792/7521 VMFA 314, MAG 13 18SEP68 - 6 MILES SOUTH OF CHU LAI AB, QUANG TIN PROVINCE, RVN. A/C HIT BY AW FIRE, FORCING PILOT TO EJECT. COND/PROG: GOOD. DIAG: IRRITATION OF RIGHT HIP. TREATED AND RETURNED TO DUTY. DO NOT, REPEAT, DO NOT NOTIFY NEXT OF KIN.

I thought I'd be flying the next day, just to show the troops that they had to hang in there. But the experience, both mentally and physically, had taken its toll. Edelen was beaten up a lot more than I was for some reason. He could barely stand. I took a day off, lay in the sun, and contemplated my navel. This is a helluva way to make a living, I thought.

What bruises we had were attributable not so much to the monumental jerk we got when the parachute opened but to the shenanigans of the ejection seat, which fired our bodies up and out of the airplane by putting about 25 g's on them. It was from that experience that I ultimately was to receive three major operations on my back, hip, and knee.

But it was really nice to be back in the harness, so to speak. I'd always admired the group commander's panache. We all called him "Animal Lead," because that's what he had put on the side of his F-4B, right behind VMFA-314: "Animal," and right under that, in slightly bigger letters, "Col. Norm Courley CO MAG 13." If you were flying high and handsome and knew where to look on the tippy-top of his aircraft's tail, you'd see "00" (we called them double nuts) and you knew it was the group commander zipping by.

Pretty soon, another F-4B Phantom was assigned me, and I followed suit. Just like Courley's lead, I had my call sign high on the side of the fuselage. "Blood," and under that, "Lt. Col. Frank Petersen CO VFMA-314." High up on its tail rode "01"—for squadron commander. Made me proud every time I strolled out and saw that. Little stuff, but it was one helluva morale booster. (The high tail surfaces of aircraft flown by executive officers bore the numerical designation "02," and operations officers, "03." Status in the hinterlands.) By the time our eyes drifted down the side of the airplane to see the Black Knight emblem—the black helmet against the gray background, the red plume flaring—we knew we were part of something damned special.

It's one thing to think you're a hotshot commander and aviator, but you simply wouldn't be effective in either role without other people to support you. My executive officer, Harry Ziegler, was one of the best. He did all the administrative work while I flew off into combat daily, but when his time came to be out there on target, he did not shrink from the combat. Another was Capt. Bernie Schmidt, my S-1 (personnel) officer. Quiet, somewhat studious, like most of the officers, in the upper 20 percent of my airplane drivers. John Herring, my S-2 (intelligence), was a little withdrawn. Then there was my eventual inheritor of the executive officer slot, Maj. E. R. Black, when Harry Z. went home. We all called him "Serb"—and he, too, was one of the best. Slightly built and serious, as in grim, Serb flew the missions, bore in on the target, and did everything. Absolutely qualified when it came to getting the job done.

Other names jump into my memory from time to time. Hinkle and Redford. Fred Shober, my maintenance officer, who'd been with me for years and years. Here at Chu Lai, he did one helluva job keeping our airplanes in the air. There was open communication between us and, as a consequence, we were close.

My memories of Fred are bittersweet now. We'd been warriors together—just real brothers in war, so to speak. Later in our careers, Fred was killed in a midair collision off the coast of North Carolina in an F-4B as he and another F-4B were flying head-to-head intercept under radar control at night. A misreading of the altimeter by a thousand feet led to the collision at the combined speeds of mach 2. An airline pilot in the vicinity saw "a bright ball of flame." We didn't even recover wreckage. I wish I could have warned him somehow.

One morning, not long after, we were in the hot pad bunker and I heard a loud boom. It sounded as if a rocket had come in, so we all rolled over and hit the deck. There were four of us. A major, a captain, a lieutenant, and me. Our eyes grew large as we looked over one another. We didn't know what that noise was. I thought I'd have a little fun with the lieutenant in the crowd.

"Junior man, go out and see what that noise was all about," I commanded.

The lieutenant blanched. Panic welled in his eyes. The skin grew taut on his face. Taking a huge breath, he leapt up and disappeared outside. Presently, he returned.

He reported that our sister squadron had been arming some air-to-air Sidewinder missiles. The hot plug on one had cooked, and that sucker went off and flew from his revetment, ricocheted off the top of our revetment, exploded, and sprayed the entire area with shrapnel. It so happened that I had been negotiating with that particular squadron commander (who was a buddy) in reference to an airplane swap. We both wanted some replacement aircraft coming in, and we had settled on what we thought was a fair split.

At staff meeting the next day, Colonel Courley, the group commander, was asked various questions about the status of operations. Solemnly, I raised my hand.

"Sir," I began, "I've agreed to the stipulations with regard to the incoming aircraft, on one condition. It's really a request from the officers and men in my squadron."

"What's that, Frank?"

"Well," I chortled, "we don't mind sharing the missions—we'll even take the dirtiest missions—but Bob Norton's people and Norton [the other squadron commander] have got to stop shooting at us. Furthermore, if Norton will agree to stop shooting at me, I'll give him the airplane he wants."

A light moment. Good for a few chuckles.

By 10 November 1968, I was heavy into the tiger's jaw again, leading an aircraft division on a barrier air patrol (BARCAP) mission. Seems the Navy had a little trouble getting their birds off their carriers. So we were given the mission to help ensure that they could do it and do it safely.

That meant we had to fly from Chu Lai all the way up to Hanoi and provide a fighter air patrol for the Navy attack aircraft that were coming into Hanoi. It was the kind of mission that could keep us in the air for four to five hours, and it called for some pretty tricky flying in between. First, it was tracking down the all-important tanker for refueling on our way to and from station off Hanoi.

The tanker had taken off long before we did. He tooled along at around five thousand feet on his outbound course. Once airborne, we began to run him down at about three miles per minute. Before we knew it, we were on him. Our fuel gauges told us we'd better fill up now or abort the BARCAP mission. We slid up behind and below the tanker, then checked in. Silently, we went through the drill, hooked up, one per side, plugged in, took a deep drink, then withdrew, sliding out to station keep while the second section completed the procedure. That done, the entire flight slid off to the right while the tanker continued its wide orbit.

Orbiting menacingly on station, we maneuvered high, wide, and handsome. Suddenly, we could see the Skyhawks coming, sliding by below us. Blustering, we rode it out, our fingers crossed, because we were really bluffing; putting up a radar image to fool the North Vietnamese. There was such a paucity of air-to-air weaponry that we flew these missions without missiles. We figured the Vietnamese never knew. It was enough, we thought, to make them think they'd be in for one helluva fight if they decided to come up to the attack. It was almost time to go home, hit that tanker, then scarf up a hot dog in the little makeshift officers' club and wash it down with a beer.

Then it happened. The voice of the shipboard radar controller brought us all to attention.

"Black Knight One, this is Crown. I've got two targets, bearing zero-two-five for sixty-five and sixty-eight nautical miles, climbing through angels one-zero [ten thousand feet] heading southeast at mach 2. Negative squawk."

The guy's voice was colorless, matter-of-fact. He wasn't trying to win an Academy Award, but what he'd just told us made our livers quiver. It was almost certainly a couple of MiG fighters, coming up to mess around—closing on us at more than eight miles per second. We got the blips coming down on us from our shipboard controller, and here we were, sitting out there over all that water without any air to air. Adrenaline surged.

We went to the book and continued the charade. Just as we were about to break into our attack positions, the MiGs did a 180-degree turnaround, a split-S maneuver, and headed back to Hanoi.

"Whew." And, "Damn." Adrenaline levels sank rapidly. We hooked up with that tanker on our way home and were pretty darned glad to see Chu Lai one more time.

The year 1968 was tough all over, including Vietnam. Being a squadron commander who flew missions daily, responsible for the whole shooting match, was tough enough, but those were cut and dried things. They could be defined, seen, touched. Within a certain context, they were things you could usually control. But the race issue within the Corps and all across the military began to be a large issue indeed and sometimes defied control. A Marine killed at Pendleton. Fraggings. Later, an aircraft carrier taken off line because of racial friction and outbreaks aboard ship.

The race issue at Chu Lai could wear you down if you weren't careful. It was quickly becoming a war within a war.

My plane captain was a black Marine sergeant. Although not many people around knew it, he was the leader of a new organization among the black troopers who called themselves the Mau Mau. In addition to the sergeant were about six or seven other black Marines and, on Chu Lai proper, a significant number of lower ranking black Marines.

The Mau Mau leader and a few cohorts decided to test me.

"Colonel?" my plane captain grunted as he stood in front of my desk. Medium height, he was darkly swarthy and exceedingly muscular. His jaw muscles twitched. Several of his lieutenants stood at his back.

"Yes, Sergeant? What can I do for you?"

"Sir, I'm the leader of the Mau Mau in these parts. I've come to request that we be allowed to paint our hootches black, red, and green—to show our African heritage and our significance. Those are our colors."

Everyone had noticed the spawning of the black power flags and black power salutes. Now, this—hootches painted black and red and green. We regarded each other for a long moment.

"Look, Sergeant," I began, "this is one squadron. I understand what your personal thoughts are about this. But if you feel that you want to paint your hootches those colors, I must alert you to the fact that when the rockets come in, they have to have something to aim at. Those huts just might make one helluva good aiming point. Now," I went on, "you've also got to realize the situation that puts me in. As the first black commander of a tactical organization of squadron size in the history of the United States Marine Corps, you're telling me to support you in something that's going to alienate the rest of the troops from you. What is the bigger issue here? For you to live in a red, black, and green hut, or for this squadron, under a black man, to operate successfully?"

The feet shuffled a bit. Torsos bobbled. Inhaled air rattled nostrils. The sergeant spoke first.

"Well, you know, boss, they're always fucking with us, and we just need to let them know that we are in power."

"Fellas," I responded, "I'm just telling you what the issues are."

We went back and forth a few more times. In the end, they gave me their total support. But they had to know where I was coming from. Combat effectiveness was the name of the game. A fragmented force, regardless of the reason, just wouldn't cut it, especially not in my squadron.

The word seemed to spread like wildfire throughout I Corps that "there was one there." A black, of field-grade rank. And that, I suppose, is why a black kid came down from the front to see me not long after.

Sitting in my tent one day, I heard the sergeant major's voice explode stridently.

"I'm sorry, troop. You can't go in there."

"Yeah," came the almost gutteral reply, "but I got to see the colonel."

I stuck my head out, took in the picture of a black Marine—dusty, big, and, under the circumstances, ugly, his rifle slung over his shoulder.

"Sergeant Major," I said, "I'll see that troop."

The trooper's eyes zeroed in on me. I saw anger and desperation written there. "Yassuh, you is the one." The words rushed now, tumbled over one another. "You got to help me. They fuckin' wid me."

"Son, have a cuppa coffee," I tried, hoping to get him to settle down a bit. A lance corporal, he was grunt Marine all the way.

"You know, Colonel, they been fuckin' wid me evah since ah been oveh heah, and it's got to the point where if I don't get some help, I'm gonna kill somebody."

His statement rang true. That kind of thing happened often in the Nam.

"Well," I said, "sit down, son. Take a load off. Tell me, what's going on?"

He took a long breath.

"Well, suh," he said, "I guess it all started when I shot the lieutenant."

Oh, shit, I said to myself. And then out loud I said, "Sergeant Major, you'd better get back in here."

As far as we could determine, the kid had been harassed ever since he'd arrived in Vietnam. He couldn't find anyone to talk to, so this was his way of letting out his frustrations. He hadn't shot the lieutenant in anger. It had been an accident. It had to have been an accident, because the kid was still walking around. Brothers in the lower ranks caught hell—people in authority were really tough on them. That was a given.

So I called his commanding officer and arranged to have an interview. We got it all ironed out. And in the nick of time, too, because that kid was really getting ready to shoot someone. A tour of the jail down in Long Binh—the LBJ—would bear out what the corporal was trying to say. More than 80 percent of its occupants were black.

The Corps needed to police itself, and quickly. There was, among the rank and file, no real understanding between black and white. The typical frontline unit was somewhere around 80 percent black—high school dropouts, caught up in the "street sweeps," as they called it—150,000 of them. Caught in the draft. Their commanding officers, normally first lieutenants and second lieutenants, also fresh-caught in the Marine Corps, all had college degrees. No meeting of the minds there at all. Putting the city with the streets. Suburbs with the streets. That, in my view, is where loads of the trouble and friction came from.

This was certainly one area in which I maintained an intense interest, even though it could become a tiring one. I always wanted to stay ahead of what was going on and, if possible, be able to anticipate what would happen next. Part of my running a tight ship was getting hands-on and dirty in some of the lower levels of the command. To see me as a commander would be to see me unable to relax.

It was impossible for me to relax, and situations like the rearing of the ugly visage of racism made life decidedly upbeat—often more than I'd bargained for. My feeling that someone out there was waiting to get me was a basic, gut feeling. Now I realize it was because of my race, my position, the fact of being first. The fact that, if I were to fail, it would be an indicator that "I told you that you couldn't handle it." So I couldn't fail—I had to succeed. I felt that it wasn't about me but about those who would follow me.

Combat zones have a way of jerking your chain. Bringing you screeching back to the reality at hand. Like the day one of my pilots and his RIO came up missing in action.

The pilot was close to me because we'd gone through training together before we went to Vietnam. Very aggressive, a skilled pilot, but he was frustrated because I wouldn't immediately make him a section leader.

"Hey, when are you gonna let me do it, Chief?" he wanted to know. He was so persistent that I relented and agreed to check him out.

"Okay," I replied, "I'll put myself on your wing and you take this mission."

So off we went, and he turned out to be a great airplane driver. He did well.

"Okay," I enthused after we returned to base, "now you're a section leader."

Well, he and his RIO were flying a mission in Laos with a guy named Manfred Reitsch. The drill called for night dive-bombing. On cue, he and company made his call sign rolling in. They never came out.

I was awakened at about five-thirty in the morning when Manfred came back and gave me the news. I got in an airplane immediately and flew to the same spot where they'd gone in. We couldn't even see a hole in the canopy of the green jungle below. Even the Air Force air/sea rescue guys over at Taklei never found anything. No beepers. Nothing.

The backseater was the son-in-law of a Congressman from Albany, New York. I'd have to make that trek when I went home. To see his relatives. To console, try to heal a bit after the fact. I wasn't looking forward to it.

That was the only crew I lost in combat. It hurt.

17: Swan Song

Near the end of my tour as commanding officer of VFMA-314, I suddenly became ill with serious flulike symptoms. After a few days of feeling out of it and being confined to bed, I began to function again. I missed the fight, the roar of the afterburners, the sound of combat. Hell, let's face it, I missed being out there where the war was. This feeling won't last long, I thought.

I was right. About eight o'clock in the evening near the end of this "feeling bad" episode, Harry Ziegler, my executive officer (XO), came by to brief me on what was taking place out where the combat glittered.

We'd just been tasked with a mission, Harry advised, "where we're going to fly way up north and hit a target, and the A-6 fighter drivers requested that we come up and help because they had taken so much fire when they attacked the area before." They wanted us to come busting into that area, do a little fire suppression, and clear the way for their attack so the path to their targets would be relatively free of hostile fire.

I was up in a flash.

"Okay, Harry, I'll lead this one," I enthused, thinking that the mission sounded really interesting. At any rate, it beat the hell out of being stretched out in the sack feeling sorry for myself.

This was a night mission, which, in spite of my enthusiasm, I knew was usually not fun. This one was to be no exception. Of course, I'd been out of the cockpit for several days. The good sign was that the weather was officially clear. After all the necessary briefings and preparations, we were airborne, firing out to harass Charlie.

The hell of it was that we were going so far north, with such a heavy load of ordnance, that we had to refuel en route. I'll never forget that night. About a third of the way to target, we met our tankers at about 10,000 feet to plug in for more fuel. Things became a bit strange almost immediately. As we refueled, the combined weight of the fuel and ord-nance really weighed us down, so we tapped afterburners just to stay on the refueling hose. It had been a real challenge just finding the tanker in the dark, but to have to tap those burners in addition was a real kick in the butt. As our afterburners flared, they gave off an unbelievably in-tense bright fire in the dark—a large version of an acetylene torch be-ing lit. The bright light they made with each "tap" screwed up our night vision. Blind for a moment, I was flying one of my country's most ex-pensive fighters into the fuel drogue of a multimillion dollar tanker.

Well, the whole thing was, at the very least, potentially explosive. Our basic engine power simply wasn't sufficient to hold us on that hose to continue the refueling connection. Too heavy. It was a cat and mouse thing. We were the cats. The tanker drogue was the mouse. The need for concentration overwhelmed. Light the afterburners. Close in. Come out of afterburner. The awesome, potentially deadly drift backward and the slow drift away from the tanker and the precious fuel. A deadly ada-gio in the sky. A dance, a playground thing. Ride the seesaw; do it again.

Touch and go, but we did it until everybody got a drink of that pre-cious nectar. Then we unplugged, regrouped the guys, and climbed back to about 25,000 feet of altitude all the way to the target in the northwest corner of Vietnam. Blood rushed as we primed for the attack.

We rolled in at 25,000 feet, pickled high—at about 10,000 feet—so we'd get a good, wide spread of ordnance on the ground. When we pulled out of our attack mode, it was like diving into a giant fishbowl. We pressed the attack forward, flying on instruments. This was no pin-point bombing. The ultimate need was for saturation time-delay bomb-ing. Cluster bombs—covering one hell of an area.

Somehow, we all got separated after the attack. There was no time to fiddle around in order to regroup, so we boogied out of there. Couldn't hang around and risk missing our refueling point on the way home. Enemy fire tried to target us, but we were so high that we were difficult to find. By the time they really opened up, we were well on our way, and our delayed-fuse ordnance began to wreak havoc. The A-6s from Da Nang came screaming in on top of them.

We made it back to the tankers, and refueling this time was no prob-lem. Everyone made it home. I was damned glad to get back home.

That was the hairiest mission I flew during my whole tour.

Norm Gourley, my air group commander, called me into his office to give me some good news. I needed some about now.

"Frank," he said, "at the end of the year and for the first time, the Marine Corps will be awarding honors to squadrons it selects as the best fighter squadrons in the Corps."

This was the prestigious Robert M. Hanson Award, which was given to recognize the most outstanding fighter/attack squadron of the year. All Marine fighter squadrons, regular or reserve, and including air group detachments, were eligible. The prize was a permanent trophy with a winged man on a pedestal bearing the Marine Corps emblem. The Marine Corps Aviation Association presents this Fighting Hawk trophy at the group's annual reunion. The trophy was established in memory of Capt. Robert M. Hanson, USMC fighter ace and Medal of Honor winner, killed in World War II after shooting down twenty-five enemy aircraft. The trophies are sponsored by the LTV Aerospace and Defense Corporation.

"You've got to get this report in, Frank," said Gourley. "I think your squadron has a pretty good chance to win this award."

This was exciting. I hadn't really thought anything about it. Then, after we'd looked at some of the records and statistics—Christ, I realized that we'd had a beautiful round. While I was commanding officer, we'd lost just one bird (and we don't think that was due to ground fire) and, of course, my bird when I'd gotten shot down.

So we filled in the requested information in terms of what the squadron had accomplished, then crossed our fingers and sent it to the Marine Corps Division of Aviation. We went back to the business of prosecuting the war and almost forgot about it.

In February 1969, I'd been a commanding officer for an unusually long time—since May 1968. A normal tour as commander of a Marine fighter squadron in Vietnam was usually six months. I'd reached that pinnacle in November 1968. Another commander would have been designated for another six months so everyone would have a shot at combat command.

I was really getting run down physically; I'd flown well over two hundred missions. And the hell of it was, I probably would've flown even more, except that the racial strife began to take up optional time. I'd lost one crew, and that ate at me. Although I hated even thinking of giving up that command, the whole thing was beginning to grind away at me.

Norm Gourley was not unaware. We discussed the issue.

"You know, Frank," he started, "we normally have about a six-month rotation. But if you want, you can stay on as commanding officer of VFMA-314 until you finish your tour here in Vietnam."

"Well, Colonel," I averred, "I don't think that would be fair and—well, what the hell—the squadron's riding high now, but just how long can you ride high?" Actually, command of VMFA-314, although tiring, was a thing that kept the blood pulsing, so I thought I'd stay put, at least until summer.

Colonel Gourley smiled, then offered me several jobs in spite of my decision.

"Frank," he said, "you've done a hell of a good job. You've flown some one hundred eighty missions, and your squadron was this, that, and the other. You were shot down. Where do you want to go?" he countered.

I thought about it for a moment. "Okay," I said with a laugh, "I'll take a shot at the DASC."

DASC (Direct Air Support Center) was the Air Force control agency in I Corps. Being a liaison officer sounded like fun. Interesting. In essence, I would be the Marine representative of our tactical air commander on the employment of Marine air at a joint operations center. The center served as a clearinghouse through which aircraft could be diverted from other missions or provide direction to other aircraft on the ground already in alert status as the tactical air and combat situations required [Momyer: *Air Power in Three Wars,* p. 260–61]. Simply put, I would be the Marine liaison officer to the Air Force direct operations center. My job would be to allocate missions as targets were generated, making sure that everyone got their fair share.

All that was good news, except that the war kept calling us back into the blue skies and putting the good stuff on the back burners. It was 28 February 1969, and I focused on a mission assignment in which I launched as section leader of two Phantom F-4B aircraft. The job was provision of support to two Marine companies engaged in combat with a large enemy force near Dong Hoi.

We maneuvered into position for the attack, located the target, and, despite big-time enemy ground fire—and pretty poor visibility, I might add—we jumped on the bad guys with both feet.

Our troops were pinned down on the east side of a road. The bad guys had them surrounded. Nobody could get to them. A forward air controller was orbiting to the south of us, pointing the way. We were carrying nape and snake (napalm and bombs with delayed-action fuses). I can remember all of it as if it were yesterday. I rolled in on the target the way I liked to, doing an inverted roll, doing a complete roll underneath, then coming back over, to give them less tracking. We used our time-worn tactic. Opened up the hole with our airborne rockets

(HVARs), then, while they were ducking and dodging, got in low and hit them with the napalm. It was effective.

This was a great break from duty at the DASC, which was sort of a let-down. The living conditions were sweet and all that, but there was really no challenge.

That's about where things were the day the word came down from on high that VMFA-314 had been selected as the top fighter squadron in the whole United States Marine Corps. That's a pretty darn good shot. Then I discovered that the Corps was going to send me back to the States to receive the award in conjunction with the annual awards banquet of the American Fighter Pilots Association that was to be held in Houston. That's when I really got excited. The award was split with Herb Lundine (the officer I replaced), because he had the unit the first six months of 1968 and I commanded it the last six months of the same year. The award was more than a high point. It was a little bit of heaven.

I called all the men in VFMA-314 together and rejoiced with them—hoisting a few in celebration of the event. I called Ellie in California to share the news about the award. The banquet in Houston would honor top aviators in both the Navy and the Marine Corps. Ellie also received notification from Washington, D.C., about the event and award. About mid-March, she wrote a letter to my mother and family passing on the good news and assuaging concerns about my having been shot down.

Dear Family:

A real fast note to let you know that I just received a phone call from Washington, D.C., stating that Buddy will be flown to the States to receive a special award for his squadron, VMFA-314. The award will be presented in Houston on March 20. He should arrive in Calif. on the eighteenth, so hopefully he will have some time to spend here. All very exciting and so glad to have some good news at long last. Don't know much about all this and neither did the man who called, but he did say it was quite an honor and that it should be an impressive ceremony.

Buddy had just called on Saturday and requested that I write to you and tell you he was fine—I had just written back to tell him to write to you himself. I know I can tell you he's fine but you'd rather hear it from him. Don't know if he will be able to stop in Denver, but if he has the time you know he will—unless you all want to fly to Houston for the big event.

Would call, but at the moment I'm nearly speechless. Loads to do and think about, so I must get this to the post office before 5:00 p.m. I'm writing the same message to Hans.

Love to all, Ellie

P.S. Buddy's Purple Heart was granted as a result of his being shot down on Sept. 10. He was rescued and supposedly received no injuries. Little late to worry about it now, so aren't you glad you didn't know before? Almost over anyway, so hang on. I know—a whole lot easier said than done.

If I recall correctly, the Marine Corps flew both Ellie and me down to Houston for the award ceremony and banquet. Bob Hope and his wife were there, and I had the privilege of meeting them. They brought Herb Lundine in, too.

At first, I found the banquet rather stressful. I'd just returned from Vietnam and had gone through many, many time zones in conjunction with that—after having been in a combat zone one day—and all of a sudden I found myself sitting at a banquet table in Houston in a dress uniform. On top of that, I had one terrific headache. Alan Shepard's wife noticed that I was uncomfortable, or in some distress. More than that, I was having difficulty hearing.

"What's the problem, Colonel?" she asked.

"Terrific headache," I responded.

Mrs. Shepard, the wife of the astronaut, reached into her purse, pulled out a couple of aspirin, and gave them to me under the table.

"Here," she said, "try these. Maybe they'll help."

I was amazed at how down to earth she was, given her husband's fame. I just thought that was great. The aspirin helped; in fact, they cleared up the pain enough so that I could get through the rest of the evening. That recovery from where I'd been was a pretty good ride.

General Barrett was the Marine Corps representative, and Lt. Gen. Frank C. Tharin made the presentation. Tharin was the deputy chief of staff, plans, and programs for the USMC. Also in attendance were the parents of Robert M. Hanson, the gentleman for whom the award was named, for his World War II exploits.

In the final analysis, although very proud and happy to have been one of the commanding officers of VMFA-314 during one of its proudest moments, I always had to go back in my mind's eye to think of the fantastic officers and Marines without whom it never would have happened.

I am certain that my counterpart CO, Herbert Lundine, felt the same way. The squadron had done herculean things. During that year, it had flown 3,830 sorties, logged more than 4,000 hours in the air, and dropped more than 8,000 tons of ordnance. Bomb damage assessment reflected 71 confirmed kills, 461 structures destroyed, 51 secondary explosions set off, 117 secondary fires, and 25 antiaircraft sites destroyed. All done against odds created by a determined enemy, the weather—sometimes seeded with great monsoons—plus the vagaries of difficult terrain, resupply, and timely troop turnover. I had flown and led more than 200 combat missions and, I am sure, Herb Lundine did his thing in combat as well. We'd run a tight, effective squadron. One in five of our troopers volunteered to extend their overseas tours under our command. A commander in a combat zone is cooking when that kind of thing happens.

Ellie and I flew back to California. I believe there was another week's leave before my return to Vietnam. No real decision had been made between us as to whether our marriage was on solid ground at that point. We discussed the issue, however, as we had done on several occasions before. There were problems. I couldn't say we were really getting along before I left for Vietnam. It was while I was there that I'd almost made up my mind that our marriage just wasn't going to work. The spark didn't seem to be there anymore.

MUTUAL VOICES
Ellie, First Wife

It was not a marriage where there was a buddy system, where I swim in my water and you swim in yours. But if I yell "trouble," you come swimming over to help me out. If I was in trouble, he was usually never around. And he felt I was never able to understand the problems that he was having in the Marine Corps. Over the years we became married against each other rather than to each other. I took upon myself his goal: his progression as the first black in the Marine Corps. I could ride on his coattails to his success. But I had to realize that would still be his success. His was a pull-up-by-the-bootstraps story. Nobody helped him. He was a very ambitious man. He had to go to every school he thought could help him climb the ladders. We were always at cross-purposes. Our values were, I think, probably a lot different.

Shortly after my return to Vietnam, I passed the command of VMFA-314 to a new commanding officer and, as planned, went up to the DASC.

But the job wasn't what I thought it would be, or was led to believe it was after talking to my predecessor.

I went from Chu Lai up to Da Nang in Vietnam and was there until the end of my tour. It was obvious that most of these Air Force guys hadn't flown combat. They had flown, instead, spotter aircraft. I remember one night in particular when an ammo barge blew up in the Da Nang harbor—or the Da Nang River—and it knocked out all the lights, flattened some buildings, and killed some people. We were stationed about a mile from there in our compound, which had previously been used by the French forces during their time in Vietnam. As the explosion reverberated across the landscape, I just rolled out and got my weapon.

I didn't know what caused the explosion. Everything was dark. I walked over to the stockade fence and climbed up. Perched there, I could see about a half block down the street. I knew that one of my buddies, a pilot with Air America, lived in that area. I thought that someone had tried to take his group out, because his was a kind of covert group. Frankly, I was worried about him.

I climbed further up the stockade fence until my head could be seen over the top. Suddenly, all hell threatened to break out.

"Who's that on the fence?" one of the Air Force guys yelled. "Somebody's trying to come over the fence."

I dropped down in a hurry, went back to my room, and went to sleep. Those guys were trigger-happy folks. I had no intention of losing my life staring over a fence at my own folks after all those combat missions I'd flown.

Life with the DASC was pretty boring after the swift, gloriously noisy, busy job of fighter squadron commander. In fact, all I seemed to do was sit at a goddamned desk, drink coffee, and look over the Air Force's shoulder. To allay the inactivity, I'd leave once a month, go down to Chu Lai, and fly more missions. That's where the action was. But I guess I did all right. The Air Force later awarded me its commendation medal.

I returned from Vietnam in July 1969. Although Ellie and I were still uncertain about the stability of our marriage, we decided to give things a try in Washington, D.C., the site of my next assignment at Headquarters, Marine Corps, as a tactical air planner/programmer in the office of the deputy chief of staff for aviation. We piddled around with the marriage for about another year or so after our arrival in Washington. Settled in a home on 16th Street in northwest Washington. But I think I knew it might be over before I went to Vietnam.

MUTUAL VOICES
Ellie, First Wife

While he was away in Vietnam, I faced some of the worst times of our entire marriage. Our marriage was going to pot, and it was in my interest to be prepared to have everything in place to be divorced in California. That was going to be most beneficial for me. I registered the cars in my name; I made sure that I'd be a California resident, and when he came back, I was just going to file for divorce. But when he came back, you know, he'd been injured, had a bad back, and he begged me—if I would go to Washington with him, I'd have a beautiful life. He didn't know I'd have a wonderful life without him. So I came back to Washington with him.

That was a bad move.

It was nice to be back among the monuments. Winter in America. Christmas with the children. The Capitol, with its huge white dome. The coming of spring again and the fragile beauty of the Japanese cherry trees setting off the magnificent Jefferson Memorial reflected in the quiet Tidal Basin. The Navy Yard Annex and work—assignment as one of the deputies in the air operations unit, dealing with aircraft purchases and long-range plans for Marine Corps aviation. I was tactical air planner/programmer for the deputy chief of staff (DCS) of aviation.

As interesting as that assignment was, I soon found that my attention to it was fractured as ghosts of my Vietnam duty began to torment me in the form of back and hip pains from the bailout after being shot down. The back and leg pain had come and gone since the accident, but now it seemed to worsen, seemingly aggravated by prolonged standing and sitting. As the chief of the Bureau of Medicine and Surgery at Bethesda Naval Hospital put it: "persisting radiating pain to the right posterior thigh . . . a right-sided posterior thigh and calf pain . . . gradually increasing." Surgeon's talk for a hairline fracture of the hip with attendant knee problems. On 10 November 1969, I was wheeled into the operating arena for surgery for a herniated disk (in the lower back at S-5), which was surgically resected by laminectomy. On 4 December 1969, I was released to limited duty for four weeks with reevaluation on 10 March 1970.

By 26 January 1970, I had completed a course designed to provide an introduction to the functional relationships and interactions between the Navy and the Department of Defense regarding acquisitions of aviation systems. A plethora of new skills enabled me to bring all of my combat and flying experience to bear as I learned more about aircraft procurement. The overview provided by the assignment was excellent.

It became obvious, for example, that you just don't go out, get into an airplane, and fly it. The whole procurement process is quite lengthy. In fact, you're buying or looking into the purchase of aircraft that might come into the fleet five years downstream.

At my job at the tactical air desk, I did a bit of everything. I worked for a while on the F-14 and Harrier projects. It was enjoyable and a really good job for an aviator: dealing with the Navy at high-level briefings, and briefing the commandant and assistant commandant on some of the intricacies of the polls and bids that we worked on. I thought I'd found a really comfortable billet, and one where I could probably flourish, all things being equal. That, however, was not to be.

General Jonas Platt (G-1) approached me one day in 1971 regarding a possible assignment shift to that of special adviser to the commandant in matters concerning procurement of Negro officers. This was being considered, General Platt noted, because the only other black Marine lieutenant colonel, Ken Berthoud—junior to me in rank, and a supply type—had initially been assigned as an assistant for recruiting but would be leaving shortly on another assignment. I'd heard the scuttlebutt, and a sixth sense warned that I might be tapped for this assignment. I didn't really want it, and I told General Platt that I didn't want to leave aviation. In fact, I was more than a little happy dealing with airplanes. It was what I was supposed to be doing, I thought.

But in the United States Marine Corps, when you're given an assignment, you might wiggle a bit in your mind, but the name of the game is to jump on the bandwagon and become effective where you've been directed. So before I could cogitate further on the matter, I found myself initially designated special adviser to the commandant for Negro officer procurement. Although I did as much as a good Marine could do and still stay out of trouble, I was dragged, kicking and screaming, into this new assignment.

Well, almost as soon as I hit the beach, I could see that a few things about the assignment had to be at least adjusted. For example, the phrase "Negro officer procurement" had to go. In my view, it connoted some sort of body purchase. Then, of course, there was the cultural "inside stuff" that majority Marines who were running the show couldn't really know—and that was that no single Negro goes into the black community (even if he represents the Marine Corps) and attempts to recruit by calling himself a "Negro procurer." My God. That's reminiscent of slavery days.

So one of the very first things I did was to have that title changed. "Minority officer selection" became the correct nomenclature for the coming effort. The second thing was to ensure that the job was expanded, so that the emphasis wasn't limited to minority officer recruitment but to provide advice on the extent of the racial problems that were seizing the services. Often I accompanied the commandant on his field trips, and I could see that these problems were very hot and heavy.

After an extensive reorganization, the office underwent further personnel changes. The commanding officer of the unit, although he was very liberal minded and knew what needed to be done, was somewhat ineffective. A nice individual, he didn't appear to be strong enough, didn't seem to have the connections or be aware of the internal maneuverings that were taking place to stymie what we were about. He was, therefore, grossly ineffective when the need arose to overcome the often artificial barriers set up to restrict our activities. Eventually, that officer retired and I was elevated to the number-one position in the shop.

It soon became apparent that I couldn't really be effective in that role while taking road trips two to three weeks in every month. Simply no way in hell. So Colonel Lederer came in to run the shop, which allowed me to function as the "outside man"—the guy who observed, advised, and was responsible for public relations for the Marine Corps within the black community, including the detection and/or solution of racial problems on Marine Corps installations.

To ensure placement of the correct emphasis on recruitment of minority officers, I pointed out to my superiors that, within the colleges, there was a population extant that could be approached; however, the need was to have minority officers as part of the recruiting team. As a result of that recommendation, the commandant of Marines, Gen. Robert E. Cushman, Jr., directed that minority officers be placed in all of the recruiting centers—especially in the large urban centers like Los Angeles, New York, and Chicago.

I was embarked on a mission unique in the annals of the Marine Corps. A black Marine Corps officer sent out with other black officers into black society and onto college campuses and Marine installations to recruit more black officers and advise solutions regarding race-related problems within the Corps. I didn't realize how special the assignment really was until I began encountering many black ex-Marines now in civilian life who remembered how racially miserable life for them had been within the Corps and who were simply flabbergasted to see a black lieutenant colonel of Marines.

As I traveled around the country, porters and cab drivers would walk up to me, their faces aglow, a kind of new hope in their eyes.

"Are you really one?" they'd almost rhapsodize. They'd never seen a black Marine officer before, especially one wearing the silver leaf of a lieutenant colonel.

The assignment lasted about a year. It was a good year, with many effective things occurring to help jump-start minority officer recruitment and find solutions to some vexatious racial problems existing in the military community. I like to think I helped somewhat in these areas. I also served as a Marine Corps representative on quite a few interservice panels discussing these issues. During this assignment, I made one trip to Europe, one to the Far East, and several throughout the United States.

But I wasn't really prepared for some of the often surprising things that awaited me as I struck off down the road as special assistant to the commandant for minority affairs.

Part Five
Attacking the Problem

18: Special Assistant for Minority Affairs to the Commandant, USMC

Our tours of college and university campuses in the United States in order to attempt recruitment of minority Marine officers were enlightening and always challenging. Confrontations with students often erupted.

"We want to know, Colonel," the rhetoric often began, with reference to Vietnam, "why blacks should be in the military in the first place." Our debates swirled around the ivied halls where the "black pride" thing was emerging—and all that rhetoric "anti" the Vietnam War. "Why are Americans fighting over there?" "Why are so many blacks involved?" We shouldn't do this; we shouldn't do that. Off campus, in the more stable civilian community, we almost always encountered respect for black Marine Corps officers. Sometimes, however, things could get pretty hot in these areas as well.

Black recruiting officers in the field would call and have me come out to speak to some of their potential constituents. One of these calls came from our guy in Seattle. Three of us were essentially walking the streets, dropping in on spots around the city and schools. Spreading the Marine Corps gospel. Our stops were usually in high schools, and also a few colleges. Later that evening, when we were just out there "showing the colors," so to speak, we were suddenly challenged by a group of vocal blacks.

"Hey, whaddya people tryin' ta do? Walkin' 'round the town tryin' ta talk somebody inta joinin' up wid some kinda Marine Corps thang?"

"Ya'll ain't nuttin. Y'ain't from 'round heah. Ain't got no bizness heah no how."

"Ummhmm. We reely oughta kick yer lil asses, tha's what."

"Ya know well as us that black folks ain't got no bizness in the military—period."

The thing was quickly becoming confrontational. Street voices. In the black part of town. Then we heard other voices of reason, which sounded pretty good to our ears under the circumstances.

"You motherfuckers," a deep voice erupted behind the badasses. "You motherfuckers don't know what in the hell you're talking about. You better leave these guys alone."

Boom. The harassment stopped as suddenly as it had begun. Black Vietnam veterans had come to our rescue and quickly put a stop to the whole thing.

Our experiences on college campuses were tolerable, with a few difficult spots here and there. First, of course, we found that the proper groundwork had to be laid before approaching a college or university. We couldn't just walk onto a campus and begin our spiel. We had to seed the territory with a group of black officers. Then we would employ a tactic developed by Capt. Jim Allen out of Los Angeles. We prepared the ground and tilled it beforehand, so to speak.

I would make a sweep by way of the state of Washington, then down to California and San Diego on one ten-day tour. When I appeared on campus, interviews on radio and television had been prearranged. I just talked and rapped about the Marine Corps and its opportunities. We found that if we went to the leaders of the various student organizations (black student unions, Chicano student unions) and made our case, things would invariably be smoother.

"We know," we'd begin, "that you folks have a bad feeling concerning the military, and specifically the Marine Corps. What we'd like to do is set up a rap session with you and some of your constituents to let you better understand the Marine Corps. To make it a more acceptable occupation for you." Once we were involved, establishment of meaningful values followed.

We could see little smiles develop across the young faces. The spiel involved both groups in at least discussing a probable game plan for the mutual good. I guess the students were always pretty respectful of me because of my rank and the fact that I had been in two wars. Tension was there, but it wasn't so unwieldy that a dialogue between them and us couldn't be established, especially if they could see that we weren't the pompous, overbearing military type. If we didn't try to support the war in Vietnam, they were always willing to hear what we had to say as long as we made sense. They would also go along with us in terms of our outlining methodologies involved in becoming a Marine officer.

I don't want to make it sound easy, because it wasn't. It was a tough sell at all of the colleges across the country. Some black, some essentially white. Oregon. Back to Washington and all over the country. Recruiting minority Marine Corps potential officer material. (Not just black men; we were recruiting from all of the minority groups.)

It was the fallout of the Marine Corps decision to meet the challenge of placement of more minority officers within its ranks. As early as 1969, the commandant of the Marine Corps had publicly ackowledged the existence of racial friction within its ranks. The paucity of black officers in the Corps was responsible in part for much of the unrest in Marine installations around the globe. Analysis of the Marine officer population in terms of comparative ratios (black to white) in the early 1970s showed one white officer for every seven white enlisted personnel, as compared to one black officer for every seventy-two black enlisted personnel. On top of that, the job codes of some black officers precluded their being assigned to troop command, thus rendering the black officer even more invisible to black enlisted personnel. Additionally, the absence of meaningful rank inhibited black officer clout. At the time, the senior black officers in the Marine Corps were lieutenant colonels, with a total of fifteen field-grade officers.

However, since the inception of the black officer recruitment program in 1967 there was a palpable increase in the black officer populations. Against a Marine Corps annual goal of a hundred minority officers, the effort yielded an annual increase of only twenty-four officers.

The emphasis on minority (primarily black) officer recruitment was not to assume that an increase in black officers would automatically bring an end to racial strife within the Corps. It would not. In fact, the Corps continued to have problems with blacks, whites, and chicanos. Animosity was rife on both sides of the racial issue—or minority affairs or human relations or whatever you wanted to call the tricky stuff. For example, it came as a surprise to some people that blacks could be as prejudiced and angry as some whites.

We were part of the Marine Corps' move to begin to attempt to change things, or try to make them better. We began to inch ahead as we visited the schools, universities, and now our own Marine Corps installations. It was a tough ball game. In some arenas, we couldn't talk about white folks and black folks without emotional outbreaks. Although Mark Whitaker [*Newsweek*, 12 November 1993, p. 52] didn't write the following until 1993, it was certainly apropos as far as what we were trying to do, for it more than succinctly described the attitudes about race we had to face.

> When it comes to discussing race, Americans might as well be watching different movies. Confronted with everything from the Reginald Denny beating trial to the Ted Danson jokes, whites see one reality; blacks see another. And the fact that both have such a hard time talking straight about their grievances only makes matters worse. How can . . . the debate [move] to more realistic—and honest—grounds? . . .

I kept saying that if we can't discuss it, we can't solve it. I kept pushing out into the rhetoric of the whole thing. We've got to realize that it's not a thing that's solved by whispering about it. We've got to grab hold of it.

Sometimes, we just had to go home and try to forget about it for a moment and face other realities. There were times I needed "home" and the peace and tranquillity that could be found there most of the time.

MUTUAL VOICES
Frank E. Petersen III, Son

Way back then I remember smoking my first cigarettes. Stole some of the old man's cigarettes and took them across the street with the hoods, I guess. Smoked and got as sick as a dog. I remember him coming over there asking those guys where they got those cigarettes. I guess he knew some of his were missing. That was one of the things I did. Another thing I did—I broke a windshield on a guy's car. Yeah. I broke a windshild. I threw a rock. I was trying to break a rock in half, and it bounced up off the ground and hit this man's window and shattered it. It must have been the heat, or whatever, it just shattered the whole windshield. The old man [my father] and the man came out and the man hollered and yelled and said I threw a rock at his car and I said I didn't. "I didn't throw anything at your car." I guess the old man finally paid for it. I guess he questioned me about it. It was an accident. He took my side, stuck up for me, told me that when I want to break rocks, go across the street in the big field and do it.

He was always there for the important stuff. He'd come through. One time we had a party. Some of the sisters were going to a party, and these guys pulled up on 16th Street in Washington and pulled a gun on some of the sisters. They ran in the house and got Dad. He went out there with nothing but his ID and said, "Look, I'm a such and so and what the hell are you doing with my daughters?" The guys got into their car and drove off. It's interesting. He's a real courageous kind of guy.

MUTUAL VOICES
Ellie, First Wife

We just were always at cross-purposes. Our values were, I think, probably a lot different. I wanted a husband and I wanted a father for my children and I wanted sort of like an additional family and he was certainly more focused on his career. People do have to sacrifice a lot to achieve. Looking back now, his career is quite an accomplishment, but it was painful at the time. I guess one of the things I said I wanted to do was go back and get the degree that I didn't get when I ran off and got married.

MUTUAL VOICES
Ernie Douglas, Topeka Friend

It was his spirit. The last time I saw him was in St. Louis. He came into a club where I was performing. And he was part of it. You know what I mean? He wasn't sitting back, being a wallflower. Get outta his way, 'cause here he come. You know. That's been his attitude. I think it's shown inasmuch as he went on to the heights of rank. Proved that he wasn't somebody that's lazy, now. Gotta get out there and get going. That was the thing I admired most about him. I knew that when he was around, something was going to happen, 'cause he wasn't gonna just sit around.

MUTUAL VOICES
Dana Charlette Petersen, Daughter, 3 September 1997

We were in Washington, D.C., it seemed, for good. I remember being really terrified in school. We'd grown up on military bases, with white neighbors. But now, we were in a black city with black neighbors, none of whom seemed to like us "because we talked white." And that wasn't all. "You think you're smart, don'tcha? You think you're cute, huh?"
My sister Gayle would get into fights. She beat up the biggest and baddest in her class. After that, they left her alone. I was the talker and shy. People would pick on me, but when they found out I was Gayle's little sister, they left me alone. That was a hard transition, made more difficult as storm clouds seemed to be gathering around our parents' marriage.

Ah, yes. Home. I guess I had known from the time I came back from Vietnam that my marriage was essentially over. We thought we'd try to inject some life into it. But a distance had come between us. A distance, in terms of emotional viability, where I thought I wanted to go with my career and her inability to keep up with me, I guess. Some of it, I think, probably was about the completion of her education. She had only one semester to go in order to complete college, but she never went back to get her degree. Instead there were many excuses. In the final analysis, I thought, the world is changing and it's time to get out there and be part of it. I always wanted my wife to make more money than I did. I don't have any hang-ups on that. Still, I mulled the matter over, not wanting to act prematurely and precipitously. But then duty called.

After about a year and a half, it became apparent that I couldn't continue with the minority recruiting and still meet the other demands of my assigned projects. We brought in a fine black officer, Solomon Hill, from Vietnam. Solomon, more than six feet tall, was exceedingly smart; he had expressed an interest in working at headquarters level, and I thought he'd be ideal as a recruiting point man. That's what we did, and we put him in charge of the minority officer recruiting program.

As wonderful as the Marine Corps' intent to bring in new minority officers was, it would, in my view, remain relatively ineffective if we couldn't increase the number of incoming minority officers for training. I thought that if we were to make a significant change in the number of minority officers recruited into the Corps, 150 men would have to be recruited per annum in order to eradicate our normal officer losses. The idea wasn't bought, nor was my recommendation that the Corps shoot for the number of black officers on deck to be around 5 percent of the total over a period of six years. I thought it a worthy goal, but the lower figure of 50 per annum was the real bottom line.

It quickly became apparent to me that if I were to remain in this race relations business in the Marine Corps, and eventually in the arenas of the other services as well, I would definitely need a "big daddy," someone of high rank to protect my back. It followed that if I did my job correctly, I'd step on too many toes, and if I told the truth, I'd pick up enemies like metal filings to a magnet.

I suppose I was lucky in that Gen. Ed Wheeler wrote my fitness report, and I could talk frankly with my immediate boss, Colonel Lederer, and advise when I thought he was about to make a mistake in these sensitive areas. I didn't mince any words in my briefings, even at the secretary of defense level. I always laid it on the line as to what I had seen on the various trips I had taken.

The tenor of the job ached for elevation to that of adviser to the commandant. The protection that provided was necessary, for with that backing I could get a feel for the problems. A decision may have to suddenly come down on a commanding general, who just might be out of step with what the Marine Corps desired.

In 1970, the name of the job changed, and I became the special assistant for minority matters to the commandant of the Marine Corps. And in the United States Marine Corps, there's no larger "big daddy" than that. Even so, the need for extreme caution rode my flanks. On the one hand, I had a feeling that if I had the necessary clout, I could probably solve the racial problems in the Marine Corps in six months— in spite of all the mysteries attached to the problems. For example, in those days, we had one hell of a lot of officers who had never encountered racial problems before, who were bewildered by them, or, at the opposite extreme, were supercautious or overly liberal.

We weren't dealing with an organized prejudicial system within the Corps. We were dealing with individuals in command and authoritarian positions who were prejudiced. Only thirty years before, blacks were just entering the Corps. Before that, racial confrontation was no problem, because blacks simply were not members of the Marine Corps and that— so the theories of the day went—automatically solved "the problem."

Now a new day had dawned. Blacks were very much part of the Marine Corps, and so were many officers in authority who remembered the "old Corps," so to speak. Remember, it was not until 1952 that I became the first black officer and aviator who came on active duty and stayed around. We had another who came aboard in 1948 and enjoyed the status for a single day before being transferred into the inactive reserves. So let's face facts. We were looking at officers trained some twenty years before, and others with significant rank trained no less than ten years before. There were no officers who could exude even a modicum of understanding when managing black troopers. Beyond that, even when some black officers came on board, some of these refused to become involved. It was a put-down to speak out, they thought. Some acquiesced, caught between pride and the demands of some commanders that problems with blacks be solved in the old, traditional ways.

These officers, both white and black, represented the focal points, I felt, at which to begin the corrective action. Not many jumped on my bandwagon, some preferring to pinpoint the "problem" as a reflection of what was going on in civilian arenas, where black social consciousness and civil rights activity were on the rise.

Although I agreed with that placebo in part, I always issued a caution to senior officers particularly, that to define our problems within the Corps that way was exactly that. The extension of that philosophical thought is to say that the Corps had exactly the same problem as did the civilian community. In short, if we have blacks who are dissatisfied, there is a reason for it. I prefer saying, unlike the civilian community, that we have a strong but small, highly disciplined microcosm of the civilian community and because of that we can solve the problems if they are present. It's a little tricky when you get into this stuff to say that we have the same problems or that our problems are a "reflection" of the civilian community, because they are really two different communities.

We'd blown it badly when it came to our decrees about the approved length of a trooper's haircut—failing to account for what caucasian hair versus black hair looked like at two or three inches in length. We quibbled, looked a little silly, and created morale problems where there probably shouldn't have been any. We went a little ballistic in the way we regarded the "dap"—the special way that black troopers greeted one another during Vietnam—probably one of the biggest mistakes we ever made. We couldn't understand, or did not know, when we demanded the closely shaved head that some black men suffered from a condition in which, if they shaved too closely, the hairs curled on themselves, grew back into the skin, and caused painful pimples, pustules, cysts, scars, keloids, and infection if not addressed properly (*Pseudofolliculitis barbae,* commonly called razor bumps, caused and aggravated by shaving). In lieu of medical attention and researched methodology for a solution, we simply discharged black Marines with this condition, saying they were unfit to serve—not the greatest of morale boosters.

To some, these were small things indeed. However, add to them all those other things involving prejudical attitudes, misinformation, or just plain ignorance on the part of many in authority, and little human engineering time bombs were set to go off all around the Corps.

The point was to disarm them by conducting as many open discussions about cultural differences as we could. To try to make whites understand that there were blacks who hated whites; it wasn't just whites who hated blacks. It was to make them understand that the officers who were leading at the unit levels were not equipped to understand the culture and mores of the blacks and the hispanics, and their cultural differences. To help them understand the fact that country and western music at the enlisted club may not be the choice for some of the minority troops, that the regulation that decreed length of hair needed to be amended to allow for cultural input, that the inability to swim like a fish hinged on the absence of facility, not because minorities simply couldn't swim.

Unfortunately, many of our commanding officers were veterans of some twenty-five to thirty years of a very strictly segregated environment. Many of them had to learn a hell of a lot in two to three years about what race relations were really all about. Many did not learn and, unfortunately, they were the ones who persisted in continuing to remain bigots and learned to go underground, so to speak, in order to operate in a more clever fashion.

In essence, we were going after old wives' tales they'd been taught all their lives about those "other" folk. I was shortly to encounter a prime example of the sad results of the passing down from one generation to another this kind of misinformation about other people not of a certain ilk.

It happened at a briefing on one of my field trips to the recruit depot, Parris Island, South Carolina, with a Marine Corps general officer in attendance. A white drill instructor (DI) was on deck addressing our expressed concerns about the high dropout rate of minority students in training, and the reasons for it. About five foot eight, on the thin side and relatively young for the position, the DI was full of himself. Just knew everything. He tried to impress us with his intelligence and points of view on the issues under discussion.

"Well, suh," he said, "it's common knowledge around these parts of the country that at least part of the problem affecting these troopers is their propensity to succumb to the aggravation of that sickle cell anemia trait that's already in their blood, suh."

"Sorry. Sickle cell anemia? In their blood? Debilitating, is it? Especially in this part of the country?"

"It's in the water, suh."

"Pardon me. In the water?"

"Suh. Yeas, suh. It's a confirmed fact, suh, that the highest rate of sickle cell anemia occurs in this area—and it comes directly from the well water, suh."

"Oh. How so?"

"Well," the sergeant continued, hand to his mouth to stifle a small cough, "it's—it's because of the wells, suh."

"The wells?"

"Yes, suh. You see, suh, they jest don't dig 'em deeply enough, suh." The sergeant finished, his face a circle of real concern and pity for his minority student charges.

It was difficult not to guffaw in the face of such abysmal ignorance, but we held it together and pressed on, to find out other reasons why the minority troopers were washing out of the training in such large numbers. They didn't fulfill the swimming requirements because, said the drill instructor, "Everybody knows their bones are thicker and heavier. Just a situation that can't be helped." And that is why, said the DI, it was well known in medical circles that "black bones being thicker, blacks are always given higher doses of radiation when being X-rayed." It was just one of those things.

This too was drivel, but the DI believed everything he was telling us. We knew all along, for example, that the lack of swimming ability on the part of these black youngsters had nothing to do with the relative weight of their bones but the fact that most of the kids came from the inner city, where there simply were no swimming pools for black people. Experience and time have also disproved the X-ray story.

We made copious notes, for if one were looking for things that served to move racism and prejudice further along, it was obvious that ignorance and misinformation ranked way up there. Until now, racism had been a thing nobody wanted to talk about. It was easier to whisper than to talk out loud. But in February 1970, it was evident that, in spite of our good intentions, racial issues throughout the Corps were red hot.

Cases in point began to proliferate. As early as July 1969, a major riot enveloped Camp LeJeune, where the Corps sent many blacks so they could be near their families on the eastern seaboard [Allan R. Millett, *Semper Fidelis: The History of the U.S. Marine Corps,* p. 599]. A plethora of incidents at the enlisted club exploded into a major riot as black Marines spread terror across the base, beating white Marines, killing one. So intense did it become that armed guards and riot units joined the base military police. Race war plagued the Corps. San Diego. Hawaii. Camp Pendleton. In February 1970, blacks in Vietnam threw a hand grenade into a crowded enlisted club at Da Nang Air Base. Sixty-two were injured and one died.

The Department of Defense began to get the drift as well, and sent out a team headed by Frank W. Render II, assistant secretary of defense for equal opportunity. Also aboard this newly formed team was Judge Howard Bennett. I was assigned to his team, and it was to be our lot to help look into the problems worldwide. The charge was to conduct fact-finding tours in Europe and Asia, in order to determine the depths of the problem of racism in the military.

Render decided to have a joint team go first to Germany and take a look at what was going on there. We knew that Germany was complaint riddled. The war in Vietnam was winding down, but still a war was being fought. Depending on the theater, lots of people were being returned home. But not from Germany. Guys there were looking at a tour in Germany, then a tour in Vietnam. Then back to Germany. And another tour in Vietnam, if the war continued.

Morale sucked. Racism and prejudice were fat cats.

19: A Circle of Cause and Effect

Colonel, what do you think the reaction would be if we took us out a senior commander? Hey! We gon' die here or die in Vietnam . . . it don't make us no nevermin'.

—Paraphrased statement of a black soldier
in a group plotting the assassination of a senior
Army officer in Germany, circa 1970

The first stop for our entire fact-finding team was the Army *kaserne* at Stuttgart, Germany, formerly the capital of the state and kingdom of Württemberg. The city, near the Neckar River, was surrounded by vineyards and woods. We called for an open forum, to which all troops could come to register any complaints about their current assignments.

The forum attracted about 150 to 200 African-American troopers. Our team of civilian and military members sat in chairs arranged on the stage as team leader Frank Render delivered the opening remarks, a kind of here's why we're here, and we'd like to have a question-and-answer period so we can address any questions you may have and speak to any concerns you may have. The base commander, unit commanders, and equal opportunity advisers on staff were also present.

Render opened it up for questions. We could feel a certain nervousness, an extenuated tension in the wide space. Some people stood; feet shuffled. Errant conversation buzzed. Suddenly, bedlam.

A young black trooper sprang to his feet, complaining of blacks' inability within the command structure to secure what they perceived as adequate justice. Nobody would really listen, he noted. Nobody cared. It didn't matter who you talked to. Nobody gave a damn. He singled me out to prove his point.

"And you there, Colonel Petersen, Marine."

The team was all sitting. I remained seated and maintained my cool, although the way he slurred the word "Marine" made for a temporary adrenaline surge.

"Now," he went on, his voice growing louder with each word, "if I were to challenge you and told you that I was gonna kick yo' ass—how would you relate to that?"

A palpable hush fell over the forum space. The base commander flinched, and I thought Frank Render's eyes went a bit glassy. Sly smiles skittered the faces of some of the troopers in the audience; some nudged the ribs of those close by in anticipation of my answer.

I looked steadily at the young man.

"Well," I started, "I'd first see if you had a brown paper bag with you."

"What?" screamed the young man, disbelief riding his face at what he heard.

"Yeah. If you're going to kick my ass, it's gonna be an all-day job— and I'd want to see if you brought your lunch."

Well, the place disintegrated into much-needed laughter. After that, all the troopers were in my corner, and the young man sat down heavily, almost ashamed he'd opened the door. The laughter took all the tension out of the meeting. The forum went on for about an hour. A long list of complaints came out of it—wrongs to right and some serious discussions about what the Pentagon needed to do to assuage problems in some areas.

I was damned glad to have had a "big daddy" back in the Pentagon on this trip. I was in deep kimchi almost from the day we arrived in Germany and especially at United States Army headquarters in Heidelberg.

Following the logic, I suppose, that if one wanted to get a line on "who's doing whom" on a military installation when it came to racism and prejudice, perhaps a good place to take a first look was inside the brig. Ratios of what kinds of people versus other kinds of people and so forth. That's what brought me to the big brig at Headquarters, U.S. Army, Europe (USAREUR), in Heidelberg. After identifying myself as part of the Department of Defense fact-finding mission as it regards prejudice and racism, I was admitted into the cell-block area.

There I found a sight I'll probably remember all my life. Let's just say I might've saved some young white boys' lives that day, because in that lockup were two white boys, lying under blankets, who had been thrashed to within an inch of their lives. They'd been beaten so badly they hardly knew their names, and now they were in shock and bordered on the comatose.

I immediately sensed what had been happening. Their cell mates were six black soldiers—the people who'd done this and who stood now across the wide cell-block room and attempted to hide in the shadows.

I yelled to summon the provost marshal, a warrant officer who was none too happy to have me poking around his territory in the first place. It was an added insult that I was a Marine lieutenant colonel, and black on top of that.

"Yes, sir?" he said, almost skidding to a stop just inside the cell.

"Please call the medics and get these men to the hospital and proper medical care."

"By—er—by whose—er—authority?" the warrant officer stammered.

"By my authority," I roared. "This is a disgrace—and right under your ever-lovin' nose, to boot. Move it."

The medics gently placed the wounded soldiers on stretchers. As we clanged the cell door shut, the black soldiers, somehow seemingly proud of what they had done to their comrades, came to life and strode threateningly out of the shadows toward the cell door. The braggadocio galled.

"Tha's all right, Colonel. Tha's all right, suh. Just leave theah lil' asses in heah—we'll take care of 'em. Yas, suh. Leave theah white asses in heah. We gon' fix 'em so's they don't nevuh has to worry 'bout black folks no mo. Don't worry. We gon' take care of 'em."

I stopped, turned, and looked at them for a long moment. I don't remember now if I said anything at all. Maybe the look, coupled with what I hoped was an expression of disgust on my face, seemed to cower them, and they slunk back across the cell and collapsed sullenly on their bunks. As I moved away, I knew we had discovered a place where a war within a war was definitely in progress, threatening to blaze into a wider conflagration.

There was no doubt in my mind that the news of my foray into the guardhouse of another service on that service's base, and my ordering the release of a prisoner without the proper authority inherent in that particular chain of command, would quickly reach the highest authority around those parts. It did—and so did the fact that it was one of "those" guys who had "told" on me—that black SOBitching Marine lieutenant colonel. Where in the hell does he get off, doin' something like that? was a question I imagined launched itself around the headquarters with varying degrees of verbal editing.

I was hoping that "big daddy" was watching, because the scythe would be swung sooner than I thought possible, and the man in charge of all American Army forces in Europe would be swinging it.

The team was split into smaller sections in order to visit as many military installations as we could. My section drew Kaiserslautern, deep in the German Palatinate and the site of a large American military presence.

This area was cause for great concern, for it was here that the black troops had built themselves a small shantytown just outside the base. There must have been at least a hundred small shacks. We walked through, and it was evident that the brothers had set up little individual homes for themselves and their honeys. Aside from the failure of commanders to control this kind of travesty outside their *kasernes*, there was also the probability (although I can't verify it) that the government was subsidizing the existence of these substandard structures, paying these troopers separate rations and quarters for living on the economy outside a military installation. On weekends the booze flowed freely, the dancers whirled, and a grand time was had by all at the huge dance hall in the center of the Vogelweh military area, the military housing complex near the center of Kaiserslautern. Although a great time was being had by all, it was a probable affront to established military regulatory protocols and a circumstance that might well figure prominently in our official reporting to the secretary of defense upon our return to the Pentagon.

I got the word that six or seven of the brothers wanted to see me in order to discuss a serious problem. The meeting was set for that night in downtown Heidelberg, in a *gasthaus* dedicated to black troops—a kind of nightclub. We knew about the Neckar River flowing through Heidelberg, the world-famous castle sitting high above, the dinner boats riding anchor at the water's edge while probable romances beckoned. But there was no time for any of these things. We had agreed to meet with these guys—"we" being an Air Force officer named Tim Boddy (who was to eventually retire as an Air Force brigadier general) and part of the task force under Frank Render. I'd invited Boddy to come along; he accepted the invitation. We changed into civilian clothing and moved out to keep our rendezvous.

It was early evening as Boddy and I entered the nightclub. The place was jumping and the jazz was pumping. The brothers were out on the dance floor doing their thing. Finally, we all hooked up and found a booth in a corner large enough to accommodate us. Initially, the conversation was something of a verbal sparring match, then things began to get serious. An aura of sinister foreboding suddenly hung over our small group.

"Colonel, suh," began one of the ranking sergeants. "No offense, suh, but we would like to see some ID from the both of you. Just to be sure you're who you say you are."

"Okay, Sergeant," I replied, and I produced my identification card. Examining it minutely, the sergeant squinted in the subdued lighting. Boddy pulled out his ID card, and the careful inspection continued.

Conversation ceased for a long moment. Small flashes from cigarette lighters and the hot ends of lit cigarettes illuminated faces. A new ambience lurched into our special corner of the big room as a dangerous excitement that wasn't there even a moment or two ago settled over the meeting. The sound of the jazz recordings gave all of it a strange tempo. In spite of what I thought was personal reserve, my foot kept time with the beat of the jazz, rocking along while dancers whirled.

"Colonel," another senior noncom began, "what would be the reaction, d'you think, if we took us out a senior commander? D'you think anybody'd listen to our problems then?"

"You mean—"

"Yep. That's what we mean," another soldier injected. "We's talkin' 'bout takin' out the main man."

The blood rushed around inside my head as my pulse gained momentum. The "main man" in this context had to be Gen. James H. Polk, then the four-star commander of all the United States forces in the European theater. I looked into their eyes, searching for verification of what I was thinking. They didn't blink. I looked at Boddy. He looked at me. These guys were talking about killing the theater commander in chief. Damn. It was a strange obverse of another melodrama also set in Germany near the end of World War II, when German generals plotted to take out an ex-corporal named Hitler who'd gone out of control.

"Well," I responded, "I think you'd get a great deal of attention—er—that's for sure." I really looked at these guys then. A very determined, very articulate group of brothers. A mixture of ranks. Corporals. Sergeants. A group of about six or seven guys. They began to tell us about some of their grievances and woes.

In essence, they had taken a good look at what they perceived to be the big picture. They were on a treadmill toward personal disaster, and no matter how much they wanted to get off, they couldn't. The Army wouldn't let them. Now, they really had nothing to lose because their tours of duty were predictable, like the rising and setting of the sun. Germany, then Vietnam, then back to Germany, and back to Vietnam again. They were on a kind of shuttle, being shifted back and forth like the cannon fodder they felt they were. It was just a matter of time before they would be killed in Vietnam. With the repeated exposure to hot combat, the odds were against them.

In Germany, they allegedly weren't in combat, but in another sense they were because of the racial climate and conditions that were then in existence. Increasing Uniform Code of Military Justice (UCMJ) punishments. More and more of their number incarcerated. Their words set off alarm bells inside my head.

"Hey," exploded one of the younger soldiers in the group, "suh, we're gonna die here or we're gonna die there."

"Yeah," a sergeant enjoined. "Why not die for what we believe in? It don't make us no nevermin'."

The sergeant's eyes burned. The intensity unsettled. He seemed to be looking at us, then he seemed to be looking way past us, at some future place he couldn't take us. Beyond Heidelberg, the river, and the castle. Beyond the USAREUR and the death of a senior commander who hadn't the slightest inkling that if these black soldiers could have their way, his sojourn on this side of death was growing shorter by the second. The possibility of that, I'm sure, had never crossed his mind.

The young soldiers felt that an assassination of that magnitude would be the only way to call attention to their plight. To create an act so breathtaking that it would bring national and international attention.

I ground out my cigarette in the small glass ashtray and stood up. Boddy stood alongside. The brothers looked steadily at us. I looked at them with compassion but with what I hope passed for steely resolve.

"Okay, gang," I started. "If that's what you're going to do, how are you going to do it? Who's going to be the leader? Who's going to do the actual deed?"

Their eyelids fluttered as they shifted about uncomfortably in the booth. For the briefest of moments their eyes lasered their comrades' eyes. Jowls grew deeper as their faces turned to stone. They stared back at me. Nobody blinked.

I leaned in, supporting myself on the table.

"Let me tell you an Aesop's fable," I continued. "About the time when all the mice got together and decided the best way to stop the cat from jumping on their asses was to put a bell around the cat's neck. Which of you will be the one to put the bell around the cat's neck?"

As I looked deep into their faces, I could tell that they weren't going to do a damned thing. Boddy and I about-faced and left. I made a note to report the existence of the plot the next day.

Because we were already in a nightclub where the drinks were flowing, the jazz still thumping, and folks still dancing their asses off, Boddy and I thought we'd hang out and enjoy the moment after all the intensity we'd just been through.

Before we could get into that, however, my mind zeroed in on a telephone call I'd gotten earlier in the day. I was to report to General Polk the next morning at 0800. I'd almost forgotten about it. Seems that the general was unhappy with me, my presence on the Department of Defense team, my style, and the fact that I was a Marine Corps officer intent on sticking my nose into the Army's business. Ordering prisoners in *his* jail released. Indeed, who in the hell did I think I was, for all of my ever-lovin' blackness?

But presently, more important things were on our horizon. Boddy and I continued to party. We met a group of black schoolteachers who took us back to their apartment. The extended party sizzled. I thought about my meeting with General Polk and his commanders for just a moment. Concern flitted by, then flew away. I had another drink and I figured, well shit, if I'm gonna die, I might as well die happy. And we continued to party until four o'clock in the morning.

Early the next morning, I called my project leader, Frank Render, and informed him of what was about to take place. The general had asked for his presence, but he'd declined. Scheduled to be elsewhere, he put me on point.

"That's all right. Go ahead and attend the meeting. You're covered—take Tim Boddy with you. Brief me later."

We pulled up in front of USAREUR headquarters. As we walked in, we noted the impressive structures and grounds, representative of the senior commander in all of Europe. When I entered the huge conference room, I knew it was going to be a real dog and pony show, because General Polk had all of his senior commanders—three stars down to one star—present and accounted for. The general appeared to be a bit nervous.

I was a fresh-caught lieutenant colonel, and I must confess I had to hold my emotions in check to keep from being blown away. There was, of course, a very real personal element of concern with that much brass around. To be the object of such minute attention by that many senior officers shot my senses through with bona fide trauma. But I surprised myself. I sat tall and looked right into their eyes as the questions came. I just seemed to go into a combat-ready alert mode—like the days in the Nam on the hot pad when the claxon blew. Turn and burn. Go for the smoke.

It was almost as if I was detached from my body, looking down on the scene as opposed to being frightened or even overly apprehensive. I knew, as far as the Corps was concerned, that I was well protected. It was also evident that a cautious approach to the sensitive subjects under discussion was being taken, and not just about the race gambit. Underneath the questions, the same approach seemed to touch on General Polk's ultimate relationships within his command.

The generals were dressed in their utility uniforms, each adorned by a wide leather belt with a great big buckle. General Polk started the proceedings, his authoritarian voice bouncing off the conference room walls. The sound of it sent little shivers skittering through my brain. I was not unmindful of the fact that to come off really badly here could have dire consequences, but I resolved to stand fast.

"Now, I want to know, Colonel, just what right you think you have to be coming into my command, giving orders to my people, and conducting what I consider to be an illegal investigation without my authority?"

I let the color subside a bit in his rosy jowls.

"With all respect, sir," I intoned, "I am here on the business of the secretary of defense, and I'm here by virtue of being a party to the assistant secretary of defense, whom I have notified of this meeting." My voice sounded louder than usual, rattling molecules of air around the room.

The remaining color seemed to drain from the general's face. He sat very still for a moment, whey-faced, his skin almost deathly white as he regarded me with a special kind of highfalutin demeanor. His eyes flickered; his gaze darted around the crowded room as his commanders silently regarded him.

Score one for the home team. Little did he know that I'd probably saved his life just a few hours ago by persuading a determined band of black enlisted men to think twice about taking him out. I wasn't about to tell him—at least not at the present time.

He recovered quickly. I could see why he'd made general those long years ago. He could stand up on his two feet, all right. This was the same West Pointer (1933) whose canny intelligence through his "line crossers," his "communications intelligence," in Korea had correctly predicted that the Chinese Communists were massing to hit X Corps and not the city of Seoul—except that no one in Eighth Army would believe him—until the hammer fell [Clay Blair, *The Forgotten War,* p. 873]. Sparring with him called for straightforward agility.

His next verbal thrust singed: I was "creating havoc within his command and inciting the troops."

"By all due respects, sir," I fired, "I must point out to you that your troops are acting unilaterally in committing acts of rebellion. Then I would surmise they not only feel they are not part of your command, but their actions show they also feel they're not even part of the United States Army."

It went on for about an hour or more with that kind of give and take, with members of his staff joining in.

"Excuse me, Colonel," began one of the general officers around the table. "I don't quite understand. Just why in the hell are you people out here in the first place?"

"I'm here by order of the secretary of defense," I replied doggedly.

"And come to think about it," chided another, "just what are you— a United States Marine—doing out here as part of this at all? This is an Army endeavor. How come you're checking us out? Why are you part of this Department of Defense team?"

"Quite simply, sir," I heard myself saying, "I'm part of the joint task force assembled by the secretary of defense, which includes all members of the various military departments."

"Well, Colonel, now that you've done all this looking at the living conditions, the social conditions, the conditions in our guardhouses and on and on—just what in the hell have you people concluded?"

"It's not a matter of what I conclude, or what you people conclude. It will be what the senior member of our team concludes. He is the assistant secretary, Frank Render. I personally feel you have some very severe problems here."

"Yes, Colonel," segued General Polk. "What problems?" A little cough gurgled up from his ample throat. "Just what is it that you people intend to report about our operations here at USAREUR? I think we're running a pretty tight ship over here."

"Well, for one thing, you have your troops living off base in isolated quarters. Troops who have managed to segregate themselves. You've also had various black power movements, which are, in effect, waging war against their white counterparts and feel that they have very little to lose by virtue of the rotation system—which is go to war in Vietnam, come back to Germany, go back to war in Vietnam. If they're going to die in Vietnam, why not choose the same opportunity here—by standing up for their rights, which they feel are being violated?"

The meeting ended with General Polk being absolutely pissed off at this black lieutenant colonel who was, of all things, Marine Corps. But as I walked out, something happened that let me know that the message had gotten across.

One of his senior commanders, a two-star general, walked out with me. Stopping on the front steps of the headquarters, he began to query me.

"Colonel," he began, "what do we have to do to stop this, to solve these problems?"

This man was genuinely interested in getting to the root of the problems, and he was obviously operating without Polk's guidance. I stopped and we chatted. I advised him that, basically, he needed to have his staff noncommissioned officers regain control of the troops, and let that extend throughout the entire chain of authority. I told him that the black troops needed a sounding board through which they could not only voice complaints but see viable results for legitimate complaints.

He didn't take notes, but he was deeply engrossed in what I had to say. So, as I left that meeting, I thought that at least someone understood what these brothers felt: that if they had to die for their country, why not make a real point on the way out? It was that serious.

The game got rougher. According to the word I received, General Polk had drafted and sent a "back-channel" message (one that cannot be deciphered over regular communications channels) recommending that the Render tour be terminated and Render himself be returned to the Pentagon. I had been singled out to be given specific attention for "inciting the troops to riot" by being kicked off the fact-finding team and returned immediately to the United States "so that appropriate disciplinary action could be taken against me," to include a probable boot out of the Marine Corps. This recommendation probably had its inception in the fact that my inclusion on the investigating team was primarily to address Navy and Marine Corps issues. From the general's point of view, I had gone outside that purview. However, Frank Render had sent a message to the Pentagon saying that I was a valuable member of the team and that he was requiring that I stay until the end of the trip.

So the airwaves were burning. That wasn't the end of the message exchanges, however.

What General Polk hadn't realized was that because of an earlier visit to the area by an assistant secretary of defense and his investigating team, a cross-channel message had been sent recommending that General Polk be removed from his command and ordered to return to the United States.

Unfortunately, the good general's nose had previously been tweaked by a judge advocate general (JAG) attorney who'd uncovered the fact that his command was showing "disparities" in the manner in which it dispensed nonjudicial punishment under Article of War 15 and indirectly sanctioned the continuation of blatant discrimination in housing available to minority troops on the economy. The command essentially failed to enforce the regulation that gave the Army the authority to place off-limits the property of landlords who discriminated because of race.

Ostensibly, with General Polk's approval as USAREUR commander, the JAG investigator was advised that "they would not enforce the regulations, except for a complaint to the secretary of the Army" [Smothers interview, 6 November 1996]. The entire ball of wax ended up being aired on *60 Minutes,* in *Time* magazine, and in the *New York Times.*

I guess it was double-whammy time for the general. Maybe he had good reason to be pissed at me, a black Marine Corps lieutenant colonel jerking him around about the status of things in his command. I'm sure he recalled that the JAG investigator and the judge who'd previously dragged his name around the block was a black attorney and Army captain named Curtis R. Smothers, slated by the fates to become my friend and personal attorney when my time came to ride straight into what appeared to be the very jaws of political perdition.

What goes around, comes around.

In time, Team Render came together, caucused, compared notes, and helped begin preparation of the Render report describing the status of equal opportunity within the United States military forces in Europe.

One good thing came of it all. We'd saved a four-star's ass—for sure.

But that was minor stuff compared to the racial auguries bedeviling the military as never before—not to mention the precarious paths my own life and career were about to take.

20: Long Knives and Alibis

Either jail them or get them out of the service.
Or jail them—then cut them loose.
—Black noncommissioned officer's view of U.S. Army
policy about blacks, circa 1970–71.
NAACP inquiry, 4/71, p. 26

"Well, Frank," boomed my two-star boss when I returned to the HQMC, "I guess you did it again." A wide smile spread across his face.

"What's going on?" I countered.

"USAREUR is in an uproar," he said, still grinning.

I took this information in good spirits, because I was well covered by the commandant of Marines, who understood and sanctioned my involvement with the investigating team.

My experience warranted personal reflection to keep on an even keel. Perhaps the Army command we'd just looked over *should* have been in an uproar. Vestiges of racism ran amok within its ranks. Our Render study focused on, among other things, the need for military reforms down the chain of command as a precursor to change. Statistics generated as a result of our investigation indicated obvious discrepancies in the numbers and percentages of blacks and their distribution across various levels, even when comparing individuals with similar records and equal times in service. Simply put, the degree of racial differentiation existing in Army occupational assignments could shock. For example, in the occupational area of infantry, review showed that of all personnel with nineteen to twenty-four months of service, 29.7 percent was caucasian and 36 percent was black. After thirty-four to thirty-six months of service, there were 12 percent caucasian and almost double the number of blacks—22.1 percent.

In technical and allied fields, the statistics showed 2.4 percent caucasians and 1.1 percent blacks involved in the former period of service; the latter period showed 3.2 percent caucasians and a steady 1.1 percent blacks. Both groups saw an increased affinity for ultimate survival; the areas of paper shuffling (administration) jumped impressively (3.1 percent caucasians and 4.4 percent blacks). The "soft" areas of service and supply increased as well (16.8 percent caucasians and 11.9 percent blacks).

The need for command reform was verified through troop interviews and was bolstered by the findings of an NAACP inquiry team that followed our visit. It was obvious that the white Army leadership had simply failed to recognize the ultimate impingement of the status quo and its conundrums about race on the roles and psyches of those it had selected as leaders. Outcomes of this failure did, in effect, operate to punish those (the blacks) who both by fact and innuendo dared resist the negative racial attitudes hiding within the status quo in any form. As a result, black consciousness had no credible existence. Black "civil liberties" did not really exist in the eyes of many Army leaders, nor was any expectation of equal treatment given anything but the shortest shrift.

Black soldiers were not bashful in coming forward with what they saw as extant problems. It all seemed, they thought, to be fallout from an intensified white consciousness regarding the black civil rights revolution then in progress. Within that consciousness, the fact of it seemed to seethe, fueling the emergence of the catch-all phrase "black militant" from white mouths. Many in that community knew that militants in any clothing were perceived to be potential threats to national security. Therefore, the most innocent gathering of more than two or three black soldiers brought arched eyebrows and quips about the Black Panthers back home and the fingering of a small knot of black GIs gathered on the company street as new "militants." A traffic stop by military police had the same urgency and intensity as a similar stop of a black man in the United States at that time. It could get you killed, such was the leaning toward the instant use of deadly force. And if that attitude was questioned, your problem was quickly explained away with the charge of "you're a militant."

In the final analysis, some facts were crystal clear. A disproportionately large number of black servicemen were found in lower pay grades and in a very few well-defined fields.

On average, black soldiers were being promoted at a slower rate than their white counterparts. Oddly, according to the NAACP's inquiry report (Report of an NAACP Inquiry Into the Problems of the Negro Serviceman in West Germany, April 1971) done after the Render study, "It was well known at the highest levels at the time"—but claimed, undoubtedly quite tongue-in-cheek—that the "factors have not been identified that account for the differences in promotion rates." If, of course, these officials were at a loss to determine the cause of the "mystery," all they had to do was simply ask the black troops, who had the whole thing down cold.

"Even though the promotion system is fair on its face," said the officials, "it fails to deal with the effects of past discrimination." That past racial design operated to confine them to only certain employment categories. As we conducted our investigation, it became clear that the attitude remained and continued to inhibit their promotional opportunities.

"The mischief resides," the officials advised, "with the Armed Forces Qualification Test." In that test, the score "determines the branch of service and the type unit to which one will ultimately be assigned." Black Armed Forces Qualification Test (AFQT) aptitude scores in those days, reported the Department of Defense, were markedly lower than those of white soldiers (23 percent of whites had scores of 30 percent or lower; more than 72 percent of black servicemen scored less than 30 percent).

This was due, of course, to what the black servicemen identified as past discrimination not having been taken into account. A difference in "educational levels" presaged by inferior school systems in the civilian arena for blacks was directly related to the difference in scoring and lack of opportunity in this military endeavor—a problem that was a primary target of the civil rights revolution. An inferior education sealed one's fate.

"When you come in," remembered a young black serviceman, "you take the AFQT. If you haven't had a good background and a good high school or college education or experience in electronics (Air Force), it's into supply, transportation, and those other soft-core areas you go.

"No matter how hard I study," he went on, "I can't advance now. On a promotional examination for the few slots that do open in my field (administration), already top heavy with black and white noncommissioned officers, I have to score damned-near perfect."

In the Army as well, substantial pay-grade differences existed between the races. Non–high school graduates scoring low on the AFQT were automatic cannon fodder for the infantry, where 30 percent were blacks and only 14 percent were whites. Twenty percent of black soldiers were at pay grade E-5 (sergeant) or higher; 27 percent of whites were there.

Where black officers were concerned, deep dissatisfaction was recorded as well. Slow advancement. Dead-end assignments. Rare opportunities for command positions, ending up in staff rather than command billets. They then became highly paid paper shufflers who found themselves hog-tied in a kind of continuing subservience not endured by battalion and brigade commanders. And even though a black might be "certified" for command, often a white "certified" officer of equal rank but with greater seniority would be placed in the same unit. The white officer thus automatically became the commanding officer because of his seniority status.

Even though there were black officers, there were never enough of them. Black soldiers constantly suggested that, to improve race relations in the military during those times, more black officers were needed—and in command positions, where junior officers would be accountable to them. In short, black officers, especially the junior black officers, were caught between the devil and the deep blue sea. On the one hand, the troops didn't necessarily look up to them, because they were considered to be powerless. At the same time, these guys were catching hell on their own because they were in a white-dominated officer hierarchy where they were constantly getting their asses kicked. It was a real-life parody on the book *The Spook Who Sat by the Door.* They were invited in and they sat down by the door so they could be seen, but they weren't allowed to do diddly-squat.

All of this was just the tip of the racial problem in the U.S. Army in Europe. A chief contributor to the problem was the military justice system as administered by that command and tagged as discriminatory and unjust. This area, I am convinced, was one that helped hurry the ultimate replacement of the USAREUR commander. We had prevented his imminent assassination. Ostensibly, incipient racism at which he winked would eventually rob him of his command.

Data given to members of our team before we left the United States for our visit to West Germany indicated that black enlisted soldiers received nonjudicial punishment at twice the rate of white soldiers for omissions punishable under Article 15* of the Uniform Code of Military Justice. Black soldiers were, according to their commanders, twice as disrespectful, disobedient, and insubordinate as their white counterparts. They were twice as guilty of assault and the generation of "provoking gestures" toward their more than likely white junior officer com-

---

*Under Article 15 of the Uniform Code of Military Justice, a soldier may choose to have a court-martial in lieu of accepting punishment. But nearly all soldiers given that choice chose the Article 15 punishment, because punishment under a court-martial could have serious, long-term effects.

manders who, not infrequently, were acting under the guidance and recommendation of a white noncommissioned officer with whom the black soldier had recently had an encounter. Available statistics on site verified that the number of blacks receiving this type of punishment was constantly higher than that of whites receiving the same punishment.

That was only part of the story. Black soldiers expounded on the extent of the prejudices they faced. Lower-ranking black soldiers were adamant in their belief that white soldiers were not punished for behavior that, if committed by a black, would bring swift, nonjudicial punishment.

"There seemed to be two sets of rules," the black troops said, "one for whites and the other for blacks."

White soldiers could have long hair; blacks could not. (Nor could they have a modified Afro, then the rage in the black community.) Any display of behavior bespeaking black awareness—the hairstyle, the dap handshake, black power salutes—could lead to almost immediate confrontation by white superior officers.

Those unfortunate black soldiers who found themselves candidates for a court-martial could also find themselves incarcerated in "pretrial confinement." Black soldiers tagged this ploy as "arbitrary and inequitable in its application." It was used, they said, "to get so-called militants out of units." Black soldiers were being held up to thirty days with no charges being filed against them. Stockade officers, when queried, advised that commanding officers "frequently failed in their responsibility to visit the detained soldier once a month, to deliver a change of clothing and to assure that he is paid." These same stockade officers found it necessary to "send letters to company commanders reminding them of their responsibilities in this area."

Nor was the problem unknown at the highest level of military authority. No less than General Polk issued directives designed to put limited reforms and maneuvers in place to resolve the issue [Memorandum, Gen. James H. Polk, "Post-Trial Confinement Population," 1 September 1970, and Memo, Gen. James H. Polk, "Reduction of Post-Trial Confinement Population," 22 October 1970] and thus reduce the numbers of Article 15 actions, including unnecessary pretrial incarcerations. Unfortunately, most attempts at such reform were either unenforced, ignored, or bypassed [NAACP inquiry, "The Search for Military Justice," 22 April 1971].

So pervasive were the problems surrounding the Article 15 system that the only full-time black Army judge in West Germany at the time,

Capt. Curtis Smothers, recommended that units publish monthly results of all Article 15 actions taken. The point was that if all such disciplinary actions were publicized, black soldiers might be less likely to jump to the conclusion that only they were being singled out for punishment. Accordingly, an order was issued by the USAREUR commander making it mandatory to publish cases involving the lower four enlisted grades.

But flies were in the ointment, and they weren't all at USAREUR headquarters.

"Equal-opportunity flying squads" were established. Their purpose was to scour the command's domains and be certain that the commander in chief's directive was being followed. Black soldiers reported that General Polk's order was largely ignored. It seems that the "flying squad" constantly had its wings clipped by officers cautioning against "undercutting the authority of the local commanders in the units they visited" [NAACP, p.19–20]. It was simply the way things were.

Said a black soldier, "If I fail to blouse my boots, or wear an Afro, I get socked. Yet, the company commander can thumb his nose at any order from General Polk he doesn't like if it deals with blacks, and nothing is done."

Of course, it was not true that every officer in USAREUR operated to defeat equal opportunity within the U.S. Army in Europe. Some tried, and others did all they could to defeat the proposition. For example, efforts by high-ranking officers were negated by lower-ranked officers who continued to indulge in racist attitudes and practiced them with impunity. It was a push-pull thing. General George S. Patton, Jr., commanding at Nuremberg, installed an educational program of seminars and dialogues for junior officers and senior noncommissioned officers. A brigade commander refused cooperation with the NAACP inquiry after we had passed through, claiming "ignorance of simple data about nonjudicial punishment in his own unit." General Harold Hayward, commanding the Berlin Brigade, appointed a black special assistant to receive and resolve the grievances of enlisted men.

Thus, black soldiers really never knew what was coming down the pike. One would expect, for example, that in the face of widespread discretionary misuse of administrative justice, black soldiers would be looking to available legal counsel to ensure preservation of their rights. Not so. A black noncommissioned officer shared the universal view of black soldiers in Europe about the judge advocate general's lawyers:

I don't want anything to do with a military lawyer. A JAG officer is in the military. He is working for the commander. He can only do so much, no matter how unbiased he is. He may want to help you. I have been in the service fourteen years, and I have never seen a white JAG lawyer do anything that great for a black man.

As far as the black troops were concerned, the bottom line was that white JAG lawyers were simply not to be trusted. They were neither free to be independent of military influence nor free from racist attitudes. Again and again, black soldiers told our teams that white JAG officers had no credibility as far as they were concerned. These were law school graduates, some coming from the best American families and law schools. Many had never been around blacks before, and seeing so many blacks in the infantry was probably tantamount to culture shock. More than that, they certainly had not spent much time with people of any color who were not high school graduates.

So the actions of these black men—wearing Afros with attitudes, greeting one another with the dap, and daring to give the black power salute—these actions were to these elite lawyers only a half step away from rebel activities. They were fallout from "that thing" going on in America, the civil rights revolution. These were H. Rap Brown wannabes, and there seemed to be an unspoken, silent outcry among them that fueled their own silent rebellion. Their bottom line was, we're not going to put up with that shit. Period.

In point of fact, the elite lawyers couldn't understand the black troopers even when they were trying to listen. Judge Curtis Smothers remembered how he and a white JAG attorney would often bring in one of these young transgressor black kids for an interview and legal counseling. The black youngster would be mad as hell and would begin to talk, the words furiously embracing the only syntax he'd ever known.

"An' de mudderfucah tried to get ovuh on me," he'd growl. The white attorney's brow would wrinkle in consternation, and perhaps he'd nod in uncomprehending assent.

"An' ah sed," the young transgressor would continue, "an' ah sed, ah'm goin' off on the mudderfucahing dude." And he'd pound powerfully on the long, polished table.

"Would you mind saying that in English," the white JAG attorney would reply. Young transgressor eyes would flash the white JAG attorney. An angry mouth would open and angrier words would pour forth. Smothers would intervene; his levity could give the entire room a different ambience, a different hue.

"Naw, let 'im talk. Let 'im talk. I understand what he's saying," Smothers would reply.

The white JAG attorney was probably glad that Smothers was aboard, and perhaps that night he would recount the tale in some bar over a whiskey sour, maybe wondering why more and more black troopers were avoiding his cohorts and him like the plague. In fact, the black troopers were spending thousands of American dollars retaining civilian lawyers to defend them in American military courts, attempting to buy themselves a fair shake from their own military. They made many American civilian lawyers living in Europe rich.

All of that wasn't the end of the miserable story about the status of black soldiers in the Army in West Germany. I knew, deep inside, that many of the ills we uncovered on our trip existed in varying degrees across the wide spectrum of America's military. Complaints about recreational facilities loomed: limited, riddled through with discriminatory practices. Enlisted clubs on military installations were alien, often hostile places for black servicemen. "White bias" permeated, according to a Vietnam vet. Soul music was played only on weekdays; prime off-duty weekend time was reserved for country and western music. There were continuing racial tensions about women, because the women being escorted by black soldiers were white German women. "Inebriated white soldiers wanted to fight," reported black soldiers, so they tended to stay away from the base clubs as much as possible. Those lucky enough to own their own motor scooter or automobile would drive far into the countryside—where there were no white American servicemen or the virulent racism that many imported—to socialize among the nationals who knew nothing of racism and could not have cared less. This allowed the black man a chance to experience real equality, if only for just one special moment of a weekend.

Particular anger was reserved for the discriminatory practices of the local innkeepers and bar owners, who quickly adopted the attitudes of their white military customers about admitting and socializing with black troops. What was extremely galling was that this combined discrimination was even more overt and complete than it was in the United States.

"White Only" and "Membership Only" bars sprang up like newly planted grass. Blacks soon found themselves segregated into one or two bars for blacks only. Striking back, blacks at one base declared their bar off-limits to white soldiers.

Complaints about these policies to USAREUR resulted in placing establishments that practiced racial discriminiation off-limits to Army personnel. In mid-1970, four such sanctions were imposed. However, it soon became evident to black soldiers that the words were only paper tigers, because area commanders were loathe to enforce the ban. In Mainz, Germany, it was said that white GIs would taunt blacks in the barracks, bragging about their great escapades in the local "off-limits" bars.

Within the year, we were off again—this time to Japan on the same kind of mission. Curt Smothers was also with us, as was the deputy assistant for equal opportunity. We found many of the same problems that we'd found in West Germany. The racial problem was found worldwide, of course, not just in Germany and the United States. Although the same kind of assignment merry-go-round existed for the troops in Japan (combat, back to Japan, back to combat), the Vietnam War was beginning to wind down.

All of this proved that large numbers of minorities were being drafted and were being assigned combat specialties as opposed to more technical specialties. In other words, they were riflemen. A large number of them were in the lower ranks, and that's pretty much where they remained. Most combat units in Vietnam were heavy in minorities.The higher you looked through the ranks, the fewer minorities you saw. I'm not just talking blacks, but hispanics and others as well. The kicker is that those units were being commanded by white noncommissioned officers and, in particular, white officers who were college graduates. Oil and water, a very difficult mix at best—one that the senior commander in the field had a responsibility to ensure worked for the good of the mission and the service.

Our studies and the NAACP study reflected the fact that black officer ranks were shrinking. Some black officers we talked with noted that perhaps opportunities on the outside were better, with more chances for advancement. At the time, the surmise was probably correct.

But another issue existed—one that many tended to overlook: In order to come into the officer ranks in the first place, you had to be a college graduate. While Vietnam seethed and boiled, most of the brothers who were in college said the same thing that their white counterparts said, and that was simply this: "I ain't going to Nam."

It was getting to be time to move on. For the moment, my Pentagon tour was just about over. I just had to tidy things up. Try, for example, to locate the paperwork for the Distinguished Flying Cross I received in Vietnam. Track down my recommendation for the Legion of Merit for my combat service. For some odd reason, the paperwork for that and several other medals I was awarded seemed to have "mysteriously" disappeared or couldn't be found for whatever reason. Nothing I did seemed to help.

I lucked out in that Gen. Keith B. McCutcheon, my old boss from the Division of Aviation, was going to take over the 1st Marine Aircraft Wing. Before he left, he asked if there was anything he could do for any of his officers while he was the commanding general. I mentioned the problems I was having in locating my awards, especially my Legion of Merit, which was never awarded. So he went out and tracked it down. Shortly after that, the award was presented. The word was that the paperwork was "misplaced." I don't want to conjecture about what the problem was. The worst thing about guessing is that I could be wrong. It's always better to search out the high ground.

I sincerely hoped I was right.

_____ Part Six

Walking a Tightrope

21: Crossroads

As 1972 beckoned, there was a bit of time to reflect on what I'd just been through as the special assistant to the commandant for minority affairs. My hope was that I had done some things and made recommendations that would help ease the racial problems within the Corps. I knew now that it wasn't the kind of duty I'd like to continue. In short, I decided that I wouldn't like to go into the field again to be the "duty black expert." To remain there would seal my fate as far as further promotions were concerned, because those, if they came, wouldn't be based upon work done in the human relations field, although that was very important work for the Marine Corps.

I also felt strongly that it was not the responsibility of black officers to handle this particular problem. They could act as advisers, but it should stop there. One of the practices I fought against was to have a commanding officer go to a black in another outfit and ask for his help in handling a race-related problem. For example, on a trip made with the commandant, the steward had been off on a toot one night and was still drunk the following morning. The commandant's naval aide and I were discussing the problem.

"Now, Frank," he harumphed officiously, "I want you to talk to him and let him know this is it."

Luckily for this aide, a major who was waiting for the commandant was listening to our conversation and injected his opinion in a timely fashion.

"Why should Colonel Petersen talk to this man?" he barked.

The naval aide flushed but immediately got the message. The impending problem was solved, and in the nick of time, for I was just about to lay into that aide when the major soothed things over.

That kind of thing is a trap that majority and minority officers can easily fall into. As a black officer, why should I handle this black non-commissioned officer and get him squared away? The point is that it is the responsibility of any Marine officer to handle that man fairly and get him squared away regardless of the color of his skin or his national origin.

It was about this time that I made a new friend and pal in the person of Capt. Curtis Smothers (he liked to be called Curt), the judge advocate general's man. Curt's work in exposing the Article 15 and housing problems in the European command had not particularly endeared him to the powers that be. Upon his return to the Pentagon, many people gave him a wide berth for fear of being swept away with him when the hammer of retribution for his Army exposé fell. As an Army captain, judge advocate general connection or not, he'd done the unthinkable—taken on a four-star general, who was at the time the supreme Allied commander in Europe, and exposed his dirty laundry for the entire world to see. No one particularly wanted to talk to Curt. In fact, "in disfavor" would have been a mild descriptor of his plight.

MUTUAL VOICES
Curtis R. Smothers, Attorney at Law

I had raised so much doubt relative to military justice—the process of what we called Article 15, showing some disparities in the manner in which it was administered—together with an effort on the housing front that the younger generation complained about—not being able to procure housing when coming to Europe. I was basically the "bad boy," a kind of pariah. I had the wonderful experience of going down the hall and watching black officers find their way into the nearest rest room—whether they had to "go" or not. Frank [Petersen] was one of the few people who would even speak to me in the halls of the Pentagon. He was one of those people to be seen with, to go to lunch with. We had an interesting series of meetings after that.

The other black officer working in the Pentagon at the time who didn't look down his nose at Curtis Smothers because of his "circumstance" was Air Force general Daniel "Chappie" James, Jr., America's first black four-star general. The three of us became good friends and socialized the Washington area with the greatest aplomb. Down the line, both Chappie and I would have need of Curt's legal expertise—and in my case, sooner than I bargained for.

After all our traveling, talking, counseling, surveying, and reporting findings, racial relations within the military seemed set to overwhelm—like wind-driven, crackling fires out west in the midst of the driest of seasons. Actually, race relations had been red hot from about 1968 and the Martin Luther King assassination until we got out of Vietnam—and then it all came home with us.

A major cause of Marine Corps problems was the need to satisfy manpower requirements during the Vietnam conflict, which brought into the Corps floods of black youth who had been exposed to the rising hue and cry of militancy and nationalism in the ghettos. In January 1970, of 301,675 Marines, 32,403 were black [Millett: *Semper Fidelis: The History of the United States Marine Corps,* p. 599]. Our self-congratulations on our handling of racial problems within the Corps had begun to wane. A major riot had erupted on Camp Lejeune in July 1969. Marine enlisted men fought one another in San Diego, Hawaii, and Camp Pendleton, not to mention tension between the forces still remaining in Vietnam.

By now the Marine Corps had firmly implanted a human relations program, which went a long way toward convincing officers and NCOs that they would have to take positive action to stop interracial tension and allay the fears of black Marines that they would be victimized by "The Man." White Marines had to be convinced that not all black Marines were potential thieves and muggers and that violence among Marines would not be tolerated [Millett, pp. 599–600].

In spite of it all, I still had to plan to carry on my career and take it as far as it could be pushed. I'd been debating for two to three years whether to stay in long enough to even make a real hard run for general officer rank. Of course, much of that strategy had to be predicated on attendance at the National War College, for that was one of the tickets that should be punched. A determined run for general officer rank for me was linked to the feeling that the Marine Corps was going to have to show a greater awareness of the problems and solutions regarding race than they had in the past. Understanding that it was the most conservative of the military services, the most highly respected, I had been most reluctant, because of my position, to talk about the things I felt should be done.

There needed to be, in my view, selection of blacks for more accelerated promotions. A policy was needed that required the Corps to look at the career patterns of selected black officers to ensure that they were on track and getting the right assignments. Something needed to be done regarding interpretation of fitness reports, not only for minorities but for all officers. At that time, it was still a problem.

Another look at the Basic School needed to be taken. Why, for example, were so many black officers coming out of Basic School with supply, transport, and service military occupational speciality (MOS) designations? I still remember an old survey we ran in which we wanted to discover how many blacks were in command billets. The answer was that of the three hundred or so black officers, only seven were in command billets. That was a pretty grim statistic. The black Marines knew the score, and they were becoming more and more verbal about it.

"Why aren't there any black commanders?" they were asking. "We don't have anyone we can talk with—why is that?" The racial climate was beginning to claw at the Corps and all the other military services—again.

I didn't want to become a general officer because I thought I was going to solve the problems all alone. I knew I couldn't do that. But perhaps I could make a positive impact on the problem. So the decision was to stick around and make a try for general officer rank if only because there was a grave need for a show of faith on the part of the Marine Corps.

A black officer named Ken Berthoud was also eligible for progression to general officer rank. He had all the tickets punched except one. He'd finished Naval War College and had his master's degree, but what he didn't have was command experience, a thing very difficult for him to come by in his field of supply officer.

Ken was about a year junior to me. It was doubtful that the Corps would be taking any blacks for upgrade to full colonel for the next four years. There were four black lieutenant colonels in the Corps at the time: Ken Berthoud, Ed House (a pilot), Clarence Davis, and myself. It did not look as though either Davis or House would go further in the Corps. That left Berthoud and myself. Considering all the vagaries—time left in service, who was the most recent senior black selected for promotion—it looked as if that was the way it would flake out. Even then, it would be six to eight years before it would happen—if it happened at all.

Even so, I still considered getting out in the event that the Corps would not be ready for a black general even then. I knew, through all sorts of grapevines, that there were general officers who were not amenable to seeing a black ascend into the hallowed halls of Corps generalship. The firefights at that level historically have been some of the biggest. Discussion of the possibility was one thing, but when considering the actuality of the idea, I could remember visions of other such ideas, great on the surface and flown, only to see them falter like a stricken bird in flight.

I was nevertheless happy to hear that I'd been selected to attend the National War College starting in July at Fort Lesley J. McNair in southwest Washington, D.C., between the Anacostia River and the Washington Channel.

This was one of the tracks on the career path I'd wanted, for it was the place, to quote Lt. Gen. Leonard T. Gerow, "concerned with grand strategy and utilization of the national resources necessary to implement that strategy. . . . Its graduates . . . exercise a great influence on the formulation of national and foreign policy in both peace and war" [Government Printing Office Catalog, National War College, George Washington University].

I should have been ecstatic about this turn of events. Instead, my life seemed to be pulled down uncharted paths onto strange crossroads. It was a time of pain, of real and imagined injustices, of highs and unimaginable lows.

For example, the beating my body had taken when bailing out of the Phantom Jet in Vietnam came home to haunt. Pain inundated my left knee. I noticed that after handball, the tendon in that knee would ache. Later, I required hot and cold packs to control the pain. Surgery was prescribed and performed at nearby Bethesda Naval Hospital, where the tendon was reattached, followed by a protracted period of recuperation.

Healing continued as my attendance at the National War College began in July with sudden exposure to subject matter beyond the ken of the mundane. Diplomatic history of the United States. Government and politics of the Middle East. National history of the Chinese Communist state. Fundamentals of national power. Foreign policies of the United States and the international communities. Ethos of the national security policies of the United States. History of Russia, history of Southeast Asia, and searching inquiry into the cultural aspects of the African continent. Often, on field trips to Europe and other destinations, I'd have to lie flat on my back as the healing process continued. Not the greatest way to fly.

It became obvious very quickly that beyond the temporary physical incapacity linked to my back operation, attendance at the National War

College full time could seriously affect my obligation to maintain my flying time, as expected of all military fighter pilots to ensure maintenance of proficiency. Unless I was careful, even my trips required while pursuing equal opportunity could have an impact in this area.

As usual, I thought that the direct way was the best way to handle this problem. So I started at the top and approached my old boss at the Division of Aviation, to ask for a waiver of the flying time requirement— at least until completion of my studies at the National War College. He agreed to cooperate and grant the waiver. I thought I was home free on the issue and pursued my studies with greater aplomb.

Of course I wanted my family to be comfortable, so we bought a home and moved from 16th Street in northwest Washington to Shepherd Park, a part of the city recycled from a neighborhood predominantly Jewish in the 1950s to one housing mostly well-to-do blacks. Many of the homes, large brick colonials on tree-lined streets with faultlessly manicured lawns, were valued at $200,000 to $300,000. Crime statistics were outstandingly low. It seemed a good atmosphere in which to mend an ailing marriage while providing security for an emerging young family. Hopefully, the change could still disturbed marital waters while my quest for a particular shining moment continued. The two points of view failed to meld, however.

Chalk it up, again, to the realization that my drive to somehow get to the top of whatever mountain I was attempting to climb required my undivided focus on the effort at hand. My attitude was not conducive to addressing the family's mantras: "How come you're never home?" and "You're never home when I need you."

Crisis was building in my life, and I seriously looked around for more peaceful environs, if any were to be had. Little did I know that it would be a long time before I'd know any real peace.

My marriage exploded. It was over, so I moved out of our new house into the home of Curtis Smothers in Alexandria, Virginia. I was looking for time without the mantras, so I could concentrate on the tasks at hand.

About the time I was beginning my stint at the National War College, in July 1972, all hell began to break loose in our umbrella service, the U.S. Navy. During the early part of October 1972, the carrier *Constellation,* off the coast of San Diego conducting refresher training exercises and testing new equipment, underwent racial confrontations and problems that ended in rioting between blacks and whites. Bitterness and acrimony between the two sides had festered for days. The blacks, believing themselves unfairly blamed as the cause of steam catapult and boiler problems, began meeting for discussions in secluded places belowdecks. The whites avoided them and began meeting in their own group. It was, it can be imagined, like a huge growl. When the two races met in the tight passageways, certain ones of them refused to turn so that sailors of the "other" color might pass.

Things weren't much better for the crew of the *Kitty Hawk*, far out in the Pacific, with 297 blacks among more than 4,000 enlisted men. Everybody, regardless of color, was upset because the ship's deployment was being continually extended due to the Vietnam War. With no liberty for a year, the *Kitty Hawk* finally put into port at Olongapo at Subic Bay in the Philippines on 11 October 1972. There, its sailors fought one another until a Marine riot squad broke it up.

Back on station, with combat flights and landings in progress, black sailors stormed out of the *Kitty Hawk*'s investigation office after being questioned about their role at Olongapo. Angry, they gave a white mess cook who was stacking trays a whipping. The Marines were called.

Commander Benjamin Cloud, Jr., the first-ever black executive officer to have that job aboard a U.S. Navy aircraft carrier, tried mightily to get a fix on the problem. Appeal. Return the dissidents' "clenched fist" salute to show his brotherliness, his togetherness. Mistakenly, he thought the problem over and appropriately localized. Unfortunately, the Marine commander (on orders from the ship's captain) sandbagged his good work, dispatching four patrols of Marines with orders to break up groups of more than three blacks and take any objectors to the ship's legal officer, by force if necessary.

Unaware of these orders, men to whom Commander Cloud had just spoken were set upon by the Marines "in line abreast, nightsticks at the ready, blocking their path" [Leonard F. Guttridge, *Mutiny: A History of Naval Insurrection*, Naval Institute Press, 1992, p. 264]. It could be termed a double cross, for Cloud had calmed down the men, reassured them—and now this. The black sailors would not be dispersed. A donnybrook ensued, swirling down and under the wings and wheels of F-4 Phantom jets lined up to starboard and port. The Marines lost, forced into the open doors between the forward and aft hangar bays as the black sailors found weapons to wield, to include tie-down chains from parked aircraft and huge dogging wrenches.

This particular incident is included here more than others because it has been written about and detailed as if this confrontation was primarily the fault of the black sailors. Perhaps in the interest of good discipline, none of it should have happened, but the ship's captain and the Marine commander, not knowing what the executive officer had achieved by talking, were determined to use force to solve a problem that apparently had already begun to be handled by Commander Cloud, thus infuriating the black sailors to new levels of anger.

Captain Paul H. Ryan, U.S. Navy (Retired), writing in the United States Naval Institute's *Proceedings* ["USS *Constellation* Flare-up: Was It Mutiny?" January 1976, p. 47], begins his piece as follows:

> Bands of marauding blacks, charging racist practices, rampaged through the ship, senselessy lashing at whites with chains and wrenches. Forty-seven men, 40 of them white, [were hurt]— three of them seriously. . . .

The thing to note here is not to excuse failure to obey orders within the military, but spending a little time getting the facts when writing about issues of this nature. Racial confrontations are volatile enough without adding fuel to the fire, even years later, by "editorial license" out of control.

Guttridge notes in his book *Mutiny: A History of Naval Insurrection* that this particular "fight" was localized, that black sailors did not "maraude senselessly . . . rampaging [through] the ship . . . lashing out at whites. . . ." That's the kind of recording that keeps the racial fires burning.

Further, Guttridge writes:

> Such are the size and intricacy of modern aircraft carriers that hundreds on board the *Kitty Hawk* . . . slept undisturbed. . . . The *Kitty Hawk* remained on Yankee Station a further three weeks, conducting daily air strikes . . . the whites and blacks of her crew working alongside one another in their customary billets, with no significant recurrence of trouble [p. 266].

On 16 October 1972, black sailors demonstrated on the fleet oiler *Hassayampa*, docked at Subic Bay. The carrier *Saratoga* experienced the same kinds of problems, the captain's decision to sound general quarters averting a major riot. Demonstrations took place aboard the carrier *Forrestal*.

Trouble aboard the *Constellation* escalated to unheard of levels. What seemed to be mutiny caused a major warship to return early to port—the first such occurrence in the history of the U.S. Navy. Black sailors swore "affinity with their black brothers" aboard the *Kitty Hawk* and threatened a "bloodbath" unless the captain came down off the bridge to talk with them. In the final analysis, the ship's captain, in wise resolve, decided to "envelop this group with a blanket of calm mature people" [Guttrididge, p. 274].

The blacks acquiesced, greatly outnumbered as the white officers and sailors surrounded them without saying a word, showing a "passive show of strength." It worked. Some of the black group still strutted and "demanded to see the captain"; others simply went to bed, played their favorite card game, or listened to music. When quiet returned, the white officers and sailors retired, restoring peace aboard the ship.

Trouble aboard the *Constellation* would spill over into the month of November, involving the naval chief of staff, Adm. Elmo Zumwalt, and the secretary of the Navy, John Warner. It was all to become pretty nasty as the U.S. Navy dealt with being threatened by near mutinies aboard its warships. I couldn't help but wonder how it all would end.

I was nearing graduation from the National War College, scheduled for the coming summer. My class was gearing up for comprehensive examinations and graduation at the end of July. I remember thinking that if I was successful, the upper reaches of the Corps would open to me at long last. It all seemed possible, especially because I'd just received the Meritorious Service medal for my work as special assistant for minority affairs on 5 September 1972.

Months later, Maj. Solomon Hill, a mutual friend, set me up with a blind date. I didn't even think twice about it. I needed the different focus about now.

Her name was Alicia Downes. She was from Philadelphia and one of five children. Solomon had met her at a convention and felt she was someone I ought to meet. And I did. I went to her apartment, was introduced. She was a lovely woman, and still is. A relationship started from there. She was living alone, had a child—a young girl—and was raising her by herself.

I was struck by Alicia's beauty. A head full of long hair. Quite a bit of American Indian forebears resided in her. High cheekbones. Reddish brown complexion. Tall, with a beautiful body. Once we began talking,

I was struck by her intelligence. We seemed to click right away. Later, I'd go by to talk. And we'd talk for long periods of time—for hours— about any number of things, sometimes into the wee hours of the morning. We became very close very quickly.

And then we lost contact with each other. It had all seemed so good, but life intervened as my personal survival as a Marine Corps officer seemed suddenly threatened from the most high places within the Corps.

22: Cabal

You don't cover your ass by putting matters in the record
that show he . . . didn't do the wrong thing.
—Curtis R. Smothers, Attorney-at-Law, Interview

It happened sometime in midsummer, when the weather was its warmest and the humidity highest in the nation's capital. Thunderstorms struck with sudden ferocity, flinging about short downpours. Wind gusted. On hot days, the temperature soared into the nineties.

The day was hot and sticky when I was served with official papers from the Corps advising that I was going to be investigated under Article 32 of the Uniform Code of Military Justice for fraudulently accepting flight pay for periods I did not fly but was required to in order to maintain flight proficiency.

My breath caught as I read the missive. Anger swept through my body. I chain-smoked and sought solitude to consider the impact. This could very well mean the end of my career. All those days and nights of work and study time. All those dreams of finally becoming a bird colonel, of ultimately becoming a general officer, star-shelled for a moment into infinity. All that combat, all that back, hip, and knee pain I was still feeling after having been blown out of the sky over Vietnam—to have someone deliver me this paper obviously generated to discredit me big-time. A paper certainly designed to drum me out of the Corps in disgrace after all the years of faithful service.

The insult deepened as I was unceremoniously assigned to Headquarters Battalion, Headquarters, Marine Corps, with nothing to do and without any specific assignment while the investigation of my "transgressions" continued. Even though I asked for job assignments (I was just sitting at home), none were given. It was the military counterpart of the corporate and public sector, where someone in disfavor is given a small desk in a dark corner with no telephone and nothing to do until the hammer falls. Rather than sit in limbo, I began the research and completed writing my master's degree thesis and got that out of the way.

One fine day I was invited to fly to California with Colonel Mickelson, the investigating officer. We were going out to interview the general officer I'd previously asked for waivers regarding my flying requirements because of my back operation.

Colonel Mickelson asked the general officer, "Did Lieutenant Colonel Petersen ask you for permission to waive his flying time requirements while you were in charge of the Division of Aircraft at the Pentagon?"

My heart sank as I watched the general lean back to search his mental computer.

"Well-l-l, no," he oozed. "I—er—I really don't—recall. There were just so many requests for waivers back then, you know," he said in a rush.

I knew the "fix" was in. This was my old boss. A guy I respected and whose orders and instructions I would have followed to the letter, who had just deep-sixed me. Yes, sir. I just knew my ass was grass if I didn't get my wagons circled in a great, big hurry.

I thought of quitting. Of walking away from the thing. If the Corps didn't need me and could so callously destroy me using what I considered trumped-up accusations, I didn't need the Corps. But then I remembered a thing I'd learned in the Corps—a thing I always said to my troopers in all sincerity and had even taught my son: "Never, ever retreat from the combat." It was a mantra, a chant, a spell, a state of being. And, of course, there was that "tiger's jaw" thing, which required a special focusing. I'd known it in combat over Korea and Vietnam. It had more than sustained me. And now, when I needed it most, the full meaning of it came rushing back.

I don't think I saw too much on the drive home to Curt's place in Alexandria. Scenery blurred. Anger rode sidesaddle with my psyche; my brain churned and turned. I sat down with Curt, who by now had quit the military and established his own law firm. Once the shock of what was occurring was absorbed, we began to analyze the situation and devise ways to get my wounded career in the Corps out of the swamp.

"Okay," said Curt, along with his law partner, Gary Meyers, "here's what we should do." Somehow, although the awesomeness of what had transpired didn't leave, nor did the anger, I began to feel better as the analysis of my situation continued.

First, we ascertained our position. We knew that being investigated under UCMJ Article 32 was the same as an appearance before a grand jury. After looking at the facts outlined in the charges, it would be determined whether the matter should be dropped or go forward to trial. Colonel Mickelson, the appointed investigator, was the one who would, after a thorough look at the facts, make that determination.

Second, the position of the Marine Corps, without quoting the full text of the papers served, was made crystal clear in the "Subject" assigned it:

> Formal Investigation to inquire into the circumstances connected with the receipt of flight pay by Lieutenant Colonel Frank E. Peterson, 511 26 19 35, U. S. Marine Corps, for periods during which he did not meet minimum flying hour requirements for receipt of flight pay in Fiscal Year 1970 and thereafter.

Third, our almost immediate conclusion was that there was, somewhere in the hierarchy of the Corps, at least a modicum of skulduggery operating, because I at least had gone to a general officer and requested the necessary waiver of flying time requirements while working as the special assistant to the commandant in areas of equal rights. Additionally, because of my back operation, I was precluded from sitting in an ejection seat. The general officer who'd indicated that the waiver would be granted was suddenly as silent as the dead of winter athwart the Arctic Circle.

Fourth, we knew that if there was room for maneuver and reason to fight this issue, we would do it.

Proceedings against me moved swiftly. It was that time of year in Washington, D.C., when you could smell fall and winter over the horizon. A slight chill pervaded, making it cool but not cold. Errant winds stirred. Trees began losing their great coats of green leaves flecked through with shades of red and gold.

MUTUAL VOICES
Alicia Joyce Downes

I saw Frank again in 1973, and I believe at that time he was in the process of going through a separation and divorce. That was the year I'd gone back to graduate school at the University of North Carolina to pursue a degree in regional economic planning. I worked for HUD in Philadelphia, then was recruited by the housing office in Montgomery County, Maryland. They offered me a position, and I went down to Washington,

D.C., to take that position as director of operations for the housing authority there. Frank was having some kind of difficulties with the Corps.

On 27 September 1973, a missive from the commanding officer of Company B, Headquarters, Marine Corps, advised me that the ongoing investigation indicated I'd received "unearned funds in the amount of $4,410—the property of the United States Government . . . resulting from [my] failure to . . . meet flight hour requirements for pay purposes . . . during FY 1970 (8 months), FY 1971 (7 months) and FY 1972 (3 months)" and directing my immediate contacting of "the disbursing officer" regarding "restitution of the subject funds." It could be prorated at an acceptable rate, or I could accept voluntary restitution. I was to do one or the other within the next seven days.

On 16 October 1973, the judge advocate general's office at Quantico signaled that it, as the supervisory authority for court-martial matters, concurred with the "findings of fact, opinions and recommendations of the investigating officer," and did, in fact, approve.

I chose not to repay through proration or accept voluntary restitution because, in my mind, I'd done nothing wrong. Accordingly, on 23 October 1973, another smoking letter arrived, noting that I had been given the chance to make voluntary restitution, had "elected not to do so," therefore my commanding officer was directed to take it out of my pay involuntarily. (An appropriate Military Pay Order was executed to do exactly that on 24 October 1973.)

With its customary efficiency, the Corps moved to transfer me from the Washington, D.C., area altogether, to proceed to the 2d Marine Aircraft Wing, Marine Corps Air Station at Cherry Point, North Carolina, for duty. However, the orders were phrased so that I could not leave until the Corps said so, and was to remain in place "upon completion of duty under instruction and on such date during October 1973 as the Director of Headquarters Support may designate," with a ten-day leave cranked in whenever I could proceed.

It would seem that the Corps smelled a court-martial in my case, at least until the investigating officer's report was in. Happily, Colonel Mickelson concluded that "not only did he not falsify his flight records, he, in fact, only lacked six minutes of flight time to meet his total flying qualification."

Right away, Smothers, Meyers, and I decided to appeal the entire action and asked for an audience with the commandant of the Marine Corps. The audience and chance to appeal were granted.

It was 28 November 1973. The trees were stark naked, the air wintry. It was almost five o'clock in the afternoon when we stepped from our car at Marine Corps headquarters at the naval annex close to the western corner of Arlington National Cemetery. The moisture in our breath made puffs in the chilly air. Inside, we mounted the stairs on our right to the second floor, turned left, and negotiated a long corridor. The commandant's office hove into view, the office to the right at the end of the corridor.

We entered to find ourselves ensconced in an anteroom. We waited and made small talk about the spit and polish of the place, the pictures on the wall, and the plaques. We sipped the coffee we were offered. After a few minutes the commandant's aide ushered us into the official inner sanctum, then into the commandant's office.

A long walnut desk sat in the far right corner. We were temporarily struck dumb by the many trophies and military items on display, not only from the commandant's military career but from commandants of the past. In my mind I could hear the shot and shell, smell the gunpowder; revisit Pork Chop Hill, Mount Suribachi, Inchon, and the agony of Vietnam as I gazed out the commandant's broad window that overlooked Arlington National Cemetery. I looked out the other window at the sprawling expanse of cosmopolitan Virginia and was glad to be home again.

It was all very military. Very polished and disciplined. The aura of it set the tone for our meeting. We were offered seats. My counsels, Curtis Smothers and Gary Meyers, sat one on either side of me. I sat somewhat to the rear of them, because they would be doing the talking and participating in the discussion in their representation of me. Across the table sat R. E. Cushman, Jr., commandant of Marines, his four stars glistening. His counsel was a one-star legal expert.

A short silence. The counsels took the measure of the other—wary, like cats come suddenly upon one another in the middle of the night. I watched, listened.

The commandant's counsel came alive. Sharp. Crisp. Spelling out a laundry list of what my counsel could not do or say. My counsel struck back, going straight to the heart of the issue.

"There can be no further proceeding in this action," I heard Curtis say, "by virtue of an investigation that disclosed that not only was there no wrongdoing, but in fact the primary issue on the table was six minutes of flying time with no evidence of any fraudulent conduct on the part of our client."

"We are afraid," chimed in Meyers, "that without a satisfactory settlement of that particular issue, we, as counsel for the defendant, have no other course but to advise him to take the matter outside the military system into the civilian judicial system."

What Curt and Gary were saying indirectly was that they intended to file countercharges and accuse the Corps of discrimination. The issue was to be resolved so that all of this would be taken out of my record. In short, the matter had to be resolved in such a way that it didn't damage my military career. If that didn't happen, they seemed to be saying, there would be a huge legal fight. The Marine Corps was smart enough to know that a trip down that road would look bad for the Corps if the issue went public.

The commandant's counsel immediately began to backpedal. Suddenly, the lawyers began to see lots of things in an eye-to-eye kind of mode.

There was an agreement that all charges would be dropped. My record would be expunged so that there would not be anything therein that could be misjudged, misinterpreted, or misunderstood by future promotion boards. It was an ecstatic time for us. We were winning—but the Corps was not going to lose the entire war. The checkage of my military pay would continue, for "even so, you still had not performed for certain periods of time. Therefore, we're going to take a certain amount of flight pay away."

MUTUAL VOICES
Curtis R. Smothers, Attorney at Law

I saw this as really an issue of command discretion. We made the visit out there and made it very clear that we were not going to hesitate to fight it and literally say what it was that improperly motivated the effort to discredit him. That was the whole thrust of the argument. The name of the game was, would they run the risk of trying to destroy Frank as opposed to looking at the fact that the investigation, with all of its smoke, didn't reveal any "intent" on his part to play games. The rules that the Marine Corps plays by in terms of computation of hours and qualifications of flying time just would not permit that anyhow. You can make a mistake as to what the log was, but you certainly wouldn't try to falsify the log. There were too many easy ways to do it. I think that someone with enough clout had gotten a hair up his ass and decided to try to "do" Frank. But as the discussions took place, it was very clear that wasn't going to hold water. It simply was not believable. You needed much more of a scheme and an attempt to defraud than what was presented. And they were contemplating charges, there's no question about that.

When we left the commandant's office, I was amazed to see a kind of comradeship seem to form among the lawyers—the two on my side and the commandant's counsel—in recognition of the expertise with which they had presented themselves in my case.

Final vindication regarding this matter was received in a letter from General Cushman on 20 December 1973. Although the Flight Status Selection Board again dinged me for "lack of motivation" in meeting the total number of flight hours required for currency in spite of my claim of approval of waiver, Cushman wrote:

> During our personal meeting of 28 November . . . you represented that your failure to meet those flying requirements was premised upon your belief that your request for a waiver had been granted . . . that you believed you were not obligated to fly any minimum number of hours. . . . Your representation that these facts constitute a sufficient basis to overcome the otherwise justifiable inferences of a lack of motivation, premised on your failure to fly the prescribed number of hours, is accepted.

The commandant's letter went on to indicate that my flying status would be reinstated and all copies of the investigation would be withdrawn from the record as would all other records in official files. At the same time, he issued a caution that I should be careful in the future.

I could breathe again for a short time. I was off on ten days' leave en route to Cherry Point. I spent some really appreciated time with my mother and sister in Denver, then went on to North Carolina for assignment in my new staff position.

I was due for consideration for promotion to full colonel. The issue was between me and another black lieutenant colonel, a supply officer. Funny, though. It was a weird, weird thing I had just been through. I thought, however, that I knew what the deal was. I knew that I was supposed to retire at that point.

I thought that the theory in someone's mind was based on the reasoning that what had just happened would force me into retirement. That would mean that there wouldn't be a black general in the Corps for at least another decade. Artful mind, that. And whoever was the driving force behind all the misery I'd just encountered was probably a bit frustrated.

Full colonel. Giddy thought. Could all of this have an impact on that?

Under ordinary circumstances, it would probably have been no contest, with my command and combat time. Somehow, I had to allow that there was more to what I'd just been through than met the eye. There were firefights in progress at the top of the Corps that could have very well presaged it.

My life had been really intense for quite a while now, and because Eleanor and I were separated and divorce was pending, I resolved to try putting it all behind me and press on.

23: Learning to Live in the Quiet Mode

With the Article 32 furor resolved, I had a delightful visit with relatives in Denver, then moved out of Curt's place down to Cherry Point Marine Corps Air Station. I'd no sooner settled into my staff job of assistant chief of staff, comptroller of the 2d Marine Aircraft Wing, when it was evident that, although there was some flying, my life was the doing and handling of budgets for the air wing. Compared to getting into the wild blue, it was dull, to say the least.

It really hadn't dawned on me that the "fix" was in, that I was already considered something of a persona non grata by virtue of the machinations taking place in Headquarters, Marine Corps, regarding the fight to see who would be the next commandant. It felt to me as if somehow my fortunes had gotten involved in that mix because someone had allowed the work I'd done on minority rights to become stuck in a rather highly placed craw. Let's face it, the powers that be thought that I had been doing a great job. In fact, they'd allowed me to continue in the assignment. I knew I'd made enemies; there was no question about it. Even so, my expectations for promotion didn't seem diminished in my own mind. When the colonel's promotion list came out shortly thereafter and I was not on it, I must confess that for a moment the adrenaline gave a squirt or two, only to give way to huge frustration.

I'd been passed over for promotion. Passed over for bird colonel.

Hell, I was more than qualified for the promotion. Combat fighter pilot in two wars. Wounded in the line of duty. I wanted to quit the Corps again. I really felt that with those qualifications I had every valid right to file a formal legal complaint about the "why" of that event.

The regulatory framework was in place to do just that, to allow someone who felt they'd been unduly challenged (or not selected) but was totally qualified. The drill was to file a petition to the Board of Correction or file suit against the Corps. My credentials were impeccable, except for what I'd just gone through. Smothers and Meyers counseled me to file the complaint.

MUTUAL VOICES
Alicia Joyce Downes

I received my degree from the University of North Carolina in December 1974. In the course of this period, Frank was transferred to Cherry Point, North Carolina. We saw each other quite frequently during that period. He would drive over. We became very close and started thinking about starting our lives together and looking at what that would mean in terms of his career.

My being passed over for colonel was big news in the black media and community. Simeon Booker, of *Jet* magazine, picked up the news as an item in his feature, "Ticker Tape, U.S.A."

Lt. Col. Frank E. Petersen was passed over by the Marine Corps in nomination to rank of full colonel—in spite of his struggle for the military . . . a combat pilot [in] Vietnam . . . recruiting minorities . . . bringing in hundreds of young blacks. It appears that the Marines 18% black enlisted men may not have a black general for another 6 years [22 August 1974, p. 11].

I can't think of many times in my life when I was more down than during this period. My attorneys still wanted me to file suit against the Corps. But I told them that wasn't what I wanted to do. What I really needed to do was to get my thinking cap on straight again. I drove up to Brown University in Providence, Rhode Island, to see my old professor pal, Dr. Bernie Bruce.

If quitting the Corps was high on my agenda, so was finding a way to stay. Bernie, as an ex-Marine officer, had been through some of the same trials and tribulations. He was, in fact, one of the clearest thinking guys I'd ever known. He could cut through the crap and see what the real deal was. So we just sat down and commiserated—networked might be a better way of putting it—looking at all the nuances of the thing. We discussed my toying with the idea of leaving the Corps, going into the Harvard Law School minorities program, where they were recruiting quite heavily to get minorities into their law school, or standing fast on first base.

It was a definite crossroads, and I had to make a decision. Bernie came through—again. He pointed out that the Corps often rigs these things to eliminate people.

"You have to see beyond the trap," he said, "and go for the gold."

Our conversation was pivotal. Bernie was one of the few people who I could share anything with—and when I wanted to get some straight scoop, he was the one. An astounding guy—absolutely astounding.

So I became determined to let the system cleanse itself. I knew that the system, although I felt it had wronged me, would do exactly that. All I had to do was sit it out and I would be all right the next time around.

That's exactly what I did, because I knew a power struggle was taking place that would yield a new commandant who would then do lots of correcting of those ills that had taken place before. If I had filed suit, I probably would've made full colonel (retroactively selected), but that would have been the end of the road. It would have been that old thing about stigma. I would've won—and I would've lost, too.

In short, I opted not to rant and rave, knowing that the power struggle was in and the enemies of old would become the friends of new.

MUTUAL VOICES
Alicia Joyce Downes

We talked, over a period of time, about the possibility of getting married. Frank is a very focused person, with very strong career goals. He knew exactly what he wanted to do with his life in terms of marriage and commitment to someone. I think he was trying to see how all those pieces would fit together. What he did was to first try to introduce me to the military. I started going to a lot of military affairs and functions with him. I think he was trying to see if this was something I could live with, because it was very much part of his life—it was really all of his life. I think that somewhere around this time we started really talking about getting married, started to feel that this was going to be a good match, that I enjoyed what I was experiencing.

Around the spring of 1975, they were thinking about sending him on an extended assignment, and I had been offered a position in New York. Frank said that he didn't want to lose me. He wanted us to be together and didn't want this separation to keep us apart. I went on to New York, but we still spent a lot of time together.

It was time to hunker down and be extremely quiet for anyone but the highest of levels within the Marine Corps. The general officer corps in the Marine Corps was divided into two camps, and it was a dog eat dog kind of thing all geared toward determining who would become the next commandant. It was an exercise rife with politics, because there was only one space to fill.

The "quiet mode" was important for me to adhere to at the time because of being passed over for promotion to full colonel. It is almost axiomatic that when that unfortunate thing happens, one's chances for advancement to star rank were practically nil. No full bull; no star.

So the other eligible black lieutenant colonel was made full colonel over me. That, of course, made tongues wag in speculation. It had become, people thought, a competition between him and me for general's rank. It wasn't that at all, and lots of people misunderstood that. The picture that many saw was that two blacks were competing as opposed to the vagaries of the system.

But I'd been passed over and another had been selected. How else could it possibly have gone? Central to this conundrum was a very senior officer (who shall be nameless here) who, I sincerely believe, had a great deal to do with the orchestration of the entire scenario I'd recently passed through as well as nonselection to full colonel. The ultimate goal of this individual seemed to be ensuring that, for years at least, there would not be any black officer ascending to general officer rank within the U.S. Marine Corps.

I think the scenario was probably planned to play out this way.

When I was passed over, I reasoned that I was supposed to be devastated and retire. Then Ken Berthoud would have been the only eligible black lieutenant colonel who could possibly be promoted to colonel and eventually to general officer rank for at least a decade. There was one promotion to star rank for supply and noncombat types about every four years. The time sequence for that to occur was askew. That was the whole scheme—and I peeped it.

So I didn't say a word. I lay back and followed the internal war for the next commandant as it played itself out in the *Washington Post.*

The letter-coding episode involves allegations that forms, individually typed . . . and sent out . . . may have been intentionally coded to make it possible to link individual Marine generals with their private views on the extremely touchy issue of who they favor to succeed [the commandant] next year. . . . Marine generals began complaining . . . and [a] Navy official estimated that roughly half of the 70 Marine generals either protested or expressed concern privately over variations in the way the response forms were typed [11 April 1975, pp. A-1, A-5].

And, still, I was as quiet as a mouse. Sure enough, after the furor at headquarters began to subside, it was maneuvered in such a way that, within a year, a female officer named Margaret Brewer became a general officer, making it the first time in the history of the Corps that a woman was promoted to star rank.

Considerable heat began to rise from certain areas of the media and many civil rights organizations as they asked a salient question.

"Why," they wanted to know, " would you promote a woman and not Petersen?"

The Brewer promotion actually began to level the playing field.

If you can make a woman a general, the quiet agitation continued, you sure as hell can make a black a general. And that wasn't the half of all the furor over my being passed over and Brewer's subsequent promotion to general officer rank from the minority community.

On 22 May 1975, Simeon Booker's "Ticker Tape, U.S.A." column in *Jet* magazine began its strut, chest stuck way out in front. Simeon wrote:

> The Marine's second black colonel, Frank E. Petersen, may take over one of the flight squadrons. . . . [He has been] recently approved for promotion and put in line to become the first black general in the Marine Corps.

By 1 July things never looked rosier. The new people at the helm of the Marine Corps made sure that Lady Luck was smiling on me as I was appointed for promotion to full colonel. In promotion ceremonies on the station flight line on 3 July 1975, I was officially promoted to full colonel by the wing commander, Maj. Gen. Ralph H. "Smoke" Spanjer, along with Lt. Col. Edward Johnson and Donald Morgan.

Wasting no time, the commander of the 2d Marine Aircraft Wing, Major General Spanjer, immediately assigned me to command Marine Combat Crew Readiness Training Group 20, stationed at Cherry Point Marine Corps Air Station, relieving Col. Clifford E. Reese, who was being reassigned to other duties. I thought it was time now to get my feet solidly planted again, and as my friend Bernie suggested, continue to "go for the gold."

MUTUAL VOICES
Alicia, Second Wife

We married in Virginia. I was still in New York on this assignment for the summer. Frank was in North Carolina. We met in Washington and Frank had a very close friend of his, Jim Smith (whom he'd met years before in Florida when he was a cadet), be his best man. It was really a small wedding. Just Jim and his wife together with us. We got married by a justice of the peace in Virginia around ten o'clock in the morning. I don't think either of us felt that we needed a big ceremony. We just really wanted to be together, wanted all these pieces that we were trying to work on to come together. I was trying to finish my degree, and he was trying to work through some things that had gone on in his life during 1974 and 1975 and get on with his career. So it was really great for both of us. We had a fast lunch after the ceremony. Frank put me on a train back to Philadelphia. He flew back to Cherry Point. We moved, with my small daughter, Monique, into Cherry Point shortly thereafter. Frank was to be the new group commander.

At that stage of my career, the ultimate responsibility was awesome. The group, comparable in size to a Marine regiment, provided specialized tactical and technical training for pilots and air crewmen assigned to the 2d Aircraft Wing. Besides having two training squadrons on board, a headquarters unit and a maintenance squadron, it also included two A-4M Skyhawk fighter attack squadrons and two attack squadrons equipped with the new vertical takeoff AV-8A Harrier aircraft. It also meant that Frank Petersen was going to be able to get into the cockpit once again and do some real flying.

Outstanding.

More importantly, there was another significant factor to be heralded that demonstrated that the Marine Corps was beginning to recognize the existence of the new equal opportunity demands of the twentieth century. My assignment as a group commander was the first such posting for a black officer in the history of the Marine Corps. I had already commanded a Marine fighter squadron in Vietnam. Putting the eagles on my tunic was heady enough, and now this. It was a great occasion, and I savored every moment.

I must confess that my assignment to Cherry Point gave me pause from time to time. It wasn't that I was having any real problems racially on station. But there was a time earlier in my career when I'd given the area short shrift. It was, after all, part of the South—the cradle of the Confederacy and all that portended. It didn't seem to be the problem some folks predicted. Life seemed to move along as it should, and I was happy for that, except for the Cadillac dealer in nearby Havelock, North Carolina, who swore he had no cars to sell me even though I could see them sitting on the showroom floor. I had to take a trip inland to Charlotte in order to buy the car I wanted.

On 30 October 1975, it all became official with the change of command ceremony. Three o'clock in the afternoon. The band sounded attention and the ceremony began. The manual of arms. The relief and appointment orders read. Colonel C. E. Reese relieved. Colonel F. E. Petersen appointed. Colonel Reese passed me the colors to signify the changing of command. Cliff Reese had a few words to say. I spoke my piece and the troops passed in review.

It was done.

Enter a new entity into my life. A gorgeous, big, heavy golden retriever. I dubbed the new guy Clyde. He was very aggressive. Clyde and I went everywhere together. We walked. We went running together. He was my absolute buddy.

MUTUAL VOICES
Monique Downes Petersen, Adopted Daughter

He's my father for all intents and purposes. He's the only father I know. I was a baby when he came into my life. How playful he used to be with me. I used to tell my mother about it a few years back, like how we'd play hide and seek and I'd go hide and he'd come looking for me—start opening up the drawers and stuff like that. I remember when I was hiding, I'd think, he knows I can't fit in that drawer. Why is he looking in that drawer for me? We had a good relationship. He and Mother kind of eloped. I was about six or seven. I was never opposed to it. When the decision came to adopt, they both sat me down and asked me how I felt. I said it was fine. I was still so young. For me, it was like a given. I had been "Downes" at school. They just put in "Petersen."

A new day. I was on the other side of a strange kind of crossroads of my life. And now, a new promotion, a new wife and daughter, a new command—and time to continue a career that had come within an ace of an ignoble end.

I looked out over the tarmac and savored the den in which those new Harrier AV-8s resided. Not only was I now going to fly, but there was the additional challenge of learning to fly an airplane new in the Corps inventory. I'd seen it coming when I worked in the Division of Aviation back in the Pentagon, and now it was there in front of me and I was one of the boss men where people would come to learn to fly it.

I could hardly wait to learn to fly it myself. I'd watched and listened to the roar for days. Listened while pilots took it airborne. It growled like no other fighter jet had ever growled into the air before. Straight up, like a helicopter, up into the air, its tandem gear hidden, the outriggers pinned back while it twirled like a merry-go-round laid out flat—hovering like a hummingbird about to take a sip from a great, big old flower, only to storm away in mountains of sound like a well raised fighter jet ought to do.

I had to have some of that, for, after all, at the time the Harrier was the single most interesting flying machine in the American military arsenal. But you don't just jump into the Harrier and expect the usual. How you were trained depended on which airplanes you'd flown before. I'd been an F-4 Phantom jockey plus. So this was going to be interesting. There were a hell of a lot of other things to worry about and learn as well as being the group commander. But that Harrier called insistently and loudly.

Anything looking that devilish just had to be tamed.

Breakout Into High Country and Tall Grass

24: Harrier Country and Beyond

It's sinister, as if the designers made a pact with the devil. . . . It's raw power held in critical balance by delicate control. . . .
—John Trotti, First to Fight: An Inside View of the
U.S. Marine Corps, p. 97

There are several routines that trainers use to teach a pilot to fly the Harrier. The training approach depends upon whether the pilot has flown or transitioned in other aircraft. Colonel Woody Gilliland, USMC (retired), remembers that, in my particular time frame, there were probably twenty to twenty-five different sorties involved in transitioning someone from another airplane. In my case the transition format was primarily from the F-4 Phantom jet and an entire group of other fighter jet aircraft I'd flown as my career progressed.

But I went out there and began to train with the rest of the guys learning to fly the Harrier. Ideally, it would have helped if I'd had a background as a helicopter pilot as well as a fixed-wing jet background. Because I'd never flown a helicopter, that's exactly where I began, learning to fly it in a hover mode. That was a challenge in itself. I finally mastered the art of it, however, and my time arrived to meet the new beastie, the vaunted AV-8.

I could tell that this was an airplane without a bunch of unnecessary paraphernalia hung on it. Everything that was needed, plus a plethora of things we'd added to the first English versions we'd gotten, all contributed to its vertical/short takeoff and land (VSTOL) design. That was its reason for being. The ability to stay close to Marine ground fighting and to operate from grass fields, roadways, pads, or wherever it was needed. Quick turnaround. Short-stage distances from the target provided the ground commander with almost immediate backup and coverage. Exhaust nozzles that swiveled. Bleed air horizontal and lateral flight controls. Blow-in doors. Huge engine inlets. Just looking at the airplane was to know that this strange craft was going to require some different operating skills.

MUTUAL VOICES
Col. Woody Gilliland, USMC (Retired)

It's a much more demanding airplane. You're busier in the cockpit as you transition from living on thrust to wing-borne flight. Going accelerated and then decelerating. It's just the opposite as you trade wing-borne lift for thrust. There's an additional lever in the cockpit that controls the nozzles, so you're working from nozzles to power, which are movements that you don't make in a conventional airplane. Normally, when you land an airplane, you're back on power, whereas in a Harrier you're really up on the power. You're asking a lot of it. Basically, it's just a more demanding airplane.

Inside the cockpit, the AV-8 looked almost like a conventional setup, until you began to check out the VSTOL controls. There was that extra control handle over on the left quadrant next to your left sporting sector angle detents, a duct pressure gauge, a nozzle pressure indicator—basic control mechanisms necessary for VSTOL flight. These are the controls that helped the Harrier become more than an airplane that flew conventionally, with an added fillip that made flying her trickier as you learned to substitute engine thrust for velocity-generated lift. It was learning to vector those nozzles to the fully vertical so that engine thrust opposed the weight of the aircraft to the point where the thrust became greater, causing the airplane to ascend from the ground like a helicopter. To go from ascent to normal flight, it was reorienting the thrust vector forward, causing acceleration so that conventional flight was possible. It was mind-blowing, because you had to erase the normal stimuli you would have in terms of flying a jet fighter, and blank that portion out, to concentrate on the new environment you were in.

My very first flight in the Harrier was a little dicey. I really wanted to be good, because, after all, I was commanding the people who trained other folks to fly these things. Unfortunately, "being good" wasn't in the cards that day. Because there were no two-seater trainers, my first flight was to be simple. Just take off in the thing and hover. That's all. Take off and hover. The control stick would control the wings and nose and keep me within a certain area within the hover. That's what I thought.

Oh, I got that baby off the ground, all right, and it roared like a banshee. In hover, the damned thing acted as if it wanted to play hummingbird, darting from flower to flower, except there were no flowers, just designated parameters of hover flight in which I was required to stay. No luck. I wandered outside the designated area, inside the area, outside again—hell, I was all over the place. That was the toughest thing I've ever done psychologically in a cockpit. I finally got my hands on that sucker and had some measure of control, I thought. Then when it was time to land, I reduced power too much, hit the tarmac hard, and damaged the nose gear.

Woody Gilliland, then a captain, thought it was great fun to see the group commander make an ass of himself.

"Yeah," Woody has since remembered, "he banged one down a little bit—damaged the nose gear. We had a lotta fun with him about that."

Although it was something of a stretch, I put on my "good-natured hat," took all the kidding and guff, and bought beers for all the guys. I was very, very careful to never let that happen again.

Level flying in the Harrier was just like flying any other jet fighter. The difficult part was going from level flight and transitioning into hover, or from hover transitioning into level flight. We had to learn a whole new set of responses and mechanical movements within the cockpit to achieve those.

It wasn't long afterward that I was considered a Harrier pilot for sure. No problem.

The year 1976 was to be a busy one for the outfit, which by now had been redesignated Marine Aircraft Group 32.

It was my largest command responsibility at that point in my career, and it included more than eighteen hundred officers and enlisted at its highest staffing point during my stint as commanding officer. Our official mission remained "the conduct of offensive air support operations in support of Fleet Marine Forces from advanced bases, expeditionary airfields, forward sites and aircraft carriers and the conduct of such other operations as may be directed." To ensure that the unit was ready, able, and competent to do that, it trained—over and above its other mission of training pilots to fly the Harrier and its other assigned aircraft.

Aerial demonstrations and static displays of the Harrier abounded and were performed all over the country, and Canada, when requested and approved. There were training deployments, to include air-to-ground and air-to-air weapons delivery; press briefings; and orientations of important visitors—congressmen as well as visiting generals from foreign countries.

Most important was our support of military exercises with mission names like Palm Tree I and II, Palm Tree III and IV, Firex, Solid Shield, Fire Support Coordination Exercises, and, in February 1976, Exercise Rum Punch, in Puerto Rico.

Rum Punch was memorable because it allowed me to do something I'd always wanted to do, and that was to visit the place my father was from, no matter how brief the visit. As part of the air staff for that exercise, we deployed to Rosie Roads (Roosevelt Field) in Puerto Rico. We had a free weekend, and Woody Gilliland and I grabbed a flight over to Christiansted on St. Croix in the Virgin Islands. Woody went his way while I spent a day, night, and half the next day wandering through my father's birthplace and hometown.

I meandered around the island, just reflecting on the fact that my dad had been born and raised there. The only person I really talked to was a cab driver. I hired him at the airport when I landed and told him I wanted to take a look at the island—just to drive around. It was an attempt to get into my father's skin, I suppose. To see what he saw, to vicariously do what he'd done when he was there. So we drove essentially the same route that my father had driven the publisher from Topeka who eventually helped him come to America. I can't really describe the feelings that welled up inside me as I did that. I suppose you'd have to do something like that yourself to connect.

After the drive, I set the cab driver up for dinner and drinks to show my gratitude. As we sat in the cafe, a sort of waterfront village in a native area, suddenly he jumped as if he'd been shot. His eyes stared over my shoulder; deep concern distorted his face.

"What's wrong?" I asked.

"That's my wife, mon," he said, groaning and pointing to a quickly approaching woman.

"What's wrong?" I asked again, concerned.

"That's my wife, mon," he repeated. "I'm supposed to be workin' and I theenk she mad, mon," he said with a gasp.

"Well, tell her I hired you and that you are working."

"Later," he insisted with wide, fanning gestures as if to extinguish all of the fires of hell. "Later, mon. Not now." He groaned, and his smile was laden with real anguish.

I could only wish him well and good luck.

During my short tour of Christiansted, I suppose one of the things that overwhelmed me the most was the abject poverty. People using the back of the house as bathrooms and so forth. Of course, these areas weren't the places the tourists went. Not at all. Later, I went where the tourists arrived and stayed. First-class, upgraded five-star hotels. I reflected on some of the social problems that I'd heard about, and suddenly I could begin to understand how, long years ago, islanders who called themselves "states' rights guys" went out onto one of the beautiful golf courses and executed a group of tourists. A yell, a scream. The act had come from a deeply abject place. When you saw the living style of the natives on St. Croix versus that of the tourists, the contrast overwhelmed. The haves versus the have nots. How poor the people were. It was striking. Murder isn't a justifiable thing; but after seeing conditions there, you can begin to get in touch with what those men must have been feeling on that fateful day.

Through June 1976, the outfit continued training and doing aerial and static demonstrations and all of those things a unit training for the ultimate does, to include more exercises to ensure skill in battle, should it come. Things really began to get interesting as training periods intensified, heralding carrier workups with CVW-19 aboard the USS *Franklin Roosevelt* by VMA-213. My own carrier qualifications were coming up too, scheduled aboard the USS *Guam* sometime in July or October.

Questionable antics by some of my younger, more vibrant officers on deployment down in Key West, Florida, got my undivided attention. It seems that they were proving that it was the sacred job of young bachelors to go out on weekend liberty and raise holy hell.

Major General "Smoke" Spanjer, the wing commander, called me in.

"Frank," the general began, "I understand we've got a little excitement down in Key West."

"Yes, sir," I said, knowing damned well that it was vastly more than "a little excitement." These jaybirds had gone into town, gotten a little loose, and ripped up some telephone booths and so forth.

"So, what do you think we oughta do?" asked General Spanjer.

"Well," I rushed, "let me make a call down to the CO at Key West and see if I can't get it squared away."

To keep it off the record, I coordinated to have the guys pay off the damage, throttle back, continue with the training, and stay the hell out of town. So it was all smoothed over. But that was part of my job as a commander. They were my people and it was my job to look after them and look to their welfare—as long as that's possible.

There were twelve of them. By 1997, one of them was a two-star general.

Sometimes, life is sweet.

On 20 July 1976, life was about to get sweeter. It was the day for initial carrier qualification flying a Harrier AV-8 aboard the amphibious assault carrier USS *Guam*. Major Drax Williams and commander of VMA-513 Detachment A led the way, making the first of forty-four landings that day.

Earlier in the day, we'd taxied our Harriers down the runway at Bogue Field and started our flights over the Atlantic to find the USS *Guam*, fifty miles out to sea. Close in, we switched our radio frequency to the ship's channels and its tower in order to receive landing instructions. The round-robins began. Land. Stand by for a clear flight deck. Launch again. Circle. Land.

To qualify in carrier landings, it was necessary for me to successfully land the Harrier six times in an outing. To maintain the qualification, another four landings had to be made. Life was good and getting better as I circled for what I figured was my last landing of the day. Tension mounted as I was directed to keep circling the ship, because the carrier deck had been fouled and was being cleaned. A Harrier had landed with a fuel jettison valve stuck in the open position, and jet fuel was spewed all over the flight deck.

Navy fire crews scrambled and swarmed over the deck with hoses, swabs, and equipment needed to cleanse the deck of a fire hazard, which could have jeopardized everyone on board the carrier. A maintenance crew fixed the fuel jettison valve on the Harrier.

While all this was going on, I was still up there in the pattern, circling and recircling the ship. I wanted to get my landings completed so I orbited some more, hoping that the fouled deck problem could be solved. An instrument check showed that my fuel was down to critical stage. It was time to do something, or it was right into the drink.

Permission was granted to proceed to our divert field fifty to sixty miles away, so I boogied for that one. Just about ran out of fuel when I touched down. It was close. I refueled and fired back out to the carrier. By the time I returned, carrier qualifications were still being done. I got into the flow of it, performed my last landing, and made a little Marine Corps history at the same time.

"Colonel Frank E. Petersen," bragged the *Cherry Point Windsock* [20 July 1976, p. 15], "commander of MAG-32, became carrier qualified in the AV-8A Harrier."

A quote from my friend Drax Williams in the same article put the icing on the cake: "Colonel Petersen," he related, "is the first group commander and colonel to ever carrier-qualify in the Harrier."

Marine Air Group 32 was the setting for an entire series of "firsts" during the remainder of 1976. The unit just seemed to hum. On 21 July, VMA-231 came under the operational control of CVW-19, conducting seaborne operations aboard USS *Franklin Roosevelt* (CV-42) and becoming the first Harrier squadron deployed aboard a CV-class aircraft carrier. An AV-8 performed a conventional landing and an arrested landing at Twentynine Palms in California. Major General R. E. Carey soloed the AV-8A on 30 November 1976, becoming the first general officer to be qualified in the Harrier.

The AV-8 was showcased across the country. In an Andrews Air Force Base air show. At the St. Louis Bicentennial Celebration. In New York at the Spirit of '76 Air Show, and at the Chicago Air and Water Show, watched by millions on television in August.

About this time, the assistant commandant of Marines, Gen. Samuel Jaskilka, sent me a message advising that they'd like to pull me from my present command and bring me to Headquarters, Marine Corps, so that I could be exposed to working with the higher elements of the Corps. That made me stop for a long moment, considering what I'd just gone through with the "headquarters" crowd. But then, the cast of characters at that level had drastically changed. Attitudes had obviously also changed, and my conscience was clear. However, being completely rational about the matter, I would have to be awfully thick not to begin to wonder what was behind this sudden invitation to labor in the headquarters camp. Obviously, some plans were afoot that could affect my career, I thought.

I was just too well raised to refuse the request. I knew it must be time to go behind the desk for a while. So, it was with a great deal of reluctance that I decided to leave MAG-32—a flying billet, one of the best in the Corps, flying the Harrier. I left the command in December 1976 to return to Washington, D.C.

There was a sizzle inside. To be tapped for that job, working for the number-two man in the Marine Corps in the most sensitive job in the

Corps, could mean being in contention to receive a star. Alicia, Monique, and I wondered about the future.

I remembered a saying attributed to Harry Truman: "If you want a friend in Washington, get a dog." After my experiences in that city, I had come by my own rule, which was: "If you want a *true* friend in Washington, bring your *own* dog."

Clyde was going with me.

25: Way Station

*There is a need for a "first," but we Americans tend to glamorize
the first black or minority associated with an event.
These titles give me a bit of a hang-up.*
—Lt. Gen. Frank E. Petersen, USMC (Retired)

It had been a long journey to this place: executive assistant to the assistant commandant of the entire Marine Corps. Once or twice I might've pinched myself. Reality check. It was really true and happening.

I hadn't really thought that much about it, but even this new position was the first time a black man had ever held the job. It was a busy, powerful position, calling for frequent contact with high-echelon Department of Defense officials and major commands. It was a "plum" assignment, no doubt about it. It kept me busy and offered a different view of how the Marine Corps really operated.

Working at the four-star level, I had access to everything that goes on in the Marine Corps and was in on the decision-making processes at a high level. Basically, the job was administrative in nature, loaded with paperwork, but it also carried a certain degree of influence. I became a kind of adviser in addition to being an administrator. If I was trusted as an adviser, then it would follow that I would wield influence by virtue of my advice.

Maybe the sweetest times were those in which General Jaskilka used me as a sounding board, asking for opinions on numerous subjects. These special times occured much more than I'd ever thought possible. I gave him my opinions, including advice in personnel or aviation matters. He came to me on many occasions for advice perhaps by virtue of my twenty-eight-year involvement in aviation matters—during which time I'd picked up some nuances, some ins and outs.

I also learned that I'd be way ahead of the curve if I gave candid answers—often not the kind of answer he would expect, because often the answers were not aligned with published policy. That was a must for me: If I felt something was not correct, I'd tell the boss why I didn't think it was. Sometimes he'd take my advice; sometimes he wouldn't. But at least I'd given it to the best of my ability and always from the center of where my particular truth lay.

It was also my responsibility in this position to supervise the normal office routines and oversee the field trips by the assistant commandant to Marine installations worldwide.

Perhaps I should refer to this special position as a kind of "way station"—on the way to my first star. That was, of course, a very private and personal observation. But I did feel a certain amount of pride by this time in my career. In spite of the roadblocks that had been placed in my way, I'd been able to accomplish goals of some pertinence. Completion of flight school. A Marine Corps commission. Managing to live through my first combat experiences right out of flight school. Of course, there were other big "pluses" for me—my first squadron, my first group, and getting to fly several types of aircraft.

I was also aware that my career was being watched by many blacks in the Corps due to the possibility of my promotion to star rank. At that time, I had to agree that the environment was ripe for the promotion of a black into that high arena. But I wanted to be sure that the selection would be based on merit as opposed to skin color. I felt that I could fly an airplane as well as my white counterparts. I also felt that, in the area of command, I had proven that I could hang tough with the best of them. In fact, I'd evolved my own thesis on the issues of management, delegation of authority, and assignation of the final responsibility.

The military, I thought, was possessed of a simple design with regard to delegating. Squadron commanders were like their civilian counterparts—corporate managers. They outlined goals they expected their subordinates to achieve, and established checkpoints on the way to meeting their objectives. In the execution of part of my responsibility for following up, I suppose I cheated a bit. I delegated authority, not responsibility, because the ultimate responsibility for the organization at hand was mine. As the commander, I instituted lower-level checks and balances through which I determined the flow of a program. If I discovered that a unit manager was not doing what he was supposed to, I fired the son of a bitch. I found that the sooner I did that, the better off things were, because as a project continued, the incompetent wielded more influence.

This doesn't mean, however, that I had to be a hard-ass to succeed in the military. As the commander, I knew and communicated with all levels—from those who managed the structure to those who pushed the brooms. A basic mistake that some managers make is that, although they sit atop a ladder, they fail to realize that weakness on the lowest rung can topple the whole enterprise. The biggest lesson I learned in developing my management style was understanding that the people I supervised were also in a competitive system and needed my recognition—which I always tried to provide.

Frankly, I felt that if I were to be given the title of "General" and the subtitle of "black General," I would have rejected the whole notion. But the Corps had come a long way since I joined back in the 1950s. Then, the question of whether or not there could be a black Marine general was purely academic. For when I went through flight training, it wasn't a question of what levels blacks could rise to. The question was, where are the blacks? In 1975, the Corps stood wide open, and not just in the aviation field.

I was not in a position to make even an educated guess as to the selection of a black general in the Corps. But if one were selected, the fact of it would make a hell of an impact. There were only two black colonels in the pipeline at the time, so it was surely to be between the two of us. I would've been lying through my teeth if I'd said that my fingers weren't crossed.

Regardless of who got the promotion, it could not help but have a beneficial effect on the morale of black Marines, officer and enlisted. When dealing with a force that was about 16 percent black without their having any representation in the general officer ranks, this was something the kids knew and thought about.

As I'd traveled around the Marine Corps on various trips, I had privates first class, corporals, sergeants, and even staff noncoms walk up to me and stop, with a special wonder and pride in their eyes.

"You're the first black colonel I've ever seen," they'd enthuse.

"Well, thanks," I'd say in return. "But there are only two of us. It's just a matter of working into the ranks."

Truly, it was a matter of longevity. Black officers in the past hadn't stayed long enough to attain the maturation necessary for high-level assignments and promotion. The computation was simple. It took twenty-seven to thirty years for an officer to progress to the rank of general. I was the first black aviator and I was a full colonel after twenty-eight years of service—so I figured I was on track.

A day that saddened and gave me pause was 25 February 1978. My good friend, and America's first black four-star general—Air Force general Daniel "Chappie" James, Jr., died unexpectedly, only fourteen days after his retirement from the military. Chappie and I had become good friends over the years. It was his philosophy that it would be a good day when we no longer felt it necessary to cite the fact that somone black was "the first" to do something in America. I'd often quoted him on that. He'd been by my home just the preceding New Year's Eve. Joviality had overflowed.

I was part of the throng who came to mourn and mark his passing at the requiem mass in the Shrine of the Immaculate Conception in Washington, D.C., on 1 March 1978. Wall-to-wall generals, admirals, and ordinary people. The crowd threatened to spill outside the great cathedral. I will always remember how Rep. Charlie Diggs from Michigan put his hand on Chappie's casket, the tears flowing. Charlie thought the world of Chappie. He loved the man. The next day, I was there in Arlington National Cemetery when they buried Chappie. It was bitter cold. I can still see Chappie's wife, Dottie, in my mind's eye; their sons and daughter; all their children and grandchildren standing at the grave site veiled with grief. Dottie and I became close in the years following Chappie's death. Chappie never got a chance to draw a retirement check. Our friendship was a book I closed very slowly, with great respect and sincere admiration. It was Chappie who'd counseled me, helped keep me in the game.

I marked it in my mind that America had lost a great patriot. It was sad, I thought, that millions of Americans hardly knew his name and what he had done for them. I knew, and resolved to honor the memory by going as far in my service as I could possibly go. It was the least I could do.

After eighteen months as the executive assistant to the assistant commandant of Marines, anticipation was in the air. New orders were coming. Different winds were beginning to blow new vistas my way.

The call was chief of staff for the 9th Amphibious Brigade on Okinawa.

In February 1979, President Carter let the cat out of the bag by announcing my nomination for promotion to brigadier general. By mid-March, the selection was approved by voice vote in the Senate along with eight other colonels to be promoted to star rank.

I'd become the first black man to achieve flag rank in the history of the U.S. Marine Corps.

Lots of Americans don't realize it, but the Marine Corps keeps combat battalions afloat in almost every major ocean in the world on a continuous basis so that when the whistle blows, it's just a matter of turning the task force in the right direction. Those task forces, like other elements of the Corps, are constantly being trained and reoriented and are, by participation in planned exercises, ready to be effective instantly.

That's how, as chief of staff of the 9th Amphibious Brigade, I found myself aboard the USS *Whitney*, part of an eight-ship flotilla, off the east coast of North Korea. An annual operation conducted jointly with Korean forces, Operation Team Spirit was designed to demonstrate continuing support of South Korea while executing joint military training exercises.

About three days out to sea, before we could really seriously get the exercise and training maneuvers under way, there came an unsettling report about a black Marine who'd been murdered on one of the ships in the fleet and thrown overboard. About a week later, Korean authorities notified us that his body had washed ashore on the east coast of Korea. It took a while, but after an investigation, we were successful in identifying the culprits. The probable murderers turned out to be four white Marines.

I knew immediately that I had a potentially explosive situation on my hands, as racially charged as anything anyone could imagine. Four white Marines killing a black Marine and throwing him overboard. Even if the racial mix had been different, it still would have been a big-time problem. Although the investigation showed that the attack was a drug deal gone bad, the fact of that gave no surcease. Because the perpetrators were white, it was doubly important that I, as chief of staff, make it really clear that there would be no pussyfooting around in the handling of the situation. I sent my noncommissioned officers into the crew holds at once, talking to the troops, explaining what had happened and what my stance would be.

I had the suspects removed from their ship, transferred via launch to the USS *Whitney*, and placed in the big brig (jail) aboard my ship. I made myself very visible during the transfer as the prisoners were brought up the gangplank in manacles and placed into lockup. I made it clear that the suspects would be handled by the book; without favoritism of any kind. I went to their ship and down into their crew compartments so there'd be no doubt who was in charge. I also visited the other ships for the same reason. In short, I wanted the brothers to see the brother locking these guys up. It was necessary, to avoid tensions.

These suspects stayed locked up, because living space was at a premium aboard ship, and in those close quarters it would have been very easy for things to get hot. The idea was to prevent a replay of the problems experienced by Navy aircraft carriers and other vessels.

That wasn't why we were out there in the Yellow Sea. Concentration on Operation Team Spirit was our real focus. But other forces over which we had no control attacked us.

It happened so gradually that not many of us noticed how bizarre the sky was beginning to look. Although it was beautiful around sunset, the sky was filled with a strange kind of foreboding. Blood red in places, green streaked above the distant horizon, deep green near the horizon. As nightfall approached, the stars seemed to dance across the sky. Stars suddenly turned silvery, then extremely white to reddish or blue. The moon was full and intensely haloed [Gary Lockhart, *The Weather Companion*, p. 540].

Christopher Columbus was the first European to write about what we were seeing over the wide sea—a hurricane. Out there, it was called a typhoon. Storm winds rising to seventy miles an hour; swirling clouds forming an eye from ten to thirty miles wide. Inside the eye, the sky was clear, the temperature mild. Around this paradise an inferno of winds circled, gusting at phenomenal speeds. The storm's diameter stretched for miles. The ocean swells grew deep and deeper. The weather fouled. The bows of our ships plunged deep into the green water.

We steamed away from our intended landing areas because of the storm. Steamed hard, trying to get out of the eye. It hung our little fleet on its fringes, and we took winds swirling at fifty knots. My ship rocked severely, plunging deep into the angry waters, the waves breaking fifteen to twenty feet high. Experiencing twenty- to thirty-degree rolls, the bows of the ships periodically disappeared underwater. We couldn't go above decks. It was just impossible. Everyone on board was seasick. Anyone in lockup was extraordinarily miserable. Sailors were upchucking all over the place.

I stood it all until near midnight, then went to bed, grabbed hold of my bunk, and held on with my gut full of water because that's the way I'd survived these things before. We were all heavy on Dramamine. It helped a little.

When you're selected for promotion to general, it is tradition in the Marine Corps that the commandant of the Corps calls to tell you about it—no matter where you are in the world. Well, it was three in the morning and here I was in the middle of a typhoon on board an amphibious troop ship doing an amphibious exercise off the eastern coast of Korea when the call came through. It was Gen. Lou H. Wilson, commandant of the Marine Corps, calling to give me the news.

"Oh, no," I gurgled when they came to wake me up. "Not now," I groused. I knew that my body would not cooperate once I began moving around. I could feel it coming on. I was so seasick that I could hardly stand up as I went to the radio room for the radio relay message from General Wilson.

"Well, Frank," I thought I heard him say, "you've done it. You've been nominated for that first star. Congratulations."

"General," I started, "you have no idea—thank you, sir." I managed to hold on long enough to say thank-you one more time, to say, "You have no idea how overwhelmed I am at the moment," and then I threw up in a wastebasket.

I couldn't wait to get back to Okinawa and tell Alicia and Monique the good news.

MUTUAL VOICES
Alicia, Second Wife

Oh my goodness, he was so excited. He was—I don't know—he was like a little boy. He was saying he just couldn't believe it. He was telling me how he was out on the ship, and he had gotten the word that he had been selected and that the boat was rocking. People all around him couldn't understand what had happened. When they found out, they all were excited for him. He came back and he was so—well, he's a very private person. He's the kind of person who'd never get on the phone and call everybody, so I always did that. I did that. I was so excited. His old friend Jim Clark was around when Frank made full bird colonel and was commander at Cherry Point. Jim had said then: "Well, you've made it. You've peaked." Jim also knew that Frank always wanted to fly, so he figured Frank had gotten where he wanted to go.

But in Frank's mind, he wanted to be a general. I believe he was shooting for that all along. That and, whenever there was a new plane, always wanting a new challenge in terms of flying—he wanted part of that, too. There would be nothing stopping him in terms of age or anything like that. He never felt restricted.

With the promotion, my tour of duty in Okinawa was interrupted and I was returned to the United States very quickly. It seemed that the Corps director of information had a newsworthy event on his plate. The U.S. Marine Corps was about to make its very first black general officer, and it was hell-bent for election to make the most of it.

I was ordered to the West Coast for a media blitz and flown into the Los Angeles area to be apprised of my publicity itinerary.

It began with a meeting with Major General Maloney, commanding general of the 3d Marine Aircraft Wing, on 19 March 1979. From there I was helicoptered to the Marine Recruiting District in San Diego to meet with Major General Schulz for a briefing on recruiting and recruit training. Around 10:30 A.M., the interviews with news media began. Kip Cooper, *San Diego Union*. Paul Cours, *San Diego Tribune*. That afternoon, it was Jack Jones of the *Los Angeles Times*.

Folks seemed to want to know what I thought about things in several arenas, and I began to tell them. I shared my feeling that after my promotion to star rank, it would probably be a long time before another black was promoted to general officer rank. I explained the dearth of eligible bodies because blacks almost traditionally hadn't chosen the Marine Corps as a career. I shared the history of it, that blacks didn't really enter the Corps until 1943, that black officers were first commissioned about 1947 but didn't stay around. I noted that I was perhaps the first black to come in and stay in, the first black to get a regular commission, and one of only two black colonels on active duty in the Marine Corps, and that the other had elected to retire after thirty years of active service.

My promotion, I pointed out, would create a gap to fill because there were only seven black lieutenant colonels in the entire Corps. And of that group, I hazarded a guess, the next black full colonelcy would be at least two to five years off—so one black general was going to be the status quo for several years.

I noted the staff positions within the Corps that had helped me immensely. I loved to fly, but if I had stayed in the cockpit, I doubt I would have been as strong a candidate for selection, because the Marine Corps does not look for ability in just one area when it is considering promotion. It was also my intent, I noted, to stay in the Marine Corps as long as I could remain competitive, and I looked forward to competing for two- or three-star rank.

One reporter asked the $64,000 question. It shocked me in a way, because it was so out of sight.

"Would you like to be commandant of Marines some day?" asked Kip Cooper from the *San Diego Union*.

I had to grin a bit, but I took a huge breath and dove in.

"Well," I said, "that would be like shooting for the moon—that would be going all the way to the top. But if it came about, I'd give it a try."

Then I told them about my forty miles of jogging every week, taking out my frustrations on the handball court, and playing chess.

I knew, though, that the big question hadn't been asked. I'd long pondered my answer. Although the question came through the barrage subtly, it gave me an adrenaline rush.

"What took the Marine Corps so long to promote itself a black into star rank?"

Another deep breath was called for, and I took it.

"The other services have used blacks since the days of the Civil War. Blacks have always been part of the Army and, of course, the spinoff from the Army, the Air Force, as a result of World War II. The Navy and the Marine Corps were the last to come aboard in terms of using blacks in key roles. It was not until 1952 that a black entered the service and stayed to go through the competitive process to the rank of brigadier general—and that black was myself.

"Quite simply," I continued, "the Marine Corps was the last to integrate and the last to have black officers."

There was, I admitted candidly, a history of real discrimination extant in the Corps, but I allowed that the Corps had begun to attack the problem. "By virtue of being last to accept blacks over the years," I posited, "there had developed the theme that the Marine Corps was a 'white man's club.' It was noted by Julius Williams, a former head of armed services and veterans' affairs for the NAACP. That was absolutely not true from the 1950s on to the present time," I averred. "Black Marines have fought and fought well, in all roles."

I explained that relations between blacks and whites had become a crucial issue during the civil rights era, and those issues surfaced quickly within the military.

"Race relations for all the services became a problem in the late 1960s and early 1970s. Recognizing this, the Marine Corps immediately moved to adopt a formalized training program for all of its members that would deal with the subject of race relations."

It was, I explained, in 1969 that I was made special assistant to the commandant for minority affairs and helped develop programs that could operate to defuse racial tensions in the Corps. They began with recruit training.

"How did that work, Colonel?"

"Well, the first thing you do is break the recruits away from their background and environment; you begin to erase the differences. You show that blacks do have likes and dislikes, that whites do have likes and dislikes. And you are, in essence, forming a melting pot. This is one of the most difficult tasks with which America is faced, I think. The military—specifically, the Marine Corps—has done one of the more outstanding jobs in this area. The signs of it are subtle. As you go off a base, look around. If you see a white kid and a black kid going off together to drink beer, you know that you've achieved a degree of success."

"But, Colonel, it hasn't all been peaches and cream, now, has it?" shot a reporter.

I admitted that there had been failures, true enough. The unfortunate episode in November 1976 at Camp Pendleton where a group of black Marines assaulted a group of white Marines whom they mistakenly thought were Ku Klux Klan members. Interestingly, however, an investigation of the charges brought against the blacks revealed that there were at least seventeen Klan members on the base. Punishments were swift.

And so went the publicity regarding this new ascendancy in my career. I was helicoptered that afternoon to El Toro Marine Corps Air Station to rest and have dinner, then was off around seven in the evening to be a guest on the *Merv Griffin Show*. As I recall, neither I nor the talk show host impressed the other. The only saving factor was Ed McMahon, another guest that night on the Griffin show, who saved the moment because he was an ex-Marine Corps fighter pilot. A low point of the day for me and the host, but scintillating conversation between the two guests.

Radio and television interviews consumed much of the following day. Twenty minutes with Larry McCormack, KTLA-TV, and the *Pacesetter* program. An interview with Chuck Whitten, on National Public Radio's *All Things Considered,* scheduled for airing on 218 public radio stations. All of it ending with a shot on KNBC's evening news program with Tricia Toyota.

Although I definitely considered my pending promotion to star rank the crowning point of my thirty-year career in the Marine Corps, I tried to downplay that aspect of it throughout this media extravaganza. More important things mattered. The fact, for example, that I was the first black to reach this position was significant because it meant a lot to the minorities in the service.

To get in touch with that calls for getting in touch with realities before inane giddiness because of a star. The armed services were not at that point without racism, although it surfaced in those days only in isolated instances. The system was clean of any institutionalized racism because it was dealt with in such a severe manner. The Corps was concerned with quality rather than quantity—an encouraging sign.

But I still remembered the day I was forced to land because of weather at the Montgomery (Alabama) Municipal Airport in my Marine Corps fighter jet during the bus boycott days. And I can still see the look on the faces of the National Guardsmen when I climbed out of the cockpit. It was as if to say, my God, now they have their own air force. The looks of astonishment and occasional negative reactions could still be found as I walked onto other Marine bases. It was extrasensory. I could feel the anger and, sometimes, hate. But even that energy had to be turned into a positive thing. It kept the kettle boiling and the pressure up. Training can't solve everything.

My promotion was walking, living proof that a black could make it.

"Will you be happy, Colonel, when you reach the day when no one asks you about that aspect of your military career anymore?" a reporter asked.

"Yes," I replied. But I felt moved to add, "But I don't think I'll see it in my lifetime."

I thought of my flight out of Tokyo on the way home for this round of publicity after the promotion was announced.

"Are you the one?" people wanted to know.

The attention has been, and is, significant because our society is still recovering from the trauma of the Civil War. I decided long ago to live with that and go seek my own destiny.

26: Brigadier

*NBC Nightly News . . . did not possess the truth on why
you were "awarded" your Brigadier star. . . . You may wear the stars,
but you will NEVER be a Marine Corps General in our eyes.*
—From a letter to Frank Petersen from an anonymous
Marine Corps "Senior Officer," 26 September 1987

Not everybody in the Corps was overjoyed at my selection for promotion. Certain of the people who already wore the stars of a general weren't applauding my good fortune. In fact, I had the feeling that some of these gentlemen just plain didn't like me. Some of the resultant slights could be really cutting and were extant long before my selection for brigadier.

For example, the guy I roomed with when we were on one of our European tours from the National War College was approached by a fellow white officer who tried to impart scurrilous gossip about me.

"What's this I hear about Frank?" he allegedly mouthed derisively.

"Dunno. What'd ya hear?" my friend replied. "What are you talking about?"

"Well," he reportedly continued in the most confidential, all-knowing kind of way, "I understand that he's a womanizer and that while you guys were out on that trip, he was up all night drinking and chasing women and just making a complete embarrassment of himself and the Marine Corps."

"He did all that shit?" my friend asked.

"That's what I hear."

"Well," my buddy said, laughing, "he must have done it between twelve o'clock at night and five o'clock in the morning, because I was with him except for those hours."

The look was hard as the gossipmonger slunk away, hands jammed deep into his pockets.

"See ya," said my friend, waving him on his way.

Conversations like this one were only the tip of the iceberg landlocking the racial hatred that until now had been kept under wraps regarding my climb up the ladder within the Corps. The hate mail was even more revealing, some of it coming, I am sure, from certain officers also wearing stars. The depth of the hate and disgust inherent in the very souls of some of these officers didn't surface until I eventually attained the rank of lieutenant general. (I'm jumping ahead of the curve here for effect.)

Being interviewed on the *NBC Nightly News* (on 21 September 1987) after that promotion resulted in the writing of one of the more hateful letters I've ever received. I quote part of that letter here and save other parts of it for later in the book.

Signed only "Semper Fi," and "A Senior Officer," because he was still on active duty at the time (26 September 1987) and said he did not "desire [the] possible personal repercussions from this correspondence," it was the usual hit, run, and hide tactic to which so many racists and bigots resort. He could not possibly have known the final outcome of my flying time situation, the resultant investigation and official decisions (unless he was part of the attempt to discredit me), because the matter was sealed forever and expunged from the official record. This individual persisted in spouting invective and hate based only on hearsay.

In excerpt, the "Senior Officer" wrote:

> Regrettably, NBC Nightly News apparently did not possess the truth on why you were "awarded" your Brigadier star, and you certainly failed to inform both the interviewer and the American public on the exact circumstances leading to your flag promotion. Since you were so demonstrative during the interview in pointing out that some white Marine Corps "Generals did not want a black General on their watch," I believe it is only appropriate, fair and honest that you now reveal the entire "Frank Peterson" story. Should you have forgotten the details perhaps a summarization of the facts are warranted.

"A Senior Officer" then continued, ostensibly as an "expert" without a smidgen of the information that would qualify him to be such:

> During the period you were eligible for promotion to Brigadier General, external pressures were placed upon the Department of Defense to promote minority officers. Since you were a Colonel, and the U.S. Marine Corps' senior minority, you were thus promoted to Brigadier General. In so doing, an investigation in which you were thus subject was expeditiously and silently terminated.

A white Colonel or a black officer, at any other time in our military history, would have been Courts-Martialed [sic], certainly not promoted, for falsifying his Aviator's Log Book, receiving remuneration [flight pay] for flights never flown from NAF Andrews and for submitting false official statements, all acts which you did but were never adjudicated because of the abrupt cessation to the investigation. Additionally, rumors of spousal abuse have circulated amongst the officer corps for years. . . .

It is obvious that "A Senior Officer" was woefully out of touch with a good many things, and further discussion here of his wild imaginings would be like talking into an empty glass.

But then, you win some and you lose some. If I was a loser in the eyes of that afflicted soul, I was a winner in the eyes of others who mattered vastly more. On 28 April 1979, the Kansas House of Representatives issued House Resolution No. 6069:

A RESOLUTION recognizing and commending Brigadier General Frank E. Petersen as the first black Marine to attain flag rank in the U.S. Marine Corps.

WHEREAS, Brigadier General Frank E. Petersen is a native son of Kansas and was reared in Topeka; and

WHEREAS, Brigadier General Frank E. Petersen was the first black Marine aviator and was the first black Marine to attain the rank of brigadier general in the U.S. Marine Corps; and

WHEREAS, All Kansans are rightfully proud of Brigadier General Frank E. Petersen's distinguished military career: Now, therefore,

Be it resolved by the House of Representatives of the State of Kansas: That we recognize and commend Brigadier General Frank E. Petersen for his distinguished military service and extend our congratulations to him on his selection and appointment to the rank of brigadier general; and

Be it further resolved: That the Chief Clerk of the House of Representatives be directed to send enrolled copies of this resolution to Brigadier General and Mrs. Frank E. Petersen in care of General Lewis H. Wilson, Commandant, U.S. Marine Corps, The Pentagon, Washington, DC 20350.

A decided upper. I simply couldn't let "A Senior Officer" and his literary efforts upset any particular applecart. It was certainly upsetting, and it hurt that someone would be so asinine and mean. But, let's face it, "A Senior Officer" didn't matter, because what the president gives, the president taketh away—and, as an old partner once exclaimed, "and the president don't care."

Promotion ceremonies for brigadier general was a day full of sweet music for my soul. It was a day I'd dreamed about and strived toward for years. And here it was, in spite of all the fire and brimstone thrown around by guys like "A Senior Officer."

By now, Alicia and Monique were on their way from Okinawa to join me in Washington, D.C., at Marine Corps headquarters for the official conferring of my first star. Alicia looked smashing in a two-piece powder blue suit. I felt a bit naked in full uniform with no insignia of rank on my epaulets. As we approached the area off the commandant's office where the pinning was to take place, I could feel the perspiration as my nerves began to twang. One look at the crowd, and I was impressed. Of course, my family was there. My daughters. My son and brother Billy. My sister. Old Marine buddies. Old Marine buddy Dr. Dale Tipton, who showed up wearing a stylish turtleneck. I was privileged to introduce him to the crowd as my "hippie friend from California." I don't think he'll ever forget that, but it was all in fun, believe me.

Suddenly, the Navy aide called attention as Gen. Lou Wilson, the commandant of Marines, made his entrance. A few well-chosen words later, attention was called to order, announcing my selection to the rank of brigadier general. I stood at rigid attention throughout. The commandant administered the oath of office.

"So help you God?" he finished.

"So help me God," I replied.

I followed his suggestion to cross in front of him and join Alicia and the aide, the keeper of my new set of stars. One star went to the commandant, the other to Alicia. Together, they officially "pinned" the stars on the epaulets of my tunic. I became a fresh-caught brigadier general as scores of camera flashbulbs lit the space with miniexplosions of light like wee lightning strikes. I could feel their heat.

The aide presented my brigadier's flag with its one glaring star to the commandant, who immediately handed it to me. I kissed my wife, left the flag with her, then seemingly floated to the lectern to give the crowd my good wishes and thanks for being there to share this day of good fortune with me.

It was then off to a reception at the commandant's home at 8th and I Streets in Washington, where a reception line waited that never seemed to end. Good words. Congratulations. Hugs and kisses. The sweat that one of my daughters loved to tease me about continued to pour off my head and ran rivulets into my shirt collar and over my face. I tried to control it, but it inundated me. It was interesting, watching the ladies get set up to float a congratulatory kiss on my cheek, then think better of it as the perspiration glistened.

Later, after all the official sound and fury, Alicia and I had a reception at the Sheraton for our family and good friends. It was there that a strange euphoria overtook me as I opened up my general's one-star flag, wrapped it around myself, and snuggled up in it.

"He took that flag," Alicia likes to remember, "and he wrapped it around himself and he sat upon this chair like he was on a throne."

Well, I don't know about that—but it had been quite a few hectic days.

And it didn't stop. Before I knew it, I was flanked by the two senators from my home state of Kansas, Nancy Landon Kassebaum and Bob Dole, there to offer congratulations on the promotion to brigadier general. Senator Dole went far afield in his statement to the Senate about the promotion. I particularly liked part of what he had to say:

> I am proud to note that among those to be confirmed was Frank E. Petersen from the Great State of Kansas. . . . [His] career has not been solely one of flying around the world in defense of our country. In 1969, the post of Special Assistant to the Commandant for Minority Affairs was created and initially filled by then-Lieutenant Colonel Petersen . . . [who] served as . . . valuable advisor . . . [leading to] solutions of minority problems. . . . I join the people of Kansas . . . and particularly those from Topeka, in congratulating . . . [him] . . . for his dedicated work and high principles . . . result[ing] in his historic promotion to Brigadier General in the United States Marine Corps.

In May 1979, I was assigned to the Pentagon as one of the deputy directors for operations in the critical National Military Command Center under the Joint Chiefs of Staff. It was a way to utilize those of us who were fresh-caught stars in joint tours involving all the services. It put us in a place where we would stand the watches and actually monitor communications coming into the Pentagon from all over the world.

The assignment was a tremendously important one, because we were on watch around the clock as the end point alert posture position for any worldwide threats that could involve the United States of America, to include threatened or real nuclear attacks against the country. Data funneled to us had been refined for validity through other central command structures operated by five joint-service, binational crews on eight-hour shifts over five consecutive days. A senior officer from each service (U.S. Army, Navy, and Air Force, and Canadian services) reviewed the data coming from satellite sensors in geosynchronous orbit, ground-based radars, and/or other intelligence sources. "Events," like a missile launch by a foreign power, were immediately assessed for geopolitical and/or threat potential. The commander in chief, North American Air Defense Command (CINC/NORAD), had scant minutes and seconds to make the threat determination. Only three answers applied: "no," "yes," or "concern" (the "maybe" option). When assessment was complete, notification was made to the national command authority—which is where we fresh-caught one-stars hung out under our boss, a three-star general, a deputy for operations under the secretary of defense. Our job was to get the word regarding the worldwide events that affected the United States to the people who could take action to counter or handle the threat.

The duty was no cakewalk. It superinundated my life. On watch eight hours, off sixteen. On the fourth day, two days off. Recycle to a different schedule. In at six. Off at two. In at two, off at ten the next morning. In at ten at night, off at six in the morning.

Shortly before I reported in, the command center was required to coordinate the removal of the bodies of the 911 victims of mass suicide from the Jim Jones's People's Temple cult at Jonestown in the Guyana jungle by Military Airlift Command (MAC). There were times during that assignment that I feared not only for my own life, because of what I knew and the things I handled, but also for the lives of my family and loved ones. I knew, since elevation to flag rank, that we all were receiving a little bit more scrutiny. It was also the time when there was some fear abroad of military generals being targeted by militant groups. It was a time of tension, not particularly calling for paranoia but for all of us to personally be constantly on high alert.

It was also the season that my ex-wife, Ellie, decided to take a shot at me through the Washington media. Columnist Judy Mann of the *Washington Post* [18 May 1979] thought the story of a "deserted wife" worth the ink, although the actual divorce had taken place years before. Under the first installment headline, "After 20 Year Hitch, She's Out of the Picture," Ellie spoke of the wedding night versus my Marine Corps orders to monitor an atomic bomb explosion, of incipient racism within the Corps, of the need for a marriage to be "a buddy system," how her house was like "an officers' club." Her "light skin," my "dark skin." Ad infinitum. I was very suprised at the venom, and a bit hurt. But I think, in the long run, I thought the world and life vastly larger than that. I was surprised that the media thought it important enough to publish. For me, it was just another thing to keep inside. Keep my head up, do my job, pursue my career, get on with my life.

In the spring of 1979 came the night watch when things of such magnitude threatened that I thought I would have a heart attack. It was about three o'clock in the morning when feed from CINC/NORAD, buried deep in Cheyenne Mountain, Colorado, displayed on our huge monitoring screens evidence that indicated early warning of incoming missiles. We're talking the probability of nuclear-tipped missiles equipped to range distances greater than three thousand miles. We'd had anomalies on our screen before that had turned out to be nothing. But on this display, the number of missiles had begun to jump. Five of them, then ten. Their numbers kept increasing until there were at least a hundred missiles in the air, all coming toward the United States.

The data we were watching was cross-checked with data from satellites in geosynchronous orbit with infrared detection capabilities, and by ballistic missile early warning radar systems. This thing looked real.

"What the fuck is going on?" I queried my crew chief.

"Boss," he opined, "I think this might be a false alarm," hope riding high in the tenor of his voice.

"But what if you're wrong?" I asked.

Only silence from my crew chief. He had no answer. I had the ball. I had to get the answers. I immediately hit a button that gave me a worldwide connection to various listening and alert posts. I began to poll them to determine if they'd experienced similar anomalies. One of the posts responded that they'd had some unusual activity in their sensor system, so I immediately went to a higher level alert—which told all U.S. forces to go to a higher posture of readiness, and especially Strategic Air Command (SAC).

There was no time to question. No reason to doubt. It was just time to boogie, get people notified, do what had to be done, because our central command centers didn't play around with this one. The answer to the question "Is this a threat to North America?" had come up hollering, "Yes." Our satellites confirmed it through infrared detection according to the data. The identified event was confirmed by ballistic missile early warning radar systems, the data said. A further check against scheduled rocket launches and tests of other known activity didn't augur a mistake.

Minutes mattered now. That perspiration thing of mine came stomping back. Rivulets of sweat began their march from the crown of my head down around the backs of my ears. My heart stormed inside my chest. Adrenaline pumped.

If my hair could've stood on end, it would have.

Now we needed to know exactly what the hell was going on, because the missiles were still in the air but we couldn't get closure points. Our data said that their points of origin were various sites within Russia. I cranked up the alert level again, and U.S. forces began to break out their defense/attack procedures. I rang up a secure conference to query what was going on. Curiously enough, NORAD, which originated part of our data input for our screens, was not getting the same signals.

So I asked Strategic Air Command, "Hold, if you can." I should have known better, because no one in the Pentagon or in most of Washington tells Strategic Air Command what to do. Their procedures are firm. When the whistle blows, they go. Screw everything else.

Those guys were rolling already. Absolutely.

We began to track down missiles, interpolate impact points. We were five minutes into this. Watching the screens intently. I knew that something was wrong.

"Hey, the missiles aren't closing. Look at the signals. The missiles aren't closing," I muttered. They were in the air, but nothing was happening. We really buckled down to try to figure things out.

And then our screens went blank.

"What in the hell?" I exclaimed.

"No idea, General," my crew chief sighed.

By this time, I'd alerted senior officials in the Pentagon, and they were on their way in. When they arrived I began to brief them, only to get a few funny looks.

"Look," I shot, "you'll just have to see what we saw on tape." Everything was recorded, thank God.

An immediate investigation was begun, SAC was debriefed, and I spent all that day in the Pentagon, going around to the various scientists, even talking to the secretary of defense and the chairman of the Joint Chiefs of Staff about the matter. I briefed the senior generals. In all, I spent twenty-four hours in the Pentagon before I could finally cool down. Then, of course, I had to go back on watch.

When I walked into the center that evening, I looked at my crew chief, and he looked at me.

"Let's hope it's quiet tonight," I said with conviction.

"I do hear that, sir," he responded.

It had been a close call. One of the closest. Training data, simulating a massive missile attack, got into the "live" warning network by mistake. Luckily, it was caught within a few minutes before response action messages were issued. I understand that since then, even more stringent measures have been taken to make certain that a similar episode never happens again. It is that kind of mistake that should never be linked to our National Military Command Center. The possible end results are too horrible to contemplate, certain to contribute to the untimely deaths of millions of innocent people.

On 6 June, the *New York Times* reported that "North American Air Defense Command computer malfunctions indicating the Soviet Union had launched nuclear missile attack on US triggers American defenses into high state of alert," noting that it was "the second such error in 7 months" [*New York Times Index Book of Record,* 1979 Je 6.14:1]. An assistant secretary of defense averred that the United States was far from ordering missiles fired or bombers into the air. "We weren't remotely close to World War III," he said. The chairman of the Joint Chiefs visited the Strategic Air Command in Omaha and the Air Force's underground complex at Cheyenne Mountain. "The White House," the article insisted, "reportedly instructed the Pentagon to get its act together," as computer specialists descended upon Cheyenne Mountain to "study computer systems thought to be responsible for nuclear alerts."

Unfortunately, it would not be the first or the last time that such a miscue would be experienced. On 10 November 1979, the *Washington Post,* in an article entitled "Missile Alert a False Alarm," would pinpoint the reasons for the miscues. "A computer foulup," it noted, "triggered a false alarm of a Soviet missile attack . . . a tape used for simulating a missile attack was loaded on the North American Air Defense (NORAD) command computer . . . for a routine test." On that occasion, "six F-101 fighters from Canada and four F-106 interceptors scrambled in response to the false alarm."

The watch was also mine on 26 October 1979, when Gen. Park Chung Lee, South Korean president, was assassinated at the Blue House by the chief of the Korean Central Intelligence Agency (CIA).

It was mine, too, on 4 November, when some ninety people, including sixty-three Americans, were taken hostage at the American embassy in Teheran, Iran, by militant student followers of the Ayatolla Khomeini who demanded the return of former Shah Mohammad Reza Pahlavi, who was undergoing medical treatment in New York City. I called the secretary of defense and advised him that the embassy had been taken over.

"By whom?' Secretary Harold Brown wanted to know.

"By a bunch of unarmed Iranian militants. The Marine embassy guards were not allowed to shoot," I explained. And that, of course, set everything in motion in the sense of coordination with state and military and the whole nine yards.

The Superior Service Medal for service rendered May 1979 through May 1980 was awarded me. The citation read in part:

> The judgement and perception demonstrated by General Petersen in response to the needs of the National Command Authorities were instrumental in coordinating numerous actions which were in the national interest. His professionalism was evidenced by the paramount success achieved in several critical military operations managed from the National Military Command Center. Brigadier General Petersen's distinctive accomplishments reflect great credit upon himself . . . the Corps . . . the Department of Defense.

Sounded great. But the night I thought the Russians were really coming was a night in hell I'll never forget.

My new assignment took me back to Marine headquarters and to a billet I considered part of my continuing learning process—director of Facilities and Services Division. As such, I found myself in charge of all the U.S. Marine military facilities worldwide, including exchanges and commissaries. It was certainly a job rife with paperwork, including the need for expert planning and programming of underway construction and stocking and furnishing our post exchanges all over the world. Once a quarter, I found myself on the road, so to speak, getting to see the operation of these facilities firsthand and to know some of the people involved. Not flying the latest fighter jet in combat, but solid.

During this period, I was invited to be the featured speaker at the annual convention of the Montford Point Marines in Atlanta, Georgia. A distinct pleasure. These were the survivors of the first group of black Marines that the Marine Corps ever allowed itself to have under the full court press of World War II. Following the order, on 7 April 1942, from the secretary of the Navy requiring that the Navy, Coast Guard, and Marine Corps allow blacks to enlist, the Marine Corps formed a battalion of nine hundred blacks. They were trained separately, at a place in North Carolina called Montford Point, adjacent to Camp Lejeune, where white Marines were trained. Montford Point was to become as synonymous with black Marines in World War II as Tuskegee was with the first black Air Force pilots. I was honored to be invited and to be thought of so well by these pioneers of the United States Marines and the odyssey of black men in the Corps.

After all the good fortune—a new wife and child, promotion to full colonel and now brigadier, I couldn't help but wonder what was next.

In 1982, I was assigned as assistant wing commander, 1st Marine Aircraft Wing, stationed at Camp Butler on Okinawa. It was obvious that big changes were coming into my life. Before the family packed to leave and after long conversation, we decided that I should legally adopt Alicia's daughter, Monique, and bring her into the Petersen fold. I was glad we did. The accomplishment of that stopped any speculation as to her background. Of course, my retriever guy, old Clyde, had to be readied for the trip. I remember that the Japanese were scared to death of Clyde. They don't have many dogs. The ones they do have are decidedly smaller than my guy. When Clyde stood up on his hind legs, his forepaws reached my shoulder. My guy. My buddy.

27: Wing Commander, 1st Marine Aircraft Wing

On my way to my new assignment, I couldn't help but reflect on how our world was shrinking. Getting to Okinawa consumed mere hours now, a walk in the park compared to my first trip to the Far East. Then, I was on a four-engine transport, and it took something like eight days from El Toro, California, to Korea.

However long it took to get there, I was damned proud to have drawn the assignment—assistant commander of the 1st Marine Aircraft Wing, a Marine Corps unit with an illustrious past. Fourteen battle streamers attached to the wing's colors bore silent witness to the seventeen years it had spent in combat throughout its forty-two-year existence. Presidential Unit Citations for action in World War II and in Guadalcanal, Korea, and Vietnam. In China and the Philippines. Vietnam Cross of Gallantry. Philippine Liberation. An outfit that, during the 1950s, proved and improved the Marine Corps doctrine of close air support, introducing the helicopter and Marine jet aircraft into combat for the first time. It was a proud wing, and I was proud to be its assistant commander. A few butterflies skittered inside my psyche, because I knew the way the Corps operated. First assignment as assistant to a billet like this was to be an understudy—like being vice president. If you do well, the odds are you'll be president one day. In this instance, a wing commander.

After Alicia, Monique, and I had gotten ourselves settled in, I went about the business of being "vice president" with gusto. The "boss" was Maj. Gen. Joseph J. Went, whose career paralleled my own in the passage of time. He began his Marine Corps career in 1952 and got his wings in 1954. He served with Marine attack, recon, transport, and fighter squadrons, commanding varied Marine organizations as his career progressed.

The name of my game was to be the best damned "vice president" that J. J. Went ever had by following the credo I'd established for myself. One, I wouldn't get in his way. Two, I would follow his directions specifically, and three, I would act as a sounding board to properly advise the boss and give him guidance in certain areas with which he may not have been completely in tune. One of the more enjoyable parts of my job as vice president was to be able to spend a considerable amount of time with the troops, traveling to all of the bases in our area of responsibility; acting as the boss's spokesperson—the same as the vice president does.

It was a great assignment, especially because I could spend lots of time in the cockpit pursuing my first love—being a Marine Corps pilot. Swinging that twin-engine Phantom jet around the sky; shades of Vietnam. I also got some time in the cockpit of the A-4M, a hot attack single-engine jet.

Alicia settled in, too, accepting a position as a schoolteacher in the local school system. But things were about to change radically. In January 1983, I was nominated for the second star—presaging movement up to the rank of major general. General Went was moving on to a new assignment as deputy commander, Fleet Marine Force Pacific.

"Friday, the Sixth of May, Nineteen Hundred and Eighty Three at Half Past Eight O'Clock, Marine Corps Air Station (Helicopter), Futenma, Okinawa, Japan," read the cover of the change of command program. The morning seemed decidedly sweet. All that pomp and circumstance. The call to attention. Adjutant's call. The "sound off" command and throatily growled "Report." The publishing of the "orders." Then the trip to the center of things on "Officers' Center." Troop the line. Honors. The 1st MAW flag is delivered. Remarks by the commanders. Went wished me well; I wished Went well. The troops passed in review. Over all of it came the strains of the Marine hymn—and then it was done. The change of command was complete.

The second star was in place.

I might sound blasé about it now. But I didn't feel blasé then, for I knew that what had just transpired marked a pretty outstanding achievement. Big-time stuff that had never happened before in the annals of the Marine Corps. A black major general who now commanded an entire air wing. And, down the line, I knew it could lead to command of a major command—and there were very few major commands in the Corps. It made the pulse race.

There was a parade, the honors, the gun salute, and a large reception in a lovely setting in a building high atop a hill.

My job as newly elected "president"—an air wing commander—got my complete attention on 1 September 1983 when the Soviets shot down a South Korean Boeing 747 passenger jet with 269 souls aboard for allegedly violating Soviet airspace.

There were no survivors.

The thing happened in our area of responsibility. We had no particular role to play initially, but because we had no idea what the United States political reaction would be toward the Soviet act, my Marines just sort of leaned forward a little bit. To let folks who might be interested know that we were in the area, so to speak. We did lots of maneuvers in the Korean area and down in the Philippines. We couldn't be missed. We were all over the Far East in so many ways.

All of it was just a smidgin above routine for us, however. We usually had small alerts when the North Koreans made a rumble. Being part of the defense forces for South Korea was part of our mission, and there was always something to respond to. At least once a month at the very least there was some kind of minor flap that would keep us on our toes.

Keeping the troops on their toes was one of my primary goals as wing commander, and I made it my business to work at realizing that. Sometimes I felt that my troops were going crazy because they never knew when the "president" was going to show up. They never knew where I was, really. My command was far-flung. I had units in the Philippines, sometimes in Hong Kong. Units in Korea and on mainland Japan.

On more than one occasion, I would fly to the Philippines and see my guys there, take off, hit an airborne tanker, land in Japan and see my people there at Atsugi, get back in the airplane, and make a mad dash over to Korea. So I'd have breakfast in Manila, lunch in Tokyo, and dinner in Seoul.

It wasn't about snooping. It was about seeing my command in real time, fixing a thing before it became an unmanageable problem. If I had to get my hands dirty with my troops or my uniform soiled in doing it, I was never too proud to tote that barge right along with them. It was about being the leader and a manager. Although I loved to fly, in this billet I was a manager as opposed to a fighter pilot. There's not another job like it in the Marine Corps. We were as close to a real combat training environment as we could reach. So touching base with my forces was my priority all the time. Even though I had capable commanders, I'm a "hands on" person. I wanted to go there, see it, and touch it. Talk to the troops myself. That's the way I've always operated.

MUTUAL VOICES
Lt. Col. Hugh Mitchell, USMC (Retired), Former Inspector General, 1st Marine Aircraft Wing, Circa 1983–84

> *General Peterson is the epitome of what the Marine Corps means when it says "leader." He had those qualities in great quantity. And one of the marks of a leader is, although the Marine Corps is not a popularity contest, do people like you? And if they do like you, they give you 100% versus 85%. And he was liked.*

For all of that, however, things happened. Things that broke my heart. Like the night we were in the middle of a Team Spirit exercise in cooperation with the South Korean forces. In that exercise, one of the assigned missions was to carry out a simulated helicopter raid on an east coast installation in South Korea. It was night, of course, and, due to radio communications problems and dense fog in the valleys, one CH-53 helicopter carrying fifty troopers became separated from the main group. The pilot attempted to find his own way up the coast and inadvertently ran into the side of a mountain.

The ship went down about two o'clock in the morning, and I wouldn't let search and rescue launch because of weather conditions. I could've easily suffered more casualties because of the dense fog permeating the landscape. As soon as first light hit, we got into the air and discovered the crash site in about an hour. There were no survivors.

A flash alert went out to Headquarters, Marine Corps, signaling the existence of a serious event in our unit. Casualty handling. Next of kin notifications. In all, there were three or four helicopter crashes during my tour.

In 1984, some white troopers, resplendent in their white sheets, tried to play Ku Klux Klan by running through some barracks in which a bunch of black troopers were billeted. News of this unhappy episode came to the attention of the commandant of the Marine Corps, who gave me a call with instructions to handle the situation. I called in my inspector general (IG) guy, Lt. Col. Hugh Mitchell.

"Hugh," I said, "I want you to go out to that detachment and find out just what in the hell's going on."

"Yes, sir."

"And Hugh?"

"Yes, sir?"

"If you run across those fellows, let them know I'm the commanding general, and give them an IQ test, will ya? People must be crazy."

"Yes, sir. Must be crazy, sir."

"Yes, they really must be. Check 'em out, Hugh."

"Yes, sir."

Well, it turned out that the guys were having a beer party. It was a detachment, which was the way they'd rotated their squadrons to the Far East. Unfortunately for them, they were on their way home, they thought, finishing up their tour.

"We were just celebrating the end of our tour, sir," one volunteered. "We were just having a beer party, and then some of the guys decided to—er—put on Roman togas, sir."

When Hugh told me, I figured they'd had to dig really deep to come up with *that* one.

"Okay," I sent the word out to them, "you just Roman-togaed yourselves into having your squadron stay here until the investigation of this thing is completed. You'll be here until I get this thing sorted out."

I wasn't about to let them go home until I found out the truth.

The completed investigation showed that it was, after all, just harmless fun. But if I had not done anything, it would have given a negative twist to it. I made it plain that that kind of action within my command was a distinct no-no.

In the early 1980s, the Corps was paying a great deal of attention to the racism within its ranks. That emphasis sometimes begged the question in my commands.

MUTUAL VOICES
Lt. Col. Hugh Mitchell, USMC (Retired), Former Inspector General, 1st Marine Aircraft Wing, Circa 1983–84

It was time for our visit from the Fleet Marine Force Pacific inspector general. Prior to the arrival of the big IG, I did my own little inspection of our Wing to be sure that we were in compliance in several areas of concern. One discovery I made was that our Wing had no race relations program going. No documentation. No race relations officer. No sensitivity training in progress.

"General Petersen, sir," I began.

"Yes, Hugh?"

*"We're about to be inspected by the fleet IG and we're all out of compli-
ance in our race relations program, sir. No program, no documentation,
no race relations officer, no sensitivity training going on, sir."*

The general looked at me for a long spell.

"Hugh," he shot, "show him my picture on the wall."

"Yes, sir."

*Well, sure enough, we were about to get dinged for lack of a race rela-
tions program, but I felt it only right to explain what General Petersen had
said. So I showed him the picture on the wall.*

*The IG's man only smiled, and I just knew we were in the soup. But
guess what? We didn't get written up. Wow!*

While in the billet of wing commander on Okinawa, I thought of the
long way I'd come. From a little black guy in Topeka who thought his
only hope in this world, once the initial tour of duty in the military was
over, was to go back and open an electronics repair shop as his father
did. From that same little black dude who found himself not only fascinated by airplanes but who longed to see what the rest of the world
was like. I saw it. The wars. The racism. And, so far, I'd gotten through
all of it to sit here, the "president" of an entire U.S. Marine Corps air
wing. And I thought, America is a strange place, to put it mildly, but
where else would I want to be?

In three decades, I had seen nothing but good changes, though there
have been some things I've questioned in terms of Marine Corps direction, and that's part of the process. It has been a chance to meet and
know some extraordinary people. Like Marine Corps pilots turned
ballplayers Jerry Coleman and Ted Williams, and Ed McMahon of television fame—all aviators along with me in Korea in the 1950s. Sixty times
on that tour I'd flown out to find the tiger and lived to tell the tale. In
Vietnam, I growled at the tiger more than three hundred times; once
he growled back in a most meaningful way and shot me down through
the vapid and bitter Vietnam air.

It wasn't about that anymore.

There's no such thing as an "old" fighter pilot, although many of us
would like to have thought so. I was under no illusions—I knew that
some of those young turks in one of my squadrons could take me out
and wax me any day of the week. But I still managed to log about ten
hours a week in the air, and that was okay for the moment. It was real,
and I was privileged in more ways than one.

There are only three Marine air wings in the system, and I enjoyed the fact that I was with the most active. I could even sandwich in a little work on my hobbies, the truest of which was tinkering with antique automobiles. Nuts and bolts. I like to get my hands dirty. Here I was deep into electronics and video equipment, trying to figure out how to do more with a particular system. Like toying with the idea of investing in a satellite dish, putting it up on my roof, and seeing how many channels I could really pull in.

And for all the pomp and circumstance, I still liked to pull off a good within-bounds prank every now and then. It tended to make life a bit more interesting.

I didn't know it but I'd caused quite a stir at Camp Butler one morning since the commandant of Marines, Gen. P. X. Kelley, was touring our area of responsibility and was scheduled to participate in ceremonies honoring some of our troops who were to be decorated. All of the troops had assembled on the parade ground waiting for the general's arrival. My troops were trying to figure out why Frank Petersen, their commanding general, was nowhere to be seen.

Whispering abounded through the ranks.

"Where's our general?"

"Dunno."

"Where's Pete?"

"Hell, man, I haven't the slightest. He'd better get his ass back here before old P. X. burns his butt."

Fifteen minutes before the general's airplane was due in, I wasn't there. Seven minutes before the general's arrival, I still wasn't there. Five minutes, and their commanding general was still nowhere to be found.

"Where the hell is the commanding general?" some of my capable commanders bleated. And with good reason. Not a man jack of them wanted to try explaining my absence to the commandant of the Marine Corps.

Well, what my troops didn't know was that I had gone up to meet the commandant the night before and greeted and hosted him when he arrived at his first stop on his tour at our base at Iwakuni, Japan. On his departure, I—in uniform—said good-bye to the commandant, walked over to where I had an F-4 Phantom parked about a quarter of a block away, and jumped into my flight gear.

He was in a propeller-driven aircraft. So my wingman and I took off after he did and passed his aircraft en route.

Now the troops on the parade ground at Okinawa could see the commandant's airplane in the distance—and still their commanding general was nowhere to be seen.

Ah, the controlled panic of it all.

I imagine that some of my troopers jumped a bit to see this F-4 Phantom, my F-4, come charging in and taxi up to within a hundred yards of the review stand. I got out, walked over in my flying togs, and assumed the position of attention as I waited—along with my troops, some of whom took long, long breaths of relief—for the arrival of the commandant of the Marine Corps to land.

The commandant didn't know what I was doing, either. It was a little joke, played on the commandant, whose eyes grew rather large to see me after he'd deplaned and I greeted him, again, on the ground.

"Frank," he began bemusedly, "what the hell are you doing here?"

"Frank," his wife intoned, "didn't we just say good-bye to you?"

"Yep. Just a little joke here."

Polite laughter. A giggle. Eyes rolled heavenward within the ranks of my troopers, who still hadn't figured it all out, and probably hadn't until now.

P. X. Kelley. Commandant of Marines. Good man. A fine sense of humor. Thank God.

My time on Okinawa was over much before I wanted it to end. It was an enjoyable tour. Lots of responsibility, but that's what I like.

Our next assignment sent us to Headquarters, Fleet Marine Force Atlantic, at Norfork, Virginia. Here, I was the number-two guy in a command that encompassed perhaps half of Europe as well as the eastern portion of the United States. A Marine division and an air wing gave it punch along with quite a few NATO commitments in the European theater.

The assignment was a relatively quiet, uneventful one. Something of a hiatus. A time to gather myself together and refocus.

And then in June 1986 came what was to be the crowning jewel of my entire Marine Corps career—command of Marine Corps Base Quantico, the most unique post in the Corps. They called it the "Crossroads of the Corps." Thousands of Marines attended professional military schools throughout their careers, but it was at Quantico that all Marine officers began their careers.

In 1968, the base had been redesignated the Marine Corps Development and Education Command (MCDEC) in the spirit of the command motto: s*emper progredi* (always forward). My new job was to oversee all of that, integrating doctrinal issues, training and education, facilities, and infrastructure support within the command in order to ensure the production of combat-ready Marine air and ground task forces.

It was a humbling experience to have been given this vast responsibility. And I was proud, damned proud, of the Corps to have entrusted the job to me.

The third star of a lieutenant general flew to my collar and epaulets.

MUTUAL VOICES
Dana Charlette Petersen, Daughter

I was there when Dad was awarded his third star. As I watched, I thought I saw something else in the face of the commandant of Marines. I had a kind of flash, an intuition thing, that said, this is the last star Dad's gonna get. I just knew it. No question. The commandant's face also said it. You could read it. It was a look that said, this is your last star— so enjoy it. It was also the first time I'd seen anybody tell my father what to do—and he did it.

28: Assignment: Commanding General, Marine Corps Base Quantico

*[There is] no way to judge the impact that . . . a Black Lt. Gen.
had on youngsters in America. It wasn't widespread, but to those of
us who were Marines [it was] almost unbelievable.*
—Maj. Gen. Jerome Gary L. Cooper, USMC (Retired),
U.S. Ambassador to Jamaica

The Indians dubbed the place Quantico. An apt name. It occupies more than 56,000 acres in Virginia on the shores of the Potomac River. Residing there is the largest training center for Marine Corps officers—the Amphibious Warfare School, the Basic School for newly commissioned officers, the Communications Officers' School, and several aviation schools, to name a few. Founded in May 1917 by Franklin D. Roosevelt, then assistant secretary of the Navy, Quantico trained nearly 34,000 officers during World War II. Weapons, new amphibious craft, and tactics are also tested there. Additionally, the FBI Academy and the president's helicopter fleet are tenants on Quantico. Its Marine Corps Air Facility was the site of the first Marine Corps air station.

Located thirty-five to forty miles south of Washington, D.C., Marine Corps Base Quantico skirts the Potomac River athwart U.S. Highway 1 and Interstate 95. Becoming its commander was the ultimate Marine Corps assignment. It meant, among other things, that I had become, as they say, "one of the chosen few." It could not have come at a more propitious time, because I had then reached my thirty-sixth year of service. It was a chance to bring much of what I had learned over the years into play while the drive and focus were alive and well. I must confess that I was beginning to get just a little bit tired. It happens to everyone, "chosen few" or not, as the years grind by.

I became the new commanding general of the Marine Corps Development and Education Command (MCDEC), Quantico, on 20 June 1986, relieving Lt. Gen. David M. Twomey, during an indoor ceremony at O'Bannon Hall because of inclement weather. General Twomey was retiring after almost four decades of service to his country. It's difficult now to describe my feelings on the verge of the most impressive command of my entire Marine Corps career.

292

The commandant of Marines, Gen. P. X. Kelley, spoke at length, lauding General Twomey's career, finally wishing him and his family the "best of everything—after the brilliant leadership, the dynamic thinking and the selfless devotion" displayed by the general during his career. We watched as the commandant pinned the meritorius award on the general's tunic.

My time had come as I strode forward for the change of command. The orders were read aloud. General Twomey was "released from active duty, assigned to the retired list of officers from the Marine Corps." And then:

> From: The Commandant of the Marine Corps. To: Lieutenant General Frank E. Petersen. Subject: Permanent Change of Station Orders. Effective 20 June 1986, you will assume duty as the Commanding General, Marine Corps Development and Education Command, Quantico, Virginia and relief for Lt. Gen. David M. Twomey. Signed: P. X. Kelley, General, United States Marine Corps.

The organization flag passed from General Twomey to me. The gunnery sergeant marched it away. Twomey and I shook hands in parting.

Now, I was in command.

"Ladies and gentlemen, please rise, in homage to Lieutenant General Petersen."

"Present H'arms!"

The band exploded with "Ruffles and Flourishes."

General Twomey delivered his good-bye speech to the crowd. His wife, dressed in a print dress, with flowers in her hair, listened with pride.

Prideful, my children sat in the row of chairs behind Alicia. Alicia sat resplendent in a blue and white polka-dot dress. I felt them there, every one of them.

Standing tall, I made my acceptance speech.

> Dave, to you and your lovely wife, Ellen, this is going to be a hard act to follow. I wish you both the very best upon your retirement. There is always a feeling of awesome responsibility when one assumes command. Contrary to what you may believe, it's a beautiful, sunny day in Virginia.

Polite laughter swept the crowd. A jibe at the quickly clearing inclement weather that had driven the ceremonies indoors.

"I realize," I continued, "the mission that is before me and I realize the responsibilities that go with the accomplishment of the mission here at the Education Center. General Kelley, the commandant, I thank you for the opportunity to command."

Applause skittered across the wide room, and it was done.

Alicia and I received guests during a postceremony reception at the officers' candidate school. A very pleasant day.

Our move from Fleet Marine Force Atlantic in Norfolk to Quantico was essentially a door-to-door move. We simply knew we had "arrived" after assignment of and moving into the commandant's quarters.

Quarters Number One, typical in the military for the senior officers' housing, was big enough for three families. The two-story house had about eight bedrooms and a large drawing room. There were also three or four fireplaces strategically placed in the well-planned space. A far cry from our house in Topeka where I grew up. The front of the grand home was graced by a large circular driveway where maybe twenty cars or so could be parked. It was sumptuous and suitable for entertainment. In fact, I think it's one of the better sets of general officer quarters in the entire Marine Corps. I'd call it a showpiece for Marine Corps Base Quantico. A beautiful piece of ground.

MUTUAL VOICES
Bernie Bruce, Ph.D., Professor

I think it was in March of 1987, I called Pete up and told him I was coming his way to visit. I drove to the gate and stopped; the sentry saluted.

"Where can I find General Petersen?" I asked.

"Quarters One, sir," the sentry replied, snapping to smartly.

So I drove up to the sumptuous quarters. I think it was a master sergeant who ran his quarters. The sergeant came to the door. I identified myself and was let in. Presently, Pete came down the long steps, just beaming.

"Boy," I exclaimed, "who'd a thunk it? Who would'a thunk it?"

He had the grill on the hill, now. He had it all. And you know Pete—smiling from ear to ear. Even cooked me some fried chicken. He did some things down there [at Quantico]—he really did some things. He's a real machine when it comes to doing his duty.

As I gave myself a tour of the house and its environs, a glance out back brought me up short. Behind the house were the remains of a small, six-bedroom house I would call a shack. It had been the domicile, in the olden days, in which the stewards who served the commanding general had lived—close by, waiting for his beck and call. The poor souls who used to live in that run-down shack were more than likely black stewards—guys who held the kind of job that Navy recruiters wanted to slide me into when I was trying to join the service back in the early 1950s.

One of my first official acts on Marine Corps Base Quantico was to have that sonofabitching house condemned and torn down. It was, after all, a derelict and, I am proud to report, had not been used for its intended purpose by recent Quantico commanders just before my time. So I had the debris removed and the spot turfed over. The act gave me a great sense of accomplishment and satisfaction.

And so to work as I began looking at what made Marine Base Quantico tick. Who did what? Correlations. Unit and mission interrelationships. Mission effectiveness. I had no sooner gotten myself a bit down that road when trouble jumped out of the box and tried mightily to bite me.

His name was Cpl. Lindsey Scott. I remembered catching wind of his sad story when I was commanding the lst Marine Aircraft Wing in Japan. Even then, a cold chill of premonition went down my spine when I read the facts of his case. I didn't know the reason at the time for the feeling, but I was sure as hell about to find out very quickly. An extremely small world.

On 6 July l987, a scant sixteen days after I had assumed command at Quantico, Corporal Scott—who was black and had been convicted and sentenced to thirty years' incarceration at Fort Leavenworth, Kansas, for the abduction, rape, sodomy, and attempted murder of the white wife of a fellow Marine at Quantico in 1983—had his conviction reversed by the nation's highest military court "because his civilian lawyer fell far short of reasonable competence in investigating the defendant's alibi. . . ." [*New York Times*, 7 July 1987, p. 18].

The case blossomed across the consciousness of America as the television news show *60 Minutes* picked up the story, including charges that Scott had been a scapegoat in the rape of that white woman from Quantico. The three-judge Court of Military Appeals unanimously set aside Scott's conviction, his thirty-year prison sentence, and the $18,000 forteiture of pay that had imposed. By that action, the court reversed the decision of the lower court that had convicted and sentenced Corporal Scott and sent it back to the Navy for possible rehearing. That meant a return to the site of the first trial—Quantico.

It quickly became a big-time *Washington Post* and *New York Times* kind of story. Black man tried initially by white general; now black man being retried under the auspices of a black general. Racial overtones slid about all over the place, a fact not missed by black activists in the area who quickly began loudly insisting that the prosecution was racially motivated.

On 22 October 1987, as the convening authority for court-martial in cases in my command, I decided to retry Corporal Scott, because we were caught between Scott's supporters and a military justice system that thought it had a good case. It was a difficult decision, but I really thought that I had, in this instance, a debt to society and the individual.

Had Corporal Scott really been denied the usual legal competence necessary to properly defend himself in a court of law? And had this woman really been raped by Scott? There were those who took both sides of that argument.

The alleged attack took place between eight o'clock and nine o'clock on the evening of 20 April 1983 at Marine Base Quantico. Scott, then twenty-five years old, said he was somewhere else, downtown in a pharmacy, buying a foot massager for his wife's birthday. Said he browsed around for fifteen to twenty minutes after that. Said he bought and drank a soft drink in a department store, then stopped for a short while at a drive-in restaurant before he went home to his wife.

The prosecution in the first case took the hard line and was more direct. Corporal Scott, they said, had come off duty as a military policeman, then had gone by the home of a fellow military policeman, kidnapped his wife at knifepoint, taken her to a deserted place on the base, raped her, and dropped her off at a different location. Unfortunately, she was unable, she had said, to retrace her steps or identify the individual who had done the deed.

When Corporal Scott discovered that he was the suspect in the case, he hired an attorney whose name he'd picked out of the Yellow Pages, one Mr. Kuhnke, to whom Scott recited the same evening's itinerary that he'd droned to the prosecuting attorneys. Mr. Kuhnke did nothing. A black woman activist, solidly in Scott's corner, actually retraced the steps that Scott said he took that fateful evening, found witnesses, and gave their names to Mr. Kuhnke. Mr. Kuhnke did nothing, and he was heard to later aver that he didn't promptly investigate or seek or interview potential alibi witnesses because he believed that "the case would never come to trial."

Mr. Kuhnke thus bought Corporal Scott a new trial, the Court of Military Review stating, as it reversed his previous conviction and sentence: "Viewing Mr. Kuhnke's performance in light of the prevailing professional norms, we can only conclude that it falls far short of reasonable competence."

As the new trial started, I immediately began to pin down all the facts of the case. I had the prosecutor and my legal assistants in to discuss the issues. I immediately went to the Naval Investigative Service (NIS) and ordered that the evidence that had been used in the first case be sent to a DNA lab near Oakland, California, one of two labs that could do that kind of testing at the time. It would be four to five months before the results could be analyzed. Unfortunately, the material had not been stored in an airtight environment, so some of it had deteriorated. But the possibility of viability still existed.

My chief lawyer and I flew to California in an attempt to get the evidence into the hands of the DNA investigators so analysis could begin. Even so, it would be a footrace to have this evidence to present before the end of the trial. In spite of the continuing absence of that evidence, the prosecution requested the judge who was hearing the case to admit DNA evidence.

The judge refused.

As shocking as that sounds today, one has to realize that back in 1986, DNA evidence was generally not being accepted by courts of law and especially in military courts.

On 19 February 1988, seven Marine Corps officers acquitted Cpl. Lindsey Scott, now thirty-two years of age, at the end of his second court-martial on charges of sexually assaulting and attempting to kill the wife of a fellow Marine in 1983.

Corporal Lindsey Scott walked. He cannot be tried again, no matter what the DNA evidence might or might not prove. Whatever its conclusion, the report is no longer debatable or a subject for further discussion.

Then there was the little matter of a case of Marine Corps embassy staff being accused of espionage, and the meteoric trial of one Sgt.Clayton Lonetree—all hanging out on my watch. As Jesus said on the cross: *"Eloi, Eloi, la'-ma sa-bach'-tha-ni?"* (My God, my God, why hast thou forsaken me? [Matthew 27:52]).

Sometimes, I wondered. We danced between the courtrooms.

Clayton Lonetree was a twenty-six-year-old Native American Marine Corps sergeant whose world was slowly falling apart because he was allegedly the first United States Marine to be publicly tried for espionage. Spencer Lonetree was his daddy's name, from the Indian tribe called Winnebago. Sally Tsosie was from Navajo stock and was Clayton's mama. His parents found it difficult to remain together; they divorced, and Clayton Lonetree was often without one or the other of his parents for long stretches of his formative years. He was a lonely youngster, that loneliness preventing close relationships with other males. The military drew him because other members of his family had done well in it. A great-uncle, Mitchell Red Cloud, won the Medal of Honor as a Marine in the Pacific arena during World War II.

In high school, Clayton fell in love for the first time. Excessive jealously dogged him, and that bright hope disappeared. His fiancée dropped him, and he was what he'd always been, lonely and alone. On the one hand, says Lake Headley in his book *The Court-Martial of Clayton Lonetree,* he "regard[ed] himself . . . an unwanted child, [and] never opened up to other males his age." On the other hand, he was obsessed with the need "to be somebody" and not remain the imagined victim of the "red apple" syndrome: white on the outside, red on the inside, proof of a thing that bugged the hell out of him—the fact that he wasn't white. He'd been "[raised] white, but I'm not," he is reported to have noted. Clayton wanted to be what he was not and struck out to try getting there.

Clayton began his enlistment in the Marine Corps on 29 July 1980. Boot training in San Diego. Infantry training at Camp Pendleton. A one-year tour at the Marine barracks, Guantanamo Bay, Cuba. He was quiet and kept to himself. A Marine Corps rifleman, he had four promotions in four years. The Good Conduct Medal flew to his tunic twice, the Sea Service Deployment Medal once. Then it was Pendleton again, where he applied for duty with the elite Marine Security Guard Battalion. That would move him up and out of the mundane world into the world of the diplomat. Maybe he could become a "Native American diplomat." Maybe this assignment would show the way.

Clayton Lonetree passed the Marine Security Guard (MSG) examination the second time he took it. After getting through the MSG School at Quantico, his choice of the embassy in which he wanted to serve was the U.S. embassy in Moscow. In September 1984 he found himself standing guard at post number one inside a glass booth at the front entrance of that embassy.

A dream come true.

Not quite. Lonetree's existence in the Marine barracks in Moscow was the same as it was for all Marines with that duty. Isolated, they lived a lonely life. Lonetree, I think, was to some degree ostracized by the other Marines. In turn, all of the Marines were ostracized by the embassy personnel, including the ambassador, who felt that the Marines were nothing more than cops. They weren't invited to social functions.

So Lonetree was caught in an age-old dilemma. His Marines didn't like him. No one liked him. But one day he met and fell in love with a Soviet translator who worked in the embassy, the beauteous Violetta Sanni, with a KGB link. She was about his age and stood about five feet seven. The story of their attraction, their subway rides, her connection with the KGB as a "Swallow" are detailed in other books, as is how he broke the rule of nonfraternization with nationals and was persuaded to provide photographs of U.S. intelligence agents to Soviet agents. In Moscow and Vienna, agreeing or attempting to obtain floor plans of the U.S. embassy, passing them and other documents to Soviet agents for considerations of money, and, finally, his conscience so rattled, confessing to an embassy official at his new posting in Vienna.

Before Lonetree knew what hit him, the Naval Investigative Service descended and, in a frenzied rush to get at whatever truth, used certain tactics that did not bode well for their reputation, branding Lonetree a spy, a person certainly guilty of the heinous crime of espionage against the United States of America. He was flown to Washington, D.C., driven to Quantico, booked for espionage, and isolated in a five- by nine-foot cell in a wing within the brig built for terrorists. Total isolation. Complete disdain from his Marine guards.

"You're a traitor, Cochise," chided one guard, according to Headley. "Here's your chow, dead man," said another. And, "Haven't they killed you yet, Indian?"

The media turned cartwheels. The CIA entered the picture as well. Secretary of Defense Caspar Weinberger was completely taken in by the media furor surrounding the espionage flap. Questioned during a press conference after Lonetree's incarceration, the secretary of defense joined the fray.

"He should be hung," Weinberger commented, "but I guess these days we just shoot them."

In all of this, my lawyers kept coming up with dead leads. Now I was curious, because nothing seemed to come up but some embassy phone directory that Lonetree had supposedly turned over to the Russian Swallows.

"Goddamn," I said to my legal guys, "we've got this kid up here on a charge that could lead to his execution on the basis of an interior phone book? And all the allegations of going through the embassy at night, unlocking the classified sections—all that turned out to be just pure bullshit?"

It was about time to order the Article 32 hearing to see just what in the hell was going on. Lonetree was still being interrogated and debriefed by the CIA and the NIS—a whole bunch of folks were taking potshots at the guy. I wanted to test my own gut feelings where Lonetree was concerned.

I called in my driver and my aide one day.

"Get the car," I said. "We're going to Washington."

Quietly. No fanfare.

Lonetree was still being debriefed and interrogated.

"I want to get a look at this guy so I can get a feel for all of this," I said.

He was in a room with one-way glass. The observation room was filled with agents, all of them posturing in their own ways. I just sat down in a corner and watched for about an hour. When I left there, I was talking to myself.

"This kid ain't done a damned thing," I heard myself mutter. I was very curious about the entire matter. All I was left with was the impression of a young Marine who wanted to "get some pootay"—and that was about the extent of it.

The Article 32 hearing began on Wednesday, 4 February 1987. Although comparable to a grand jury or a preliminary hearing in civilian law, the Article 32 hearing was different in that the defense could have its say and there was no skilled prosecutor present to sidestep evidence that he didn't wish introduced.

"Sergeant Lonetree," bounced the sonorous voice of Maj. Robert J. Nourie, who would be submitting recommendations to me at the end of the hearing for my decision as to whether we would press charges against Sgt. Clayton Lonetree at a formal court-martial, "have you seen these charges against you?"

"Yes, sir," Clayton replied. "I have."

29: Circus

I recognized from the outset that an espionage Article 32 hearing and a subsequent trial that could result in a death sentence for Sgt. Clayton Lonetree just might, to put it mildly, create a frenzy among the media. I was glad that we'd had the foresight to take steps to effectively control that situation before the hearings began. I didn't want to exclude the media, so we had closed-circuit television piped into a small house situated up the hill from Hockmuth Hall, where the Article 32 hearing was taking place, so that reporters could effectively follow the proceedings, except when security matters were being discussed. The transmission would be stopped at those times during the hearing.

Aside from the need for a certain amount of "guarded secrecy," because it had been floated that the outcome of this case could affect national security, there was simply not enough room for everybody inside the windowless room with walls of gray concrete in which the hearings were to be conducted.

So the closed-circuit television idea worked for a good many reporters. But the aura of a circus began to exert itself as Lonetree's relatives, friends, and supporters appeared and began staging pow-wows in front of the flagpole right outside my headquarters window. Beating drums and tom-toms and all that stuff.

My military police didn't want them to do it, and wanted me to head 'em up and move 'em out.

"No, no," I said. "Let them do that. It's a peaceful demonstration."

I wasn't concerned about their harming the base—I had enough manpower to control that—but I was concerned about the appearance of an overpowering military justice system. My bottom line was that if they felt some emotional gratification from being able to beat those drums, then by all means beat the drums.

• • •

Out in California, the long arm of the NIS flexed. Late in the afternoon of 20 March 1987, two NIS investigators were more than excited.

"We've got ourselves a spy," one of the duo is reported to have crowed.

The two were finishing up three grueling days of grilling Cpl. Arnold Bracy, a black Marine previously stationed with Sergeant Lonetree in Moscow. Bracy had violated the nonfraternization rules by not reporting his latest contact with an embassy cook, a Miss Golotina. For this, Bracy was reduced in rank from sergeant to corporal, lost a dream tour to Caracas, and was reassigned to Quantico in May 1986 and finally to Twentynine Palms, California, where he worked as a mechanic.

Whatever the NIS investigators had induced Bracy to sign as a "confession," he immediately repudiated. Bracy called himself a "dummy" for signing the sheets placed before him. The investigators responded, "That's okay—we'll prove it later." Bracy and Lonetree, they suggested, were in on the espionage together—two Marines escorting Soviet spies through highly sensitive areas of the United States embassy in Moscow, shutting off security devices as they went. If this was true, then a huge spy drama was about to unfold, compromising U.S. protocols and perhaps secrets galore.

Now Bracy resided in Quantico's brig. The evidence against him would have been damning had there been any. Before I knew it, we had about fifteen to twenty Marines locked up, all pulled from embassy duty, sent back to the base to await trial and a charge. Because the charge was espionage, they were all locked up.

But in all of this, my lawyers kept coming up with dead leads. It all still seemed to come down to Clayton Lonetree. Now, I was even more curious. It appeared that all these other kids were being slam-dunked, because nothing seemed to come up but some embassy phone directory that Lonetree had supposedly turned over to the Russian Swallows.

If I was simply curious, on 1 May 1987, the *Washington Post* hollered.

> It would be one thing if, at the conclusion of investigations involving . . . Marine Embassy Guards, an announcement were to be made that there would be no prosecutions because no violations of law had occurred. But if some unfortunate . . . official has to stand up a few weeks from now and announce that there will be no prosecutions because military investigators botched the cases, there will be hell to pay. . . . The whole investigation was begun . . . not because intelligence agents had uncovered any viola-

tions, but rather because Sgt. Clayton Lonetree turned himself in in Vienna and began to talk. Important decisions were made early and, it is alleged, without careful consultation with the people who would eventually be responsible for the prosecution. What work has been done—or left undone—to secure evidence that would substantiate statements that some of the accused and some witnesses now seek to retract? [Lake Headley, p. 136–37.]

On 12 May 1987, Major Nourie closed the Article 32 investigation. His report was sent to me for my review and ruling as the convening authority for court-martial determination. As I was trying to formulate some opinions, the Washington press and some of the Washington senior personnel were making utterances that this was the worst spy case in the history of the United States.

Well, I was more than a little pissed. So I called the senior legal officer at headquarters.

"Look," I said, "can you guys give me some help up there? I can't try this case with all this outside influence being exerted subtlly or otherwise. These guys are innocent until proven guilty, and I need a break down here. If they're going to try this case, goddamnit, have them come on down here and take over the command."

Well, all the media pronouncements didn't exactly stop because of my outburst, but the barbs from Marine-controlled sources did seem to relax for the moment.

By 16 May, my review was complete.

Essentially, I ruled that eleven of twenty-four charges against Lonetree be dropped, including the accusation that he allowed Soviet agents to roam freely through the embassy during "moonlight tours." There was no evidence to support the charges that I recommended be dropped. What they had done, in essence, was to throw a blanket over the whole thing, hoping that something would stick. Many of the charges were without substantiation. I also removed the death penalty provision, which, until now, had hung heavy over Clayton Lonetree's head.

By now, over in Bracy country, I was also becoming quite pissed. What in the world was going on with Cpl. Arnold Bracy? Was he in cahoots with Lonetree in escorting Soviet agents through the embassy in Moscow? Lonetree was saying that even if Bracy said such a thing, it was untrue. Was it as William Kunstler—the famous civil rights lawyer, the principal civilian lawyer handling the Lonetree case, and one of Bracy's attorneys—suspected? That "the NIS, in quest of a witness to assure a conviction, had contrived a case against another minority—a black Marine—thinking if they put enough pressure on him he would roll over and testify against Lonetree" [Rodney Barker, *Dancing With the Devil*, p. 152].

Bracy was having none of that.

"Now wait a minute," I'm afraid I roared. "Somebody made these charges, and where is the evidence? Where," I repeated, "is the evidence?"

Finally, the senior legal guy came in with the beginnings of a partial solution.

"General, I've got to tell you something. We can't find a damned thing on Bracy. He hasn't done a thing. It appears his confession isn't valid and he was apparently coerced."

The news was incredulous. My hackles rose.

"I want that man out of jail in seventy-two hours," I grated.

"But, General, we can't do that," my chief legal guy said.

Stuff came unglued.

"Whoa. You've got an innocent Marine locked up and you're telling me you can't do what? I want him out of there in twenty-four hours," I growled. "Don't give me that bullshit."

The press was contacted and, with representatives of the NAACP present, the world was apprised of the fact that Cpl. Arnold Bracy was not guilty of espionage. Too many inconsistencies and contradictions. Flawed investigative techniques. No really hard evidence pointing toward conspiracy with Sergeant Lonetree or anybody else to commit treason against the United States of America.

So on 12 June 1987, Corporal Bracy was released and allowed to walk away. Subsequently, some of the other Marines caught in this "spy" scenario were also released.

Corporal Bracy let his discomfiture with the media be known.

"The media," he rasped, "tried to play it up like we [Sergeant Lonetree and Bracy] we were like peanut butter and jelly." They weren't even friends, Bracy asserted, saying that Lonetree got into trouble a lot and nobody really liked him much.

On 20 July 1987, the *New York Times* wrote: "Last month conspiracy charges against the two marines were dropped for lack of evidence. . . ." ["Spy Case: Tracing Collapse," p. A-1].

There was no rest for the weary, it seemed. Authorities now brought a brand-new prisoner right into my brig—one of the terrorists responsible for the 1985 highjacking of the Italian cruise ship *Achille Lauro* in the open sea as it approached Port Said, Egypt, with some four hundred souls aboard. The terrorists, before the televised world, had begun killing people and dumping them into the sea. An international terrorist was in my brig, with both wrists broken. I was concerned, not because I couldn't protect and deliver him to trial, but because I couldn't protect the base population should reprisals be mounted against Quantico. My base was wide open. No perimeter fences.

Even though I increased my security, military police were covertly keeping an eye on me as the commanding general for reasons of safety. As Alicia and I were about to leave a cocktail party on base one evening, I was approached by a security officer.

"Boss," he said sotto voce, "you can't go now."

"What? Why not?"

"There's a report that someone was seen sneaking toward your quarters with a rifle. There are military policemen in your house now—searching it and searching the grounds."

Well, that certainly slowed things down for the evening. Luckily, it worked out all right. But the next morning I demanded that this prisoner be removed from my brig and my base—at once and in a hurry. A terrorist reprisal attack could have resulted in hundreds of Americans, including dependents, being killed.

He was moved.

Wednesday, 22 July 1987. Eight in the morning. The pretrial aspects of Sgt. Clayton Lonetree's trial were set to begin. A white van brought him from the brig to Lejeune Hall. Television cameras watched his hand-cuffed arrival like fat crows perched on a fence. Five military policemen, two grasping him by the arms, marched with him over hard concrete and up the wide steps into the red brick building as shadows gobbled them up. My security was tight. Armed military police patrolled the perimeter. Metal detectors electronically regarded all persons entering the courtroom. The press was relegated to the house on the hill with its closed-circuit television.

Lonetree's family came to bear witness. Spencer, his daddy. Sally Tsosie, his mother. Mae Washington, his auntie, carried a single feather in her hand. His grandma, Alice Benally, was resplendent in her torquoise and silver jewelry. Sam Lonetree, Clayton's grandfather, shocked the court when he showed up at the trial in full Indian head-dress and carrying a peace pipe and rattles. Proceedings stopped; the court stilled in awestruck silence. For the moment, Sam was shaman and priest, come to drive out the evil spirits in that place. Asking for good luck in this war of words surrounding his grandson as he chanted a prayer to the Great Gods. He gestured and beseeched deliverance for his kin from all the Great Spirits residing at every point of the compass: north, south, east, and west. Deliberately, he walked over to Clayton and brushed him with the feather of an eagle, a sacred symbol of the Great Spirit. He turned and, with great dignity, departed the courtroom to join his compatriots outside, where together they denounced the court-martial at every turn to anyone who would listen.

The number of Indian sympathizers had grown steadily on the parade grounds outside the courtroom. Red Crow, from South Dakota, beat tom-toms while he chanted to the spirits of the Sioux. A Chippewa activist rally was in progress by the Iwo Jima memorial at the entrance to Quantico. Twenty Indians from varied tribes participated [Barker, p. 169–70, 199].

At nine o'clock, proceedings began. After considering the results of the Article 32 hearing, and considering the documents presented (I had ruled that there was sufficient evidence to proceed with a court-martial; the most dramatic evidence had been dropped), Bracy's hearsay was deemed inadmissible. The ultimate prosecution was restricted to non-capital punishment. Beyond that, it was incumbent upon me to stay more than an arm's length from any of the investigations and further negotiations with the suspect(s). The pretrial ground on. Introduction of motions. Strenuous objections. Plea bargaining. Jury selection. Challenges.

As the pretrial wore on, I went downstairs one day to get a haircut. As I sat in the barber's chair, William Kunstler spotted me and came over. We had a brief conversation. I'd known him before only by reputation. He'd come to speak at my grade school in Topeka, the school providing the basis for the Brown v. Board of Education landmark court decision concerning civil rights in American school systems. I knew that Kunstler had played a key role. In our current situation, I knew he couldn't "cross the line" with me, and I sure as hell wasn't going to cross the line with him, either. So we had a nice little friendly conversation. That was the extent of it. What I didn't know, however, was that Kunstler went running back and got his chief investigator, Lake Headley.

"I just talked with the general," he said, probably gushing. Like it was some big thing. He then asked Lake Headley to come down to meet me.

In his book *The Court-Martial of Clayton Lonetree* [pp.158–59], Headley says that I "rose" from the barber's chair to greet him "with a warm smile and firm hand." But then he goes on to really gild that lily far too much by quoting me way out of context.

"I was a youngster in Topeka, Kansas," I am alleged to have said, "when Mr. Kunstler came to my school and talked about Brown. He's one of my Gods." I certainly never referred to Kunstler as "one of my Gods," nor did I ever regard him as such. Headley rushed on, optimizing common courtesy into inordinate "respect for Kunstler, whom he had listened to as a black schoolboy three and a half decades ago," and that "respect" literally "gleamed on my face." In point of fact, we were all happy that Kunstler did come to my school and talk. Somebody needed to—but to thus achieve the status of a God? Ill timed, a bit of nonsensical braying.

But as Headley goes on to point out, there did exist a certain irony in the observation that the fate of Clayton Lonetree, an American Indian, now lay, within a certain context, in the hands of a black man whose chance for opportunity in American society and ultimate ascension to his current position had been championed by the same attorney who now defended a descendent of that oldest of American minority cultures. There was nobody in the area more cognizant of that than I.

My need to remain totally objective in my demeanor and decision-making processes was tantamount by virtue of the fact that Bracy, Lonetree, and I were all people of color, and the mounting interest in and the sensitivity associated with the rape case that just preceded these cases left no place for posturing or the spouting of pithy aphorisms on issues of race. Facts in evidence were all that mattered.

Clayton Lonetree's trial began on 11 August and ended on 21 August 1987. All eight Marine officers constituting his jury convicted him of every charge on the charge sheet. They say he trembled; his whole body shuddered; his face went grim. Word was that when they led him outside to go back to the brig, though, he smiled as he passed by his mother, who held fast to an eagle's feather.

"Innocent," they say she shouted as their eyes met.

"He took it like a Marine," marveled Kunstler.

Sentencing came around ten minutes to four on the afternoon of 24 August 1987. The black president of the court, Lieutenant Colonel Allen, said the heavy words.

> Sergeant Clayton J. Lonetree, it is my duty as president of the court to inform you that the court sentences you to be reduced to

the grade of E-1; to be fined $5,000; to forfeit all pay and allowances; to be confined for 30 years and to be dishonorably discharged from the Naval Service.

It was just about during this time that an old ghost from Vietnam began to bug me again, that fractured left hip I sustained bailing out of my F-4 Phantom when we'd been shot down. The pain came and went; sometimes it could get extreme. I knew that I was getting close to the end of my tenure in the Marine Corps and figured it was time to go and have some of the elective surgery I'd been putting off for years. So it was up to Bethesda Naval Hospital for a total left hip replacement.

The operation kept me away from my desk for two to three weeks, but I continued to work because my driver brought me papers that were important where I could sign off. When necessary, I communicated with my command by telephone. After several weeks, I was back on line.

We had one more deal to attempt with Clayton Lonetree, with the carrot of probable sentence reduction held far out in front for compensation for his cooperation. Our deal was that if he would admit to everything that he knew, then a reduction in the length of his ultimate incarceration would be granted. We had to make sure that we milked this guy dry.

What we found out was that there wasn't anything else. There was, at first, an offer of a two-year reduction in his sentence, which the defense considered a joke. But it was that or be ordered to cooperate and receive no immunity. Clayton gave exactly the same story that he'd given in the first place—the same story he'd given during the court-martial and for which he had passed every lie detector test he was given in the process.

Years down the pike, Lonetree's appeal process would work. He'd really fallen in love those years ago with Violetta Sanni, regardless of her reputed KGB connections. And she had fallen in love with him. Through twists of circumstance that only the fates understand, the two of them came together again, as man and wife, after Sgt. Clayton Lonetree was eventually released from prison.

Some say that the heavy sentence imposed on Sergeant Lonetree was given primarily because of the panic and hysteria existing in official governmental entities at the time. That's for history to decide.

It was indeed a tough several months, coming into a new command with two of the highest-profiled espionage cases in which U. S. Marines were allegedly involved. Again, as the convening authority for court-martials on Quantico Marine Base, I couldn't interfere or inject many of my own opinions into those cases. A conflict of interest would have been immediately apparent. So it was my job to see that a correct and secure arena existed in which those matters moved forward to their logical conclusions. It wasn't easy, not by a long shot.

Practically every unit aboard Quantico Marine Base had to be tapped for support and involvement, from ensuring adequate physical security of the base by increasing its presence, to adequate media control and coordination. Proper control of suspects detained under my control was paramount, I thought, and to these ends I formed an internal Security Task Force, required to deal with every conceivable concern—from the handling of television reporters to the provision of closed-circuit viewing of the trial for the general public. To ensure adequate protection of sensitive classified data, it was necessary that I served as the classification/declassification authority when considering transmission of data to agencies outside the scope of the Department of Defense.

The Lonetree trial was a volatile, wild thing. Sometimes, I thought I'd pull out what hair I had left. But we made it through the trial with no major difficulties. Some have given me credit for the guidance involved in all of it. But without my Marine Corps troopers, both officer and enlisted, handling such a sensitive issue that had international exposure in the professional and military fashion that we did, it would never have been possible. That's why, when some folks asked me about how that Lonetree trial went, I was able to arch one eyebrow and smile, acknowledging it as "very emotional and difficult" but really "a piece of cake." It wasn't that, but a tribute to the Marines assigned to my command at that time.

I would rather have spent my time in a cockpit than behind a desk. The thrill of flying is something that drives me to fight to stay in the cockpit. And as I sat through these investigations, hearings, and trials, even though with three stars, I probably would have given up a month's pay to rove around with the young aviators and fly their stuff and live in their world.

As commanding general of Quantico Marine Base, however, all that flying on a regular basis was quickly becoming a thing of the past. Here, almost as never before, an awareness of my oath of office always came to the fore. Being an officer was an awesome responsibility. I believe I fulfilled that responsibility during those trying days and months. I was behind a desk, and there were miles and miles to go before this tour was over.

Alicia learned a few lessons too as the wife of the Quantico Marine Base commanding general.

MUTUAL VOICES
Alicia, Second Wife

It was an experience you'd definitely have to live through. Frank has always thought that the military was like any other corporation. It had its hierarchy, its structures, jobs, and occupations. I always could see some of that, but thought it was that and a lot more. It was a totality of all your social as well as your business experience. You didn't leave at five o'clock. There were all these things you had to do in the evening. They became part of your social life, part of your family life. I think Quantico was the epitome of that [because it was the training facility] for very key elements of the military schools. The FBI Academy. Embassy officer training. I found that, as the wife of a general officer, nothing that you do is done obscurely. They always know you. Everywhere you go, everyone knows you. People that you don't know, know you. So you have to maintain a certain appearance at all times.

I did work as a teacher, which was atypical for a military wife. Higher ranking wives discussed their concern with me in terms of my ability to perform the "other" duties of a high-ranking officer's wife. In fact, one of the general's wives telephoned to specifically speak to me for that purpose. There was "concern" that the responsibilities that went along with the position of wife of the commanding general "might be neglected" and did I intend to quit my job? I said I had a career that was important. I enjoyed what I was doing. And we did have a steward, a driver, and Frank had an aide. Some of that helped a lot and helped with the responsibilities that went along with my position. But I did them both. When [the Quantico] schools turned over their classes, they brought their families and wives along. I got the wives together so they could meet each other. On a regular basis, I was having either a coffee or tea, getting the wives of the various training schools together. I spoke to new officers' wives about what it was like to be an officer's wife and what they could expect in the military. Some of them seemed to be a new breed [contrary to the belief of older wives who thought they shouldn't work but did volunteer work] and were coming in with degrees and career goals. They wanted to know how to make those things work. They'd come up to me and talk privately. "We know what you've done,"

they'd say. "How did you manage to do it?" I could only mirror Frank's
point of view: wives can and should have careers. It makes for happier mar-
riages [when wives] are doing things that matter.

And there were the constant dinners and receptions for important vis-
itors to Quantico in our home. The stewards and aides helped plan, sched-
ule. And I'd be off evenings, planning even more things for the wives, both
military and FBI. There were other types of tours also, luncheons to plan.
A dinner involving husbands and wives. Finally, I think there was some
resentment on the part of some of the older wives about my coming into
Frank's career when it was already a status position. Many of them had
begun with their husbands as lieutenants, seeing them struggle up the lad-
der. And here I was—with all these benefits. But there was always Frank.
Out front. He was very unusual. Strong, extremely intelligent. Very secure.
His approach was not only to excel but to do it in the way he thought was
the right way to go. [And for that] he was extremely respected. Because of
that, I never [experienced] any direct racism, for example.

With the furor of the espionage trials slowly disappearing, it was time
to look closely at the primary mission of the billet, the adequate training of Marine Corps officers. Part of that mission had already begun in
between the investigations, trials, and demonstrations, and now it began in earnest—looking at the organization that provided the training
and tweaking it for maximum effectiveness to produce the very best for
the U.S. Marine Corps.

30: Toward Renovation

It is ironic that in your current posting you are in charge of training our future officers, and yet you failed to uphold the truth and honor taught to these young officers within your command at Quantico.
—A Senior Officer, Letter to General Petersen, 27 September 1987

I began looking at the organization of Quantico Marine Base the moment I arrived and was in place. The investigations and trials on deck tended to slow the "look" a bit, but soon it was obvious that four or five fiefdoms were in existence. No central glue held the thing together. Everybody seemed to be doing his own thing.

The first mandate was the consolidation of financial responsibility into one office that answered directly to me. I knew full well that if you controlled the money, their hearts and lives would follow. To facilitate this, I created a new position called the chief financial officer for the entire base, thus moving the authority for decision as to how dollars would be spent up the chain of command from subordinate commanders. Now all major money decisions had to come through my office.

With that as a start, everything began to fall in line.

The change was made after about two months of patient observation. It was evident that everybody was operating his own little bailiwick; they were all kings in their own little courts. For example, bidding processes for goods and services were awry. Several were in place; none were centralized. A low bid at point A might have been the high bid at point B. Cronyism was rampant.

I have nothing against civilian workers. Many are among the best folks we've got on our bases, but some of them had been in their positions for more than thirty years. These guys knew the system far better than anyone just wandering through for a few months.

It was really necessary to take these kinds of approaches when assessing the command to which I'd been posted as the "new kid on the block." This was the Marine Corps human development center, its pride and joy. The presidential helicopter fleet and the FBI Academy also resided there. More than twenty thousand men were involved with an annual budget of more than $250 million. It was basically like running a small city, serving as mayor, city manager, police chief, and budget director—the whole bit. It was necessary to be serious, because the bottom line was that I was the guy who went to jail if anything went radically wrong. Nobody else.

That said, before moving further with organizational changes, I thought that an extensive study of the command would be in order, having as its focus the future needs of the country with respect to the role of the Marine Corps mission. Intrinsic to the study was the goal of the possible expansion of the Quantico role, ensuring increased involvement in the development, structure, design concepts, doctrine, and systems requirements expected to impact Corps operations well into the next century.

Fallout from this directed study resulted in a recommended organizational change targeted to solve some of the ills immediately apparent after my first review of the Quantico systems. The resultant study was submitted to the commandant of Marines, who reviewed and approved its recommendations for implementation on 10 November 1987, the 212th birthday of the Marine Corps.

Under the aegis of that study, the former Marine Corps Development and Education Command (MCDEC) became the Marine Corps Combat Development Command (MCCDC), a designation that many believed more accurately reflected the pivotal role that Quantico played in the Marine Corps mission.

The new concept was designed to increase overall Marine Corps proficiency and efficiency in training, education, planning, matériel requirements identification, and concept and doctrinal development.

Central to the reorganization were five discrete, functionally related centers under Combat Development Command. Established were the *Warfighting Center,* the Marine air-ground task forces proponent, which developed, assessed, and brought forward concepts, plans, and doctrine. It ensured coordination with other services, commands, and allied entities in the development of joint/combined warfighting doctrine. The *Training and Education Center* developed training systems and programs for the education of regular and reserve Marine personnel and units. The *Intelligence Center* was tasked with threat analysis, intelligence awareness development, and support to the Marine Corps Combat Development Command. The *Wargaming and Assessment Center,* which was the focal point for all wargaming, manual or automated, acted as the center point for simulation, modeling, and assessment for MCCDC operating forces. Finally, the *Information Technology Center* developed and publicized information about Marine doctrine, training, and force structure related to task force deployments.

We made important improvements on Quantico Marine Base that upgraded the quality of life for the Marines, sailors, and their dependents assigned to the command. A new Seven-Day Store and Gas Station, a complete car care facility, was dear to my heart as an inveterate automotive tinkerer. The Hostess House was completely repainted and recarpeted. The base theater was renovated. For working households, we increased the capacity of our child care center by providing space for forty-five more children than before, at an affordable price. Beyond that, we developed and put in place the Family Day Care Homes Program, designed to allow for supervised child care in individual homes. Quantico was the first Marine Corps base to establish this program. At the end of my assignment, about forty homes provided this care for about 110 children.

The beat went on.

Gymnasium facilities were improved and billeting was expanded. Our commissary facility was made larger by consolidating four remote warehouses into one storage facility. By eliminating duplication of effort and improving stockage routines, we saved more than $250,000 in labor costs. An updated commissary operation was put into place, featuring centralized management, lower costs to consumers through increased buying power, and automated operations, including a mechanized locater system.

Realizing that Quantico was the Marine Corps' premier facility for the qualification and training of Marine Corps officers, we made sure that our training facilities and programs came in for their share of attention and redesign. Training coordination requirements needed updating and further refinement. An officer billet was established to address these deficiencies in training areas and ranges. We left a legacy of congressional approval for a $4.3 million project to upgrade three existing training ranges and create two additional ones. Headquarters, Marine Corps, also approved $3 million for the construction of a modern Military Operations in Urban Terrain training facility and a fire observation training device at the Basic School.

We also gave new priority to the maintenance and repair of overseas training areas that had suffered from neglect, decay, and failure to be adequately included in successive budgets. It was also within our purview to assess how we were doing environmentally on Quantico in hazardous waste management, solid waste disposal, and landfill operations. Installation of an integrated data automation system (MIDAS) greatly enhanced productivity in the workforce through office automation and allowed for the realization of interactive processing and data distribution throughout the command.

I was proud to be able to host and pull off two of the largest Marine Corps Marathon events to be held in the history of that race, with more than eleven thousand participants each. In June 1987, for the first time in its history, the Marine Corps Marathon was given live television coverage from start to finish, which afforded the Corps positive publicity.

It was gratifying to be able to actively participate in the graduation ceremonies held by the Marine Corps schools on Quantico, especially when it provided the opportunity to speak to the new officers. It gave me immense satisfaction to reiterate the primary message: "For a successful career in the military, you must be well aware of the contents of your oath of office." The words are meaningful, and in realizing their meaning and accepting the awesome responsibility of being an officer, one also accepts the military as a profession. "As an officer," I used to say, "you have a responsibility to exercise the powers invested in you in a way that is fair, impartial, and good for the nation."

Beyond the Marine Corps schools on Quantico, I was often invited to speak at universities and colleges, on several occasions at commencement ceremonies.

It was an honor in the spring of 1987 to be invited as the commencement speaker at Virginia Union University. My speech, written by Carlos C. Campbell, was filled with statements of hope and promise for the young graduates in the audience. A section of that speech reminded that what had been done on Quantico Marine Base to improve its operation on many fronts had its ultimate muscle in the people assigned to my command.

If any of you would ask me to explain each and every medal on my chest without looking at them, I doubt if I could do that. I never sought out a single medal. I only focused on being prepared to do what was necessary to the best of my ability. If you asked me to describe the missions that I have flown in combat in Korea or Vietnam, I would tell you about the courage of my squadron mates, officers and men alike. I would tell you about Marines who returned to battle after being treated for wounds sustained in com-

bat; I would tell you that they were the best, that they were prepared and always faithful, because that is what I remember most
vividly.

That spirit lived on at Quantico from the first day of my command.
It was my job as the commanding general to light the spark, to be sure
that the torch, once lit, reached established goals. My Marines, officers
and men alike, saw to the reaching of the defined goals. And that is why,
in September 1987, the letter I received from a "A Senior Officer," was,
as the oldsters used to say, just "water off a duck's back," because the
record belied the hate.

A record of almost thirty-seven years of honorable service to the Marine Corps and my country was my testament. I was one of the few men
who had fought in two wars and, by now, was close to being the Corps'
senior aviator on active duty who participated in the Korean War combat. When the time came, they gave me an award and called me the Silver Hawk.

Before I knew it, I was designated the Grey Eagle, this time the Navy's
senior aviator and, by virtue of designation as an aviator in October 1952,
having superseded all other aviators in the Air Force and the Army as
well. I was only the sixth Marine to ever get the award. The trophy was
of a miniature aircraft carrier with an eagle landing on deck with the
inscription: "In recognition of a clear eye, a stout heart, a steady hand,
and a daring defiance of gravity and the law of averages." I even received
the trophy in miniature to keep for myself.

As an aside, that inscription has never been a lie.

Historically, my life was full of those little bomblets that Air Force general Daniel "Chappie" James, Jr., warned my people that they would one
day be better off without. But it had happened. First black aviator in the
United States Marine Corps. First black commander of a tactical Marine
Corps fighter squadron. First black base commander. First black Marine
Corps group commander. First black wing commander. First black Marine officer to attain flag rank.

I earned the Purple Heart I wore on my tunic. It wasn't given because
of a pinprick, but because of 37mm antiaircraft shrapnel tearing my
Phantom apart, forcing my ejection like a corkscrew from a shrieking
fighter jet with a force of about 20 g's at about 640 feet per second, cracking my left hip, slicing my nose, herniating my spine, attenuating my
knee into postures it could not long tolerate. The broken hip singed
and burned for years. I limped. Sudden pain sometimes shot down the

middle of my back as if someone had skewered my spine with a hot poker.

"A Senior Officer" can go to hell.

Some people seem to think that my career was an ego trip with its history-making properties. I hasten to point out that was not my ultimate purpose. I didn't want to be held up as a role model for blacks, or deal with the racial issue at all. I did want to prove myself an effective commander and pilot rather than a black commander or black pilot. It turns out, however, that the latter is exactly the direction in which my career had turned. It wasn't my goal, but in the final analysis, I am proud that it is being read that way. Perhaps we're on our way, albeit painfully, to that place and time in which we will have truly lived up to the stated ideals of our country and there will be no need to highlight "firsts" in anything.

There have been memorable tours, especially those where I was in command, such as when I took over Marine Aircraft Group 32 at Cherry Point, when we were involved with the AV-8A Harrier aircraft. I still consider the Harrier a pilot's dream. We could take off from grass fields or highways and even fly backward. I was involved with the early development of the Harrier and still feel that it's the way of the future.

Assumption of command is a hell of a responsibility. If you look at the cost of matériel, training, personnel, and salaries and bounce that against a corporate figure, you're looking at a minicorporation. It's a responsibility that the government and the American people have entrusted to me on several occasions.

I believe that the Marine Corps has become a better service during the time I've been a member of it. Hopefully, my being there had a little to do with that. We have been able, for example, to be more selective about who we enlist in the Corps. Certainly the economy is a factor, but I still don't see it as the driving force. I believe there is a resurgence of the military in the eyes of Americans. As I see it, a young high school senior who has no job and doesn't really have any definite plans toward college should take a good, hard look at serving in the military for a few years. These people would have a few years to get some training, learn a skill, and see the world. As far as I'm concerned, the military is one of the best things going.

But having said that, the need continues to exist to ensure the maintenance of an effective Marine Corps and presence. That requires the enlistment and retention of quality Marines regardless of rank, officer and enlisted. My point of view, which has evolved over the years, hasn't changed one iota. Don't take the money if you don't do the job. In short, don't be what I call a "foot shuffler." The Corps numbers the days of those people and separates them like chaff from the wheat, ensuring that the chaff blows away.

One does get tired, no matter how great the love for the work attending the career path chosen long ago. It was 1988 and I keenly felt that the time had come to officially bid the United States Marine Corps a fond adieu. Somebody once confided, "When you pin on the first star, that's the time to think retirement." Well, I'd pinned on three. I'd gone about as far as any senior officer could possibly go minus the billet of the commandant of the Marine Corps, and we all knew that was a position supremely unattainable at that time, no matter how much the Corps had changed its way of thinking about race and skin color.

Although retirement from the Corps came to mind from time to time, the thought was more properly akin to that of a butterfly winging its way into a garden for a few bright seconds, then over the fence and out of sight. Then came the change at the top of the hierachy—a new commandant of Marines. And the idea of retirement was no longer simply my call.

General Al Grey became the new guy at the top, and the scuttlebutt among us senior general officers began. Al was a tough, tobacco-chewing warrior. We all knew that change would certainly be coming, and as the days flew by, the fact of it became undeniable. We all knew that, at the time, the Marine Corps had, on average, the oldest general officer corps of any of the other services. We read the tea leaves and knew pretty much what was coming. A new commandant required a new, fresh team, young enough to allow him to make new, younger general officers. Officers that he could advance or recommend for further advancement.

The need for me to retire became all the more necessary because a three-star general, such as I was, represented 1 percent of 1 percent of all general Marine officers. There just weren't that many of us.

General Grey was trying to inject that necessary new blood into the general officer corps. He had the reputation of being something of a rebel. Chewing that tobacco. Holding the opportunity of relating directly to the troopers dear to his heart. I knew him pretty well, having been his deputy when assigned to Fleet Marine Force Atlantic down at Norfolk.

So I just about knew what the real deal was when he visited me in my office at Quantico.

"Well, you know, Frank," he began, and I knew that the retirement butterfly I'd seen flying around in the garden of my mind wasn't coming back over the fence anymore. That sucker was long gone down the road to somebody else's garden.

"One of the problems I'm facing, Frank, is the age of our general officers."

He didn't need to draw me any pictures. My counterparts and I had already discussed the possibilities. No need to dawdle.

"Al," I started, "I know what you're up against. Look, I've been at it now for thirty-seven years nonstop. And quite frankly, I'm looking at my usefulness in a civilian world in a large company executive position. If I stay here, I'll be sixty or so when I get out, and who the hell's hiring sixty-year-old guys?"

I was already fifty-seven.

"So, Al," I continued, "you just tell me when you want me to go."

So we selected a date and went forward with it. Just like that. Deep inside, though, I must confess an errant dream I'd often had of making a run for the position of assistant commandant, which would have given me a fourth star. I figured I had the political clout, and it was a political move that have a fairly decent chance of succeeding. I'd had that dream before, and each time I'd been against kicking up that kind of internal fight within the Corps. Ah, it would have been yet another "first" as a black. But then I'd gone on record as having enough of this "being the first" and I really meant it. Let somebody else be first, for goodness sake.

Now it was time to retire from my beloved United States Marine Corps. I was going to miss it, no doubt about it. That particular challenge. Getting the sense of what was going on around Quantico Marine Base. Wandering around it evenings and weekends in nondescript blue jeans and tennis shoes. Amused when passersby suddenly recognized me. Dropping by the auto hobby shop, turning another bolt on my '59 Jag, which I had sequestered there. Talking cars with the old car aficionados. Making mental notes of what I'd seen. Things to look into or change maybe next Monday morning.

Time now to give up cherished temporary possessions. The Grey Eagle award I passed on to Adm. Ronald J. Hayes, CINC United States Pacific Fleet, in ceremonies in the Pentagon. We laughed and made pleasant asides when I passed on the Silver Hawk award to Lt. Gen. John H. Hudson, deputy chief of staff for manpower, U.S. Marine Corps.

From time to time in the days that followed, those great airplanes I'd flown over the years thundered and pirouetted in my mind. F-4U Cor-

sairs, the A-4 Skyhawk, the quirky Harrier. Magnificent, roaring, screaming F-4 Phantom jets; the F-8 Crusader and the full-throated F-15 Eagles;
the F-16 Falcons and the F/A-18 Hornets.

I remembered the acrophobia and how I'd whipped it. Korea, its
people and that piece of dog I'd eaten. Vietnam and the Vietnamese.
USO shows. My Marines, the good ones and the questionable ones—
always remembering the sober thought about them all: that whatever
their basic orientations as human beings, they were always Marines first,
and when the chips were down they'd all be present and accounted for.

Lieutenant General Victor H. Krulak, who came along before I
showed up, said in his book, *First to Fight: An Inside View of the U.S. Marine Corps* [p. x]:

> When trouble comes to our country, there will be Marines—
> somewhere. . . . They have maintained themselves in a high state
> of readiness and can therefore address the threat in a meaning-
> ful way and do it at once . . . in a lean, serious and professional
> way. . . . They believe themselves capable . . . the faith and confi-
> dence is almost mystical.

I was more than gratified to have been a part of that. When I drove
out the gate of Quantico on my way to Topeka and St. Louis, I saw something that made me twice as proud to have been a part of it all. As I drove
by one of the sports fields, I saw a group of boys playing football. The
group included white, black, yellow, and red kids. That's the norm
around Marine bases these days. No problems there. You don't see
groups separated by skin color anymore. Finally, minorities were beginning to get a fair shake in the military. In fact, the military led civilian life in this respect.

I like to think I helped that come about.

In the last days of my career before retirement, I received a steady
stream of telephone calls discussing possible future careers. Perhaps
some of that was fallout from the fairly intense notoriety I had engendered in the Washington, D.C., press, not just because of the court-martials but also because I was the only black general in the United States
Marine Corps. That fact alone tended to give me a fairly high profile.

One of the job offers came from a black agent, one Herb Smith of
Cleveland, Ohio. He'd called, "just testing the waters." My focus had begun to be set on companies in California and its aircraft industries. In

fact, a tentative interview had already been set up with a firm in the San Francisco area.

Other impressive mail began to arrive in my offices at Quantico.

6 April 1988. A letter from William L. Ball III, secretary of the Navy. "Speaking for the entire Department of the Navy [to] extend my appreciation and thanks as you bring your superlative career to a close. In the past four years, you have served our nation and the Corps with great distinction."

1 July 1988. A letter from the commandant of the Marine Corps, Gen. A. L. Grey, "thanking you on behalf of all Marines for your many accomplishments. . . . Please accept . . . personal congratulations on your tremendous career and . . . achievements."

7 July 1988. The Honorable Ben Blaz of Guam read a glowing congratulatory piece into the record of the House of Representatives, ending it with, "Mr Speaker, with the retirement of Lt. Gen. Petersen, there is indeed the passing of an era . . . an era of superior service, characterized by courage, determination, and total commitment to Corps and to Country. . . . [He] will be missed, but . . . always remembered for his pioneer spirit. The era which begins now is a better one for his contributions."

7 July 1988. A letter from President Ronald Reagan, proferring congratulations upon my retirement after thirty-eight years of service. "Throughout your military career, you have played a critical role in the perservation of America's security and freedom, as well as in the pursuit of world peace. Your legacy of achievement will serve as a shining example for future generations of cadets and officers. I am proud to speak for all Americans in thanking you for your dedicated service."

8 July 1988. The retirement date stared us down. My hometown relatives weren't with us. They'd come out east for my promotions, but advanced age prevented the trip now. But my youngest brother, Hans, had come all the way from Texas. Alicia and Monique were there. My children by my first marriage were there, as were scores of my friends.

When I'd announced my retirement, I planned to sort of slide out gracefully, the way I came into the service. When the announcement reached the Pentagon, it was released to the wire services, and calls began pouring in. I finally called a last press conference in Ellis Hall on Quantico.

I discussed my views on racism and prejudice in and out of the Corps. The future for more black generals in the military. My own job plans. I was reminded—rather gleefully, I thought—that some blacks have had problems when retiring from the military and finding civilian employment and big trouble in the job market.

"My feeling," I replied, "is that maybe not everyone takes the same approach. I'm going to make a good, hard run at it, and if in fact I find that employment is out of the question, I'll try another alternative. I've worked since I was fifteen years old. I'll open a shoe-shine shop if that's what it takes."

That seemed to quiet the threatened cacophony a bit.

"All my life," I continued, "I've been able to plan what I'm going to do, or at least what I want to do. Now it's all variables, not constants. I don't like that at all. It drives me buggy. Whatever my new job, it will be meaningful and challenging. I do not plan to be a figurehead."

That done, before I knew it I was one of the focal points in a huge retirement and change of command ceremony on the parade grounds of Quantico. Bright flags flew fitfully. The band fired up. More than four hundred Marines participated in the ceremonies as I stood tall in front of the colors performing a hand salute, giving honors to Gen. A. L. Grey, the commandant of the Marine Corps, and other distinguished guests. I relinquished my command to Lt. Gen. William R. Etnyre and received a Distinguished Service Medal after my thirty-eight years of service.

I didn't know how emotional I felt until the commandant spoke. I didn't think it would be emotional at all. But it was. Extremely emotional. I just about bubbled over inside when he addressed the approximately two hundred first lieutenants then attending the Basic School for new officers. They were situated in their own section of the stands.

"Take a look at this man," General Grey bellowed. "Take a look at him, because what you're seeing here is a part of Marine Corps history."

The emotion welled inside.

MUTUAL VOICES
Dana Charlette Petersen, Daughter

The day he retired was such a sad day. It was hot as all get out. A couple of troops had passed out. The ceremony was long. I felt like Daddy was trying to stay composed. He'd already cleared out the big house and was living in temporary quarters. It wasn't just a retirement—it was like stripping away all the luxuries, the pomp and circumstance, the status. It had all ended. It was really awful, because when it was over, I think he might have gone to a reception for a really short time, and then he was gone. He

even had to put his dog, Clyde, to sleep, because he was so old. Dad loved
that golden retriever. And we all said: "Well, if he can put his dog to sleep,
damn. If he could do that, what could he do to us?" He was gone, and we
didn't see Dad for months after. He was gone.

They gave me my flag. They gave me the medal. And off I went. It
was over. And on 1 August 1988, the deal was officially done. Thirty-eight
years come and gone. I thought I'd relax for a month and try to figure
out what kind of clothes to put on in the morning, because I'd no longer
be wearing a uniform.

My brother Hans and I packed lightly and drove to Houston so I
could kick back at his house for a few days, regroup, and never look
back. Alicia and Monique went to Philadelphia to spend some time with
her parents.

I should have paid more attention to Hansy on our drive to Houston. There was something wrong, but I guess I was so wound up in my
own thing, I missed it. It was the hoarseness. The coughing and, later,
the inability to eat and swallow properly. But we were so glad to spend
some time together again that I missed it. Hansy just wasn't up to speed.
We smoked, drove fitfully, drank, and stopped to eat.

I kept on doing my thing. Looking for that next connection. I
thought I was about ready to accept the offer with the firm in the San
Francisco area.

Herb Smith, the Cleveland agent, tracked me down after a few
weeks.

"Look, Frank, I think I've got a thing lined up for you," he enthused.

"Herb," I replied, "I'm just about to go for a final interview with a firm
in San Francisco."

"Look, before you do that," Herb said, "would you consider working
for Dupont?"

"Dupont?" I replied. "I don't think I know too much about Dupont."

"They're in Wilmington, Delaware."

"Where the hell is Wilmington, Delaware?" I quipped.

At any rate, Herb got me up to speed and gave me a plane ticket. I
met with him in his office in Cleveland, then flew from there to Wilmington, where I had my interviews. Of course, by the time I arrived, I
knew quite a bit about the Dupont Corporation.

The chief executive officer of Dupont at the time was a gentleman
named Ed Woolard. He had been in the military, in the Army I believe.
Stayed in about two or three years and came out a sergeant or some-

thing. But he was now in the position of taking over the Dupont Corporation. I was so impressed with this guy because he was a straight shooter. Only two or three years younger than I. The two of us just clicked.

So I decided to go with Dupont. Herb worked out a lucrative contract with them, and I was more than pleased to slide into that new world. Alicia and I moved to Wilmington, and the new career began.

Unfortunately, a few storm clouds began to gather at home. Alicia and I couldn't seem to see eye to eye about how our life was to be structured. I guess I wanted my wife with me in this new, retired setting. But Alicia decided she wanted to go back to school to work on her doctorate. There were some other minor problems. It just wasn't working out, and, sadly, we went our separate ways. But we're still good friends in spite of it all.

MUTUAL VOICES
Alicia, Second Wife

You know, making that bridge into civilian life after the military and trying to decide how we wanted to make that work was hard for a while. Frank went on to a new career. We kept struggling to try to make things work. It just didn't. If you have a break in communications, it's difficult. Differences about directions. Not knowing where we were going. I decided to go back to school to work on my doctorate. Frank began at Dupont. It's hard to say. We never really worked through our communications problems.
But we're still friends.

Epilogue

Second Lieutenant Frank E. Petersen . . . was more of an oddity than the pfc. Or was it the fact that Petersen was the Corps' first black aviator that caused so many double takes? Flying Corsairs out of K-6 [Pyongtaek], he often landed at P'ohang, for interviews or to receive awards. But oh, how he could fly! He ended his tour with six Air Medals . . . a Distinguished Flying Cross. In 1968, he became the first black Marine to command a tactical air squadron, flying Phantom jets in Vietnam with Marine Fighter Attack Squadron 314, adding 17 more Air Medals and a Purple Heart. He continued serving Corps and country, retiring as a Lieutenant General.
—Tom Bartlett, "Swinging with the Wing"
[*Leatherneck* magazine, May 1993, pp. 25–26]

Hooray! Retirement. A word synonymous with rest, relaxation. An entree to leisure. Wrong.

As I looked over my command standing at attention at my retirement ceremony, I was filled with a mixed emotion of frustration and reflection. The latter took me backward in time to thirty-eight years before when I first entered the service as a seaman recruit. Fast forward through two wars, through countless hours in the cramped spaces of a fighter cockpit, hanging from a parachute in Northern I-Corps Vietnam with a new understanding arriving in a flash inside the words "Oh, shit." Unnamed friends who are no longer alive.

The former thought was framed by the rigid, formal military way of doing things. For example, I hate parades. From the first time to now. I simply hate the things. Standing in the ranks, broiling in the hot sun (always). Sweaty. Silently cursing the "Old Man," who always walked too slowly, pompously inspecting the ranks. I've always felt that a simpler way of changing commanders would be for the old and the new commander to meet in an office, shake hands, and get on with it. Recalling my time as an enlisted man, I know that group would drink to the idea.

I had an impish urge to issue my last three-star order: standing the troops to parade rest, grant them all a three-day pass, and end the parade. Strangely, impish urges sometimes play tricks, and highlight almost-forgotten memories in bright shafts of color not seen or imagined in years.

And that is how, as I stood tall, contemplative of a playful order, I wondered if my maternal great-grandfather, Cpl. Archie McKinney, formerly of the 55th Massachusetts Infantry, would have thought it a lark if *his* commanding officer had given everyone a three-day pass on the day he returned to Fort Sumter, South Carolina, in 1865 after the Confederates had gone, as he and others like him retired from the Union Army.

The twin facets of our retirements from the military, albeit more than a hundred years apart, assumed a special grandeur in my mind. The two of us had become an ongoing exercise in the engineering of a special human cultural experiment where, in spite of sometimes gargantuan imperfection, a black man and a kinsman could retire from the military of the United States of America, one at the lowly rank of corporal and a great-grandson with the rank of a three-star general. I savored the memory, for I knew that if Great-Grandpa McKinney had been a member of the 55th Massachusetts Infantry, the odds are high that neither of us would be enjoying this mental tête-à-tête.

Yes. The three-day pass idea would have been spectacular then as it might have been had I done it now. But I was not the Big Cheese present that day. That was the commandant of the Corps, Gen. Al Grey.

One did not upstage the commandant of the Corps.

Prior to my retirement, an executive search firm for possible post retirement employment had contacted me. An interview with the Dupont Corporation was arranged after a two-month respite. No duty periods. No emergency phone calls. No wake-ups at 0600. Perfect for a paced review of the data given me about the corporation. The French background of the Dupont family. How it earned its reputation by manufacturing gunpowder, supplying the Union Army. From gunpowder to prowess as a chemical company, until today it is the largest chemical company in the world. A family representative still sits on the board of the corporation.

After a tour of corporate headquarters in Wilmington and meeting with senior officials, I signed on and exchanged USMC green for corporate Armani suits. Several things impressed me straightaway. First, I was gratified to know that, for a change, I was *not* the first black executive Dupont had ever hired. Several had preceded me; one was to become a senior vice president. And at the same time that I was hired, so was a black retired Navy admiral. Additionally, the company had also hired a former black U.S. ambassador.

I was also struck by the similarity of corporate America to the military structure. The same pecking order. Go-fers. Sniffers. There were two significant differences, however—the working orders and the pay.

I was particularly impressed by the chief executive officer, Ed Woolard. A tall, impressive Southerner who had a real love of people and a superb manner in dealing with them. He possessed a steel trap of a brain, evident in his ability to be decisive and analyze things correctly. Also inbred was an uncanny ability to see through bullshit. If I were to describe him in a single sentence, I'd say: "He talks slow but he thinks fast."

Once, Ed asked me how I would compare corporate America to my military experiences.

"The structure," I replied, "is essentially the same, but you don't work the troops hard enough and you pay them too much money."

"I'm glad you brought that to my attention," he shot.

Now it was my turn to think quickly and in a hurry.

"Present company excluded," I quipped.

The coughing and hoarseness that my youngest brother, Hans, had exhibited as we drove to Houston after my retirement, and later, suddenly assumed ominous proportions in 1990. A growth in his throat was responsible. He'd let it go. He knew something was there but he remembered Mom's self-healer routines. A cure for everything in the world. "Swallow Vicks." Vicks was a waste of time. By the time he felt that he should have a chat with a doctor, the cancer had already spread. Too late for radiation. Too late to operate.

I went to Houston at every chance to be with him. I saw him becoming progressively weaker, then finally hospitalized indefinitely. Our whole family knew it was just a matter of time. Our whole family knew. I was out of the country when it happened. My sister Anne called.

"Okay," she said heavily. "Hansy's gone."

While I was en route home, the family began the funeral arrangements. Perhaps another quirk, but I hate funerals. I've hated them since day one. To me, it's a rite of passage that has little significance to the real world.

As I headed home, I remembered Hansy with great affection. He and I were always close. We three boys in the family were all rebels of a sort. Billy, the middle, was the rebel with flair. Hansy was the youngest, and

I always felt that I was to protect and teach him the way. No matter where I was stationed, sooner or later Hansy would show up, even on Okinawa. All of the boys were always close, but Hansy and I seemed closer.

The circumstances of Hansy's death seemed unfair somehow. He was four years younger, and here I'd gone through two wars, three major operations, and he's gone while I'm still here. And his death was a slow, lingering thing, more than six or seven months of suffering.

We lay Hansy to rest in the cemetery plot reserved for members of his wife's family in Houston.

Trauma in my personal and family life continued to haunt. This time, it was Mom. With regrets, we'd placed her in a rest home in Denver near my sister, Anne, and her family. She had reached the age where she was showing signs of senility and loss of memory.

"And which one of my sons are you?" she'd ask when I'd come to visit.

"Mom," I'd reply, "I'm the one in the Marine Corps who became a general."

"Oh, yes," she'd exclaim. "We've got a general in the family."

It took her some time to get her thoughts together, but the brain was still cooking. Things would come and go. The previous Christmas when I was visiting, I'd asked her some questions about her sister in an attempt to see how much she was really losing her mental faculties.

Suddenly, her eyes cleared.

"That's your aunt," she snapped, looking directly at me. "And don't you ever forget it." I jerked to attention.

On her birthday about a month earlier, Mom's sister and her husband had gone to see Mom. They confirmed the fact that she was indeed eighty-seven years old.

"My," she'd beamed. "I've certainly lived a long time, haven't I?"

Shortly after, my faithful sister, Anne, called me again. The rest home had called. Mom passed away in her sleep. We had her cremated, and closed the book on a generation plus one of Petersens from Topeka.

I went into the Dupont Corporation at the director level, working for a senior vice president. My assignments were varied but began with logistics and matériel evaluations, which involved taking a look at their education and training programs. There had been some concern within the company over the processes involved in bringing their executives up to professional level. Also involved was a look at the logistics of their corporate real estate holdings. All of this from a worldwide point of view.

As I moved out to accomplish my duties as an old Marine would approach them, I ran smack dab into what I term "the culture" of the corporation. Little or no flamboyancy. No display of exaggerated wealth. A reluctance to engage in overspeak. So I found myself to be outspoken when compared to that culture. Their culture involved walking softly without carrying a stick. So when I began making observations and pointing out what I considered to be errors in their management style, a backlash began.

The corporation was constructed so as to have business compartments within the corporate structure, and I found that each business compartment competed against the other to see who could best bring the bottom line forward. In the accomplishment of that, they were draining internal assets, resulting in a rush to buy outside consulting assistance. I found that consultants were having a field day taking a program, selling it to a "compartment," leaking the success of that program to another compartment, who would then buy the same program at a different price, thus maximizing their profits. I pointed this out to the boss.

"Do you realize," I asked, "how much you're paying in the education and training of your corporate executives?"

Because of compartmentalization, no one had ever taken a look at the total price. And then I gave him a number, *which exceeded the total Marine Corps' annual training budget.*

"Oh, shit," he said.

We went on to discover that their capital assets, also subdivided among these same internal business interests, were equally out of kilter. A few eyebrows were raised. The assets included a castle in the French Alps, a marina in California, and a graveyard that no one knew existed.

About a year later, I was promoted to vice president in charge of corporate aviation, and I was back around my first love—airplanes. Dupont had one of the largest corporate fleets of any American company, located at four different sites in the United States. Company travel—intercontinental as well as domestic—involved some seventy pilots along with several hundred support staff.

I didn't know it at first, but several of the pilots were ex-military. They became a bit exercised when I was appointed, because they'd seen an article about me in *Air and Space* magazine referring to my having been designated a Grey Eagle. Some apprehension was immediately apparent, I understand.

"Uh-oh, here comes a three-star Marine Corps general."

"Yeah. Wonder what the hell he's gonna have us doing?"

They needn't have worried. My Corps training made me know at once that this wasn't a job you can learn or master sitting in an office. The need was to fly with the crews, understand what they were going through, and thus get a much better feel for the effectiveness of the whole organization. The same as a fighter squadron commander.

No F-4s or Harriers. Now it was Gulfstream. Lears or Hawkers. Here today, India tomorrow. Nonstop from Pisa, Italy, to Philadelphia. A corporate executive and his wife. Executives flying the maximum aircraft capacity. Catering, ground handling, and flight briefings by contract. Roll the need into the computer and contracted services roll in to make your landing rights, your overflight rights, and the whole ball of wax.

I love traveling, and in this position I went to places I never went while in the Marine Corps. France. China. Africa. Flying over the wide expanse of the Sahara Desert, sweating out the possibilities in the event of engine failure or emergency. I'll always remember the thrill of an African headman in Gabon who discovered that I was a vice president on the Dupont staff. A *leadership position*. How he stuck to my shoulder the whole time we were there. Very proud of the fact that an African American was, to some degree, "runnin' the show, mon." He made certain that everyone knew that *this* was the man.

In 1992, the famous Montford Point Marines decided to honor me with a big celebration for my accomplishments. The setting was the huge officers' mess at Bolling Air Force Base in Washington, D.C. I tried to dissaude the guys from doing it. True, I'd always supported the Montford Point Marines, but I thought it was about time to stop looking at past heroes and begin creating new ones. Being a hero doesn't last forever. My philosophy on retirement was not to look back over my shoulder but to look at something new on the horizon.

The affair was big indeed, with more than four hundred souls in attendance. A sit-down banquet, with Gen. Carl Mundy, the commandant of the Marine Corps, as the guest speaker. It was, without a doubt, one of the greatest honors afforded me in my whole life, and it was sincerely appreciated.

In April 1997, I retired from Dupont, mandatory for executives reaching age sixty-five. Senior executives whom I had grown to respect and admire hosted me at dinner. Not surprisingly, several had served in the military. Of particular note was Jack Kroll, successor to Ed Woolard as chief executive officer. Jack had served as a naval officer on the staff of Adm. H. Rickover, the father of the U.S. Navy's nuclear submarine. He'd been one of the first to serve as a nuclear physicist for a man noted for his imperial manner and his ability to chew up and spit out junior officers. Jack had survived.

Dupont was a wonderful company with many great people. Realizing that it had been a white-dominated corporation, I was most impressed by their willingness and desire to change to meet the demands of the twentieth century in hiring practices. I could only applaud their efforts to include women and minorities into the hierarchy. Their understanding of the changing world became apparent as they became a multinational company. They understood that the peoples of the world, not just those of the United States, would be driving factors.

Most of all, I was impressed at how their senior executives made an effort to understand what I was saying one day in Africa at a social function as our corporate executives and their wives visited the country leaders in their homes.

"You know," I noted, "all of the women who went in to look at the house were white. All of your hosts were of color. Isn't it interesting that they were not also included?"

It was gratifying to watch the light go on and illuminate a countenance.

At age sixty-five, there was time now to look back on the road I'd traveled. Time to reflect on the many social changes the nation has seen. I see myself—first, the young native of Topeka; then as an eighteen year old in Pensacola, known by many varied descriptive terms (the most innocuous of which were "colored," "Negro," "black," and "African American"), angry at "white only" drinking fountains, being restricted to riding in the back of the bus and to "colored" entrances to movie theaters, being unable to enter the bar of the San Carlos Hotel (or the hotel itself) where all other cadets congregated on weekends.

I fondly remembered my particular act of retaliation as I "paid the racists back" on a dirt airfield in Alabama outside a hamburger shack while on a cross-country training flight by trying to blow away the shack, its inhabitants, and everything around it with my prop wash as I spooled up for takeoff. Later in my training, another black cadet entered the program (about par for the course in those days—one black per year). I advised him that on his cross-country training flight to "X" field, he would be well advised to carry a sandwich in his flight suit and stay in the cockpit.

It all has become a strange multicolored kaleidoscope of memories now. Combat tours. Korea and cold, harsh winters. The Yalu River. MiGs and heavy ground fire. Vietnam and hot, sweaty odors and muggy days. My strong belief in fighter pilot mythology—"big sky; little bullet"—shattered in September 1968 when I was shot down. Fast forward to final retirement. My children firmly advising me that "power boating was okay" but it was "time to quit flying—sell the aircraft."

How my kids dealt with my military success was interesting. They had a harder time than I did. Their problems, especially in school, resided in the fact of my being the only black officer. They encountered things that I didn't know about until years later. And I think there was some name calling. In fact, all our kids were very light skinned and some of them even had sun-bleached blond hair. My first wife, Ellie, handled most of these things, but the children were resentful of the school systems because many times they were the only blacks there. Of course, the constant change of bases and assignments sometimes operated to create memories of events that were warped, negative, and never should have happened the way they did.

I think back over the marriages, what went wrong, what was right. Both are wonderful ladies; both are still friends. The many moves—some twenty in all—testified to the truth of the old military saying that "if you don't like where you are, wait a year." Now I'm able to share some of these experiences with the kids. I describe a world that is difficult for them to comprehend. My grandson listens, his facial expressions reflecting the unspoken words.

"Granddaddy General is pulling my leg again," bolsters his need to believe.

I think of the irony of titles, such as "the first and only black pilot in the United States Marine Corps." "Black General." Black whatever. A title that connotes progress, or a report card on the lack of progress. I can't help but imagine, however, that all of that "first" stuff has made some kind of memorable impact someplace in some hearts around the country.

MUTUAL VOICES
Brig. Gen. Clifford L. Stanley, Director of Public Affairs, Headquarters, USMC
Even after his retirement from the Marine Corps, Lt. Gen. Frank Petersen continues to be an inspiration to thousands of Marines, particu-

larly those in the African American community. I first met then Lieutenant Colonel Petersen when I was a new second lieutenant at the Basic School. He was already looked up to by many young officers because of his down-to-earth insight and his influential leadership. At a time when racial tensions were particularly high in the military, Lieutenant General Petersen held key billets that allowed him to advise and influence the commandant of the Marine Corps and other senior leaders on minority personnel issues. As the first black promoted to general officer in the Marine Corps, he inspired many junior officers to believe that "it could be done." For me, he had set the standard as a true professional, mentor, and role model.

MUTUAL VOICES
Brig. Gen. George Walls, USMC (Retired)

One of the high points of my career was when General Petersen was commander of the 1st Marine Aircraft Wing in Okinawa. I was privileged enough to go out there and serve under him as the wing engineer squadron commander. It was a great experience. He's the kind of leader who gives you your marching orders and lets you go do your job. I appreciated that. Of course, if you did not do your job, his reaction would be just as swift and deadly as it was when he was giving you guidance at the beginning. General Petersen was always straightforward and to the point and when he got done telling you what he wanted, there was not too much question about that. Also, if you failed to live up to his expectations, he let you know. And that's the kind of thing most of us appreciate in a leader. You always knew where Frank Petersen was coming from; he was always the same and you could count on him to be that way.

MUTUAL VOICES
Frank Emmanuel Petersen III, Son

Well, I think he's done some exceptional things. I think he is one of the rare ones [who has been] afforded the opportunity and been able to capitalize on [them]. A lot of people get those chances but fall by the wayside. His timing; putting himself at the right place and the right time. You know, all those guys [the Montford Point Marines] are heroes and they really talk about him as a legend. He gave a helluva lot. It cost the family; it cost a lot of things. It was a strain for everybody, and we're not unique in that regard. We've all accepted it, have dealt with it. He was never distant with his emotions. He was always there. If there was a rainstorm or thunder, he'd call to make sure we were all right. He never stopped telling me to take care of my mom. To be good. He's always been there. One day he said, "You know, we communicate without even talking." And I said: "You know, Dad, I think you're right." Emotionally, we've never been separated, even on those birthdays when I wondered if he'd be there. Most of the time, he was, and sometimes he didn't have a gift. Once, I waited up for him all night, and finally went to bed. I ran downstairs, and he didn't have anything for my birthday and I broke down in tears. As far as a father in the traditional sense, he was a good pilot, but in comparison to what other fathers are doing, he clearly surpasses them. We always had good schools, good homes. He was always there if we had a problem.

The year 2000 approaches with much hoopla on diversity and love. Yet the "first and only" card is still in the deck. The hope is that inroads made will become even wider. So I've arrived at the last stage in life where the actors are always center stage. My first Social Security check puts me on the wonder.

"Is that all I rate?" a small voice somewhere inside loudly asks. "I tell you what," it rants on, "give me an eight-year lump sum settlement and you keep the rest."

And now, a beautiful home on the shores of Chesapeake Bay. Peaceful. Restful. Tranquil. Quiet broken only by the frequent arrival of my kids. Dana, who thinks I think I'm "reviewing the troops" when I ride my mower around my land. Or others of my children who still think perhaps I don't know how to buy my dress ties. But I think they'll all say I'm their friend, their good father, and a better listener these days. It's peaceful. Tranquil. Gallon buckets of quiet.

I can't stand it. What next?

Only the natural course for me. I've started a business that addresses aviation safety issues. What else?